The Wahhabi Mission
and Saudi Arabia

For Stephen, Gary, and Neil

The Wahhabi Mission and Saudi Arabia

David Commins

I.B. TAURIS
LONDON · NEW YORK

Paperback edition published in 2009 and reprinted in 2013 by I.B.Tauris & Co Ltd
6 Salem Road, London W2 4BU
175 Fifth Avenue, New York NY 10010
www.ibtauris.com

Distributed in the United States and Canada Exclusively by
Palgrave Macmillan, 175 Fifth Avenue, New York NY 10010

First published in Hardback in 2006 by I.B.Tauris & Co Ltd.

ISBN: 978 1 84885 014 9

A full CIP record for this book is available from the British Library

A full CIP record for this book is available from the Library of Congress

Library of Congress catalog card: available

Typeset in Palamino by Steve Tribe, Andover
Printed and bound by CPI Group (UK) Ltd, Croydon, CR0 4YY

Contents

Preface to the paperback edition   vii

Preface   ix

Acknowledgements   xiii

Map of Arabia   xvi

Introduction   1

1. Islam Began as a Stranger and Will Return as a Stranger   7

2. Holding Fast Against Idolatry   40

3. Abd al-Aziz ibn Saud and the Taming of Wahhabi Zeal   71

4. Wahhabism in a Modern State   104

5. The Wahhabi Mission and Islamic Revivalism   130

6. Challenges to Wahhabi Hegemony   155

Conclusion   205

Al al-Sheikh   210

Chronology   211

Glossary   213

Notes   215

Bibliography   263

Index   275

Preface to the paperback edition

Wahhabism – the official religious creed of Saudi Arabia – has stirred controversy since its genesis more than two hundred years ago. Presently, it figures in arguments over Islamic belief, worship, and manners throughout the world. Saudi embassies and multilateral Muslim institutions, funded by Riyadh, disseminate Wahhabi teachings. Saudi universities and religious institutes train thousands of teachers and preachers to propagate Wahhabi doctrine, frequently in the name of reviving 'Salafi' Islam, the idea of a pristine form of Islam practised by the early Muslim generations. From Indonesia to France to Nigeria, Wahhabi-inspired Muslims aspire to rid religious practice of so-called heretical innovations and to instil strict morality. While Wahhabism claims to represent Islam in its purest form, other Muslims consider it a misguided creed that fosters intolerance, promotes simplistic theology, and restricts Islam's capacity for adaptation to diverse and shifting circumstances. The upshot is fierce debate that reproduces two-hundred year old arguments between Wahhabis and their Muslim rivals.

In Saudi Arabia, Wahhabism's spokesmen endorse the royal family's claim to rule as defenders of the faith. Modern Saudi rulers have erected a formidable set of institutions that enable Wahhabism to dominate public religious practice. But identification with the Saudi state, however beneficial in material terms, jeopardises Wahhabism's credibility by inclining its most eminent figures to compromise religious principles for the sake of dynastic interest. In the 1990s, the gap between idealism and pragmatism spawned the *Sahwa* (Awakening) movement of religious dissent. Its suppression left open the field of religious opposition to extremists, who waged a violent campaign under the banner of al-Qaeda in the Arabian Peninsula. The shock of suicide bombings in Saudi cities and the sobering effects of imprisonment led the Sahwa sheikhs to condemn the religious militants. The militants' methods horrified ordinary Saudis, and by the end of 2007, security forces gained the upper hand. Yet religious dissent is unlikely to dissipate as long as the Wahhabi establishment pays more attention to correct performance of ritual and personal morality than to pressing economic and political issues.

Wahhabism confronts challenges from liberal Saudi opinion as well. The kingdom's integration with the global economy, most conspicuously through its petroleum sector, produced a cadre of technicians and managers more at ease with non-Muslims and their manners than the strict Wahhabi code can countenance. Chambers of commerce, eager to expand the private sector's participation in global trade, and government agencies engaged with international bodies also harbour Saudis with liberal views, although likely to maintain them in private. The substantial Shiite minority and Sunnis preferring a less austere religious regime comprise yet another constituency for curtailing Wahhabi influence. Whether a robust liberal tendency will ever emerge to challenge Wahhabism's domination of public life remains an open question. For the time being, liberal Saudis lack firm institutional ground and depend on royal toleration for breathing space.

Wahhabism's future standing is related, in part, to the resources available to the Saudi Arabian government. High oil prices have boosted the Saudi economy after the lean years of the 1990s. Steadily growing global demand for petroleum would ensure abundant resources for Wahhabi institutions. It is not clear, however, that material benefits alone will blunt appeals to make religion relevant to the public interest, deflect challenges from Islamic dissidents, or satisfy yearnings for a more liberal climate. Nevertheless, religious universities continue to prepare Saudis for careers as judges and lawyers in the Islamic law courts, as teachers in public schools, as preachers at mosques, and as proselytisers abroad. It is likely that Muslims in Saudi Arabia and throughout the world will contend with Wahhabism for many years to come.

Preface

What is the Wahhabi mission?[1] To answer that question is to risk taking a position on a controversy that has divided Muslims for more than two centuries. A neutral observer could define the Wahhabi mission as the religious reform movement associated with the teachings of Muhammad ibn Abd al-Wahhab (1703–1792). He and his followers believe that they have a religious obligation to spread the call (in Arabic, *da'wa*) for a restoration of pure monotheistic worship. Thus, the mission's devotees contend that 'Wahhabism' is a misnomer for their efforts to revive correct Islamic belief and practice. Instead of the Wahhabi label, they prefer either *salafi*, one who follows the ways of the first Muslim ancestors (*salaf*), or *muwahhid*, one who professes God's unity. On the other hand, a Muslim critic would say that Wahhabism is a deviant sectarian movement started by an ambitious, misguided religious leader from a remote part of Arabia that has spawned heretical movements since early Islam. Muslims sharply disagree on this question of definition because the pivotal idea in Ibn Abd al-Wahhab's teaching determines whether one is a Muslim or an infidel. In his opinion, Muslims who disagreed with his definition of monotheism were not heretics, that is to say, misguided Muslims, but outside the pale of Islam altogether. Therefore, Wahhabi disputes with other Muslims are not comparable to those between Catholic and Protestant during the Reformation.

It is well known that Muslims profess belief in one God, and that such belief is a cardinal tenet of Islam. The profession of faith (*shahada*) states, 'There is no god but God, and Muhammad is the messenger of God.' The controversy between Ibn Abd al-Wahhab and his critics turns on the implication of the first clause and its sincere proclamation. Most Muslims throughout history have accepted the position that declaring this profession of faith makes one a Muslim. One might or might not regularly perform the other obligatory rituals – the five daily prayers, fasting, almsgiving, and pilgrimage – and one might or might not scrupulously conform to Islamic ethical and moral standards. But as long as one believed that God is one and that Muhammad is His messenger, then any shortcomings would render one a sinner, not an unbeliever.

Muhammad ibn Abd al-Wahhab did not accept that view. He argued that the criterion for one's standing as either a Muslim or an unbeliever was correct worship as an expression of belief in one God. He noted that in the time of Muhammad, the Arab idolaters acknowledged that God was the Creator and the Lord of all creation, yet they were the Prophet's worst enemies, and the Qur'an states that they will suffer eternal torment in the Fire for their disbelief. But how can that be if they believe in God the Creator? It is so because, according to the Arabian reformer, belief in one God has a second aspect that one absolutely must affirm in order to qualify as a Muslim, and that requires one to devote worship purely and exclusively to God. Any act or statement that indicates devotion to a being other than God is to associate another creature with God's power, and that is tantamount to idolatry (*shirk*). Muhammad ibn Abd al-Wahhab included in the category of such acts popular religious practices that made holy men into intercessors with God. That was the core of the controversy between him and his adversaries, including his own brother. In the course of composing polemical epistles and treatises, a host of ancillary disputes sprouted forth.

One of the peculiar features of the debate between Wahhabis and their adversaries is its apparently static nature. A set of arguments and counter-arguments emerged in just a few decades after Muhammad ibn Abd al-Wahhab began his public mission in the 1740s. Since then, the two sides have added what each considers convincing proof texts from the Qur'an and the Sunna (the Prophet's exemplary conduct and sayings) to support their positions, but the main points in the debate stay the same. This struck me in fall 2001 when I read an exchange between an Omani and a Saudi scholar that went over the same ground that rivals had covered for more than two centuries. I mentioned this to an Egyptian scholar and he asked me why I would want to study something that does not change. I replied that when I began my research, I did not know if or how Wahhabism had evolved. As a western student of the subject, I was a bit shocked to find the same points getting rehashed in a twenty-first century publication, and my reaction was one of both bemusement and admiration. The former stemmed from a prejudice favouring dynamism and evolution in the realm of ideas. The latter came from a historian's wondering about the power of practices and discourses to endure through an era of profound transformation. I was at a loss to fathom it or to categorize it. My initial thought was that it represented a sort of fossilized discourse, but that is not true. It is not a fossil. It is alive and meaningful and moving to its partisans. Part of the historian's challenge is to decipher the logic and dynamism of ideas and relationships that are remote from his own time and culture.[2]

Acknowledgements

Five years ago, I decided to study the history of Wahhabism in the nineteenth century. And I wanted to research the topic in Saudi Arabia. The trick was to find a host institution and the means to support a period of study there. I was very fortunate to apply for a residency at the King Faisal Center for Research and Islamic Studies at the King Faisal Foundation shortly after it began to host foreign scholars. A Fulbright Grant for the Middle East, North Africa, and South Asia Regional Research Program funded my five-month stay in Riyadh in 2001–2002. I am grateful to Juan Cole, Michael Cook, Philip Khoury, William Ochsenwald, John Voll, and Neil Weissman for encouraging the project at that early stage. I owe a deep debt of gratitude to the King Faisal Center's directors, staff, and researchers for their hospitality and assistance. The words 'institutional host' fail to capture what the Center meant to me. I cannot imagine more gracious hosts than Dr. Yahya Mahmoud ibn Junayd, Director of the Center, and Dr. Awadh al-Badi, Director of the Department of Research and Studies. Mr. Syed Jameel efficiently and cheerfully performed the sorts of administrative and logistical tasks that a newcomer might demand. All three men and their associates went out of their way to make a stranger feel welcome.

It was a special pleasure to get reacquainted with a friend from graduate school days at Ann Arbor, Dr. Abd al-Rahman Shemlan, whose warmth and wisdom have deepened over the years. To Abd al-Rahman I owe fond memories of spending Id al-Fitr in Unayza with his family and friends. Dr. Abd Allah al-Askar introduced me to his colleagues at King Saud University and invited me to visit his family's home town, al-Majma'a, affording me some glimpses of Najdi life outside Riyadh. I met Dr. Khalid al-Dakhil fairly late in my stay, but we kept in contact after my departure and got reacquainted in fall 2003 when he was a resident scholar in Washington, DC. By that time, this project was a bit further along and I used Khalid as a sounding board for ideas, confident that he would offer me frank criticism, often for leaping to unwarranted conclusions. Dr. Fahd A. al-Semmari, Secretary General of the King Abdulaziz Foundation for Research and Archives, supported my efforts to sustain academic exchange by kindly lending the Foundation's support to a panel of Saudi and American scholars at the Middle East Studies Association's 2002 Annual Meeting.

One of the special delights of research is the fortuitous encounter. On a visit to the King Fahd National Library I met Abd Allah al-Muneef, curator of the manuscript section. He led me to several important sources on nineteenth century Wahhabism. Abd Allah also kindly introduced me to fellow researchers Dr. Suheyl Sapan, curator of the Library's Ottoman and Turkish section, Abd al-Rahman A. Al-Shuqeir, Muhammad Rashid, and Rashed M. Bin Asakir. At the very end of my stay in Riyadh, I met Mr. Saud Sirhan. Thanks to all of these men, my time in Saudi Arabia turned into a fascinating intellectual and cultural journey.

Lora Berg, cultural affairs officer at the United States embassy in Riyadh, and Karim Chaibi offered their friendship, which was essential to keeping me going during the tumultuous fall of 2001. It was an honor to become acquainted with Dr. Igor Timoreev, a fellow researcher at the King Faisal Center. To him I owe delicious memories of chocolate mousse and conversations about modern Saudi history. In Cairo, Dr. Ann B. Radwan, executive director of the Binational Fulbright Commission, and Nevine Abd al-Salam provided valuable support for my research efforts. On returning to the USA, a Dickinson College Sabbatical Supplement Grant made it possible to continue research in spring 2002.

The roster of colleagues and friends who have read and commented on portions of this book includes Khalid al-Dakhil, Natana DeLong-Bas, Abd al-Aziz Al-Fahad, Hala Fattah, James Gelvin, Dina Khoury, and Steven Weinberger. My brothers Stephen and Gary Commins read chapters and offered valuable suggestions. My friend Chuck Nyren gave me smart pointers on writing style that I doubt were put to very good use. I owe Susan Lindt for her steady encouragement of this project, from conception to completion. Tina Maresco and Sandra Gorrity in the interlibrary loan department at Dickinson College kept the pipeline of books and articles flowing. When I decided to include a map, my associate Michele Hassinger assured me it would be a snap and produced one for me. I may not have turned my project from early Wahhabi history into a general survey were it not for prompting from Iradj Bagherzade and Turi Munthe of I.B.Tauris. I also thank Hanako Birks at I.B.Tauris and Steve Tribe for taking this work from rough manuscript to polished publication. I appreciate the criticisms and suggestions of two anonymous readers for improving the manuscript. Saudi Aramco World kindly granted permission to reproduce photographs from its Public Affairs Digital Image Archive. This project became a preoccupation during my daughter Marcia's final year of high school. She tolerated the inexorable spread of books, papers, and files at home and her dad's eccentric tales of discoveries in the Arabian past.

If this book has any merit, it comes from the colleagues, friends, and family members to whom I owe so much. Its flaws belong to the author.

David Commins
Carlisle, PA

Introduction

In the early 1740s, Muslim religious scholars in Mecca took note of a new doctrine coming out of Central Arabia.[1] The author of that doctrine, Muhammad ibn Abd al-Wahhab, declared that Muslims had reverted to idolatry. Naturally, the religious scholars (*ulama*) took exception and wrote treatises attacking his views as well as his qualifications to comment on theology. As the controversy between Wahhabism and its critics unfolded, the latter formed an explanation for the 'errant' doctrine's origin that found its way into standard histories. It goes something like this.

Muhammad ibn Abd al-Wahhab came from a remote backwater of Arabia where the tradition of scholastic learning was shallow. A handful of ulama studied at cosmopolitan centres like Cairo or Damascus and then returned to Najd (Central Arabia), where their knowledge was magnified by the depth of ignorance surrounding them among an illiterate population of townsmen and nomads. Members of Ibn Abd al-Wahhab's lineage, including his grandfather, father and brother, belonged to this unsophisticated but earnest cluster of ulama. As long as they followed the lead of more learned colleagues in Syria and Egypt, the townsmen of Najd benefited from their guidance on ritual, family law and property transactions. Sheikh

Muhammad followed the family tradition of religious study, but he misunderstood passages in the Qur'an and the Prophet's tradition (*Sunna*), leading him to break with the mainstream of Muslim thought. Some of the more fanciful descriptions of his life stem from an effort to depict him as a deviant thinker. For example, an early nineteenth-century biography reports that he spent a number of years studying in Iranian towns, which would have been centres of Shiite learning as opposed to the Ottoman Empire's tradition of Sunni learning. Perhaps the author wished to imply that Ibn Abd al-Wahhab had absorbed heretical (from an Ottoman viewpoint) tendencies from Iran's Shiite scholars. Some Muslim authors averred that Ibn Abd al-Wahhab's views were not the result of an innocent intellectual mistake but an intentional distortion of Islam that suited his thirst for power. Thus, he considered genuine Muslims to be infidels, whose life, property and honour were fair game for his and the Saudi dynasty's expansionist wars. He was able to stir up religious enthusiasm because he was living in the midst of ignorant nomads, easily swayed by a clever preacher and eager to plunder settlements and towns. Apart from the obviously tendentious character of this view, it is utterly mistaken about the relationship between Arabian nomadic tribes and the Wahhabi movement, which in fact regarded nomads as ignorant barbarians in need of religious instruction.[2]

Of course, the Wahhabis have a very different view of their own history. They might encapsulate it in a Prophetic tradition where Muhammad said, 'Islam first appeared as a stranger and will one day return as a stranger.' By this is meant that when Muhammad first preached in seventh-century Mecca, the idea that people owed all worship and devotion to one God was utterly foreign to the Arabs. Islam was not merely strange. It was contrary to the beliefs, customs, mentality and desires of Muhammad's audience. After years of courageous and determined effort, Muhammad gained many followers, forged them into a community and mobilized them to prevail in a political and military struggle for supremacy in Arabia. But, according to the Hadith, Muhammad foretold a time when Islam would become as alien to mankind as it had been when he began his mission. Muhammad ibn Abd al-Wahhab believed that he lived during such a time. And it was not merely a matter of finding lax adherence among the rustic inhabitants of his native Najd, for he travelled to and spent time in the cosmopolitan Holy Cities, Mecca and Medina, the latter especially renowned as a centre of religious

learning that attracted pupils and scholars from the breadth of the
Muslim world, from Morocco to the East Indies. Wherever he went,
he found that people had lapsed into religious ignorance, *jahiliyya*, a
barbaric state wherein they did not recognize their violation of the
imperative to devote all worship to God alone.[3] Sheikh Muhammad
concluded that Islam was as much a stranger in his time as it had
been eleven centuries earlier when God had first revealed the Qur'an.
His call (*da'wa*), the essence of the Wahhabi mission, was to revive
pure devotion of worship to God alone. For Muslims who agree with
this account, 'Wahhabism' is merely a rebirth of Islam at the end of a
period of decadence. The paradigm of religious decline and revival is
a common one in Muslim thought. In this respect, Ibn Abd al-Wahhab
conformed to a cultural model of a reformist preacher. Moreover, his
correspondence and the Wahhabi chronicles depict him as arriving
at his convictions on his own, indeed, through inspiration, not
under the influence of any teacher he encountered in his travels. The
controversy between Wahhabis and other Muslims centres on his
standing as an inspired reformer performing a necessary task or as an
eccentric man whose deficient educational formation made him stray
from the mainstream and form a sectarian movement.

Historians need not choose sides in the argument between Wahhabis
and their foes. But historians love to argue and I might start some
arguments with a new framework for making sense of Wahhabism.
It is time to push past questions about its origins and the emphasis
on its relationship to the Saudi dynasty, as significant as they are.[4]
Whatever historical forces caused its emergence, Wahhabism has
been around long enough to make one wonder about the secrets
of its endurance during a transformative phase of history. It is not
merely a matter of dynastic support. True, the doctrine's initial
establishment required that support because Wahhabism overturned
an ancient tradition of religious learning and that was achieved, in
part, by force. Many ulama left their homes in Najd and resettled
in southern Iraq, where they incited Ottoman ulama to wage a
propaganda war against the Wahhabi doctrine. In turn, Wahhabi
sheikhs discouraged travel to Ottoman lands, whose inhabitants they
deemed idolaters, and subjected visitors to close scrutiny for hints of
doctrinal contamination. The uprooting of the old scholastic tradition
and the quarantine on travel made it possible for Wahhabism to attain
a monopoly on religious thought and practice in most of Najd. Thus,
by the mid 1800s, the Wahhabi mission formed a regional religious

culture with its own doctrine, canon, leadership, cadre of ulama and centre of learning. Its dependence on dynastic power had diminished so that when Al Saud collapsed in the 1880s and 1890s, the mission did not collapse with it. True, Najd's new rulers did not make a show of supporting the doctrine; but they did not try to suppress it either. Wahhabism was not merely the dominant doctrine in Najd. It was practically the only one.

If Wahhabism isolated itself from the rest of the Muslim world and other Muslims regarded it as a heretical innovation, how did it attain so much influence outside Saudi Arabia in the twentieth century? A sequence of developments created an opening in the wall separating Wahhabis and other Muslims. In the late nineteenth century, an Islamic revivalist tendency appeared in the Arab East and India. The revivalists had much in common with the Wahhabis. Although not identical, these doctrinal cousins were dedicated to resisting western cultural influences, so differences were submerged and contacts cultivated. Most significantly, revivalists published works to revise Wahhabism's reputation in the eyes of the Muslim world. The next step in the rapprochement came in the first decades of the twentieth century when the founder of Saudi Arabia's modern kingdom, Abd al-Aziz ibn Saud, took steps to integrate his realm into regional and global political and economic systems. In pursuit of that policy, he suppressed the mission's most zealous current, employed non-Saudi Arabs as advisers and invited Americans to develop his land's reservoirs of petroleum. Wahhabi ulama disapproved of the foreigners' arrival but were powerless to block it. Ibn Saud's pragmatism and political independence at a time when European powers exercised direct rule over most Arab lands raised his kingdom's stature. During the same era, popular religious organizations such as the Muslim Brothers surfaced in Egypt and spread to other Arab countries, widening the revivalist niche that viewed Wahhabism with favour. In the 1960s and 1970s, Al Saud adopted an Islamic foreign policy and created religious institutions to proselytize abroad. In that effort, the Wahhabis joined hands with the Muslim Brothers and revivalist organizations in Pakistan. As a result of that alliance, Wahhabism reached new heights of influence far beyond the confines of its historic homeland. The anti-Soviet Afghan jihad of the 1980s represented the peak of Wahhabi-revivalist collaboration and triumph.

Throughout the decades of rapprochement between Wahhabism and Islamic revivalist movements, it seemed that the Wahhabi mission's connection to the Muslim world was a one-way street, with Saudi ulama propagating the Najdi doctrine abroad and retaining its monopoly at home. But Saudi Arabia's integration into regional politics and its need for expatriate workers to manage the modern sector of its economy exposed it to the full range of Arab political and religious tendencies. Given the popularity of nationalist and leftist parties in the 1950s and 1960s, it made perfect sense to ally with conservative religious organizations like the Muslim Brothers. The decision to offer asylum to Muslim Brothers fleeing persecution at the hands of secular Arab regimes was part of an effort to consolidate the bastion of Islam against atheist currents. No one could have foreseen that the Muslim Brothers would successfully spread their ideas in the kingdom and erode Wahhabism's hegemony. As long as Muslim revivalists supported Al Saud, their doctrinal differences with Wahhabism could be muted and the extent of revivalist inroads into Saudi religious culture undetected. Wahhabism's soft spot was its political doctrine, which dictates obedience to a ruler unless he commands a believer to violate Islamic law. This puts Wahhabi religious scholars in the position of either defending rulers or offering quiet, behind the scenes criticism. Muslim revivalists have no compunction about openly denouncing rulers or even striving to depose them. The economic downturn of the 1980s and the infiltration of western culture soured many Saudi citizens' views of their rulers' leadership. Revivalist thought offered a platform for political dissent missing in Wahhabism. The alliance between doctrinal cousins shattered in 1990 when Riyadh responded to Iraq's invasion of Kuwait by requesting military assistance from the USA. The kingdom's erstwhile revivalist friends suddenly turned into sharp critics, accusing Al Saud of betraying Islam by inviting infidel troops to occupy the land of the holy places. Saudi dissidents, who had assimilated the revivalist ideology, echoed that criticism and accused the Wahhabi leadership as well of betraying Islam for the sake of an illegitimate dynasty. Dissidents preached to receptive ears at mosques and recordings of their sermons found a large market. Wahhabi hegemony faced its most serious challenge since the early nineteenth century. In the following decade, Wahhabi religious leaders tepidly defended Al Saud against the angry bromides of dissident preachers, confident of their popular backing.

The 11 September 2001 attacks on the USA led to intense scrutiny of Wahhabism and its global influence. The involvement of Saudi citizens in the attacks and suspicions that Saudi institutions helped fund al-Qaeda led many to conclude that Wahhabism contributed to anti-western violence and therefore to call on the Saudi government to reduce its influence. But were Osama bin Laden and al-Qaeda the fruit of Wahhabi schools in Saudi Arabia? How could that be the case when bin Laden considered Al Saud traitors who must be overthrown? In the autumn of 2001, a Wahhabi cleric appeared on a Saudi television news programme to explain why killing civilians is prohibited in Islam and why Osama bin Laden could not proclaim a jihad (that power is held by the sovereign). Young men called the station and defied the Wahhabi cleric: the 11 September attacks were part of a righteous jihad against the West; bin Laden was the 'commander of believers' and therefore perfectly justified in launching a jihad.

In 2003–2004, Saudi cities were the scene of a wave of suicide bombings, killings of westerners and gun battles between Saudi security forces and militants. Was this mayhem the outcome of revivalism's inroads in the kingdom, a sign of Wahhabism's diminished authority? Or were Wahhabis divided between loyalists to the dynasty and zealots who had jettisoned traditional political theory? In that event, we would be witnessing its fragmentation. Furthermore, members of Al Saud decided it might be time to trim Wahhabism's domination by holding a series of National Dialogues that included Shiites, Sufis, liberal reformers and professional women. At present, the indications are not good for true believers in Wahhabi doctrine. But as its history demonstrates, the doctrine has survived crises before. The question that history cannot answer is what will be Wahhabism's future.

Chapter One

Islam Began as a Stranger and Will Return as a Stranger

The Wahhabi religious reform movement arose in Najd, the vast, thinly populated heart of Central Arabia. Contrary to common belief, the movement did not bear the stamp of nomadic or tribal Arabia. Rather, it emerged from oasis settlements. To make sense of the movement's origins, then, we must situate it in the context of Najdi society and that society's place in the wider Muslim world.

Najd before the Wahhabi Mission

For centuries before the rise of Wahhabism, Najd was, to outsiders, a virtually forgotten land, an abode of disorderly, uncouth and irreligious nomads, a hole in the imagination of Islamic civilization's great urban centres in Istanbul, Cairo and Damascus. It lay beyond the Muslim heartland's cultural horizon even though it was adjacent to the Holy Cities, the spiritual core of Islam. Few Muslims traversed the Central Arabian desert to reach the pilgrimage centres at Mecca and Medina. Instead, pilgrims from North Africa, Egypt and Turkey would gather in Cairo and Damascus to journey in caravans that skirted the Red Sea coast. From the vast Indian Ocean basin, pilgrims sailed under monsoon winds to Yemen and Red Sea ports. The exceptions to this avoidance of Najd's parched landscape were pilgrims and merchants from Iraq and Iran, for whom the land route was close at hand.

Najd's isolation also obtained in the political sphere, as none of the great Muslim land empires had ruled it since the weakening of the Abbasid caliphate in the tenth century. The Ottoman Empire at its height in the sixteenth century surrounded the region on two sides, projecting its authority like two arms, one down the Red Sea coast to Yemen in order to secure the Holy Cities and another down the Persian Gulf to guard against Portuguese interlopers and to fend off Persian advances in Iraq and on the Gulf's western Arabian shore. The Ottomans saw no reason to invade and subdue Najd – it lacked valuable economic resources, it posed no strategic threat and it offered the sultan no prestige. Istanbul regarded the peninsula as a primitive frontier zone whose primary importance was as the site of Islam's Holy Cities. The sultan claimed to be their guardian on behalf of all Muslims, both inside and outside his domain. As long as the Ottoman-commanded pilgrim caravans made the journey safely, Istanbul was satisfied with arrangements managed by sharifs of Mecca with nomadic tribes. Interfering with or obstructing the pilgrimage, however, would pose a threat to the sultan's prestige and provoke a strong reaction. Except for the rare successful nomadic raid on pilgrim trains, Ottoman sultans had little reason to worry about that quarter of their realm in the early 1700s. They were far more concerned with the empire's weakening posture with respect to European powers.

Local Arabian powers west and east of Najd played a more active role in its political affairs. In Hijaz, the sharifs of Mecca, who acknowledged the Ottoman sultan as sovereign, had complex relations with the tribes and settlements of Najd. The sharifs tried to develop stable alliances with powerful tribes and extracted tribute from settlements; such arrangements, however, were rarely durable because of the tribes' view of alliances as temporary opportunities. In al-Hasa, the Banu Khalid tribe was dominant and vied with Meccan sharifs for influence over Najd. In the early 1700s, the Banu Khalid enjoyed several decades of preponderance among the region's tribes and oases.[1]

Najd occupied a marginal position in the Muslim world. If we take a different perspective, that of Najd looking outward, the picture shifts. The central Islamic lands loomed large in its economic activities and a substantial section of the settled population regarded the major cities as vessels of religious and cultural ideals. Nomads and oasis dwellers derived part of their livelihood from trade with neighbouring regions (Iraq, al-Hasa, Hijaz, Syria) and from servicing trans-Arabian caravans with guides, escorts and camels. Nomads raided settled areas in adjacent lands for plunder. Nearby Muslim lands provided a model of civilized life that oasis dwellers regarded as exemplary and one dimension of that model was religious learning.[2]

Najdi society was divided between nomads and settled folk (*hadar*). The nomads belonged to several tribal groups organized by ties of kinship, both real and fictive. Each tribe grazed its sheep, goats, horses and camels in a more or less well-defined domain. They exchanged animal products for food crops and for goods made in settlements or imported there. They also sold transportation and security (against raids by other tribes) to merchant and pilgrim caravans. In contrast to the interdependence that characterized economic relations between nomads and settled folk, they were usually separate in the political sphere. Each tribe had its own leading clan, from which was selected a sheikh. Tribes made alliances with each other and oasis settlements, but again, such alliances were temporary. An important difference between the nomadic and settled realms lay in the degree to which kinship figured as a factor in social relations. It is only a slight overstatement to say that for residents of oasis settlements, tribal bonds seldom figured in their political or economic pursuits. One might consider them to be detribalized because of their immersion in an environment that fostered ties related to landed property and commercial wealth rather than common shares in livestock.[3]

The domain of the sown, the oasis settlements of Najd, depended on date palms and cultivated crops. Traders profited from long-distance caravans in the trans-Arabian trade. The political order bore a superficial resemblance to the nomadic one in that the settlements had chiefly lineages that commanded armed retinues to collect land rent from poorer townsmen. The Arabian chronicles record political events in the larger settlements as unending battles for pre-eminence between chiefly lineages or within rival branches of the same lineage. The scale of political power was small, both in terms of population and area under the sway of a chieftain. At the most, the chief of a large settlement might dominate smaller neighbours by levying tribute and designating an ally to act as his surrogate. More commonly, settlements were completely independent or even divided into two rival segments.

Since the fifteenth century at the latest, Najdi religious scholars (ulama) looked to learning centres in Hijaz, Egypt, Syria and Iraq to provide the most eminent teachers for itinerant Arabian pupils and to supply authoritative texts on Islamic sciences. The record on Najdi ulama prior to the mission is thin, but we can discern four significant patterns. First, just a handful of oasis settlements had any religious learning worth mention at all. Second, in those settlements, certain family lineages specialized in maintaining and transmitting the scholastic tradition. Third, the focus of learning and practice was applied Islamic jurisprudence (*fiqh*). Fourth, the majority of ulama followed the Hanbali school of fiqh while a handful belonged to the Shafi'i and Maliki schools.[4] These aspects of Najd's scholastic tradition, singly or in combination, do not explain the rise of the Wahhabi mission, but the mission does bear a Hanbali stamp and it is firmly associated with the region's most prominent scholastic lineage, known as Al Musharraf. While we know few details about the ulama, we know even less about the religious lives of ordinary Najdis apart from what Wahhabi critics wrote about their deviance from proper Islamic practice. The religious climate seems to have accommodated a variety of traditions: different Sunni schools of law, coexistence between local custom and norms of Islamic law (*shari'a*) in everyday life and indifference to the sectarian allegiance of Shiite pilgrims from Iran and al-Hasa passing through the region to perform the hajj.[5] Wahhabi sources characterize Najd as a land of such lax observance and moral degradation that a revivalist mission was necessary, but the handful of chronicles that predate the mission take no note of such decadence.

To summarize conditions in Najd around 1700, society was divided between nomadic and settled populations, both organized in small scale, autonomous, ephemeral polities, as tribal groups or chieftaincies. The arid and semi-arid region provided sufficient vegetation and rainfall for raising livestock and growing date palms; a steady stream of merchant and pilgrim caravans traversed the peninsula, adding a locally significant surplus to the economy. A small number of settlements hosted scholars, mostly from a handful of lineages, who looked to cosmopolitan centres as repositories of Islamic sciences.

The Mission of Muhammad ibn Abd al-Wahhab

A prominent scholarly lineage named Al Musharraf provided religious leadership as teachers and judges in several oasis settlements.[6] The modern Saudi historian Abd Allah al-Mutawa has identified ten ulama from Al Musharraf in the period before Muhammad ibn Abd al-Wahhab.[7] Abd al-Wahhab ibn Sulayman Al Musharraf (d. 1740) was the chief jurist in al-Uyayna. He had two sons who pursued religious learning, Sulayman and Muhammad. Because the latter would launch the Wahhabi reform movement, historical sources provide much more, often contradictory, detail about his upbringing than his brother's.[8] Of course, he acquired the standard introduction to reading and writing through instruction about the Qur'an and then proceeded to the usual range of Islamic sciences, with emphasis on jurisprudence. The variants in his life story begin with descriptions of his travels to pursue learning.[9] For at least two centuries, Najdi religious pupils journeyed to Cairo, Damascus and the Holy Cities to study under leading Hanbali authorities and then return home burnished with the prestige of their academic affiliation.[10] That Muhammad ibn Abd al-Wahhab travelled widely was not extraordinary. It is attested by all the sources, but the details vary not only on the sequence of his travels, they diverge as well on the extent of his journeys. Saudi sources confine his travels to Arabian towns – the Holy Cities and a town in al-Hasa (just east of Najd) – and the southern Iraqi city of Basra. Other accounts report lengthy tours in Baghdad, Mosul, Damascus and several Iranian towns. A close study of the various sources leads to the conclusion that somebody was misinformed.

Some historians suggest that Ibn Abd al-Wahhab's studies in Medina formed his outlook. In the early eighteenth century, ulama in Medina were part of an intellectual trend that was sweeping the Indian Ocean's Muslim rim: the revival of Hadith (reports about the Prophet Muhammad) studies and a concomitant desire to bring the practices of Sufi orders into conformity with rules of Islamic law.[11] The list of Sheikh Muhammad's teachers in Medina includes one of the Hadith-revivers and some sources report that this teacher urged him to dedicate himself to a campaign to purify religious practices at odds with the Sunna.[12] On the other hand, his doctrine bears little similarity to the teachings of other eighteenth-century religious revivalists and the very notion of a common revivalist impulse during that era is not firmly established.[13] Another possibility is that he arrived at his ideas during his stay in Basra in the 1730s. The southern Iraqi city was passing through a turbulent period that included spells of Persian invasion and battles between Ottoman and Persian armies. Basra has a large Shiite population, something unknown in Najd and it is possible that Sheikh Muhammad reacted against Shiite veneration for the imams when he first encountered it.[14] There he began public preaching against what he deemed illegitimate ritual innovations (singular, *bid'a*) and violations of man's duty to devote all worship to God alone.[15] According to Sheikh Muhammad's grandson, it was during his study with Basra's scholars that God revealed to him hidden aspects of God's unity and His attributes. This special divine inspiration set him apart from other scholars of his time and moved him to compose the seminal treatise for Wahhabism, *The Book of God's Unity*, on the basis of Hadith collections he found in Basra.[16] The chronicler Ibn Ghannam placed the writing of that treatise in Huraymila, but Wahhabi sources concur that gifted inspiration is the wellspring for his monotheist manifesto.[17]

This brief essay is of tremendous significance for the Wahhabi mission and the subject of enduring controversy between supporters and detractors. It represents the core of Sheikh Muhammad's teaching and the foundation of the Wahhabi canon. The essay deals with matters of theology, ritual and the impact of actions and speech on one's standing as a true monotheist. It has nothing to say on Islamic law, which guides Muslims' everyday lives. This is a crucial point. One of the myths about Wahhabism is that its distinctive character stems from its affiliation with the supposedly 'conservative' or 'strict' Hanbali legal school. If that were the case, how could we explain the fact that the earliest opposition to Ibn Abd al-Wahhab came from other Hanbali scholars? Or that a tradition of anti-Wahhabi Hanbalism persisted into the nineteenth century? As an expert on law in Saudi Arabia notes, 'Ibn Abd al-Wahhab produced no unprecedented opinions and Saudi authorities today regard him not as a mujtahid in fiqh [independent thinker in jurisprudence], but rather in da'wa or religious reawakening... The Wahhabis' bitter differences with other Muslims were not over fiqh [jurisprudence] rules at all, but over *aqida*, or theological positions.'[18]

The Book of God's Unity contains 67 brief chapters. The first six chapters define monotheism and idolatry in general terms; the following chapters comment on the meaning of Qur'anic verses and the implications of hadiths to establish clear lines of permitted and forbidden beliefs, practices and utterances. The typical chapter has a text, usually verses from the Qur'an and hadiths, sometimes only one or the other, to illustrate a particular aspect of the main theme.[19] After the authoritative text, there is a list of issues that Muslims should consider based on those texts. In most of the essay, Sheikh

Muhammad's voice is muted; his 'authorship' consists of selecting Qur'anic verses and hadiths to juxtapose with a set of issues that seem to be salutary lessons the reader should draw from the religious texts. One gets the impression that each chapter functioned as a text for oral lessons with a circle of pupils or for public sermons. It is not a sustained discourse on monotheism and idolatry as one might expect from its title. Rather, it consists of discrete bits radiating from the axial concept of monotheism. For the sake of analysis, it is possible to divide the treatise into clusters of thematically related chapters. For instance, seven chapters deal with popular superstitions that imply human effort to manipulate supernatural forces rather than to trust in God: sorcery, soothsayers, breaking spells (reciting the Qur'an is permitted, other methods are not), divining evil omens and astrology.

The first chapter, 'On God's Unity', begins with five passages from the Qur'an commanding man to worship God and forbidding him to worship any other being. In particular, the verses state that God created mankind and the *jinn* (invisible spirits mentioned in the Qur'an) so that they should worship Him; God sent a prophet to every people to teach them to worship God and to avoid *taghut* (often translated as idolatry); God commanded that men shall worship only Him; God commanded men to worship Him alone and to 'associate' none with Him; the Lord has forbidden men from 'associating' any other being with Him. The Arabic term for 'associating' a creature with God is *shirk* and in Islamic usage it has the sense of idolatry or polytheism.[20] A large portion of Wahhabi discourse focuses on listing acts that constitute shirk. There follow two hadiths. In the first one, the Prophet's Companion Ibn Mas'ud[21] reported that the Prophet's will, or his legacy to the Muslims, was a verse from the Qur'an, already cited among the five verses, forbidding association with God. The second Hadith is a report from the Companion Mu'adh ibn Jabal where he relates that he was once riding on a camel behind the Prophet when the Prophet asked his Companion if he knew what God's creatures owe Him and what He owes His creatures. The Prophet then answered his own question: God's creatures owe Him exclusive worship and not associating any other being with Him; God owes his creatures not to punish any who do not associate any other being with Him. Finally, Sheikh Muhammad listed twenty-four *masa'il*, issues or salutary lessons, in the texts. They are stated in very brief form: The wisdom of creating the jinn and humans; the wisdom of God sending prophets; the religion of all prophets is the same and so forth. The issues include doctrinal points (all prophets taught the same core religious belief), the significance of specific verses in the Qur'an and the Prophet's modesty in sharing a donkey with another rider.[22]

Perhaps the most distinctive facet of Sheikh Muhammad's teaching and hence of the Wahhabi mission, is the insistence that proclaiming, understanding and affirming that God is one do not suffice to make one a Muslim, but that one must also explicitly deny any other object of worship. In the *Book of God's Unity*, he developed that point in Chapter Six, which stands out from the others in consisting largely of his own commentary on Qur'anic verses and a single Hadith. The verses state that idolaters call upon beings that themselves worship God, that Abraham declared he would not worship the idols of his folk, that Christians take men of religion as lords alongside God and that some people associate other beings with God. It seems that the Hadith is the key text in this chapter. The Prophet once declared that, 'Whoever affirms that there is no god but God and denies all other objects of worship, safeguards his blood, property and fate with God.' Sheikh Muhammad discussed the Qur'anic verses in a straightforward manner: they affirm the imperative of rejecting any hint of idolatry. He then stated that the Hadith is a clear explanation of the meaning of 'There is no god but God,' namely, that pronouncing, understanding and affirming it do not makes one's blood and property safe from attack. One must also deny any other object of worship and if that denial is ever compromised, then the safeguard against attack is lifted. He emphasized this point, 'It is indeed a grave problem, singular in its seriousness and importance, which has in these texts been made absolutely clear and its solution established without question.' It would be only a slight overstatement to assert that most of the animosity between Wahhabis and other Muslims boils down to this single question of what exactly makes one's life and property inviolable from attack.[23]

In addition to making idolatry a justification for war, Muhammad ibn Abd al-Wahhab underscored the perils of idolatry in the afterlife. According to the Qur'an, God forgives any sin except that of associating another being with Him. The Prophet once said that if someone died in the act of invoking God's associates for help, then he would enter the Fire. According to another Hadith, on the Day of Judgment, whoever did not associate another being with God will enter heaven and whoever did associate another being with God will enter the Fire.[24] Since idolatry has such dire consequences in this life and the next, it is essential to recognize the various forms that idolatry can assume. For instance, according to Sheikh Muhammad, making a vow to any being but God is a form of idolatry. The proof texts for this point are two Qur'anic verses. One enjoins believers to fulfil their vows. The other relates that God knows all the vows that one makes. The Hadith proof text states, 'Whoever vowed to obey God, let him fulfil his vow; whoever vowed to disobey God, let him not fulfil it.' In the absence of any texts that condemn vows to other beings, it seems that Sheikh Muhammad extracted the chapter heading, 'Vows to other than God are Idolatry,' from the implication of these texts rather than their clear sense.[25] He had stronger textual support for the position that seeking the help of any being but God is a form of idolatry. Several Qur'anic verses emphasize the futility of calling upon other beings; in a Hadith, the Prophet urges believers to not seek help from him against a hypocrite who was hurting some believers but to turn instead to God. Sheikh Muhammad interpreted the verse which commands believers not to call on other beings for help to mean that such practice constitutes major idolatry, even if one appeals to a righteous person for purely decent purposes. He also considered the texts to show that 'calling on anyone is a kind of worship of the person called.'[26] This last point would become a hugely controversial issue between Wahhabis and other Muslims. Ibn Abd al-Wahhab insisted that 'calling upon' (al-du'a') is the essence of worship. Other Muslims argued that one's intention and expectation determined whether 'calling upon' constituted worship or an innocent way to seek God's favour.

Another major point of contention is intercession, the belief that a particularly righteous individual might intercede with God on behalf of a believer at the Last Judgment. Five Qur'anic verses state that man has no intercessor apart from God, that the angels may intercede only with God's permission and that none but God has the slightest bit of power. Of course, Muslim critics of the Wahhabis seized the exception in the verse, 'None intercedes with God except as He is pleased to allow' and they asserted that their intercessionary requests were directed to those God 'is pleased to allow'. Sheikh Muhammad cited a Hadith reporting that the Prophet will not ask to intercede but will bow to and praise God; only then will God say that he may intercede and grant his intercession. While he considered this a proof against intercession, other Muslims interpreted the same text to indicate its permissibility.[27]

Muslims commonly sought the intercession of dead holy men at shrines erected over their graves. It should be no surprise, then, that Muhammad ibn Abd al-Wahhab justified the destruction of shrines. To support his position, he adduced a Hadith condemning Christians for worshipping at graves and placing images in churches. He blamed Shiites for importing into Islam the practice of constructing mosques at graves. (He also exhibited his anti-Shiite bias by using the insulting term *Rafida*, or 'Rejecters'.) A second Hadith bars the believers from building an edifice over the Prophet's grave for fear they would turn it into a mosque. Yet another one forbids imitating People of the Book in their custom of worshipping at prophets' graves. By analogy, Sheikh Muhammad declared that one may not pray at any grave, since to do so could lead to its conversion into a place of worship.[28] The most controversial point to arise from his discussion of worship at graves had to do with custom in Medina, where Muslims visited and prayed at the Prophet's tomb. Ibn Abd al-Wahhab cited hadiths that prohibit prayer at the Prophet's grave and concluded that while one may visit his grave, one must not pray there or in any cemetery for fear it could lead to idolatry.[29] The Wahhabis' enemies accused them of disrespecting the Prophet whereas the Wahhabis insisted they were closely following the Prophet's own example.

One last detail in *The Book of God's Unity* is worth mention. It expresses Muhammad ibn Abd al-Wahhab's sense that he lived at a time in history when Islam had become a stranger. This concept is embedded in three hadiths. The Prophet foretold that the believers would follow the path of Jews and Christians; he did not fear the prospect of an enemy conquering the believers but that of misguided leaders restoring idol worship and the appearance of false prophets; and the Prophet predicted that one group of believers would remain steadfast and not succumb to either false prophets or misguided leaders. Sheikh Muhammad concluded that the hadiths meant that idolatry would spread among the believers but that one group would stay true to God's message and eventually prevail.[30]

That perception pervaded Wahhabis' sense of their history as one of an enterprise facing resistance and onslaught from powerful political forces. The first Wahhabi chronicler, Husayn ibn Ghannam, portrayed Muhammad ibn Abd al-Wahhab not merely as a heroic figure, but as a solitary one in the early stages of his reformist effort.[31]

It followed that Ibn Ghannam's narrative of Sheikh Muhammad's life would echo standard Muslim accounts of the Prophet Muhammad.[32] According to the earliest Wahhabi chronicler, Muhammad ibn Abd al-Wahhab's mission began in Basra, where he issued the call to affirm God's unity and to reject idolatry. At the urging of Basra's ulama, the ruler expelled him during the peak of the most intense summer heat. He departed on foot and when he was about halfway to the nearby town of Zubayr, he nearly perished from thirst, but a kindly man chanced upon him. This Good Samaritan gave him water to drink and then put him on his donkey until they reached Zubayr. He eventually made his way back to Najd and the settlement of Huraymila, where his father had moved to become the religious judge (*qadi*) after a falling out with the chief of al-Uyayna.[33]

Sheikh Muhammad devoted himself to further studies of the Qur'an and other Islamic sciences, but he also began to criticize illegitimate innovations in ritual that in his view amounted to idolatry. It seems that his father sharply disagreed with him: the Wahhabi sources mention a dispute between them and add that Sheikh Muhammad kept silent until his father's death in 1740. At that point, he launched his public mission, 'forbidding people from depending on any being but God, whether they are saints, holy men, trees, or idols'.[34] He soon attracted a following in Huraymila and from nearby towns in the district known as al-Arid. He gave instruction on his treatise on God's unity, copies of which then spread. But once again he encountered political interference. The chronicles provide more detail on events and circumstances in Huraymila than in Basra. The town was divided between two clans from the same tribe. One of the clans was renowned for its immorality and plotted to murder the sheikh because of his campaign to 'forbid wrong and command right'. The clan's supporters made an attempt on his life one night but he escaped. Shortly thereafter, he moved on to al-Uyayna.[35]

For the first time, Sheikh Muhammad enjoyed open political support because al-Uyayna's amir, Uthman ibn Mu'ammar, endorsed his mission and ordered his townsmen to obey it. The amir signalled his close relationship to the sheikh by marrying his aunt to him. Jawhara bint Abd Allah ibn Mu'ammar is one of the few women mentioned in early Wahhabi sources. With support from the town's chief, the reformer resumed his mission of combating popular veneration of trees, stones, tombs, shrines erected over the graves of Companions and holy men, and places where folk slaughtered animals to seek good fortune. Amir Uthman supported a campaign to eliminate physical structures associated with intercessionary practices.[36]

Two episodes illustrate the disruptive impact of Sheikh Muhammad's mission. First, he personally destroyed a dome over the grave of a Companion, Zayd ibn al-Khattab, brother of the second caliph, Umar. This action embodied his aggressive attitude toward idolatry. Second, he commanded the stoning of a woman who willingly confessed to adultery. That the sources report this incident in some detail suggests that the punishment was rare. The report of the episode conveys the depth of Sheikh Muhammad's commitment to applying shari'a rules in a community that previously displayed a lax attitude on such matters. In the chronicles, there is something of a 'Yes, it is hard to believe, but it is true' tone to the account of the stoning. The woman came of her own volition, admitted to adultery, then repeated and affirmed her admission. Before deciding her case, Sheikh Muhammad made certain that she was of sound mind, asked her again if anyone had forced her to make this admission and only when she repeated her confession a third time did he order her grim punishment, putting her to death.[37]

It was not long before opposition to the mission again appeared. This time, it came not from a clique of immoral clan leaders (as the Huraymila foes are characterized in Saudi sources) but from religious scholars who rejected Sheikh Muhammad's views on proper worship and strict morality. In the Wahhabi sources, they are depicted as unable to defeat him through argument based on the Qur'an and the Sunna, so they resorted to lies and slander, but that tactic failed as well. Finally, the religious scholars contacted the region's distant overlord, Sheikh Sulayman ibn Uray'ar, the ruler of al-Hasa and persuaded him that the reformer's mission posed a threat to his right to collect taxes. Ibn Uray'ar then commanded Amir Uthman to expel Sheikh Muhammad. Thus, he departed from al-Uyayna as he had from Huraymila and Basra on previous occasions: as a persecuted figure in need of political shelter.[38]

In 1744, Muhammad ibn Abd al-Wahhab arrived in al-Dir'iyya, an oasis settlement under the rule of a clan known as Al Muqrin, but later to become famous as Al Saud. Unlike Huraymila and al-Uyayna, the sheikh had no family connection to al-Dir'iyya. It seems that he moved there because a member of one of its prominent clans had joined his circle of disciples and invited him upon his expulsion from al-Uyayna. He initially resided with his pupil's family and relied on them to pave the way for an introduction to al-Dir'iyya's amir, Muhammad ibn Saud. One chronicler states that a Bedouin wife of the amir persuaded him to meet with the refugee sheikh. At their first meeting, Ibn Abd al-Wahhab declared that the people of Najd were living in the same religious ignorance as were the Arabs when the Prophet Muhammad first preached Islam a millennium earlier. Muhammad ibn Saud declared his readiness to back the mission against unbelief and idolatry but insisted that the reformer accept two conditions. First, that he pledge to continue supporting Ibn Saud if their campaign to establish God's unity triumphed. Second, that Sheikh Muhammad approve of Ibn Saud's taxation of al-Dir'iyya's harvests. The reformer agreed to the first condition, but as for the second, he replied that God might compensate the amir with booty and legitimate taxes greater than the taxes on harvests. This was the origin of the pact between religious mission and political power that has endured for more than two and half centuries, a pact that has survived traumatic defeats and episodes of complete collapse.[39]

By the time of his arrival in al-Dir'iyya, Muhammad ibn Abd al-Wahhab had already been forced to move three times and he had seen dissolve one political alliance sealed by the ordinarily reliable tie of marriage. This time, however, he had far better fortune. Between 1744 and the sheikh's death in 1792, Ibn Saud and his descendants gradually expanded their realm to encompass all of Central Arabia. Saudi-Wahhabi conquest took place through a long series of raids that saw advances, retreats and renewed advances. The scale of violence in the fighting was small in comparison to wars fought between the Ottomans and the Persians in the central lands of the Middle East.[40] The effect on Arabia, however, was dramatic. For the first time since the rise of Islam, much of the peninsula would become unified under one political authority that enforced a single interpretation of Islam.

Muhammad ibn Abd al-Wahhab taught a cadre of ulama dedicated to the mission and he fought his own war of words against ulama who rejected his claims to revive true Islam. Throughout its history, the Wahhabi mission has confronted a constant barrage of criticism from Muslims who considered it a heresy. An early polemical adversary was Sulayman ibn Suhaym (c.1718–1767), a native of al-Majma'a, a town that boasted more religious specialists than most others in pre-Wahhabi Najd. At some point, Ibn Suhaym moved to Riyadh, quite close to al-Dir'iyya and became the settlement's religious leader.[41] Riyadh proved to be the most difficult nearby town for the Saudis to conquer, holding out for a quarter century under its own capable leader, Dahham ibn Dawwas.[42] Ibn Suhaym had begun his polemical campaign against the mission while Sheikh Muhammad was still in al-Uyayna. He labelled the reformer a misguided innovator in religion and urged ulama in surrounding lands – the Holy Cities, Basra, al-Hasa – to compose treatises against the reformer.[43] It is worth pausing to examine Ibn Suhaym's objections to Sheikh Muhammad because they would remain part of anti-Wahhabi rhetoric for generations.

Ibn Suhaym criticized Sheikh Muhammad for specific actions like destroying the tomb of Zayd ibn al-Khattab even though there were practical, not idolatrous reasons for erecting a tomb. The area was too rocky to dig a grave, so the Prophet's Companions had to set up a stone tomb to protect Zayd's corpse from beasts of prey. Sheikh Muhammad had also levelled a mosque in the tomb's vicinity for no reason but sheer whim. Ibn Suhaym accused the reformer of burning two famous religious works for containing allegedly idolatrous expressions. A more extensive set of objections centred on Sheikh Muhammad's definition of an unbeliever. This issue would become a permanent and perhaps the most emotionally charged part of Wahhabi polemics. After all, what could be more divisive in a mono-theistic religion than the claim that to be a believer one must adopt a particular view and that all others are infidels? Ibn Suhaym accused the reformer of declaring that whoever did not agree with his position is an unbeliever and that whoever agrees with his position is a believer, even if he is morally deficient. Along similar lines, he claimed that Sheikh Muhammad had declared prominent and venerated Muslims to be unbelievers, including the Sufi masters Ibn al-Farid and Ibn Arabi. In addition, he regarded as unbelievers descendants of the Prophet (known as *sayyids*) who accepted vows from Muslims; and he considered anyone who did not view these men as unbelievers to be unbelievers as well. Finally, he is supposed to have declared that whoever makes a sacrifice to a being other than God in order to ward off the evil intention of invisible spirits (jinns) is an unbeliever. Nearly as sensitive as the charge of unbelief was the mission's position on some practices that express respect for the Prophet Muhammad. Ibn Suhaym wrote that Sheikh Muhammad wished to raze the Prophet's tomb in Medina and dismantle a well-known ornamental feature, a golden water spout (*mizab*) on the *ka'ba* (the central cube-shaped structure in the Grand Mosque of Mecca) to replace it with a plain wooden one. He also said the reformer considered a special prayer for the Prophet on Thursday evening and Friday to be an innovation that leads to eternal punishment in the Hereafter.

Ibn Suhaym suggested that Muhammad ibn Abd al-Wahhab came to hold errant views because he lacked proper scholarly training. He claimed to know of a letter that Sheikh Muhammad sent to his missionaries swearing that he did not acquire his insight into the truth about God's unity from his father or any teacher in al-Arid or elsewhere. Ibn Suhaym sarcastically asked, then where did he get this so-called knowledge? Did God inspire him? Did he have a dream? Or did Satan teach him? Along similar lines, Sheikh Muhammad supposedly stated that people had been completely misguided and ignorant concerning God's unity for the past six hundred years.

If Ibn Suhaym is one of the earliest authors to attack the Wahhabi mission, Sheikh Muhammad's response to his charges is one of the first formulations to defend it, setting forth clarifications and denials.[44] For instance, in an epistle that Ibn Abd al-Wahhab sent to a religious teacher in Ibn Suhaym's home town of al-Majma'a, he called his adversary a liar for accusing him of wishing to level the Prophet's tomb and to replace the golden spout at the ka'ba. He also denied ever saying that people had been misguided for the past six hundred years or that he rejected the weighty tradition of learned jurists from the four Sunni legal schools. In addition to the 'sheer fabrications' that Ibn Abd al-Wahhab denied, there were a number of points that, he declared, were distortions of his positions. For instance, on the matter of levelling domes above tombs, he cited a prominent medieval authority who considered it obligatory to destroy sites of idolatry in general and from that broad principle, he concluded that any structure erected over a tomb must be levelled.[45] When it came to the issue of burning certain books, he said that he had not done so but he warned against allowing any book to become dearer than the Qur'an. Sheikh Muhammad's epistle to al-Majma'a affirmed that he held that one does not become a Muslim until he knows the true meaning of 'there is no god but God,' that he teaches that meaning and that its essence is knowing the full implication of the term 'god' in that phrase. He affirmed that he considered an unbeliever whoever sacrificed meat to ward off jinn and whoever made vows to a lower creature in order to get closer to God. He regarded a special prayer for the Prophet on Thursday and Friday as an illegitimate innovation even though praying for the Prophet in general is permitted. Glorification of the sultan was, in his view, an illegitimate innovation.

Ibn Suhaym's points against Muhammad ibn Abd al-Wahhab surfaced in other critical writings, including a treatise by the reformer's own brother Sulayman.[46] We do not know whether Sulayman was older or younger than his famous brother.[47] He followed their father as the qadi of Huraymila in 1740 and he held that post until the town fell to Saudi forces in 1755. During those years, the town wavered between allegiance and opposition to the Saudis. Huraymila's chief embraced the Wahhabi mission in 1745 and its townsmen participated in some Wahhabi military expeditions against nearby settlements. Huraymila withdrew support from the Saudis a few years later, in 1752.

The sources are mute on Sulayman's position toward the mission before 1752, when Huraymila withdrew from the Saudi fold. It appears that he quietly, if not clandestinely, opposed his brother's teachings and that when Sheikh Muhammad discovered his activities, he rebuked him in a letter. Sulayman then replied with a letter in which he gave his views on the mission at the same time he pledged to withhold support from any military action against his brother. Nevertheless, he soon publicly proclaimed hostility to the mission and his loyalty to its political enemies. In 1754, Sulayman sent an epistle warning against his brother's deviations to be publicly recited in al-Uyayna's mosques and meeting places. According to the Saudi chronicler Ibn Ghannam, Sheikh Muhammad ordered the killing of the man who recited Sulayman's epistle.[48] Sheikh Muhammad also composed an essay to rebut his brother's epistle.[49] It was because Sulayman had turned Huraymila into a centre of doctrinal opposition that Ibn Saud mustered forces for its definitive conquest the following year. When Huraymila fell in 1755, Sulayman wisely fled north to al-Zilfi since his brother had condemned him as an atheist and enemy of religion. Saudi sources do not mention him again until al-Zilfi's subjugation in 1781. Its townsmen brought him to al-Dir'iyya at Sheikh Muhammad's order. There, he was placed under house arrest and remained until he died in 1793. Later reports claim that Sulayman eventually repented his errors, but those may well represent efforts to smooth over the historical record.

Sulayman's 1754 anti-Wahhabi treatise elaborated some of Ibn Suhaym's criticisms of Sheikh Muhammad.[50] First, he accused his brother of undertaking independent legal reasoning (*ijtihad*) without the necessary scholarly qualifications. He did not argue that qualified scholars have no right to do ijtihad, but that his brother's handling of proof texts from the Qur'an and the Sunna was deficient.[51] If Sheikh Muhammad had discussed his views with other ulama, he would have avoided erroneous conclusions. Second, Sheikh Muhammad wrongly branded Muslims as infidels.[52] On this matter, Sulayman anticipated a perennial controversy between Wahhabis and their Muslim adversaries. The Wahhabis would always maintain that they never regarded Muslims as infidels while their opponents insisted that the fundamental problem with Wahhabism is its exclusion of Muslims from the community of believers. Sulayman asserted the common view that to proclaim the creed (There is no god but God and Muhammad is the messenger of God), to perform the obligatory acts of worship and to believe in God, His angels, books and messengers qualify one as a Muslim. In contrast, Sheikh Muhammad argued that if someone violated God's unity by invoking a dead or living holy man or by a similar practice, then that person was guilty of idolatry even if he sincerely proclaimed the creed. According to Sulayman, the Muslim consensus viewed such violations of God's unity as 'lesser idolatry', which falls short of apostasy, for which one may be put to death.

In discussing the question of branding others as infidels (*takfir*), Sulayman claimed that the two medieval Hanbali scholars, Ibn Taymiyya and Ibn al-Qayyim, had endorsed this view of lesser idolatry.[53] Indeed, much of the essay consists of excerpts from their writings to refute Sheikh Muhammad's positions.[54] This was a clever rhetorical stroke because the reformer relied on those two scholars for many of his positions.[55] Sulayman mined their works for passages that contradicted his brother's views. For instance, in one place he wrote that he cited Ibn Taymiyya because his brother had drawn on his work to justify takfir for invoking saints and making vows to them; Sulayman then cited a specific passage to rebut that position. He went on to note that even if somebody committed 'major idolatry', the religious authorities had to make that clear to him before he could be held responsible, because he might have erred out of ignorance.[56] At numerous points, he accused his brother of rupturing Muslim unity and in so doing, going down the same misguided path as the Kharijites of early Islamic times.[57] This would become a standard charge in Muslim polemics against the Wahhabis, as they were said to accuse an entire town of infidelity and judge it as apostate and a land of war. Thus, Wahhabis fought other Muslims with no justification but their own mistaken notion that these Muslims were idolaters.

Muhammad ibn Abd al-Wahhab responded to his brother's challenge.[58] He insisted that invoking and making vows to holy men indeed constituted major idolatry and that it was proper to deem as infidels anyone who failed to view such practices as idolatry. He also reiterated that Ibn Taymiyya and Ibn al-Qayyim held this view and that it would be true even if they did not. He then stated that if one admits that these practices are major idolatry, then fighting is a duty as part of the prophetic mission to destroy idols. Thus, the idolater who calls upon a saint for help must repent. If he does so, his repentance is accepted. If not, he is to be killed.[59] The essay includes hadiths enjoining affection for believers and enmity toward infidels.[60] In the end, the debate between the brothers was not settled by the stronger argument but by *force majeure* through Saudi conquest, carried out in the name of holy war, or jihad.[61]

Had the religious controversy been confined to an exchange of heated epistles among the ulama of Najd, Muhammad ibn Abd al-Wahhab's mission would have passed unnoticed by Muslims outside Arabia. The success of Saudi military expansion, however, forced the wider Ottoman world to take notice. For the Wahhabis, the conquests were justified as religiously sanctioned warfare, or jihad. Sheikh Muhammad's writings on that subject fall into two categories: legal discourse on the conditions of waging jihad and epistles to towns calling on them to accept the mission and Saudi sovereignty.[62] His position on jihad is adumbrated in the *Book of God's Unity*, where he interpreted two hadiths to validate war against people who rejected a summons to Islam. In the first Hadith, the Prophet advised the leader of an expedition to Yemen's People of the Book (Jews and Christians) to call on them to perform the obligatory prayer (*salat*) and to distribute alms. If they agreed, then the Muslims would not attack. The second Hadith reports Muhammad's words before a battle against a Jewish oasis (Khaybar). He told Ali to call Khaybar's people to Islam and to their duties to God. Muslims at war with the Saudis could argue that the hadiths pertained to Jews and Christians, not to fellow Muslims. The key text in the *Book of God's Unity* is actually Sheikh Muhammad's explanation of monotheism (*tawhid*) and what exactly 'There is no god but God' means. In his view, if one's denial of any associate with God should ever weaken or fail, then his life and property are liable to attack.[63]

The essence of Ibn Abd al-Wahhab's justification for fighting the people of Arabia is reiterated in many brief epistles and treatises.

The main points are as follows. The unbelievers (*kuffar*) of the Prophet's time affirmed that God is the creator, the sustainer and the master of all affairs; they gave alms, they performed pilgrimage and they avoided forbidden things from fear of God. But all that did not suffice to make them Muslims or prohibit shedding their blood and plundering their wealth. Rather, they were unbelievers liable to attack because they failed to devote all worship to God alone; they sacrificed animals to other beings; they sought the help of other beings; they swore vows by other beings. Whoever seeks the help of any being but God is an unbeliever; whoever sacrifices an animal to any being but God is an unbeliever; who makes a vow to any being but God is an unbeliever. It was in order to wipe out such idolatry that the Prophet fought them, killed them, plundered their wealth and permitted taking their women. Ibn Abd al-Wahhab noted that the unbelievers may well profess God's oneness as the creator and the sustainer. But if they call on the angels, or Jesus, or the saints to get closer to God, then they are unbelievers. Even if they pray night and day, live an austere life and donate all their wealth, they are still unbelievers and God's enemy because of their belief in Jesus or some saint.[64] Sheikh Muhammad did not, however, endorse fighting unbelievers before they had received the call, understood it and then rejected it. He admitted that many idolaters of his time were merely ignorant folk who could be guided to correct belief and worship.[65]

Sheikh Muhammad set forth three conditions for launching a jihad in a treatise on the subject. First, when a Muslim force happens to meet an enemy force; second, when an enemy force approaches Muslim territory; third, when the legitimate leader (imam) deems it necessary.[66] While the first two conditions refer to specific situations, the last one essentially leaves the declaration of jihad to the discretion of the imam. To initiate a jihad, one must first call on the adversary to embrace Islam, an action that sounded reasonable to adherents of the mission, but to its Muslim foes, it was presumptuous and utterly unjustified to call on them to embrace Islam. To convey the insult to other Muslims, consider this scenario.[67] Saudi forces take some captives. All such men would have considered themselves to be Muslims combating a Saudi attempt to subjugate their town. Such a situation was not unusual in the climate of endemic strife between Arabia's towns. In this instance, however, the Wahhabi captors call on the prisoners to embrace Islam. The prisoners consider themselves to be Muslims and find the notion that they are actually idolaters insulting. Sheikh Muhammad stipulated that the prisoner may embrace Islam and go free; he may accept Muslim rule and pay a tax of protection (a rule applied to Christians and Jews); if he does neither, then he is to be executed. Is it any wonder that Muslims detested Sheikh Muhammad and his followers when they justified executing Muslim prisoners of war? At one time, a Muslim had written to him asking for an explanation of his attacks.[68] In his reply, Sheikh Muhammad declared that it was proper to fight any idolater, which in this instance apparently referred to someone who did not accept his definition of monotheism, for he wrote that if someone received correct instruction but rejected it, then he was to be fought. Since early Islamic history, Muslims have differed on the essential point of what constitutes correct belief, but at most times, such differences did not result in military conflict or the adoption of coercive measures as in an inquisition. The Muslim consensus had been weakest along the divide between Sunnis and Shiites, but among Sunnis themselves, violent conflict over doctrinal matters was a rarity and it was unquestionably the Sheikh's castigation of Sunnis as idolaters that fostered a legacy of hostility that would endure for generations.

Under the canopy of expanding Saudi power, Wahhabism became the dominant religious doctrine in Najd. Converting the region was a gradual process with a deep impact on the ulama. When Muhammad ibn Abd al-Wahhab settled in al-Dir'iyya, he sent epistles and copies of treatises to various Najdi towns in a campaign to persuade their ulama to embrace his call. This effort apparently had some effect, for when a settlement entered the Saudi fold, some of its ulama declared their allegiance. In several instances, however, most of the ulama refused, and emigrated under pressure.[69] In addition to fostering a new doctrinal orientation, the mission created a new focus of religious authority in the person of Muhammad ibn Abd al-Wahhab, who transmitted his standing to his descendants. Wahhabi hegemony meant that al-Dir'iyya would be the centre of religious scholarship. Henceforth, religious pupils commonly made it their destination rather than older seats of learning in Najd or Ottoman lands.

The most important centre for religious learning had long been Ushayqir, a town in the Washm region north of al-Arid. In the sixteenth and seventeenth centuries, no other town approached it in the number of ulama it produced or the number of pupils who travelled there to attend religious lessons. If one compared Ushayqir to Cairo or Damascus, the number of its ulama and pupils is quite modest, but the Arabian context is the relevant one. In the seventeenth century, Ushayqir was the birthplace of eighteen ulama and the adopted home of fourteen others. It was also the home of Al Musharraf, the most eminent scholarly family and the lineage of Ibn Abd al-Wahhab. After Ushayqir came under Saudi-Wahhabi authority in 1766, ambitious pupils and scholars no longer came to study with its ulama but tended to go to al-Dir'iyya instead.[70] Ulama opposed to Wahhabism departed and by around 1800, the town's ulama were thoroughly Wahhabi. Doctrinal polarization in Ushayqir during the initial encounter with Wahhabism is evident in some details about four of its ulama. Two went to al-Dir'iyya to study with Sheikh Muhammad: one of them became a qadi for the Saudis in Huraymila and al-Hasa; the other became a teacher in Ushayqir. On the other hand, one scholar left the town when it came under Saudi rule in 1766 and went to Damascus, where he spent the last twenty-five years of his life. A second scholar was pressured to leave Ushayqir, but rather than emigrate from Najd, he resettled in Unayza, a northern town that had not yet entered the Saudi fold.[71]

Other towns in Washm followed the same pattern. Wahhabi converts entered the mission's service as teachers or judges while opponents felt pressure to emigrate: the qadi of Tharmada was killed in a Saudi raid;[72] a scholar from Uthayfiya who composed a polemical attack on the mission emigrated to al-Hasa;[73] another anti-Wahhabi author, this one from Far'a, moved first to al-Hasa, then Zubayr and finally Kuwait, where he became the earliest known qadi.[74] In the later decades of the first amirate, Washm's ulama were almost entirely lined up with the Wahhabi mission. There were eleven ulama from the region, and we have no evidence that any opposed it. Instead, there was a trend toward consolidation through ties of marriage to Sheikh Muhammad and study in al-Dir'iyya. One man from Al Musharraf entered the Sheikh's study circle, married his daughter and returned to his town as the qadi.[75] His son, the Sheikh's grandson, followed him as qadi.[76] The son of an early Ushayqir Wahhabi served the mission as qadi in al-Hasa.[77] Within Ushayqir, a new scholarly lineage allied to the mission arose.[78] One last shift of note in Washm was the rise of Ushayqir's neighbouring town Shaqra to prominence as a regional centre of learning.

The picture in a second region, Sudayr, reinforces the impression one gets from Washm that Saudi rule brought pressure for conformity to the mission and the departure of its critics. One of the prominent scholarly lineages, Al Shabana of al-Majma'a, had risen to prominence in the seventeenth century. When Saudi power subjugated the town in the 1770s, members of the lineage loyally served the Wahhabi mission.[79] On the other hand, members of another scholarly lineage, Al Suhaym, rejected Sheikh Muhammad's call. Muhammad ibn Ahmad ibn Suhaym wrote a treatise against it and his son Sulayman, author of the anti-Wahhabi epistle, became the imam at Riyadh's princely court. Sulayman's son left Najd when Saudi forces overran Riyadh and continued the anti-Wahhabi tradition in Zubayr.[80]

Another town in Sudayr, Harma, harboured more ulama opposed to the Wahhabi mission than any other in Najd: at least five, perhaps six, of that town's seven ulama. Abd Allah ibn Isa al-Muwaysi (d. 1761)[81] was one of Muhammad ibn Abd al-Wahhab's best-known adversaries. He studied with Hanbali ulama in Damascus and became the qadi of Harma upon his return. When the Saudis conquered the town in 1779, they exiled its ruling clans[82] and four anti-Wahhabi ulama emigrated to Zubayr and al-Hasa, where they perpetuated the anti-Wahhabi tradition.[83] The only individual in Harma to support the mission, Abd Allah ibn Ahmad al-Busaymi, studied in al-Dir'iyya and permanently settled there, perhaps because of hostility toward the Wahhabis in his native town.[84]

In the less populous settlements of southern Najd, we find the same pattern. The one exception to Wahhabi conversion is the northern region of al-Qasim. The sources offer little detail about the attitude of its ulama toward Muhammad ibn Abd al-Wahhab, but they consistently point to opposition. An ambiguous but suggestive example is Dukhayl ibn Rashid, who belonged to a chiefly lineage in the town of Unayza and succeeded his father as amir in 1760–1761.[85] He later abdicated that position in favour of his brother and travelled to Damascus to pursue religious learning. By the time he was ready to return to Unayza, it had come under Saudi rule, so he went to Mecca instead. Perhaps Sheikh Dukhayl rejected Ibn Abd al-Wahhab's doctrine, but he may have moved to Mecca for political reasons: He belonged to a chiefly lineage that resisted Saudi power until it was completely defeated.[86] Sheikh Humaydan ibn Turki provides a clear instance of opposition to Wahhabism. The mission's ulama called him an unbeliever and Saudi persecution caused him to move to Mecca.[87] Sheikh Salih ibn Sa'igh's critical stance toward the Wahhabis is evident from polemical verse he wrote against a well-known poem praising Muhammad ibn Abd al-Wahhab.[88] A review of fifteen ulama from Unayza turns up just one individual who embraced the Wahhabi doctrine, for which he was first rewarded by the Saudis with an appointment as amir and qadi of a small settlement near Unayza. He was eventually killed in an anti-Saudi revolt in 1782.[89]

Establishing Wahhabi hegemony over religious life entailed more than purging its opponents. It also required a corps of ulama who embraced its doctrine, often after studying with Muhammad ibn Abd al-Wahhab and his sons. The descendants of Sheikh Muhammad, who became known as Al al-Sheikh (House of the Sheikh) played the central role in perpetuating the Wahhabi mission and assumed an unrivalled position of prominence as a hereditary line of religious leaders for two centuries. Abd Allah (1752–1826) was the most prominent of Sheikh Muhammad's four sons and the one who inherited the standing of supreme religious leader.[90] The other sons achieved distinction and contributed to the lineage's proliferation. Quite a few of their descendants figured prominently in later Wahhabi history.[91]

Just as Abd Allah's father had served as chief adviser to the early Saudi amirs, so did he occupy a highly influential position with later amirs as counsellor and chief of the religious estate, overseeing the appointment of qadis and teachers throughout the growing realm. He also continued his father's vocation of discursive combat against doctrinal adversaries, authoring treatises to rebut the attacks of Shiite scholars in Yemen and Iran. Sheikh Abd Allah had the honour of joining the Saudis' victorious campaign to seize Mecca and entered the holy city in 1803. He later set down a description of negotiations over its surrender and occupation.[92] In one of his essays, he made a special effort to persuade Mecca's ulama of the mission's place in the mainstream of Islam's Sunni scholastic tradition. He stated that Wahhabis follow the Hanbali school but did not reject the other Sunni schools; he did, however, declare that he considered Shiite traditions beyond the pale, expressing in that respect, a common Sunni prejudice. In order to give specific substance to his claim of Sunni affiliation, he noted that Wahhabism derived its positions from well-known authorities on Qur'anic exegesis and Hadith. This was contrary to charges against the Wahhabis that they interpreted the Qur'an to suit their particular views and accepted only those hadiths that reinforced their positions.[93]

The adoption of a controversial doctrine set Najd's tradition of religious learning at odds with that of neighbouring regions and

therefore brought about a new relationship between those areas.
Ambitious pupils formerly travelled to the Holy Cities, Damascus
and Cairo to pursue specialized training that would set them above
pupils with purely 'provincial' Central Arabian learning. In Wahhabi
Arabia, study with 'the Sheikh' and his entourage conferred status.
It became far more common for itinerant pupils to make al-Dir'iyya
their destination to imbibe the mission's doctrine and essential texts
and then return to home towns as its agents. Fewer pupils left Najd
and most of those who did adopted anti-Wahhabi views. It is not
clear whether they held such views to begin with and left Arabia
because they did not wish to study with Wahhabi sheikhs or if they
adopted anti-Wahhabi ideas from their teachers. It is clear, however,
that travel to study outside Najd became a common feature of anti-
Wahhabi pupils and scholars.[94]

The Wahhabi Mission and the Muslim World

In the 1780s and 1790s, the Saudi amirate's expansion brought it
to the borders of the Ottoman Empire's Arabian possessions in al-
Hasa and Hijaz. In doing so, the Wahhabi mission assumed a more
threatening aspect to Ottoman ulama in those regions and they urged
Istanbul to take action to suppress the Najdi movement. In 1793, for
example, an Ottoman qadi in Medina collected the signatures of more
than 50 officials on a letter to Istanbul.[95] He compared the Wahhabis
to a tenth-century Shiite sect, the Qarmatians, who were notorious
in Islamic history for raiding Mecca and stealing the black stone
embedded in the Ka'ba. By 1802, the Ottomans were mounting a
doctrinal campaign, sending official tracts refuting Wahhabi positions
and likening them to the Kharijites of early Islamic times.

In the same period, Wahhabi sheikhs dispatched epistles to religious
scholars in various parts of the Middle East – Syria, Egypt, Tunisia and
Morocco. Only in the Moroccan sultan's court did the proselytizing
effort find a favourable reception in official circles, primarily because
the attack on excessive respect for holy men as constituting idolatry
bolstered the ruler's position against marabouts, primarily small
town holy men whose religious prestige often conferred political
influence.[96] Elsewhere, loyalty to Istanbul and confidence in the
cosmopolitan Islamic consensus fuelled the sense that the Wahhabis
represented a rustic, misguided and fanatical – and hopefully
temporary – intrusion.[97] An exception to the anti-Wahhabi chorus
in Ottoman lands turns up in the work of the celebrated Egyptian

chronicler Abd al-Rahman al-Jabarti.[98] Whereas Ottoman writers disparaged Muhammad ibn Abd al-Wahhab, the Egyptian author described him as a man who summoned men to God's book and the Prophet's Sunna, bidding them to abandon innovations in worship.[99] To the Wahhabis' discredit, al-Jabarti reported the 1803 massacre at Ta'if, where Wahhabi forces slaughtered the men and enslaved the women and children.[100] But when it came to doctrinal matters, he reproduced an epistle that the Wahhabis had sent to the religious leader of a Moroccan pilgrim caravan. The epistle set forth their views on idolatry, intercession, festooning the graves of holy men and adhering to the Sunni mainstream. It emphasized that the Wahhabis did not bring anything new but followed classical authorities.[101]

The conquests of Medina and Mecca had shocked the Ottomans and alarmed many in the Muslim world. But in al-Jabarti's account, the Wahhabis took Medina without any fighting and then prohibited things forbidden by shari'a: they banned tobacco in the marketplace (implying that they tolerated private consumption) and razed the domes over all graves except for that over the tomb of the Prophet.[102] In Mecca, again, the Wahhabis banned smoking at pilgrimage sites, prohibited silk clothing and ordered attendance at the congregational prayers. Al-Jabarti drew an unflattering comparison to the Meccan sharifs when he mentioned that the Wahhabis abolished illegal taxes that the sharifs had collected, like special dues for the performance of burials. In general, the new regime brought greater security and prosperity to the Holy Cities.[103] The Wahhabis' enemies accused them of disrupting the pilgrimage, but al-Jabarti reported that the Syrian caravan of 1807 was blocked only because the Ottoman commander refused to promise conformity with shari'a prescriptions for correct performance of the pilgrimage rites.[104] For those pilgrims who did reach Mecca that year, the Saudi leader ensured their safety. He also maintained low prices – contrary, it seems, to the sharifian regime's customary gouging of pious Muslim sojourners.[105] In similar fashion, al-Jabarti cleared the Wahhabis of charges that they obstructed the pilgrimage from Egypt and Syria in 1809. Moroccan pilgrims passing through Cairo on their way home told the historian that they had no difficulty with the Wahhabi regime. He concluded that the rumours about their wrongdoings originated with corrupt Meccans and Medinans who had profited by extorting gifts and fees from pilgrims.[106] The Meccan sharif in particular was singled out as a corrupt and duplicitous hypocrite.[107]

Whereas most Ottoman ulama reached their conclusions about the Wahhabis through hearsay or the occasional doctrinal work that might land in their midst, al-Jabarti met two Wahhabi sheikhs who visited Cairo in September 1815 on a diplomatic mission. They were free to roam the city in the company of official escort.[108] As religious scholars, it was natural that they should visit al-Azhar, Cairo's ancient seat of religious learning. They may have been disappointed to learn that the Hanbali legal school had become extinct in Egypt. Nonetheless, they purchased copies of famous works on Qur'anic exegesis and Hadith collections. Al-Jabarti described them as articulate, learned, mannerly and displaying substantial understanding of religion and Islamic jurisprudence.[109]

Wahhabi-Ottoman polemical hostility turned into a political confrontation after the Saudi conquest of Mecca and Medina in 1803 and 1805. The Central Arabian power was no longer a mere nuisance to the Ottoman sultan; it was now a dire threat to his standing as the guardian of Muslim holy places. The crisis first required the recovery of the Holy Cities and then eradication of the ideological challenge posed by the Wahhabi mission. At that moment in Ottoman history, however, the sultan did not have at his direct command the military resources necessary for these tasks; he did, however, have a promising instrument in the ambitious, energetic governor of Egypt, Muhammad Ali. The latter had arrived in Egypt in 1801 with the Ottoman-British expeditionary force that would end France's three-year occupation. In the complicated power struggle that followed, Muhammad Ali emerged as the strongman. His dynastic aspirations drove him to experiment with forms of economic production, administrative organization and military tactics that would transform Egypt into the eastern Mediterranean's major power. Istanbul's request that he retake Hijaz offered the opportunity to secure his position as a valuable vassal; it also presented the possibility of building his own empire under the cover of serving his overlord. For their part, the Saudis had confronted and thwarted Ottoman military expeditions dispatched from Iraq to dislodge them from eastern Arabia, so the prospect of another invasion may not have alarmed them. The difference was that Muhammad Ali was embarking on the Middle East's first successful experiment of military and administrative modernization and that made him a far more formidable enemy than any they had previously encountered. Nonetheless, the daunting logistical task of equipping and moving an army from Cairo to Arabia, then maintaining it among a hostile population and finally mounting and sustaining sieges on fortified strongholds deep in Najd meant that Muhammad Ali's first military adventure would take a full seven years.

In August 1811, an Ottoman naval expedition seized the undefended Red Sea port of Yanbu, which served as a base for resupply and headquarters to regain the Holy Cities. Saudi and Ottoman forces first clashed in December between Medina and Yanbu. The Saudis ambushed their foes and forced them to retreat in disarray. Following this inauspicious beginning, the Ottomans regained their balance and marched in better order to Medina, which the Saudi defenders evacuated in November 1812 after a brief siege. The Saudis withdrew as the invading force approached Mecca in January 1813. A stalemate set in for the next two years, during which Muhammad Ali cemented his authority in Hijaz. In 1815, the Ottomans made their first major thrust into Najd, marching into al-Qasim, where inconclusive fighting led to a truce. Talks resulted in an Ottoman withdrawal to Hijaz.[110]

In al-Dir'iyya, Wahhabi leaders watched the crumbling of the mission's domain with alarm and bitterness over the reversal of history's course. The early sense of a beleaguered, lonely vanguard battling for truth returned, now tinged with revulsion at fair-weather friends abandoning the Saudi bandwagon in the face of Ottoman forces. During the 1815 truce, the Saudi ruler Amir Abd Allah marched north to punish disloyal towns and chiefs in al-Qasim. For urging the Ottomans to invade Najd, he razed the walls of two towns and seized their chiefs, transporting them to al-Dir'iyya.[111] Notwithstanding this exemplary punishment, men from the district went to Cairo to incite Muhammad Ali to resume his war against the Saudis.[112] Such betrayal may account for the resentment expressed in the writings of a talented young member of Al al-Sheikh, Sulayman Ibn Abd Allah ibn Muhammad (1785–1818). In two brief epistles that he apparently composed during the war, he gave Wahhabi polemics a stronger xenophobic accent by elaborating on two related questions: Is it permitted to travel to the land of idolatry? Is it permitted to befriend idolaters?[113]

In the treatise on travel to the land of idolatry, he wrote that it is permissible on two conditions. First, one must openly practise one's religion. Second, one must refrain from befriending the idolaters. The rationale for this ruling is that God commands believers to bear enmity toward idolaters; whatever may cause one to neglect this command is not permitted. Travel to conduct trade with idolaters may incline one to placate them, as often occurs in the case of 'corrupt' Muslims.[114] He stated that there is no difference between a brief sojourn of one or two months and a long one. It is forbidden to stay even one day in a land where one cannot openly practise religion and refrain from befriending the idolaters if one is able to depart. The proof texts for this position are a verse from the Qur'an and a Hadith. The Qur'anic verse is *al-Nisa'* 140:

> He has already revealed unto you in the Scripture that when you hear the revelations of God rejected and derided, sit not with them until they engage in some other conversation. Lo! In that case you would be like unto them. Lo! God will gather hypocrites and disbelievers, all together, into hell.

Sheikh Sulayman held that this verse means that if a Muslim willingly sits with infidels while they ridicule God's revelation and he does not condemn them and leave them, then he is like them because remaining in their company connotes approval of disbelief, which itself is disbelief.[115] The Hadith proof text related by the Companion Abu Da'ud is particularly important because it would appear in numerous Wahhabi writings for the next two centuries: 'Whoever associates with the idolater and lives with him is like him.'[116] Sheikh Sulayman explained this to mean that if a believer associates with idolaters, assists them and shares a dwelling with them such that they consider him one of them, then he becomes one of them, unless he openly practises his religion and refrains from befriending them. He then noted that that was what befell the believers who remained in Mecca after the Prophet's emigration (*hijra*) to Medina. Even though they claimed to be Muslims, they resided in Mecca and the idolaters considered them to be part of their group. Indeed, they went with the idolaters to fight the Muslims at the battle of Badr. Some Companions thought they were Muslims. So after the battle they said, 'We have killed our brothers.' But then God sent down the Qur'anic verse, *al-Nisa'* 97:

> Lo! As for those whom the angels take (in death), they wrong themselves.

Experts in Qur'anic exegesis interpreted the verse to mean that such men were infidels and that God will not forgive them, except for those whom the Meccans compelled to join them.

Sulayman ibn Abd Allah devoted a separate treatise to the requirement that believers refrain from offering loyalty to idolaters.[117] On this topic, Muhammad ibn Abd al-Wahhab had written that devoting all worship to God and abandoning idolatry did not make one's religion complete unless one also showed open enmity toward the idolaters.[118] The sheikh had also composed a brief epistle condemning as idolaters folks who lived in Mecca, Basra, or al-Hasa when those areas were at war with the Wahhabis.[119] His grandson composed a more extensive treatise consisting of a brief discussion and twenty-one proof texts, mostly from the Qur'an. In the discussion, he stated that whoever pretends to agree with the idolaters' religion is an infidel, even if one does so out of fear and a wish to placate them. The only exception is for a believer who has come under their power. If they torture or threaten to kill the believer, then he may verbally agree with them as long as he maintains faith in his heart.

The proof texts establish five main points. First, the central theme is the duty for believers to bear enmity toward infidels and idolaters (*al-Mujadala* 22, *al-Tawba* 23). From this duty it follows that believers may not offer them loyalty (*Al Imran* 28, *al-Maida* 51, 55, 80–1, *Hud* 113, *al-Mumtahana* 1–3) or obedience (*Al Imran* 149, *al-An'am* 121). Third, God has ordained these duties to protect the believers from straying from His guidance because idolaters wish to lead believers away from the true religion (*al-Baqara* 120, 145, 217, *al-Kahf* 20). Fourth, merely keeping company with them will make a believer become like one of them (*al-Nisa'* 140, *al-A'raf* 175, Abu Da'ud's Hadith). The apprehension that social pressures arising from daily interaction with infidels would either force or tempt a believer to abandon the true religion is behind the obligation to remove oneself from their midst, in other words, to emigrate (perform hijra). Lastly, worldly temptations could weaken believers' resolve and leave them vulnerable to backsliding (*al-Nahl* 106–7, *al-Hajj* 11, *al-Tawba* 24, *Muhammad* 25–8, *al-Hashr* 11, *al-Ma'ida* 52–4).

Hijra is not prominent in Muhammad ibn Abd al-Wahhab's writings, but he did consider it a duty for Muslim who may not practise their religion, according to a Hadith stating that hijra will not cease until repentance ceases and repentance will not cease until the sun rises in the west, i.e. Judgment Day.[120] Later Wahhabi writers would remain concerned with the implication that hijra from the land

of infidels to Muslim territory is obligatory. For Sulayman, the key to
the matter lies in *al-Nisa'* 97:

> Lo! As for those whom the angels take (in death) while they
> wrong themselves, (the angels) will ask: In what were you
> engaged? They will say: We were oppressed in the land.
> (The angels) will say: Was not God's earth spacious that you
> could have migrated therein? As for such, their habitation
> will be hell, an evil journey's end.

Sulayman's discussion of the verse begins with a terse rhetorical
question, 'In other words, what group were you with? The Muslims
or the idolaters?' He then remarked that this verse concerns Meccans
who had embraced Islam and refrained from joining the hijra. When
the idolaters went out to the battle of Badr, they forced them to go
along and the Muslims killed them. When the Muslims realized this,
they regretted it and said, 'We have killed our brothers.' And then
God revealed this verse.[121] In alluding to the Wahhabis' fair weather
friends, Sulayman asked what this meant about folk who once
followed Islam but then showed agreement with idolaters and entered
into obedience to them, gave them comfort and assisted them? They
forsook Muslims (*ahl al-tawhid*, that is, the Wahhabis), faulted them,
insulted them and mocked them for their perseverance, patience and
struggle on behalf of monotheism. Further, they willingly assisted the
idolaters (the Ottomans). Such folk are worse in their disbelief and
more deserving of punishment in the Fire than those in Muhammad's
time who chose not to join the hijra out of attachment to their homes
and from fear of the infidels.

Thus, in Sulayman's view, the Ottoman-Saudi military confrontation
was not merely a struggle between enemy political forces but a facet
of the struggle between belief and unbelief, between monotheism
and idolatry, between those who love God and His messenger and
those who hate God and His messenger. The principles governing
the early nineteenth-century war were the same as those revealed
by God in the Qur'an to guide His messenger and the believers in
their struggle against idolaters, unbelievers and hypocrites more
than one thousand years earlier. While one might consider Sulayman
harsh in his condemnation of weaker spirits who bowed to superior
military force, one cannot accuse him of failing to remain true to his
convictions. After the surrender of the Saudi leadership at al-Dir'iyya

in September 1818, he refused to declare submission to Ibrahim Pasha, who then ordered that he be tortured and executed.[122]

The Ottoman-Saudi truce ended in confused circumstances. Fighting between allies of the two adversaries offered Muhammad Ali a pretext to launch a campaign led by his son Ibrahim Pasha in autumn 1816. From his headquarters in Medina, he advanced slowly and methodically into Najd, co-opting tribal leaders with gifts, replenishing his forces from Egypt and letting the effect of his impressively armed troops gradually stretch the loyalty of Saudi vassals to breaking point. The historical route for armies invading Najd from Hijaz ran to al-Qasim, where Saudi forces mounted stiff resistance at al-Rass. They withstood a siege for three months in summer 1817 before surrendering. Al-Qasim's two other chief towns (Unayza and Burayda) fell by the end of the year. In the first months of 1818, Ibrahim's forces easily overran Saudi defences on the march to al-Dir'iyya. The invaders arrived at the capital in April and would spend the next five months fighting skirmishes and waiting for the defenders' supplies to run out. Finally, on 11 September, the Saudi ruler, Amir Abd Allah, surrendered to Ibrahim Pasha, who sent the deposed ruler to Cairo. Muhammad Ali then transferred him to Istanbul. In December, the sultan ordered his execution and public display of his corpse.

Back in Najd, Ibrahim Pasha rounded up survivors of Al Saud and Al al-Sheikh for deportation to Egypt. According to an Ottoman document listing the exiles, the Saudi princes, children, slaves and retainers numbered over 250 and the Al al-Sheikh entourage counted thirty-one.[123] Elsewhere in the former Saudi domain, Ibrahim's forces ousted Wahhabi religious officials and restored former oasis chiefs who had been eclipsed in the Saudi amirate. When the Ottoman commander finally received orders to withdraw to Hijaz in June 1819, he evacuated the entire population of al-Dir'iyya and had his men raze all structures and cut down the oasis's trees, rendering it unfit for habitation.[124] Glimpses of the general devastation wrought by the Ottoman forces appear in the account of the first European to traverse Arabia, a British officer named G. Forster Sadleir. He had journeyed from India to Arabia to strike an alliance with Ibrahim Pasha against south-eastern Arabian sheikhs preying on Britain's maritime trade in the Persian Gulf. Sadleir spent much of 1819 trying to catch up with Ibrahim's evacuating army. On the way, he passed by way of al-Dir'iyya in August. He noted that the deserted town's date groves

and enclosing walls were completely destroyed; refugees from the
razed capital were camping in groves around Riyadh.[125] Ibrahim's
ruthless prosecution of the war, al-Dir'iyya's levelling and the exile
of the amirate's political and religious leadership gave the same
impression to a sojourning European as it did to Arabian Bedouins
and townsmen: The Saudi amirate and the Wahhabi mission had
been crushed once and for all.

1. THE RUINS OF AL-DIR'IYYA.
SOURCE UNKNOWN, *SAUDI ARAMCO WORLD*/PADIA.

Eighteenth-century Arabia underwent a profound shift from a world
of dispersed political and religious authority to their unification under
the Al Saud/Al al-Sheikh alliance. 'Profound' may not do justice to
the depth of change. In the light of nearly 1,000 years of political
fragmentation, it was an astonishing rupture. Muhammad ibn Abd
al-Wahhab's doctrine on monotheism and idolatry, rendering other
Muslims idolaters who must convert to Islam, was just as radical a
departure from Najdi history. His failure to secure steady support
in Huraymila and al-Uyayna led to his forced departure from both.
If he was going to succeed at converting 'jahili' Najd to Islam, he
needed political backing. He got that from Al Saud in al-Dir'iyya and
his monotheist mission rode the Saudis' robust military energy to

hegemony over Najd and much of Arabia. The establishment of an official doctrine and the suppression its opponents profoundly altered the culture of religious learning. The old centres of learning declined and Ottoman towns, deemed nests of idolatry, no longer represented the acme of scholarship. Instead, ulama and religious pupils flocked to al-Dir'iyya, where Al al-Sheikh, Najd's new religious leadership, taught the official doctrine. Having mastered Wahhabi tenets, the ulama dispersed to oasis settlements to preside over religious life. Since the Wahhabi movement owed its dominance to Saudi might, it was natural that it would suffer when the Saudis encountered a superior enemy. The conquest of the Holy Cities occurred when Istanbul's authority in the provinces was at its nadir. But it so happened that the Middle East was on the verge of a new historical phase. Muhammad Ali represented the vanguard of rulers who would build more powerful armies with a longer reach than before. Thus, when the Ottoman sultan sought Muhammad Ali's assistance in regaining the Holy Cities, he set in motion the downfall of both the Saudis and the Wahhabis. While the Egyptian governor moulded and mobilized a military force capable of destroying the Saudi amirate in Najd, he did not have the capacity to consolidate a stable regime in that remote region. After a brief occupation, he withdrew his forces, opening the way for a Saudi restoration.

Chapter Two

Holding Fast Against Idolatry

In 1800, nearly the entire Arabian peninsula was under the sway of the first Saudi amirate, supporting and supported by religious scholars enthusiastically propagating the mission calling to proper observance of God's unity. For fifty years, the teachings of Muhammad ibn Abd al-Wahhab had polarized Arabia's Muslim scholars. The Saudi amirate had provided political backing and economic sustenance to Wahhabi religious scholars. At the end of 1818, the first Saudi state was utterly destroyed, al-Dir'iyya razed, its political leader, Abd Allah ibn Saud, dispatched to Istanbul for public execution. At that juncture, the Wahhabis' enemies might have reckoned that Muhammad Ali's forces had rid the Muslim world of the sort of heresy that periodically arose on its less civilized fringes. But just a few years later, the Ottoman army would withdraw, the Saudis would regain power in al-Arid and the revivalist mission would recover. The second Saudi amirate, however, never attained pre-eminence over Arabia as the first one had. Instead, its leaders deftly manoeuvred between powerful neighbours. To the east, the British Empire at its apogee limited Saudi movements in the Persian Gulf and created a string of protectorates from Bahrain to Oman. To the north, a rejuvenated Ottoman Empire gradually put together a network of military and administrative institutions that fortified its Arabian frontier. To the west, Muhammad Ali's Egypt turned into a conquering machine that would briefly resubjugate Najd before settling for a hereditary dynasty in the Nile Valley and yielding to an Ottoman restoration in Hijaz.

In addition to facing harder political frontiers, Wahhabism confronted determined religious adversaries pursuing a polemical campaign to contain and marginalize it, a campaign that benefited from Ottoman backing. Al Saud's political quiescence meant that Wahhabi ulama lacked the means they had used to spread their call in the eighteenth century. Expansion through jihad was out of the question. Instead, they dug in to vigilantly guard against any trace of idolatry that might crop up or infiltrate from neighbouring Ottoman lands. Travel to those lands became a controversial issue due to fear of doctrinal contamination. As long as the ulama had the firm backing of Saudi rulers, they could maintain doctrinal hegemony. When Saudi authority faltered in later decades, Wahhabism's foes tried to exploit the opening and opened their own campaign against the mission's ulama.

Executions, Exiles, Refugees

For the leaders of the invading Ottoman-Egyptian army, the war against the Saudis had strategic and religious purposes: The expedition aimed not only at crushing Saudi political power but the Wahhabi mission as well. Official Egyptian correspondence expressed sectarian hostility to the Najdi reform movement, as in a letter from Muhammad Ali to the Ottoman court at Istanbul (October 1820) reporting on the first attempt to revive Saudi power undertaken by Mishari ibn Saud. The letter uses the following terms to refer to the mission: the Wahhabi sect (al-ta'ifa al-wahhabiya), polluting presence of the Wahhabis (lawth wujud al-wahhabiya), Khariji swords (suyuf al-khawarij), this despised sect (hadhihi al-ta'ifa al-makruha) and the despised Khariji sect (ta'ifat al-khawarij al-makruha). The letter has a tone of embarrassment or apology for the reappearance of a Saudi pretender after what Muhammad Ali presumed to be their eradication in the wake of Ibrahim Pasha's devastating invasion. But Ibrahim had to withdraw his forces from Najd in the face of a drought that made it impossible to provision his troops. Muhammad Ali's explanation (or excuse) implied that the Ottomans would have preferred a longer occupation to prevent a Saudi revival. He noted that Ibrahim Pasha had 'purified the Hijaz of the polluting Wahhabi presence', that a small band of Wahhabis remained scattered between al-Hasa and Medina and that it would be an easy matter to destroy them once and for all.[1]

And so it appeared at the end of 1818: As al-Dir'iyya lay in ruins, the mission's supporters must have been devastated and demoralized. Beyond destroying the Saudi capital, Ibrahim Pasha's campaign depleted the ranks of Al al-Sheikh and other prominent figures in the Wahhabi establishment. Sheikh Abd Allah ibn Muhammad Al al-Sheikh had been the religious leader since his father's retirement from public life in the early 1770s. The Egyptians spared his life and dispatched him to Cairo, where he died in 1826. His son, Sheikh Sulayman, the author of stern epistles against consorting with idolaters, suffered torture and execution in al-Dir'iyya for refusing to surrender to Ibrahim Pasha. Sheikh Abd Allah's nephew, Abd al-Rahman ibn Hasan Al al-Sheikh, accompanied the train of captives to Cairo, but he would return to Najd in 1825 to revive and lead the Wahhabi mission for several decades. Two more of al-Dir'iyya's qadis fled to the remote amirate of Ra's al-Khayma on the south-east tip of Arabia.[2] Seven additional qadis were executed by the Egyptians or killed in combat,[3] and eight men from ulama families were either killed in combat or executed.[4] Before departing al-Dir'iyya, Ibrahim received instructions from Cairo to transport members of Al Saud and Al al-Sheikh along with their families, slaves and servants.[5]

Attrition further diminished the ranks of Wahhabi ulama through emigration. One of Sheikh Muhammad's grandsons, Abd al-Aziz ibn Hamad ibn Ibrahim ibn Musharraf, had been a qadi for the last two Saudi rulers and an envoy to Yemen and Egypt. Perhaps because of his visit to Egypt, where al-Jabarti reported that he made a positive impression, he was permitted to leave al-Dir'iyya and move Unayza, where he became qadi in 1819. He appears to have stayed only a year before emigrating, probably on the occasion of a subsequent Egyptian incursion. This time he left Najd and settled in the southern Iraqi town of Suq al-Shuyukh, where he died in 1825.[6] A nephew of Sheikh Muhammad, Abd al-Aziz ibn Sulayman ibn Abd al-Wahhab ibn Musharraf, managed to reach his native town of Huraymila safely, but in 1821 an Egyptian military leader plundered his home and tortured him. He then migrated to al-Hasa, where he died in 1848.[7] Abd al-Aziz ibn Hamad Al Mu'ammar, son of a leading teacher and himself a qadi at al-Dir'iyya, lost his brother Nasir to the Egyptian campaign. After the Saudi surrender, he moved to a small town (Sadus) where the amir was a kinsman, before heading to Bahrain. The ruler of Bahrain made him welcome, so he settled there. Abd al-Aziz ibn Hamad Al Mu'ammar acquired some fame for authoring an essay to rebut the book of an English missionary. He died in Bahrain in 1828.[8]

Altogether the Wahhabi mission lost some two dozen ulama and men from ulama families in the Egyptian invasion and its aftermath. On the other hand, a similar number survived the onslaught and made possible the mission's transmission to a new generation of Najdi religious pupils. Thus, the war diminished but did not destroy the network of religious teachers and judges that had spread since the middle of the eighteenth century. Members of Al al-Sheikh fled to the far south-eastern tip of Arabia at Ra's al-Khayma, the base of the Qasimi 'pirates', who were allied to the Saudis. The entire train of refugees may have numbered three hundred,[9] and included two al-Dir'iyya qadis and four other ulama.[10] Their sojourn with the Qasimis was brief. In December 1819, a British naval raid demolished the town and the refugees moved on to Qatar. Another member of Al al-Sheikh, Abd al-Malik ibn Husayn, took refuge in the southern Najdi settlement of al-Hawta. When the Saudis recovered power, he and the refugees to the Gulf region converged on Riyadh to revive the Wahhabi mission.

Seven other survivors provided continuity between the first and second Saudi amirates. Their importance resides in their standing as qadis, the highest religious officials in their respective localities. After Abd al-Rahman ibn Hasan Al al-Sheikh (exiled to Cairo), the most prestigious sheikh to bridge the two eras was Abd Allah ibn Abd al-Rahman ibn Aba Butayn. He had been the qadi of Washm for the first amirate. It appears he remained there during the war. In the second amirate, he was the most prestigious Wahhabi figure in the politically sensitive region of al-Qasim for more than thirty years. He was a prolific writer in polemical exchanges between Wahhabis and their foes.[11] Several men returned to their native towns after the fall of al-Dir'iyya. Abd Allah ibn Sulayman ibn Ubayd was the qadi at Ha'il in northern Najd. When Egyptian forces occupied Ha'il, he moved to his native Julajil in Sudayr. When Amir Turki restored Saudi power, he made Ibn Ubayd the qadi of Sudayr, but only briefly, as he died in 1825.[12] Uthman ibn Abd al-Jabbar ibn Shabana was the qadi in Sudayr (probably at al-Majma'a) in the first amirate and he seems to have remained there throughout the years of crisis. He witnessed the Saudi restoration but died shortly afterward in 1827.[13] Ahmad ibn Ali ibn Du'ayj became the qadi at Marat in Washm when his predecessor was killed in battle in 1817. He stayed there during the war and ensuing turmoil and then served as qadi until his death in 1851.[14] Qirnas ibn Abd al-Rahman ibn Qirnas had been the Saudi qadi in Medina, then became qadi in his native al-Rass (in al-Qasim), but he fled when Ibrahim Pasha's army passed through on its withdrawal from Najd. He returned to become qadi in the second amirate until his death in 1846.[15] The qadi at Burayda, Abd al-Aziz ibn Abd Allah ibn Suwaylim, a native of al-Dir'iyya, remained at his post until he died in 1829.[16] Muhammad ibn Muqrin was qadi for the region surrounding Huraymila in the first amirate and he continued in that post for the second one until he died in 1851.[17]

Reviving the Wahhabi Mission

When Ibrahim Pasha withdrew from Najd, the pre-Saudi political pattern of local contests between chieftains resumed as if there had never been a powerful Central Arabian amirate. Chieftains from lineages that had been ousted by the Saudis began to fight each other. Into this struggle among small factions stepped a Saudi survivor. Turki ibn Abd Allah seized and held Riyadh for a few months in 1820 before an Egyptian force advanced, laid siege and appeared to have cornered him, but he somehow escaped.[18] To discourage future Saudi comebacks, Ibrahim Pasha ordered the massacre of some 200 former residents of al-Dir'iyya who had attempted to repopulate the oasis. This brutal measure ended any prospect of it recovering from the recent devastation and further embittered the area's inhabitants toward the Egyptians.[19] Over time, frequent Saudi raids and the cost of maintaining garrisons drove Ibrahim Pasha to concentrate his forces in just two towns. In spring 1823, Turki rode out from a remote region of southern Najd to harass Egyptian garrisons and reconquer towns one by one. By summer 1824, steady military pressure and logistical strains caused Muhammad Ali to completely abandon Najd to the founder of the second Saudi amirate. Turki made Riyadh his capital. By the end of 1825, he consolidated authority over central and southern Najd up to al-Qasim. In the next five years, Turki firmed up his authority over the northern parts of Najd and the eastern Arabian littoral. What had appeared in 1818 to be the eradication of the Wahhabi mission's political face turned out to be an interlude.

Like his ancestors, Turki ibn Abd Allah supported Wahhabism. One of his first tasks was to reconstitute its leadership after the decimation, exile and flight of the most eminent ulama. Once the Saudi banner flew over Riyadh, like a magnet it drew surviving scholars and teachers eager to resume their ordained roles as bearers of divine truth. These men harboured grim resentment toward the Egyptian foe, not merely for religious error as before the war, but also for turning so many of their fellow Wahhabis into martyrs. Members of Al al-Sheikh in Cairo and the Persian Gulf made their way to Riyadh and one of them, a grandson of Muhammad ibn Abd al-Wahhab, became the top religious authority in the amirate.[20] Most of the qadis in the second amirate's early years had previously served the first one.[21]

As a young child, Sheikh Abd al-Rahman ibn Hasan (b. 1780) had some acquaintance with his grandfather, Muhammad ibn Abd al-Wahhab. He studied with his uncles and other pupils of his grandfather.[22] During his exile in Cairo, he attended lessons at the Azhar with scholars from the other Sunni legal schools, a significant detail in view of the common assumption that Wahhabi scholars hold themselves aloof from their peers. In the twentieth-century Wahhabi biographical tradition, Abd al-Rahman figures as the most learned scholar of his era, in part because of his sojourn in Cairo, where he studied religious sciences in greater depth than was possible in Najd because of the Azhar's massive library and outstanding scholars. In his capacity as head of the Wahhabi religious establishment, he appointed qadis and teachers, gave lessons, advised the ruler, composed religious tracts and led the polemical campaign against the mission's Muslim detractors. Among his religious writings is a commentary (*sharh*) on his grandfather's *Book of God's Unity*.[23]

The second Saudi amirate entered a fresh period of turmoil when one of Turki's cousins, Mishari ibn Abd al-Rahman, had him assassinated in Riyadh outside its chief mosque in May 1834. At the time, the murdered ruler's son Faysal was leading a military campaign against Bahrain. Upon receiving news of Turki's demise, he rallied loyal governors to confirm their allegiance. In just three weeks, he seized Riyadh, captured Mishari and put him to death. Faysal spent the next few years coping with challenges from Bahrain, restive tribal leaders and southern Najdi oases. None of these local nuisances posed a threat to Saudi authority in its heartland, but a second Egyptian invasion would turn the Saudis and Wahhabi ulama into refugees once again.

In 1831, Muhammad Ali invaded Syria and expelled the Ottomans. He followed that with an effort to extend and consolidate his possessions in Arabia from Hijaz southward into Asir and Yemen. To round out his Arabian realm, Muhammad Ali decided to remove Faysal and to rule Najd through a Saudi puppet, Khalid ibn Saud, who been exiled to Cairo in 1818. Faysal's effort to forestall the invasion with a pledge of allegiance to the Egyptian ruler failed. When Egyptian troops advanced into Najd in spring 1837, he retreated to al-Hasa. Even though Khalid claimed the mantle of Saudi legitimacy, his obvious debt to an Egyptian master caused the Wahhabi ulama to leave Riyadh and move to southern strongholds around al-Hariq beyond the Egyptian army's reach. An Egyptian effort to subdue al-Hariq in July 1837 utterly failed. For the moment, Egypt's vassal Khalid ruled Central Arabia from al-Arid to al-Qasim while Faysal kept a tenuous grip on al-Hasa and southern Najd. At the end of 1838, an Egyptian expedition captured Faysal at his stronghold south of Riyadh and he was sent to Cairo. With firm control over Syria and most of Arabia, Muhammad Ali ruled more securely over Najd and the Persian Gulf than he had twenty years before, but his empire quickly crumbled in the face of European pressure to relinquish it in exchange for international recognition of his heirs' right to rule the Nile Valley. The military might behind Khalid ibn Saud evaporated in spring 1840 and a scramble for power erupted not long after the dust had settled behind the retreating Egyptian expedition.

Muhammad Ali's agents took a less intrusive approach to the second occupation of Najd. First, they ruled through a member of Al Saud. Second, they adopted a softer approach to Wahhabi ulama who chose to stay in areas under their power. Rather than exiling or executing them, the Egyptians left them alone. Consequently, some quietly accepted the political shift from Faysal to Khalid, but others chose to emigrate from what they considered an infidel land.[24] The latter embodied the defiant, uncompromising spirit articulated by Sulayman ibn Abd Allah in his treatises during the Ottoman-Saudi war. The spokesman for this outlook was Hamad ibn Atiq, originally from the Zilfi region located between al-Arid and al-Qasim.[25] In 1836, Ibn Atiq went to Riyadh to study under Sheikh Abd al-Rahman ibn Hasan and other Wahhabi sheikhs.[26] When Egypt invaded and installed Khalid ibn Saud, Sheikh Abd al-Rahman accompanied Faysal first to al-Hasa and then to southern Najd.[27] Ibn Atiq joined them in southern Najd.

During the second Egyptian occupation, Hamad ibn Atiq wrote a treatise, *The Refutation of Ibn Du'ayj*.[28] This work reflects the animosity that sprang up between ulama who emigrated from Riyadh and those ulama who chose to live under Khalid, thus accepting Muhammad Ali's authority. According to Ibn Atiq, Ahmad ibn Du'ayj, a qadi in Washm, a region under Egyptian control, falsely claimed that the Wahhabi mission held that anyone who lived in a land conquered by idolatrous troops must emigrate or be considered an infidel. Ibn Atiq wrote that not a single scholar of the Najdi mission (*al-da'wa al-najdiyya*) had ever expressed such a view. He contended that Ibn Du'ayj wished to alienate folk from the mission by spreading lies, as his (unnamed, perhaps Ottoman Iraqi) teachers had done.[29] Furthermore, Ibn Atiq asserted that Ibn Du'ayj exonerated the infidels and their leaders of apostasy. It seems that Ibn Du'ayj claimed that the infidels (Egyptians) did not force anybody to renounce his religion or to do something that defiled his religion. Ibn Atiq accused Ibn Du'ayj of wishing to get along with both Muslims and infidels instead of openly declaring enmity to idolatry even though he knew that these people (the Egyptians) tried to destroy Islam, deported its imams (referring to the exile of Al al-Sheikh in 1819) and killed many ulama for refusing to apostasize (including Sulayman ibn Abd Allah).[30] Ibn Atiq criticized Ibn Du'ayj for claiming that the only reason he lived in the land of infidels was to safeguard his life, property and family. He noted that the Qur'an does not admit such worldly reasons as excuses and that emigration from the land of the Turks (Ibn Atiq's term for the Ottoman-Egyptians), whose unbelief is widely known, was obligatory.[31] In setting forth what Ibn Atiq deemed an accurate version of the Wahhabi position on living under idolatrous rule, he asserted that people who reside in the land of idolaters fall into three categories. First, those who choose to reside there, enjoy the company of idolaters, approve their religion and assist them in fighting Muslims. Second, those who reside there for worldly reasons, do not openly practise religion and yet do not give allegiance to idolaters. Third, those who openly practise religion or are compelled to reside among idolaters. Most of the treatise is a discussion of these three categories.[32]

Ibn Atiq considered the first category, those who willingly fall in with the idolaters, to be infidels. The proof texts consist of two hadiths: Do not take Jews and Christians as allies in preference to believers. Whoever keeps company and lives with idolaters is similar to them.

Ibn Atiq also cited Muhammad ibn Abd al-Wahhab's definition of one category of infidel as a person who remains in a town whose folk are fighting the Muslims. Those in the second category are not infidels but sinners because they stay with idolaters for the sake of wealth or preserving family ties; they do not openly practise religion yet they refrain from giving allegiance to the idolaters. It appears, then, that merely associating with idolaters does not entail unbelief. It is a sin, however, to remain in their land even if in one's heart one hates the idolaters. We have already seen the proof texts for this point in Sulayman ibn Abd Allah's treatises: al-Nisa' 97 and the Hadith, 'Whoever associates with the idolater and lives with him is like him.' The one difference is Ibn Atiq's citation of the medieval exegete, Ibn Kathir, who noted that this verse applies not only to the particular case of Muslims who remained in Mecca at the time of the emigration to Medina but applies generally to those who reside among idolaters, are able to emigrate and are unable to practise their religion openly. Ibn Kathir stated that according to this verse and the consensus of scholars (ijma'), such a believer has committed a forbidden act (haram). God did not allow love or attachment to Mecca, the most noble place on earth, to excuse one from the duty to emigrate. Those in the third category are free of any blame. They openly practise religion or are compelled to reside among idolaters.

One essential condition for residing among idolaters without falling into the category of unbeliever is to practise religion. Ibn Atiq elaborated on what exactly that entails and he set the bar high. One must openly declare that one has nothing to do with the religious practices of one's hosts. This means telling the idolaters among whom one lives that they follow falsehood, not true religion. The proof text is the Qur'anic verse, 'O unbelievers, I do not worship what you worship.' This verse obliges one to say, 'You are unbelievers, you practise idolatry, not monotheism.' Ibn Atiq emphasized that openly practising religion does not mean that one may remain silent about others' idolatrous worship. The people of Zubayr, Kuwait, Egypt, the Persians, the Jews and the Christians do not prohibit correct prayer in their lands. But openly practising religion is more than merely performing correct worship. It also entails proclaiming enmity to unbelievers and declaring to them that one has nothing to do with them or their religion. As for believers forced to reside among idolaters, the proof text is the Qur'anic verse, 'Those who live among idolaters will have the Fire as their abode except for those who cannot find a way out.' Ibn Kathir noted that such folk wished to escape the idolaters but could not. Ibn Atiq concluded this section by declaring that this is the position of the leading Wahhabi scholars and not what the liar (Ibn Du'ayj) ascribed to them because of his loyalty to the infidels and his prejudice against the mission.[33]

The substance of Ibn Atiq's attack on faint-hearted ulama echoed Sulayman ibn Abd Allah's treatises on travel to the land of idolatry and befriending idolaters. For the rest of the nineteenth century, strict enforcement of this aversion to mixing with idolaters – and in Wahhabi terms, most Muslims fell into that category – would remain the norm in Wahhabi discourse. It would also serve to mark the difference between true believers in the mission and those who for various reasons adopted a more tolerant view of non-Wahhabi Muslims. Indeed, a gap opened between ulama who spent their lives in the pure domain of Wahhabi sovereignty, no matter how circumscribed, and those who either acquiesced to foreign rule or even travelled to the outside for trade or study.

The abrupt Egyptian retreat in early 1840 opened the way for yet another power struggle in Najd. Khalid's nearly complete dependence on the Egyptian garrison in Riyadh spelled his doom. The first challenge to his rule came from a fellow Saudi, Abd Allah ibn Thunayan, who spent the years of Khalid's rule in southern Iraq with a powerful tribe. Ibn Thunayan rallied local allies of Faysal and attracted the backing of Al al-Sheikh, who considered Khalid illegitimate for his reliance on 'Turks'.[34] By the end of 1841, Khalid had retreated from Riyadh to al-Hasa, leaving the way open for Ibn Thunayan to occupy the capital with the blessings of the Wahhabi ulama.[35] At some point, however, it seems the Wahhabi ulama turned sour on Ibn Thunayan and they turned to Faysal. In 1840, he mysteriously escaped his captivity in Cairo.[36] In the next three years, he rallied his dynasty's historical religious allies and patched together a coalition of regional chiefs while Ibn Thunayan's position in Riyadh weakened. A large force of oasis troops and nomadic horsemen advanced on Riyadh. Faysal's men overwhelmed Ibn Thunayan's small band of loyal defenders. He threw Ibn Thunayan into prison, where he died in circumstances whose details are murky. The chroniclers' consensus is that Faysal had his kinsman murdered. This episode ended twenty-five years of turmoil and opened an era of stability.

Once the political scene was settled, Wahhabi ulama moved to reconsolidate the mission, with Sheikh Abd al-Rahman ibn Hasan in Riyadh presiding over a network of qadis and teachers vetted for their firm loyalty to his grandfather's teachings. Attention to the slightest wisps of suspicion is evident in the confirmation of a qadi in Burayda in al-Qasim. The issue arose in part because the town's Wahhabi qadi under Amir Turki died in 1840, when the area was under Egyptian rule. Nonetheless, a Wahhabi succession to the post transpired under the auspices of the mission's pre-eminent sheikh in al-Qasim, Sheikh Qirnas. His choice of Sulayman ibn Muqbil (c.1805–1887) raised eyebrows in Burayda. Even though he had studied under Wahhabi teachers in Unayza and Riyadh (including Abd al-Rahman ibn Hasan), he had also spent ten years in Damascus as a pupil to Hasan al-Shatti, a well-known and outspoken Hanbali opponent to the mission.[37] A group of townsmen expressed doubts about Ibn Muqbil's doctrinal correctness, but Qirnas succeeded in convincing them to accept his recommendation. When Faysal returned to power in 1843, Abd al-Rahman ibn Hasan summoned Ibn Muqbil to ascertain his views on seeking the intercession of saints and visiting their tombs. The meeting dispelled any reservations about a man who had spent years in the questionable company of Damascus's ulama. It also underscored the determination of Riyadh's guardians of doctrine to enforce their views.

Enforcing Doctrinal Conformity

In the eighteenth century, the Wahhabis purged Najd of ulama opposed to their doctrine. For the most part, the purge was complete. Its dependence on Saudi power, however, meant that anti-Wahhabi ulama might exploit political soft spots to perpetuate the old scholastic tradition of Najd, which shared the religious outlook of Ottoman ulama. The Burayda qadi incident was symptomatic of al-Qasim's doubtful doctrinal correctness and a sign of Saudi weakness in the region. The amirs of its two main towns, Unayza and Burayda, repeatedly defied Saudi authority and tolerated religious non-conformity, even dissent, during Faysal's rule. Burayda's Amir Abd al-Aziz Al Abu Ulayyan belonged to a lineage that had loyally served the Saudis for four decades under the first amirate, but he so frequently tested the limits of Faysal's authority that the Saudi ruler finally captured him and put him to death in 1861.

In Unayza, members of Al Sulaym rose to monopolize the amirate for much of the nineteenth century, more because of their ability to triumph in local factional struggles than Al Saud's confidence in their loyalty, which was sporadic and opportunistic. These amirs first displayed an independent spirit in April 1847, when the Meccan sharif marched into Najd at the head of an armed force and entered Unayza without encountering any opposition from the 'Saudi' amirs there or in nearby Burayda. The absence of resistance is in itself noteworthy. Even more remarkable was the presence of Khalid ibn Saud in the sharif's entourage. The sharif spent two months in Unayza, evidently on good terms with the Al Sulaym amir. Faysal then gathered a large force and threatened to attack the sharif, but the latter agreed to withdraw in exchange for a pledge by Faysal to pay tribute to Istanbul.[38] Not long after the sharif left, Faysal dismissed Unayza's Al Sulaym amir and appointed a man from a rival lineage.

Two years later, Unayza and Burayda rose in revolt against Faysal. In this instance, Al Sulaym supported the Saudi cause in the hope of regaining their former position. Once Faysal defeated the rebels, however, he tried a new approach to governing the region by appointing his brother Jiluwi as amir for all of al-Qasim, with a seat in Unayza.[39] This arrangement lasted until an uprising expelled Jiluwi in 1853. That revolt ended through negotiation when Faysal agreed to restore Al Sulaym to the amirate.[40] A third Unayzan revolt erupted in 1861, after Al Saud had executed Burayda's amir. Faysal dispatched a large force to crush the uprising at the end of 1862. The humbled Amir Abd Allah al-Sulaym went to Riyadh to obtain Faysal's forgiveness and the Saudi ruler obliged.[41] But this did not mean that Unayza's amir had converted to the Saudi cause. An Italian traveller, Carlo Guarmani, met him in March 1864, described the amir as 'the bitterest enemy of the Derreieh (sic) princes' and observed that he did not 'even attempt to conceal' his hatred for Faysal ibn Turki.[42]

All of this thrust and parry between overlord and vassal was common in Ottoman provinces and perhaps these incidents were part of the redefined relationship between the Ottomans and the Saudis. The Meccan sharif's probe into Qasim reminded Faysal of Istanbul's claim to tribute at the same time it offered al-Qasim's amirs the opportunity to cultivate ties with an Ottoman representative, presumably as leverage against Faysal. In this context, the uprisings of 1849, 1853–1854 and 1861–1862 represented bids to redefine the towns' standing in Arabia's fluid field of power relations. In the eyes of the Wahhabi leadership in Riyadh, however, the amirs' independent streak posed an obstacle to efforts to wipe out traces of religious dissent. The first Saudi amirate had succeeded at consolidating the

Wahhabi mission in most regions of Najd by expelling or silencing its doctrinal adversaries and by installing qadis and teachers loyal to the mission. In this way, the towns of Sudayr and Washm went through the turmoil of the Ottoman war, occupation, fragmentation, Saudi restoration, Egyptian invasion and Saudi succession struggles with their Wahhabi character unshaken. Al-Qasim was altogether different. The old scholastic tradition persisted there, in part because of the amirs' indifference, in part because the region's merchants participated in long-distance trade with Iraq, Syria and Hijaz, where the remnants of Arabian opposition to the Wahhabis formed a community of embittered exiles committed to discrediting the revivalist doctrine.[43]

Resistance to Wahhabi doctrine in Najd was rooted in connections between al-Qasim and a network of Najdi émigré ulama concentrated around Zubayr, where religious and political adversaries to the first Saudi state formed an enclave in the last quarter of the eighteenth century. Zubayr had long-standing economic and social ties to Najd. Chroniclers mention emigration to Zubayr, Basra and Kuwait during periods of drought in the eighteenth century.[44] In the era of Saudi expansion, political and religious opponents migrated to Zubayr, Basra and Baghdad. The immigrants became known as the Uqaylat. They entered different niches in Iraq: Some joined Ottoman regiments in Baghdad; others participated in local trade; yet others prospered in long-distance caravan trade between Aleppo, Iraq and Arabia.[45] The Uqaylat attained prominence in Zubayr, where they soon dominated its political and economic life.[46] They handled overland trade among Syria, Iraq and Arabia and they profited from the increase in commercial exchange throughout the Persian Gulf-Indian Ocean region. Therefore, historical patterns of communications, a burst of Najdi emigration and opportunities to participate in commerce made southern Iraq a powerful magnet for Najdi traders, especially in al-Qasim. Part of the stream of travellers between Arabia and Iraq consisted of religious pupils and scholars following a custom of journeying to pursue knowledge (*al-rihla fi talab al-ilm*). The distinctive aspect of the path between al-Qasim and Zubayr is that it connected a region where Saudi authority was weak to a town whose ulama brimmed with hostility to Wahhabism.

Zubayr's historical religious character made it a natural lightning rod for Muslims opposed to one of Wahhabism's fundamental positions: condemning the supplication of dead holy men at their graves. The town had grown up around the grave of an early pious figure, the Companion Zubayr ibn al-Awwam. Muhammad ibn Abd al-Wahhab disapproved of veneration for the Companion, likening worship at his tomb to Christian worship.[47] Also in the town's vicinity were the graves of Zubayr's son Talha and of al-Hasan al-Basri. At the latter two sites stood the sort of domes so offensive to Wahhabis. Political sentiments compounded this religious aspect. Zubayr, whose population had long consisted mostly of Najdis, became a refuge for clans and ulama expelled from their towns for refusing to embrace Wahhabism. Therefore it was natural for the town to become a centre of anti-Saudi sentiment.[48]

Two early, influential anti-Wahhabi ulama in Zubayr were Muhammad ibn Ali ibn Sullum (1748–1831) and Ibrahim ibn Jadid (d. 1816). Ibn Sullum travelled from his home in Sudayr to al-Hasa in order to study under Muhammad ibn Fayruz (1724–1801). This man was a contemporary of Muhammad ibn Abd al-Wahhab and the author of anti-Wahhabi treatises.[49] In Zubayr, Ibn Sullum became the most prominent figure among the Najdi émigrés.[50] His circle of students included men who reproduced criticisms of the Wahhabi mission well into the nineteenth century. Ibrahim ibn Jadid's ancestors may have been political refugees from the Saudi conquest of Sudayr who emigrated to Zubayr, where he was born. Like Ibn Sullum, he studied in al-Hasa under Ibn Fayruz. He too became a renowned teacher in Zubayr, imparting a dose of enmity to the Wahhabi mission in his lessons to pupils. Some of these later brought Zubayr's anti-Wahhabi tradition to Mecca.[51]

Zubayr's mood of religious enmity to the Wahhabi mission harmonized with its disposition to support Ottoman efforts against the Saudis. Its leader in the 1790s and early 1800s was a political refugee expelled from his native Najdi town, Huraymila.[52] Zubayris assisted Ottoman-inspired raids against the Saudis in 1785 and 1797;[53] religious and political leaders solicited Ottoman assistance for the construction of fortifications against Saudi attack.[54] In 1803, Saudi forces stormed Zubayr, leaving many dead and razing the structures at Talha's and al-Hasan al-Basri's graves (Zubayris constructed new embellishments after al-Dir'iyya's fall fifteen years later). The attack could only have deepened the rancour harboured by its survivors, such as Sheikh Ibrahim ibn Jadid, and hardened their determination to impart their antagonism to the next generation of religious students.[55] The Zubayri tradition of hostility toward the Wahhabi mission, fed by springs of political and religious resentment, would intersect with the old Najdi tradition of religious learning at Unayza.

The connection between Unayza and Zubayr hinged on the former's involvement in long-distance trade. Unayza's merchants prospered in commercial ventures connecting al-Qasim with the Red Sea, the Gulf and the Indian Ocean. Its wealthiest merchant lineage, Al Bassam, had first gained renown in the sixteenth and seventeenth centuries as religious scholars in Ushayqir, Najd's major centre of learning before the Wahhabi era.[56] Members of Al Bassam established commercial agencies in Jeddah, Basra and Bombay. The extent of their commercial interests is well represented by Abd Allah ibn Abd al-Rahman al-Bassam (1824–1907). His trading interests took him to Baghdad, Basra, Bombay, Zanzibar and Mauritius.[57] Bassam's friend Abd Allah al-Khunayni spent much of his life at Bombay and Basra. When the British traveller Charles Doughty met him in Unayza in the late 1870s, he told the English traveller that he preferred to reside at Basra because he did not like living in the shadow of 'Wahaby straitness and fanaticism'.[58] Not all of Unayza's long-distance traders shared this outlook. Doughty mentions a branch of Al Bassam, also widely travelled, that hewed to the Wahhabi mission.[59] Nonetheless, contact with merchants and attendance at mosques outside Najd exposed Unayzans to religious perspectives that reinforced the old scholastic tradition, which complemented the cosmopolitan commercial and cultural interests of Al Bassam merchants. Members of this lineage displayed cultural interests that fell beyond the scope of Wahhabi teachings. Abd Allah ibn Abd al-Rahman al-Bassam[60] was a respected authority on history, genealogy and the pedigrees of horses. Another member of the clan, Abd Allah ibn Muhammad (1858–1927)[61] read widely in history, literature and politics. These two men and their relatives used their wealth to purchase rare manuscripts and amass large book collections.[62] More generally, Al Bassam showed a proclivity to patronize the old scholastic tradition and attend the lessons of its teachers.[63]

Unayza's broad cosmopolitan horizons explain the tendency of its religious pupils and ulama to leave Najd for religious studies. Such journeys violated the Wahhabi taboo against travel to the land of idolaters and provided a channel for anti-Wahhabi views to reach Najd. Unayzan religious students travelled to Iraq, Syria and Hijaz far more frequently than students from any other region. By contrast, Wahhabi pupils and ulama made Riyadh their chief destination.[64]

The old scholastic tradition's ties to Ottoman lands are evident in the career of an opponent to Wahhabism, Abd Allah ibn Fa'iz ibn Mansur Aba al-Khayl (c.1786–1835).[65] During the Ottoman war of 1811–1818, Aba al-Khayl went to Mecca, where he studied with two men who had come from Zubayr's anti-Wahhabi milieu.[66] In 1824, after the evacuation of Egyptian forces and before Turki restored Saudi authority in al-Qasim, Aba al-Khayl returned to Unayza. At the request of the town's notables he became the qadi as well as prayer leader and preacher at the congregational mosque. He held the posts for three years until Wahhabi ulama spread rumours to the effect that he considered Riyadh's ulama to be deficient in learning. A second aspersion against him claimed that he corresponded with the noted adversary of the Wahhabis, Muhammad ibn Sullum, to obtain his assistance in setting a horizontal sundial (*mizwala*). The implication was that Wahhabi ulama lacked the expertise for the task.[67] Upon his removal from the qadi post in 1827, Aba al-Khayl returned to Mecca, but he may well have spent the next few years dividing his time between there and his hometown. Another report about him has bearing on the role of the prominent merchant family Al Bassam in supporting the old scholastic tradition in Unayza.[68] The first documented expansion and renovation of Unayza's congregational mosque, Masjid al-Jarrah, occurred in 1831–1832, when a local notable took the initiative to improve one part of the building. That same year, a member of Al Bassam undertook the expansion of a different portion of the building and entrusted the supervision of the project to Sheikh Aba al-Khayl.[69] The episode indicates the role played by Al Bassam in patronizing a member of the old scholastic tradition.

Aba al-Khayl's ties to local and Ottoman networks of sheikhs and pupils illustrate the impact of personal links in sustaining Najd's old scholastic tradition. He reared his nephew Muhammad ibn Ibrahim ibn Uraykan (1815–1854),[70] so it is not surprising that he studied in Iraq under Muhammad ibn Sullum and his sons. Ibn Uraykan later settled in Mecca, where he became devoted to the famous Sufi teacher Muhammad al-Sanusi. Sheikh Aba al-Khayl's pupils also included two men from an established family of scholars, Al Turki, whose ancestor had opposed the mission. Abd al-Wahhab ibn Muhammad ibn Humaydan ibn Turki (d. c.1840)[71] studied under Aba al-Khayl and then around 1818–1819 travelled to Baghdad and Zubayr, where he attended the lessons of the anti-Wahhabi scholar Muhammad ibn Sullum.[72] Ibn Turki became an authoritative teacher and mufti in

Unayza for a time, but he departed, perhaps for Mecca, at the time
of Saudi restoration in 1824. The old scholastic tradition and study in
Zubayr with the Wahhabis' foes also formed the outlook of Uthman
ibn Mazyad (1785–1863).[73] He first studied under Aba al-Khayl and
Abd al-Wahhab ibn Turki. In the early 1820s, he travelled to Zubayr
to study with Ibn Sullum and with a Naqshbandi sheikh, Uthman ibn
Sanad, a famous adversary to the Wahhabis. Ibn Mazyad's affiliation
with the Qadiri and Naqshbandi Sufi orders almost certainly took
place during his sojourn in Iraq.

Apart from the names of sheikhs, their teachers, pupils and travels,
details about the old scholastic tradition are scarce and sometimes
the evidence is more suggestive than conclusive. An epistle by the
Unayzan sheikh, Muhammad ibn Ibrahim al-Sinani (1793/4–1852/3),[74]
offers a bit more colourful detail than the networks embedded in
biographical dictionaries. Al-Sinani wrote that when he was a
religious student, opponents to the Wahhabi mission had urged him
to avoid reading Muhammad ibn Abd al-Wahhab's books. Their term
for Ibn Abd al-Wahhab's essay *Kashf al-shubuhat* (The Exposure of
Specious Arguments) was *Jam' al-shubuhat* (The Collection of Specious
Arguments). Sinani wrote that if someone had asked him to read it,
he would have refused.[75]

The most prominent Unayzan anti-Wahhabi sheikh during the
second Saudi amirate was Muhammad ibn Humayd (1820–1878).[76]
His maternal lineage, Al Turki, was of some local renown for its
religious scholars, including two men who had earlier opposed
the Wahhabis.[77] One of them, Abd al-Wahhab ibn Muhammad (d.
c.1840), authored a chronicle of Najd where he expressed antipathy
toward the Wahhabis.[78] For example, his entry for 1737/38 notes that
Muhammad ibn Abd al-Wahhab appeared in al-Uyayna, located in
the valley of Musaylima, the seventh-century false prophet who
contested Muhammad's claims. The chronicler repeated Sulayman
ibn Abd al-Wahhab's argument that the Najdi reformer had declared
Muhammad's community to be infidels on the basis of a misguided
reading of Qur'anic passages and Prophetic traditions pertaining to
infidels and Jews and it was sheer whim that led him to declare
infidels all pious scholars who did not agree with his deviant
innovation.[79] It is true that Ibn Humayd studied under prominent
Wahhabi ulama in Unayza, but then his pursuit of learning took him
to Mecca, Yemen, Syria and Egypt. In Mecca, he came into contact
with the Zubayr trend through Muhammad al-Zubayri and with a

Meccan sheikh, Ahmad ibn Zayni al-Dahlan (1817–1886), the author
of important historical and polemical works that are sharply critical of
the Wahhabi mission.[80] Ibn Humayd's learning, his personal contacts
with Ottoman sheikhs and the compatibility of his religious outlook
with Ottoman hostility toward Wahhabism made him suitable for the
post of Hanbali imam and mufti in Mecca and thus a member of the
empire's religious officialdom.[81]

To specialists in nineteenth-century Arabian history, Ibn Humayd
is known for his four-volume biographical dictionary of Hanbali
ulama, which added to a rich Hanbali tradition in that genre dating to
the tenth century.[82] In general, biographical dictionaries are a major
source for the history of Muslim scholars. They typically consist
of brief entries that report subjects' years of birth and death, their
teachers and pupils, texts and religious sciences they studied and
offices they held. A biographical dictionary might focus on the ulama
of a particular region, a single law school, jurists, Sufis, theologians,
or a centennial period. Ibn Humayd's biographical dictionary contains
843 entries on Hanbali ulama and covers over 500 years (750 to 1291
AH). Instead of following the customary practice of listing scholars
in the chronological order of their deaths, he placed his subjects in
alphabetical order.[83] The bulk of the entries are verbatim or nearly
verbatim renderings from a handful of sources whose authors lived
and wrote in Egypt and Syria, so most of the men in Ibn Humayd's
collection come from those regions, with a mere handful from parts
of Arabia.[84] Najdi Hanbalism thus appears as a peripheral offshoot,
whose religious pupils and ulama regarded the Syrian and Egyptian
schools as the wellsprings of learning.[85] Arabian pupils and ulama
travelled north to acquire advanced learning; we find no instances of
traffic in the opposite direction.

Ibn Humayd wove a polemical bias into his work by seamlessly
blending a more cosmopolitan Hanbali heritage with passages
disparaging the Wahhabis.[86] For the middle to later parts of the
eighteenth century, Ibn Humayd included twenty-four Arabian
Hanbalis, all of them either indifferent or bitterly opposed to Wahhabi
doctrine. For that portion of the nineteenth century covered in his
work, he composed entries on twenty-one men, roughly half of
them from al-Zubayr. The picture of Muhammad ibn Abd al-Wahhab
and his movement that emerges from Ibn Humayd's pen has three
components. First, members of the reformer's own illustrious Al
Musharraf lineage – his father, brother and grandson – rejected his

teachings. Second, he had his enemies assassinated. Third, Wahhabis lacked the ability and perspicacity for sensitive diplomatic missions and polemical works.

Ibn Humayd portrayed Muhammad ibn Abd al-Wahhab as the black sheep of Al Musharraf. Ibn Humayd acknowledged the learning and virtue of Al Musharraf as a scholarly and moral legacy passed down from generation to generation.[87] He described Muhammad ibn Abd al-Wahhab's grandfather Sulayman ibn Ali (d. 1668/69) as the foremost Najdi scholar of his time.[88] Having admitted the merits of Sheikh Muhammad's ancestors, Ibn Humayd depicts him as a wayward member of the lineage. The reformer's father Abd al-Wahhab ibn Sulayman (d. 1740) disapproved of his son's unwillingness to specialize in jurisprudence as his ancestors had done, disagreed with his views on doctrine and declared that he would be the cause of wickedness.[89] Ibn Humayd included reports of the well-known opposition Muhammad ibn Abd al-Wahhab faced from his own brother, Sulayman. According to Ibn Humayd, the fraternal disagreement spurred Sheikh Muhammad to plot against his brother's life, because if somebody disputed his teachings and he could not kill him openly, then he would send an assassin to dispose of his adversary in bed or in the marketplace under cover of darkness because he considered anyone who disagreed with him to be an unbeliever and therefore it was legitimate to shed his blood. Ibn Humayd claimed a madman used to go about town striking whomever he met, so Sheikh Muhammad ordered that this madman be given a sword and sent to his brother Sulayman while he was alone in a mosque. When the madman saw Sulayman, he was overcome with fear and dropped the sword (a sort of divine blessing for Sulayman).[90]

Ibn Humayd also figured as a participant in a polemical controversy that erupted over the visit of a Baghdadi religious scholar to Unayza.[91] Da'ud ibn Jirjis al-Naqshbandi (1816–1882) visited Unayza, not long after its rather shaky incorporation into Riyadh's political orbit in the mid-1840s.[92] Ibn Jirjis looms large in the roster of doctrinal adversaries to Wahhabism. He criticized Wahhabi doctrine in a pair of essays and triggered a flurry of replies from several Wahhabi scholars. It seems that the controversy began when he first came to Najd, perhaps en route to performing the pilgrimage some time in the 1840s.[93] He stopped for a time in Unayza, where he studied with the Wahhabi qadi Abd Allah ibn Aba Butayn and obtained a licence authorizing him to teach. It appears that Ibn Jirjis intended mischief all along, as in the course of teaching he vindicated certain verses of a famous poem of devotion to the prophet Muhammad, *al-Burda*, which the Wahhabis considered expressions of idolatry – a position set forth in Ibn Abd al-Wahhab's *Book of God's Unity*.[94] The Baghdadi scholar also disputed a number of Wahhabi tenets on intercession by citing passages from the works of medieval writers, Ibn Taymiyya and Ibn al-Qayyim.[95] There followed a series of treatises by Aba Butayn and Abd al-Rahman ibn Hasan against Ibn Jirjis and his defenders.[96] In addition to the formal polemics, Abd al-Rahman's son Abd al-Latif, who would become the next supreme religious leader, sent an angry letter to the people of Unayza to rebuke them for hosting Ibn Jirjis:

> There occur among you matters that cause pain for the believers and joy for the hypocrites... most of you honour Da'ud the Iraqi even though he is famous for enmity toward monotheism and its supporters.[97]

Abd al-Latif enumerated the harmful views that Ibn Jirjis openly espoused in Unayza: Supplicating the dead is not a form of worship but merely calling out to them, so it is permitted. Worship at graves is not idolatry unless the supplicant believes that buried saints have the power to determine the course of events. Whoever declares that there is no god but God and prays toward Mecca is a believer. He continued:

> This man enjoys friendly relations with your town and is accustomed to going there. Among its nobility and dignitaries are some who honour, befriend and support him and who accept his specious arguments. The reasons for this are hatred, heretical tendencies and refusing to accept God's light and guidance, which are known in al-Arid.[98]

In a separate letter to a Wahhabi partisan in Unayza, Abd al-Latif urged him to have arguments against Ibn Jirjis publicly recited at Unayza's mosques and to advise the townsmen of their duty to show enmity toward the Iraqi. He also asked for the names of the men who had invited Ibn Jirjis so Abd al-Latif could show them to Amir Faysal, who had said that Ibn Jirjis was not allowed into the region.[99] Thus did the Wahhabi leadership strive to eliminate idolatrous beliefs and practices in the domain of belief, not merely through instruction and preaching, but also through exhortation to display animosity toward anyone espousing dangerous beliefs. The demand for the names of Ibn Jirjis' Unayzan associates to pass on to the Saudi ruler underscored the political power propping up Wahhabi discourse's claim to a monopoly on religious speech.

Outside of Unayza, there was only one other major Najdi opponent to Wahhabism during the rule of Turki and Faysal. Uthman ibn Mansur (1788 or 1796–1865) was one of the most curious and controversial Najdi scholars of his era. His early teachers were local Wahhabi sheikhs in Sudayr and Washm. Around the time of the Saudi-Ottoman war, he went to Basra and Baghdad, where he studied under some anti-Wahhabi sheikhs.[100] His travels then took him to the Holy Cities, where he may also have encountered ulama hostile to the mission, but his exposure to 'idolatrous' teachers did not automatically put him on the wrong side of the Wahhabi establishment. He served both Amir Turki and Amir Faysal as qadi at several locations. Faysal, for instance, gave him jurisdiction over all of Sudayr because of his reputation for justice and integrity. Ibn Mansur's broad learning in literature as well as religious sciences made him a popular teacher as well. That Faysal trusted his discretion and judgment is evident from his appointment to the sensitive post at Ha'il (c.1849), the seat of Faysal's powerful ally, Talal ibn Rashid. It appears that Ibn Mansur clashed with the Rashidi amir when he sided with a group of townsmen in their dispute with Talal and that led to his removal. He then moved to his native region of Sudayr, where he spent the rest of his life.

In addition to his public career as a judge and teacher, Ibn Mansur composed a number of religious treatises, including a commentary on Ibn Abd al-Wahhab's *Book of God's Unity*, reportedly at the urging of Amir Faysal. By most accounts, the Wahhabis of his era considered it a correct commentary. In the estimation of Abd al-Rahman ibn Hasan, it had only one defect, namely, Ibn Mansur mentioned the noted anti-Wahhabi scholar Muhammad ibn Sullum. A more critical evaluation was voiced by Abd al-Rahman's son, Abd al-Latif, who declared that Ibn Mansur's defective understanding led him to commit countless errors in his commentary.[101] The second opinion probably reflected a new, revised Wahhabi consensus that formed when it became evident that Ibn Mansur had abandoned the mission and taken the side of its Ottoman critics. The timing and details of this shift are invisible in the sources, but the shift itself is unmistakable and obviously infuriated the Wahhabi establishment because it represented betrayal by an insider, something more threatening to Najd's discursive uniformity than critics from the outside. The key piece of evidence for his betrayal is a treatise condemning Wahhabi leaders for their declaration of other Muslims to be infidels.[102] The inclusion of an elegy to a prolific anti-Wahhabi writer (Da'ud ibn Jirjis) can only have irritated Riyadh's ulama all the more. The response was an outpouring of treatises by the two senior members of Al al-Sheikh (Abd al-Rahman and Abd al-Latif) and several other sheikhs.[103] In addition to a wave of polemics, the Wahhabi establishment combated Ibn Mansur by suppressing copies of his treatises. When he died in 1865, his book collection was sent to Riyadh, apparently to inspect its contents and remove from circulation 'harmful' writings, such as his work condemning the Wahhabis for considering Muslims to be infidels.[104] Two years later, another copy of his anti-Wahhabi treatise surfaced in Burayda and Sheikh Abd al-Rahman wrote to a Wahhabi sheikh there, advising him to send it to Riyadh for safekeeping.[105]

The suppression of Ibn Mansur's writings and the containment of the old tradition to Unayza were significant in two respects. First, both were reminders that the Ottoman religious establishment continued to regard the Wahhabi mission as anathema and would support Najdi dissidents. Second, the appearance of a group of dissenters in the single region whose amirs barely tolerated Saudi rule underscored the political underpinnings of the rival scholastic traditions. From these two points, it follows that as long as the Saudis maintained a firm grip over their domain, the Wahhabi tradition could purge opposing ulama and impose their hegemony over religious practices and discourse. In the last years of Faysal's rule, there was little reason to anticipate the stormy decades that would close the nineteenth century and shake the mission's political foundations.

Wahhabism and Saudi Dynastic Strife

Amir Faysal's reign after his return from exile in 1843 marked the apogee of the second Saudi amirate. On the face of it, when he died at the end of 1865, there was little reason to expect Al Saud to wage a fierce succession struggle. His son and designated heir Abd Allah had long served as chief military lieutenant, but his younger half-brother Saud openly challenged him. In doing so, Saud triggered a protracted military contest that sapped the Saudis' power, paving the way for the fall of the second amirate in 1891 to the Rashidi amirate based at Ha'il. The story of the Saudis' self-destruction and of the Rashidis' triumph conformed to a familiar pattern of Najdi dynastic politics. For the Wahhabi ulama, however, the succession struggle raised an unprecedented and knotty issue: namely, which candidate to support. Part of the problem lay in the ulama's tendency to accord allegiance to the ruler, regardless of how he came to power, as long as he declared support for Wahhabism. But some ulama insisted on a strict juridical view that branded a rebel against the legitimate ruler (imam) as a usurper. Further complications arose from Abd Allah's decision to seek Ottoman assistance against his brother because he broke a taboo against making an alliance with idolaters. The upshot was a rare feud among Wahhabi ulama on a political issue.[106] A second aspect of the problem was that Al al-Sheikh went through its own succession crisis when Abd al-Latif ibn Abd al-Rahman suddenly died in the middle of an intense phase in Al Saud's internecine fighting. Yet another ramification of the crisis was that it gave Wahhabism's adversaries in al-Qasim the opportunity to incite the Rashidis against Wahhabi ulama.

Shortly after Abd Allah's accession, Saud asserted his own claim on the grounds that twelve years earlier Amir Faysal had deputized him to govern southern Najd. The Wahhabi leader Abd al-Rahman ibn Hasan denounced the rebellious amir for breaking ranks with the legitimate imam, who had received a public oath of allegiance.[107] The only ground for rebellion in Wahhabi doctrine is if a ruler commands believers to violate religious duties.[108] He also wrote directly to Saud, upbraiding him for making alliances with enemies of Islam.[109] Saud tried to sway Hamad ibn Atiq to back him, but the veteran sheikh denied Saud's claim to legitimate authority in southern Najd. Saud argued that he had paid allegiance to Abd Allah under compulsion. Ibn Atiq dismissed that as irrelevant because Abd Allah's succession had already been publicly and properly conducted. In the end, he called on Saud to submit his dispute with Abd Allah, including his claim that Abd Allah denied him rightful properties in al-Hasa, to Al al-Sheikh for resolution.

When fighting between Abd Allah and Saud intensified in 1870, Sheikh Abd al-Rahman had died (1869) and his son Sheikh Abd al-Latif had become the leader of the Wahhabi mission. He handled the delicate task of negotiating Riyadh's surrender to Saud's forces when Abd Allah abandoned the seat of Saudi power. Citing the doctrine of necessity, Abd al-Latif recognized Saud as the new legitimate ruler even though he had previously labelled his cause 'the banner of religious ignorance' (jahiliyya).[110] His commitment to Abd Allah may have been diluted by the beleaguered ruler's bid to forge an alliance with the Ottoman governor of Baghdad. The Wahhabis condemned any such move that might bring the 'infidel' Ottomans into Arabia and they made no allowance for Abd Allah's desperation in the face of Saud's threat.[111]

In early 1871, an Ottoman force occupied al-Hasa, whence Abd Allah moved to plot his return to Riyadh. The Wahhabi leadership adopted an uncompromising stand on Abd Allah's relationship with the Ottomans. Abd al-Latif issued epistles condemning allegiance to infidels as a violation of God's explicit word in the Qur'an. On the contrary, it is an obligation to sever ties with them, to wage jihad against them and to grow closer to God by hating them. To help them, to bring them to Muslim lands, to give them allegiance and to choose to live among them amount to clear apostasy.[112] The idea that a ruler might seek help from an idolater is based on a weak Hadith, which in any case stipulates that the idolaters may not have power over believers. In a letter to Hamad ibn Atiq, the Wahhabi leader described how the Ottomans spread immorality like alcohol and sodomy and permitted the notorious anti-Wahhabi of Baghdad, Da'ud ibn Jirjis, to spread idolatry.[113] Abd al-Latif wrote to Saud, urging him to launch a jihad to rescue Muslim lands from the hands of God's idolatrous enemies.[114]

The proximity of Ottoman power hardened the discourse of separation that flourished during earlier wars against the Ottomans and the Egyptians. As the leading Wahhabi sheikh, Abd al-Latif faced a peculiar difficulty at this stage because Wahhabi ulama cited his father Abd al-Rahman's fatwas and epistles that deemed travel to and residence among idolaters permissible in certain circumstances. Both Abd al-Rahman and his pupil Hamad ibn Atiq had noted that travel to and residing among idolaters were permissible if the believer openly practised his religion. Abd al-Latif argued that the present circumstances were different because the Ottomans in al-Hasa were a direct military threat and thus were the enemy camp of an aggressive, belligerent power.[115] He viewed laxness toward the infidels as an opening for unbelief to enter the abode of Islam. Consequently, he denounced offering hospitality to anyone who lived among infidels. As a Hadith puts it, 'Whoever honours an innovator [of prohibited ritual practices] has assisted in destroying Islam.'[116] The Qur'an commands believers to not befriend any who make a plaything or a game of religion (*al-Maida* 57–8), as the Turks do when they accompany the call to prayer with drums, bugles and flutes.[117] The matter was a practical one because Abd al-Latif feared the influence of Najdis going to al-Hasa and befriending the Ottomans. Such men would return to Najd and persuade their countrymen that the Ottomans were benevolent rulers worthy of allegiance.[118] Such a prospect was made more likely by the willingness of Wahhabi ulama in al-Hasa to cooperate with the Ottomans. In one epistle, Abd al-Latif censured one such sheikh for forgetting his allegiance to monotheism and departing from the way of Muhammad ibn Abd al-Wahhab even though the Ottomans suppressed Islam by implementing European laws and permitting Shiism to flourish.[119] In another piece of writing, he lamented the Najdis' succumbing to Satan's tricking them into accepting the worst infidels in all of God's creation (the Ottomans) who include in their company English soldiers, deny God's very existence and assert the eternity of the world.[120]

One Wahhabi scholar, Muhammad ibn Ajlan, considered Abd Allah's invocation of Ottoman assistance to be permissible. Ibn Ajlan came from Riyadh, where he studied with Sheikh Abd al-Rahman before Amir Faysal appointed him qadi for two districts in southern Najd in 1858. During the succession struggle, he sided with Abd Allah and even travelled to Baghdad on his behalf to solicit Ottoman help against Saud. Thus, it was natural that he composed a treatise defending Abd Allah.[121] Abd al-Latif rejected Ibn Ajlan's position without qualification.[122] In one letter, the Wahhabi leader expressed surprise that a man of Ibn Ajlan's learning would say such things, but that he hoped his treatise would not become widely known. Its circulation in southern areas prompted him to write to Ibn Ajlan directly to turn his attention to hadiths that disallow seeking help from idolaters and to correct his misunderstanding of Ibn Taymiyya's recourse to Egyptians and Syrians against the Mongols.[123]

While the ulama settled the proper doctrinal response to the return of Ottoman power, the political situation continued to evolve. Saud's position in Riyadh crumbled in 1871 and he quit the town, deputizing one of Abd Allah's uncles. The Ottomans then thought they were in a position to annex both al-Hasa and Najd, so Abd Allah secretly returned to Riyadh to fight for his patrimony's independence. In a facile reversal, Abd al-Latif quickly recognized Abd Allah as the legitimate ruler. He explained his switch by declaring that he had nothing to do

with Abd Allah when he brought the Ottomans to Arabia, but that
the Saudi contender had since proclaimed repentance and remorse.[124]
If Abd al-Latif imagined that matters were now settled, he was to
be disappointed by Saud's return two years later to again oust Abd
Allah and to find himself compelled to pledge allegiance to Saud.
But the rebellious amir died soon afterward in Riyadh, whereupon
Abd al-Latif and the leading ulama consecrated Faysal's youngest
son Abd al-Rahman as the new leader.[125] But Abd Allah would not
relinquish his claim to rule and he again marched on Riyadh in early
1876, whereupon Abd al-Latif persuaded Abd al-Rahman to yield to
Abd Allah in the interest of uniting against Saud's sons, who were
busy rallying support against their uncles. This concluded nearly ten
years of internecine fighting. During that time, the Rashidis in Ha'il
had seized the opportunity to annex al-Qasim to their realm. Thus,
in 1876, Abd Allah ruled over a much diminished domain consisting
of Riyadh and adjacent districts.

Unlike the messy and prolonged strife within Al Saud that followed
Amir Faysal's passing, the succession of religious leadership in Al al-
Sheikh from one generation to the next transpired with no visible
sign of controversy. When Abd al-Rahman ibn Hasan died in March
1869, his son Abd al-Latif naturally emerged as the supreme Wahhabi
leader. He was perhaps the most learned individual during the
second amirate, something he owed at least in part to his upbringing
in Cairo and his studies at the Azhar for thirty years. After he joined
Faysal's court in 1849, he composed several polemical works and
dozens of epistles. As Abd al-Rahman grew old, he passed the
mantle of Al al-Sheikh leadership to his son. Abd al-Latif witnessed
the unravelling of Saudi cohesion and strove to hold together the
Wahhabi religious establishment during the rapid political twists
and turns that by chance came on the heels of his father's death.
The record of his letters to ulama in Najd and al-Hasa testify to his
efforts on that score. It was a stunning blow to the mission when
he suddenly died in January 1876, just days after a Saudi pretender
brazenly shot a political enemy in Riyadh's mosque right after Abd
al-Latif had led the late afternoon prayer. The incident so shocked
him that he apparently suffered a heart attack and died five days
later.[126] This time the matter of succession to the mission's leadership
was not so rapid or easy for reasons on which the sources are mute.
Nor is it exactly clear how Abd al-Latif's son Abd Allah became the
choice for religious leadership.

When Abd al-Latif had returned to Arabia from Egypt in 1848, he first moved to heavily Shiite al-Hasa, perhaps to buttress the Wahhabi mission there against local ulama. He married the daughter of a Wahhabi sheikh at Hofuf, where Abd Allah was born and spent his boyhood, studying in the household of his maternal uncle, Sheikh Abd Allah ibn Ahmad al-Wuhaybi. Then, in 1861, his father brought him Riyadh. When his father died, Abd Allah was a rising figure in the religious establishment, but perhaps too young to hold the respect of men his father's age. According to one account, he chose to withdraw from Riyadh because of his grief over his father's sudden demise and anxiety that chronic strife among Al Saud might destroy the political foundations of the Wahhabi mission.[127] Abd Allah withdrew to al-Aflaj in southern Najd, where he spent the next three years in the company of Hamad ibn Atiq. In the meantime, Riyadh's foremost ulama, primarily his father's pupils, felt the need for a member of Al al-Sheikh who was both learned and respected and they considered Abd Allah to be the one qualified for that role. Hamad ibn Atiq urged him to return to the Saudi capital to take over his father's position as leader of the Wahhabi religious estate. For the next forty years, until his death in 1920, Abd Allah ibn Abd al-Latif taught, wrote epistles to ulama and counselled Saudi rulers on political matters. He represented a generational bridge between the second and third Saudi amirates. In the early 1900s, he rallied Wahhabi support for the reviver of Saudi rule, Abd al-Aziz ibn Saud. They sealed their relationship with a marriage between Abd Allah's daughter and Abd al-Aziz.[128]

Wahhabi Ulama under Rashidi Rule

The exhausting Saudi civil war had given the Rashidis, trusted vassals during Faysal's reign, the opportunity to extend their sway in northern Najd. A key step in their expansion came in 1876, when Burayda's amir, Hasan Muhanna, formed a pact with Muhammad ibn Rashid. Soon, their combined forces were raiding central Najdi areas still loyal to Riyadh: in 1881, Sudayr's main towns went over to Ha'il. In 1884, Rashidi forces overran central Najd, leaving Riyadh and southern Najd as a rump Saudi principality. The next turn in Saudi self-destruction came in 1887, when Saud's sons seized Riyadh and jailed Amir Abd Allah; Ibn Rashid then intervened, forced the rebels to retreat south, brought Abd Allah to Ha'il as his 'guest' and appointed his own deputy to govern Riyadh. The second amirate's

last gasp came at the Battle of Mulayda in 1891, when Ibn Rashid
crushed an alliance of Faysal's one surviving son, Abd al-Rahman,
and the amirs of al-Qasim, whose calculations that Ha'il's ascent
would result in greater autonomy were confounded by Ibn Rashid's
determination to cement his authority over all of Najd. The battle
was a disaster for the anti-Rashidi allies and it spelled the end of the
second Saudi amirate.[129]

The Wahhabi mission's attitude toward the Rashidis during their
bid to conquer all of Najd is evident in a letter by Abd Allah ibn Abd
al-Latif. He wrote that the Rashidis were enemies of monotheists and
that they sought the support of infidels (the Ottomans) by inviting
them into Najd. There is no doubt about the Rashidis' infidelity and
the duty to fight them.[130] The odd thing about this verdict is that the
Ha'il amirs had been partners to the Saudis in the second amirate
and, as such, had received Wahhabi qadis, teachers and preachers
without qualms. A European visitor to Ha'il in the 1840s described
the Rashidis as true Wahhabis, enforcing the duty to pray at a mosque
and forbidding idolatrous acts.[131] When the Rashidis broke away
from Riyadh to establish an independent amirate, they did not expel
Wahhabi ulama, but they did adopt a more relaxed attitude toward
enforcement of ritual duties and religious law.[132] While the Rashidi
rulers were indifferent to the struggle between Wahhabi ulama and
their adversaries in al-Qasim, the latter viewed the Rashidi takeover
as an opportunity to undermine the mission. The initial reaction of
Wahhabi ulama to the new political arrangement was to abandon
Burayda in 1876 when its amir withdrew allegiance from the Saudis.
This act assumed a religious hue from the Wahhabi perspective. Abd
al-Latif ibn Abd al-Rahman reported to Hamad ibn Atiq that Burayda's
ruler had seceded from the Muslims to side with God's enemies.[133]
In Burayda itself, a prominent Wahhabi sheikh, Muhammad ibn Abd
Allah al-Salim, clashed with the amir, Hasan al-Muhanna, because
the sheikh had declared loyalty to Al Saud. As a result, the sheikh
had to flee to Unayza and soon other ulama and religious pupils
joined him there, symbolizing Wahhabi repudiation of Hasan al-
Muhanna. A few years later, the Wahhabi qadi of Burayda, Sulayman
ibn Muqbil, moved to Mecca when Hasan al-Muhanna turned down
his request to retire, presumably to avoid serving under an infidel
regime. Ibn Muqbil deputized a fellow Wahhabi, Muhammad ibn
Umar al-Salim, who in his turn also departed for Mecca when the
amir tried to appoint him as qadi.[134] It is not exactly clear how or

why, but around 1885, Amir Muhanna prevailed upon Muhammad
ibn Abd Allah al-Salim to return to Burayda as its qadi.

Around the same time, perhaps because of the return of a
Wahhabi qadi to Burayda, a controversy erupted there on two well-
worn issues: the permissibility of seeking the intercession of holy
men with God and travel to the land of idolaters.[135] The leader of
the anti-Wahhabi side was Ibrahim ibn Jasir (1825–1920), a Buraydan
sheikh who had initially studied under local Wahhabi scholars (the
Al Salim cousins) and then travelled to Iraq, Syria and Mecca.[136] Back
in Burayda, he quarrelled with his former mentors over the issue of
political allegiance to the Ottomans, travel to the land of idolaters
and intercession. While the Ha'il amirs did not directly meddle in
religious matters and took no measures to suppress the Wahhabi
mission, their neutrality gave an opening to al-Qasim's anti-Wahhabi
party to rally its followers, who included members of Al Bassam.[137]
According to the Wahhabi sheikh Sulayman ibn Sihman, Ibn Jasir's
deviation from Wahhabi doctrine vindicated the mission's ban on
travel. He noted that a Najdi scholar had gone to Syria for study and
upon his return had declared it permissible to seek the intercession
of holy men and to address prayers to them. The adoption of such
views, he observed, was just one of the evil consequences of travel
to the land of idolatry.[138]

When Abd al-Aziz ibn Mit'ab became the Rashidi amir in 1897,
religious controversy again erupted in Burayda. A prominent
Wahhabi sheikh, Abd Allah ibn Muhammad ibn Mufadda, withdrew
to a village when he heard that the Rashidi amir had accompanied
an Ottoman official to Burayda.[139] Anti-Wahhabi ulama came into the
open, hoping to persuade the Rashidi ruler to curtail the mission's
influence. The most vocal adversary to Wahhabism was Abd Allah
ibn Amr (c.1870–1908).[140] Ibn Amr came from Burayda or a nearby
town, studied for a time in Riyadh and travelled to study in Aleppo.
In March 1897, he urged the Rashidi ruler Muhammad ibn Rashid to
take action against Wahhabi leaders Abd Allah ibn Abd al-Latif, his
brother Ibrahim and Muhammad ibn Abd Allah al-Salim. Ibn Amr
accused the Wahhabis of fomenting ill will in al-Qasim because of
their arrogance and their habit of judging folk to be infidels (takfir)
with insufficient cause. He claimed that Najd was full of people
who considered Abd Allah ibn Abd al-Latif the most authoritative
religious figure and who deemed anyone who disagreed with him to
be an infidel. Ibn Amr asserted that the Wahhabi sheikh considered

travel to nearby lands an act of infidelity. In this critic's opinion, such dogmatic extremism began with Hamad ibn Atiq, who passed it on to Abd Allah ibn Abd al-Latif and another member of Al al-Sheikh, Hasan ibn Husayn. Most religious pupils accepted the Wahhabi position even though it is clearly mistaken on the bases of Islamic law and reason. Ibn Amr sided with those who believed that self-professed Muslims in the Ottoman Empire were indeed believers and not infidels; consequently, he felt under no obligation to bear hostility toward the empire, to forbid travel to its lands, or to emigrate from Ottoman territory.

This controversy raged in al-Qasim for a number of years but the Wahhabi camp held its ground in the adverse political climate. True, the Wahhabis lost control over influential religious positions, such as when Muhammad ibn Rashid dismissed Unayza's Wahhabi qadi (Salih ibn Qirnas) after the Battle of Mulayda in 1891 and replaced him with the less ardent Abd Allah ibn A'id.[141] Yet the Rashidi amirs did not thoroughly purge them because they had no interest in uprooting Wahhabi influence. There would be no repetition of the Ottoman-Egyptian efforts to stamp out Wahhabism. Outside of al-Qasim, the Rashidis left Wahhabi ulama in place as qadis throughout Najd, including the amirate's capital Ha'il. By the 1880s, generations of Najdi townsmen had lived in a Wahhabi milieu. The strict monotheistic doctrine had been naturalized as the native religious culture.

If we view Wahhabism in the broader perspective of the Middle East in the nineteenth century, we see that it remained a marginal phenomenon, entrenched in hostility toward traditional Ottoman ulama. Wahhabism retained hegemony over Najd's religious life because of the political shelter provided by Saudi power. In turn, the Saudi realm could maintain its independence vis-à-vis Istanbul because of physical and technological factors: Its geographical isolation, its lack of valuable resources, the limits of nineteenth-century communications, transportation and military technologies made conquest and pacification too costly for both Cairo and Istanbul. These outside powers decided to leave the Saudis alone so long as they did not revive the first amirate's impulse for expansion through jihad and refrained from attacking Hijaz, Iraq and Syria. This meant that Amir Faysal could concentrate on holding power in Najd and portions of the Persian Gulf coast. Within that protected space, Wahhabism became firmly anchored as a distinctive regional religious culture wherever Saudi power could ensure conformity. In al-Qasim, where restless amirs repeatedly challenged Riyadh, representatives of Najd's old scholastic tradition, bolstered by contacts with Ottoman ulama in Hijaz and Iraq, were able to persist and to transmit that tradition to their religious pupils. When Saudi power crumbled in al-Qasim in the 1880s and 1890s, anti-Wahhabi ulama saw an opportunity to incite the Rashidis against Wahhabi ulama, a task made easier by the latter's loyalty to Al Saud. But the Rashidis themselves never adopted an anti-Wahhabi religious policy. Some amirs viewed the Wahhabis as troublesome but not insufferable; others embraced the mission's doctrines and views on proper worship. Moreover, Rashidi power in Najd turned out to be ephemeral, as the ruling family split into rival factions that proved as self-destructive as those of Al Saud in the 1870s and 1880s. Instability at the court in Ha'il put the Rashidis at a disadvantage in the early 1900s when a new Saudi leader emerged to restore, once again, his family's power in Najd.

Chapter Three

Abd al-Aziz ibn Saud and the Taming of Wahhabi Zeal

The modern kingdom of Saudi Arabia is very much the product of the leadership of Abd al-Aziz ibn Saud. While his father, uncles and cousins languished in exile in Kuwait, he led a band of raiders to wrest Riyadh from Rashidi control in January 1902. In the next thirty years, he undertook a military and diplomatic campaign to expand his domain to encompass the lands that today make up the kingdom of Saudi Arabia. His accomplishments laid the foundation for the establishment of Wahhabism as the official religion of a twentieth-century Arab nation. Abd al-Aziz ibn Saud was the first powerful ruler in Riyadh since his grandfather Faysal died more than 30 years before. During that long interregnum, Wahhabi ulama adjusted to difficult political circumstances and dissident ulama exploited the lack of dynastic backing for the mission to challenge it, especially in al-Qasim. Ibn Saud put his stamp on the religious estate by restoring Al al-Sheikh to their customary pre-eminent role, rehabilitating ulama who had fallen afoul of local amirs and stamping out dissent. The consolidation of Saudi political power injected new energy into the Wahhabi mission and allowed it to finally attain uncontested supremacy in Najd. Wahhabi ulama, however, paid a price. Ibn Saud calculated that survival in the international arena required that he curb Wahhabism's xenophobic impulses embodied in the doctrine restricting travel to the land of idolaters. He sent his sons on diplomatic missions abroad, surrounded himself with Arab advisers from the Arab east and invited westerners into the domain of belief to assist in its economic development. When devotees of doctrinal purity challenged Ibn Saud's pragmatism in the late 1920s, he crushed them. Thereafter, Wahhabi ulama could grumble about his policies, but they accepted their role as guardians of ritual correctness and public morality while acceding to Ibn Saud the right to pursue what he deemed necessary for the kingdom's and his dynasty's welfare.

Imposing Wahhabi Hegemony

The expansion of Ibn Saud's authority over Arabia spanned thirty years. In the decade after he seized Riyadh, he battled the Rashidis to regain control in Najd, from al-Qasim to the southern regions. In 1913, Saudi forces overran al-Hasa and ended Ottoman rule there. During the First World War, Ibn Saud formed an alliance with Great Britain that brought him arms and funds for his struggle against the pro-Ottoman Rashidis, who fell to Saudi arms in 1921. The next object of Ibn Saud's expansionist project was Hijaz with the Holy Cities. The Hashemite sharif of Mecca, Husayn ibn Ali, had colluded with Great Britain to launch an anti-Ottoman revolt in 1916. The British were allied to both Husayn and Ibn Saud, so they gingerly avoided encroaching on one another as both viewed the Ottomans as their primary enemy. Husayn sent his forces to lay siege to an Ottoman garrison in Medina while Ibn Saud whittled down Istanbul's Rashidi ally in Ha'il. After the guns fell silent in Europe and the common Ottoman enemy was removed, the fluid political space of western Arabia and the territorial ambitions of Ibn Saud and Husayn made a clash unavoidable. Sharif Husayn established an independent Hashemite kingdom and soon found himself on the verge of conflict with Ibn Saud, whose allies raided along the ill-defined boundary of Najd and Hijaz. The British were in an awkward position of having two Arabian allies on a collision course and wound up adopting a neutral posture. In 1924–1925, Saudi forces prevailed, the Hashemite kingdom collapsed and Ibn Saud added Hijaz to his realm. In 1932, he proclaimed the establishment of the Kingdom of Saudi Arabia.

The restoration of Saudi power made it possible to consolidate Wahhabism as the ruling doctrine. Political considerations dictated the pace and extent of efforts to impose Wahhabi norms. In al-Qasim, for instance, Ibn Saud's determination to once and for all crush its independent-minded amirs coincided with the ulama's eagerness to stamp out the pocket of dissidents. By contrast, Ibn Saud's handling of Hijaz showed sensitivity to the sentiments of foreign Muslims and European powers with colonies with significant Muslim populations. Consequently, he opted for a lighter touch in the Holy Cities. While the appointment of Wahhabi sheikhs to head religious institutions no doubt offended local religious leaders there, he refrained from completely satisfying the mission's zealots. Likewise, the need to stabilize the situation in al-Hasa with its large Shiite population dictated an approach of half-measures designed to meet the external requirements of conformity with Wahhabi norms without forcing Shiites to embrace the mission and risk chronic unrest.

In the contentious climate of al-Qasim, the Saudi restoration afforded the opportunity to silence anti-Wahhabi critics. Ulama and pupils aligned with the Wahhabi faction led by Al Salim had suffered intermittent persecution at Rashidi hands since the 1870s. The region's subjugation to Riyadh tilted the balance in favour of the Wahhabi camp once and for all. Thus men like Fawzan ibn Abd al-Aziz Al Sabiq (1868–1908), who had fled Rashidi rule to Qatar, joined Ibn Saud's military expeditions and triumphantly entered Unayza in the ruler's company.[1] On the other hand, Wahhabism's most determined foe in the region, Buraydan sheikh Abd Allah ibn Amr, would pay the ultimate price for his strident opposition to the Wahhabi mission. After Ibn Saud conquered al-Qasim, Wahhabi ulama issued a fatwa condemning him to death for opposing the mission and for undermining the legitimate ruler (*wali al-amr*) by forging a document proclaiming the nullification of Burayda's oath of allegiance to Ibn Saud and affirming the town's affiliation with the Ottomans.[2] Ibn Saud is generally known more for his inclination to clemency than ruthlessness, but in this instance, he implemented the fatwa and had Ibn Amr put to death in Riyadh in 1908.

A much less clear set of circumstances surround Ibn Saud's treatment of a man who had vigorously, even courageously, advocated the mission while residing in unfriendly surroundings. Apparently, adherence to Wahhabi doctrine did not always suffice to gain Ibn Saud's favour. Ahmad ibn Isa (1837–1909), the son of the Wahhabi qadi for Shaqra in central Najd, studied under the most eminent ulama of the second amirate, including members of Al al-Sheikh.[3] Rather than follow his father into the religious estate, he settled in

Mecca to pursue long-distance trade in cotton goods. In the holy city, he was well situated to serve as a nodal point for connecting the Wahhabi mission to revivalist movements that were emerging in the second half of the nineteenth century in India and Ottoman lands. According to Wahhabi sources, Ibn Isa strove to salvage the Najdi religious mission's reputation, which had been distorted as a result of Saudi wars with the Ottomans, Egyptians and Meccan sharifs. In particular, he is credited with converting a wealthy Jeddah merchant to Wahhabi views on worship and doctrine. He then persuaded the merchant to pay for the printing and distribution of classical works by Ibn al-Qayyim and Ibn Taymiyya, when the Muslim world was beginning to revive its classical intellectual heritage through publishing such works. This same merchant also helped publish a treatise by a Baghdadi scholar in sympathy with the Wahhabis on a number of doctrinal points,[4] and he handled the shipment of books from a prominent ally of the mission in India.[5] Besides spurring the circulation of scholastic props for the mission, Ibn Isa wrote polemical works to rebut Wahhabi adversaries like the Baghdadi Ibn Jirjis and the Meccan Ibn Dahlan. Another report has him persuading the sharif of Mecca to dismantle a number of tombs that were objects of popular devotion. Ibn Isa also figures as the teacher of various Najdi religious pupils who resided in Mecca.[6] Furthermore, he used his influence in Najd during the Saudi civil war of the 1870s by urging rival members of Al Saud to resolve their conflict. After spending much of his life in Mecca, he finally returned to Najd in either 1899 or 1905,[7] and became the qadi of al-Majma'a for the Rashidi amir Abd al-Aziz ibn Mit'ab. When Ibn Saud conquered that town in 1908, he dismissed Ibn Isa, probably for having accepted an official position from the Rashidis and in spite of his noted contributions to the Wahhabi cause in unfriendly Ottoman Hijaz. The cause of his dismissal is not completely clear because one of his kinsmen, Ali ibn Abd Allah (1833–1912), likewise served as a qadi for the Rashidis but kept his post under Ibn Saud.[8] He remained in al-Majma'a, living in poverty until his death in 1909.

Ibn Saud exhibited his more typical tendency to leniency in two other instances. Sheikh Abd Allah ibn Musallim al-Tamimi (1851/2–1923) had studied in Riyadh with Wahhabi scholars, but seems to have resented the standing of Sheikh Abd al-Latif's sons in the 1880s and considered himself more knowledgeable, so he went to reside at Ha'il and rallied Rashidi forces against the Saudis. Nonetheless, after

Ibn Saud captured Ha'il, he merely sent al-Tamimi back to his native town in southern Najd (Hilwa).[9] In a second case, a sheikh obtained not just forgiveness but even entered the official religious institution. Sulayman ibn Muhammad al-Adwani (1849–1942) was born in Julajil, studied in Baghdad,[10] traded between Iraq and India and settled in Zubayr. He became involved in early twentieth-century politics in support of Kuwait's rulers against the Rashidis. When Ibn Saud rose to power, al-Adwani went to Riyadh and apologized to the ruler for his previous opposition. Ibn Saud forgave him at the behest of Sheikh Abd Allah ibn Abd al-Latif and appointed him to various posts.[11]

After al-Qasim, the next major region to fall to Saudi forces was al-Hasa in 1913. Its trading ports and fertile oases made it a key possession for the treasuries of the first two Saudi amirates. Its loss to the Ottomans in 1871 was a significant factor in the second amirate's collapse. Its recovery, however, presented a knotty problem because of the Wahhabi view of its Shiite population as infidels. Of al-Hasa's major towns, al-Qatif was almost entirely Shiite while Hofuf and Mubarraz were about evenly split between Sunni and Shiite. To carry out a purge of Shiite ulama along the lines of al-Qasim's 'purification' would have triggered unrest when Ibn Saud was bent on further expansion into the Rashidis' domain. The primacy of political considerations led him to seek declarations of loyalty from Shiite religious leaders and to target for punishment individuals who yearned for the Ottomans to return. Of the latter, he had a leader in al-Qatif executed and his family's properties seized. Ibn Saud satisfied both his need for revenue and Wahhabi sentiment by imposing a special tax on Shiites in lieu of their participating in jihad. When it came to al-Hasa's religious establishment, he left local judges and teachers in place for several years. Then he appointed a Maliki scholar sympathetic to Wahhabi doctrine, Isa ibn Akkas, to serve as qadi. Religious pressure on the Shiites increased in 1920 when Ibn Akkas died and the ruler appointed a more traditional Wahhabi judge.[12] Around the same time, emissaries of the zealous Ikhwan movement (see below) arrived in al-Hasa and pressed for a ban on the observance of Shiite religious holidays (Ashura and the birthdays of the Imams and the Prophet). The Ikhwan clashed with Ibn Saud's governor, Abd Allah ibn Jiluwi, a man renowned for his iron-fisted control. He apparently considered the Ikhwan a threat to order because of their moral vigilantism and he responded with vigorous measures. In two separate incidents that a British observer noted in

1920, Ibn Jiluwi punished the Ikhwan for assaulting local girls whose dress violated their sense of the allowable.[13]

The standing of al-Hasa's Shiites came into play when tensions mounted between Ibn Saud and the Ikhwan. The Riyadh conference of January-February 1927 brought together Ikhwan leaders, Wahhabi ulama and Ibn Saud. The Ikhwan conceded the point that only Ibn Saud had the authority to order a jihad and in doing so accepted his decision to prohibit raids against Iraq and Transjordan. Having compromised on what might be termed foreign policy, the Ikhwan insisted that in domestic affairs their religious views should prevail, including the forced conversion of al-Hasa's Shiites. To implement that decision, Shiite religious leaders gathered before the Wahhabi qadi and vowed to cease observance of their religious holidays, to shut down their special places of worship and to stop pilgrimages to holy sites in Iraq. The region's governor, Abd Allah ibn Jiluwi, carried out the decision and heard public declarations by Shiite ulama that they were renouncing idolatry and converting to Islam. Wahhabi ulama ordered the demolition of several Shiite mosques and took over teaching and preaching duties at the remaining mosques in order to convert the population. In the face of humiliation and persecution, some Shiites emigrated to Bahrain and Iraq. In one instance, a local religious leader spurred Shiite villagers to rise up against Saudi tax collectors, but the revolt did not spread and was easily suppressed. The intensive phase of Wahhabi coercion lasted about one year. When Ibn Saud decided to curb the Ikhwan, he permitted the Shiites to drive away Wahhabi preachers. Thereafter, the Saudi ruler tolerated private Shiite religious ceremonies and permitted the Shiite religious establishment to serve their following without interference. Wahhabi judges and teachers had a very small presence. On the other hand, the Shiites were not allowed to construct new mosques or religious schools.[14]

Integrating a largely Shiite region into a Wahhabi polity was largely a matter of devising a regime that would satisfy Riyadh's religious leadership without stoking widespread resistance to Saudi rule. The absorption of Hijaz presented a different set of challenges because of the Holy Cities' significance for all Muslims and Ibn Saud's desire for international recognition as their legitimate guardian. His approach to territorial expansion combined patience, diplomacy and opportunistic moments of aggression. We see this mix in the conquest of Hijaz. In 1924, his forces stormed Ta'if and perpetrated an awful massacre. Ibn

Saud then negotiated the peaceful surrender of Mecca. The following year, his forces occupied Jeddah and Medina after a prolonged siege and negotiations with Hijazi notables.[15] Ibn Saud ensured continuity in local administration by including dignitaries from Mecca, Medina and Jeddah on advisory bodies that he placed under his son Amir Faysal (later King Faysal); he also appointed Hijazi ulama to the District Council.[16] For the most part, he retained and modified late Ottoman and Hashemite instruments of governance that were untested in Najd but of obvious utility. In this respect, he retained bureaus to manage the pilgrimage, public health and education.[17]

With respect to religious policy, Ibn Saud aimed to absorb the Holy Cities in a way that reassured the Muslim world that a new Wahhabi regime would not disrupt the pilgrimage or disturb the large number of foreign Muslim residents. At the same time, he had to satisfy his Wahhabi constituency that idolatry would be stamped out. The region had been part of the Ottoman Empire for four centuries and consequently its religious culture was pluralistic, with the four Sunni legal schools, various Sufi orders and a tiny Shiite community around Medina. Therefore, Ibn Saud had to strike a balance between accommodating customary arrangements and upholding Wahhabi doctrine. Hijazis naturally regarded the reintroduction of Saudi rule with much apprehension, but other than an initial sweep conducted by the Ikhwan against domes on tombs in Mecca, Ibn Saud's keen awareness of broader Muslim sensibilities resulted in a mild touch.[18] When he negotiated the surrender of Medina and Jeddah, for instance, he agreed to keep the Ikhwan out; he also forbade them from permanently settling in Mecca.[19] For their part, Wahhabi leaders pushed for a more thorough reform of local custom than Ibn Saud had instituted in al-Hasa, where he preferred to leave the Shiites to their own devices. Thus, at the leadership level, the customary pluralist Ottoman culture in Hijaz gave way to a uniform Wahhabi regime of prayer leaders, judges and teachers hewing to a single doctrine. The Ikhwan pressed for strict adherence to Wahhabi norms, but Ibn Saud was willing to take a more relaxed approach to matters like smoking tobacco and worship at shrines. A typical illustration of Ibn Saud's balancing of incompatible tendencies was the way he established an early form of Wahhabi religious police (the Committee for Commanding Right and Forbidding Wrong). He appointed a native Meccan to supervise the new body to ensure proper observance of ritual and morality but also to temper the Ikhwan's zeal.[20] In general,

Ibn Saud designated local dignitaries in Mecca and Jeddah to enforce loosely the Wahhabi prohibition of tobacco, alcohol, playing cards and the phonograph. The outcome of this approach was the preservation of a more relaxed atmosphere in Hijaz than in Najd. Standards would stiffen when Ibn Saud arrived for the pilgrimage with a retinue of Wahhabi ulama and then slacken with his departure. Visitors report it was easy to find alcohol in Jeddah, public smoking in Mecca and singing in public places except during the pilgrimage season.[21]

The most sensitive issue facing Ibn Saud in Hijaz was the annual pilgrimage. He had to reassure the Muslim world that he was a responsible custodian of the Holy Cities at the same time as he satisfied the religious standards of Wahhabi ulama. For the benefit of pilgrims, he introduced tighter regulations on pilgrimage guides and the fees they could charge; he improved public health by instituting a quarantine to prevent the outbreak and spread of contagion (a chronic danger when crowds gathered in unsanitary conditions); and he even pioneered the use of automobiles to transport pilgrims from Jeddah to Mecca over the objections of Wahhabi ulama who considered them a prohibited innovation. In another sign of Ibn Saud's willingness to disregard Wahhabi sensibilities, he allowed Shiites to perform the pilgrimage. These steps succeeded at boosting the pilgrim traffic in the late 1920s. Taxes and fees on the pilgrims were lower than under the Hashemite regime but still provided an important source of revenue for the revival of Saudi rule.[22]

The political demands of consolidating a freshly forged kingdom prevailed over religious principles when it came to Ibn Saud's handling of Sufi activity in Hijaz. Sufi orders occupied an important niche in the pluralistic Ottoman religious culture, and the towns of Hijaz, including the two Holy Cities, were in this respect typical. Their distinction lay in the annual influx of pilgrims from all corners of the Muslim world. The constant mixing of believers from the Caucasus, the Malay Strait, the Niger Delta and so forth fostered a climate of religious diversity – and, from the Wahhabi perspective, idolatry – that the Saudis might tame but not suppress without offending much of the Muslim world.[23] In a sense, then, incorporating Hijaz posed a different problem for Ibn Saud than it had for his ancestors in the early 1800s, when political circumstances and slower communications gave the first amirate's rulers more leeway to impose Wahhabi doctrine. Caught between the ulama's insistence on purging Hijaz of idolatrous practices and the political imperatives of internal consolidation and external accommodation, Ibn Saud navigated a course of tacitly countenancing the Sufi orders and their practices as long as they were discrete. True, there was an initial spate of Wahhabi destruction of domes and Sufi convents, which caused an exodus of Sufi sheikhs to other parts of Arabia. Yet the Holy Cities continued to harbour branches of Sufi orders, as long as their sheikhs avoided notice by holding lessons in private homes. This leniency probably stemmed from two factors. First, Ibn Saud's need for correct relations with London may have smoothed matters for Muslims from British-ruled Sudan and India. Second, Islamic law safeguards private space from intrusions by public authorities.[24] The upshot may be described as a 'don't ask, don't tell' policy toward Sufism that permitted it to endure in Hijaz, as a handful of sheikhs and their disciples kept the orders alive in the decades after Saudi conquest.

In addition to dealing with Hijazi Sufi orders, the Saudi authorities contended with a pocket of Shiites in Medina and its environs. These Shiites formed three distinct groups.[25] The best documented and most ancient one consisted of a branch of the Prophet Muhammad's descendants, known as the Banu Husayn because of their descent from the prophet's grandson, the second Shiite imam Husayn. For more than five centuries, the Banu Husayn ruled Medina as an autonomous principality, recognized by a succession of dynasties, including the Fatimids, the Ayyubids, the Mamluks, and the Ottomans.[26] The second group, known as Nakhawila, occupied the opposite end of the status hierarchy as date cultivators residing in villages outside the city walls;[27] in fact, there are reports from Ottoman times that they were not permitted to sleep within Medina's walls.[28] The earliest extant description of the Nakhawila, by a seventeenth-century Moroccan visitor, attests to their frequent gatherings at the tomb of the sixth imam's son, Ismail ibn Jafar al-Sadiq, for weekly meals and occasional circumcisions.[29] Around 1900, another visitor reported observing the Nakhawila performing Shiite rites to commemorate the martyrdom of Imam Husayn.[30] The third group consisted of nomadic tribes that roamed near Medina and that were associated with the Harb tribe, especially its sub-section the Banu Ali. The Harb and Juhayna tribes were openly Shiite until the Saudi conquest, but they did not have a particular affiliation with either Twelvers or Zaydis.[31] The Banu Ali section of the Harb tribe switched to the Saudi side when it became apparent that it would defeat the Hashemites, so the degree of their commitment to and identification with Shiism is open to question.[32]

The different approaches Ibn Saud took toward al-Qasim, al-Hasa and Hijaz reflected his sense of how to consolidate political control over these regions and demonstrated his flexibility in adapting policy to local circumstances. At the same time, he had to keep an eye on the demands of Wahhabi ulama, who would have preferred a more thorough eradication of Shiism and Sufism. The religious leadership, however, apparently recognized the utility of Saudi revival and was willing to go along with his political compromises of Wahhabi purity. Nevertheless, Ibn Saud did have to contend with an uncompromising strain of Wahhabism that assumed a militant dimension in the form of the Ikhwan movement.

Curbing Wahhabi Zeal: Ibn Saud and the Ikhwan

Around the same time that Ibn Saud regained al-Hasa, there emerged in obscure circumstances a zealous movement known as the *Ikhwan* (Brethren). Wahhabi ulama went out to domesticate nomadic tribesmen, to convert them from idolatry to Islam and to make them soldiers for Saudi expansion. The Ikhwan became zealous religious warriors united and motivated by idealism more than allegiance to Ibn Saud. Eventually their devotion to a strict conception of the line between believer and infidel clashed with Ibn Saud's state building imperative. The result was a rebellion by some of the Ikhwan against their creator, who crushed them and in so doing reasserted dynastic power over the religious mission.[33]

Wahhabi ulama had always viewed the nomads as bearers of religious ignorance, jahiliyya and thus as raw material for conversion to Islam. In this respect, the notion that Wahhabism developed from and somehow reflected a tribal nomadic setting is utterly wrong. For that matter, the Saudi dynasty never had a comfortable relationship with nomadic tribes either because they were unreliable allies, fair weather friends at best. One Saudi researcher has even argued that Wahhabism represented a movement of Arabia's settled population against Bedouin domination of trade routes and 'protection' taxes.[34] This reading of history emphasizes Muhammad ibn Abd al-Wahhab's view of the Bedouin as infidels to be subdued and converted, tasks that the first Saudi state temporarily achieved. One of the secular virtues that Arabian chroniclers ascribed to the Saudi rulers was the taming of the Bedouin. To meet the threat of nomadic raids, Wahhabi ulama in the second Saudi amirate endorsed measures ordinarily not allowed in Islamic law, such as collective punishment against tribes for the deeds of their members. The attenuated, ephemeral power of the first two Saudi states left Arabia's tribal nomads in command of their domains when al-Dir'iyya and Riyadh collapsed. Thus, when Ibn Saud embarked on the reconstruction of dynastic power, the social and political landscape he encountered in Najd largely resembled the one facing the Saudi rulers over a century earlier.[35]

Who exactly conceived the idea to gather nomads in agricultural settlements and teach them to be proper Muslims is not clear; some sources attribute it to Ibn Saud himself while others see it as beginning with the ulama and then winning his support. Perhaps it was an invention born of the necessity to pacify once and for all Arabia's inner social frontier in order to bring security for Najdi townsmen by removing a perennial source of political instability. Tribal leaders had always proved susceptible to blandishments from Saudi foes and just as ready to attack as to rally to the Saudi banner. Perhaps the full significance of founding the first colony was not immediately apparent to Ibn Saud and the Wahhabi ulama. The sources do not suffice to reach a conclusion on the matter. Indeed, while the Ikhwan have drawn more attention from historians and writers on Saudi Arabia than any other aspect of early twentieth-century religious developments, there remain disagreements about fundamental points like their relationship to Ibn Saud.[36] The significance of Ikhwan military power for the success of Ibn Saud's conquests is another disputed point.[37] That Ibn Saud envisioned a military purpose for some of their settlements is evident from their location at forward positions poised for campaigns against the Hashemites in Hijaz and Rashidi strongholds at Jawf and Ha'il.[38]

The common understanding of Ikhwan settlements emphasizes a few elements. First, a single settlement was called a hijra (pl. *hujar*), a site populated by emigrants. The very term *emigrant* emphasized a religious purpose – to emigrate from the abode of idolatry to the abode of Islam. Muhammad ibn Abd al-Wahhab did not emphasize hijra in his writings, but he did support the position that it remains a duty for the believer until Judgment Day, according to the Prophetic tradition that emigration will not cease until repentance ceases and repentance will not cease until the sun rises in the west.[39] Emigration had long been a major theme in Wahhabi discourse, especially since Sulayman ibn Abd Allah's treatises during the Egyptian-Ottoman invasion of Arabia. It remained a central part of Wahhabi polemic in the nineteenth century, when ulama argued against travel to and residing in idolatrous lands. The essential idea was that it was nearly impossible to be a Muslim while living among idolaters and under their authority because social pressures would influence the believer to conform to the idolaters' ways. Therefore, emigration was a duty, just as it had been for seventh-century Muslims to quit Mecca and move to Medina. The creation of colonies for tribal sections, however, marked a new sort of emigration. Before Ibn Saud's experiment, the customary template in Wahhabi discourse for emigration had been to divide the world into internal and external spaces: the internal was the abode of Islam under Saudi rule; the external was the abode of idolatry under Ottoman rule. In the early twentieth century, the creation of hijra's gave the emigration template a different twist by implying that internal spaces harboured idolatry – the Saudi domain was dotted with islands of idolatry. The hijra offered a means to depopulate these islands, assemble the nomads in settlements of belief and assimilate them to Wahhabi religious practice.

A second element in the common view of the Ikhwan has to do with religious indoctrination. Along with removal of a tribal section to the hijra, the section's sheikh went to Riyadh for instruction in Wahhabi tenets while ulama taught the tribesmen in the hijra. The settled Bedouins' first exposure to formal Islamic tenets thus came directly and exclusively from Wahhabi teachers. The hijras also had religious zealots, called *mutawwi'a*, to enforce public morality and punctual observance of prayer. Specific evidence on the kind of instruction imparted to the Ikhwan is fragmentary, but the sources do mention that they studied a short 'catechism' by Muhammad ibn Abd al-Wahhab and a treatise by a contemporary figure, Sulayman ibn Sihman.[40] More detail emerges in the portrait of a prominent Wahhabi sheikh from Burayda, Umar ibn Muhammad ibn Salim.[41] He used to spend two to three months each year at the best-known hijra, al-Artawiya, and at others to give religious instruction. When he visited, as many as thirty religious students accompanied him to continue their studies under his guidance. Moreover, when Ibn Salim taught at al-Artawiya, people from the towns of Sudayr and Washm would join his circle along with the Ikhwan (described by Ibn Salim's biographer as emigrants, *alladhina hajaru*), a detail that contradicts the common view that complete segregation separated hijra residents from other Najdis. Ibn Salim kept up this routine until 1926, when some Ikhwan demonstrated dissatisfaction with Ibn Saud's pragmatic policies toward Muslims of Hijaz. The particular instance regarding

Ibn Salim is of more than marginal interest because it confirms the idea that at least some Ikhwan were instructed in conventional Wahhabi teachings. Ibn Salim's Wahhabi biographer emphasizes his impeccable credentials as a member of a solidly Wahhabi lineage (both his father and his uncle endured Rashidi persecution in al-Qasim for proclaiming Wahhabi doctrines) and a close pupil of the era's leading Wahhabi figure, Abd Allah ibn Abd al-Latif.[42]

Another prominent Wahhabi teacher to visit the hijra at al-Artawiya was a member of Al al-Sheikh, Hasan ibn Husayn (1849–1921).[43] A Wahhabi biographer omits any mention of his involvement with the Ikhwan, but does note that he was a qadi at Aflaj and Riyadh during the Rashidi years.[44] Hasan ibn Husayn maintained the strict view on forbidding contact with idolaters. In a brief epistle, he reiterated standard views on the land of infidelity with specific reference to Kuwait and the Iraqi town of Zubayr.[45] He noted that the ulama affirm that wherever the signs of idolatry appear is deemed an infidel land. Zubayr contains a dome on the grave of an early Muslim Companion and the townspeople worship at the dome, an act of idolatry. He cited Sheikh Abd al-Latif's view that Muslims who migrated to al-Hasa deserved to be considered infidels because they had moved from the land of Muslims to the land of idolaters, which constitutes an act of apostasy. The same ruling would apply to emigrants from Najd to Zubayr. Another factor in Zubayris' infidelity is their voluntary submission to 'satanic law', probably a reference to the Ottoman Empire's reformed legal order. Sheikh Hasan then gave a number of customary conditions of infidelity: taking idolaters as allies and lending them assistance; offering sacrifices to jinn, as he claimed the Kuwaitis and Zubayris did; failing to consider Ottoman infidels as such and claiming that they are Muslims; and detesting the Islamic (Wahhabi) mission and ridiculing it. Like earlier Wahhabi ulama, he concluded that the wealth and blood of such infidels are permissible and that none would dispute this conclusion except those who believe that merely professing the creed constitutes belief even if one commits acts of idolatry.

Given these views, which were the core of the late nineteenth-century controversy in al-Qasim between Wahhabi ulama and their foes like Ibn Amr, it was natural to find that the Ikhwan at al-Artawiya would quarantine anyone who travelled to Kuwait.[46] What is more puzzling about the Ikhwans' separatism was their much-noted intolerance toward other Wahhabis. If they learned doctrine from men like Umar ibn Salim and Hasan ibn Husayn, that distinctive degree of fanaticism must have stemmed from other factors.[47] A handful of anecdotes suggest that a rigid separatist impulse characterized fringe elements in the nineteenth century. For example, Abd Allah ibn Muhammad ibn Dakhil (1845–1906) of al-Majma'a studied with Al al-Sheikh in Riyadh, the Al Salim cousins in Burayda and at mosques in Mecca and Medina.[48] He settled in his ancestral town of al-Midhnib in 1883 to become its qadi (he came from the chiefly lineage) and teacher, drawing a large number of students. He wrote a treatise forbidding a student to study under anybody not loyal to the Wahhabi mission. The Rashidi ruler Abd al-Aziz ibn Mit'ab removed him because he would not declare support for the Ha'il amirate, but Ibn Saud restored him when he conquered the area shortly before Ibn Dakhil's death. Another indication of a tendency to ostracize is the report that a Najdi scholar from the same period, Ibrahim ibn Duwiyan (1858–1934), had few students because he was not an enthusiastic proponent for the mission.[49] Finally, we find a connection between the late nineteenth-century xenophobic thread in Wahhabi thought and the Ikhwan in the case of Muhammad ibn Abd Allah ibn Salih ibn Isa (d. 1929), from a prominent clerical family in Shaqra. On one occasion he rose during the Friday sermon at Unayza's chief mosque to accuse the preacher of uttering an idolatrous phrase when he alluded to the Prophet as the 'remover of affliction' (*kashif al-ghumma*). After the congregational prayer, the town's amir asked a group of ulama if the phrase really did amount to idolatry and they replied that Ibn Isa was exaggerating, so the amir expelled him from town. He later became known for inciting the Ikhwan.[50]

In the absence of more detailed sources, a clear understanding of how the Ikhwan adopted an extreme doctrine on separation from others will remain elusive. A demographic trait of the hijras, however, suggests that a social factor might have played a role. The settlements were not melting pots for the blending of Arabians from different tribes and their transformation into homogenized Saudi subjects. Instead, each one was populated predominantly by members of a single tribal section.[51] On the face of it, this was to be expected: When a tribal section agreed to settle at a hijra, it would prefer to remain in its home region.[52] As a consequence, the renowned solidarity of tribal nomads would not have been diluted at all by this particular form of sedentarization by tribal sections. The persistence of tribesmen's loyalty to their traditional leader rather than to the Saudi ruler also makes sense in this context.

In addition to the significance of hijras and religious indoctrination, a third point that historians emphasize is the conversion of nomads to the rigours of a sedentary economy. They no longer depended on their herds for their livelihoods, but they did not take to agricultural work with enthusiasm. Nor, it seems, did many pursue productive work in crafts or trade. In other cases of forced sedentarization (the Ottoman Empire and Iran), the central authority strove for a double benefit from the process: an increase in security for settled folk and an increase in rural economic production that the treasury might capture as revenues. If Ibn Saud expected a fiscal dividend, he was to be disappointed. The hijras became consumers of dynastic largesse in the form of regular and occasional subsidies in coin and kind.[53] Eventually, the exhortations of Wahhabi ulama spurred some Ikhwan to assume productive work as a fulfilment of religious duties.[54]

A fourth element in discussions of the Ikhwan is their propensity for warfare. While they abandoned their former pastoral occupation, they did not give up the martial bent of nomadic tribes. What had formerly been mundane raids for lucre now had religious sanction.[55] But in contrast to the conventions of nomadic combat, where warriors did their utmost to minimize killing and severe injury and refrained from attacking non-combatants, the Ikhwan became noted for ferocity in battle. Indeed, they earned notoriety for routinely killing male captives and they sometimes put children and women to death in spite of reprimands from their ruler.[56] The pretext for such slaughter was the Ikhwan's notion that the nomads they fought, particularly from 1912 to 1919, had to convert or be put to death.[57] That they deemed themselves qualified and authorized to judge for themselves which nomads required conversion is evident from their letters to leaders of tribal sections that did not quit nomadic pastoralism.[58]

Tensions between Saudi dynastic power and Ikhwan religious zeal unfolded in two phases. First, between 1914 and 1926, Ibn Saud and the Wahhabi leadership exhorted the Ikhwan to moderate their attitude toward other Najdis living under Saudi rule. Second, between 1926 and 1930, a handful of Ikhwan leaders rebelled against and attempted to overthrow Ibn Saud. In the first phase, Ibn Saud sent letters and treatises to hijras and dismissed a number of teachers. Ikhwan zeal was expressed in disdain not only toward the usual targets of Wahhabi contempt – infidels residing in neighbouring lands – but also toward those tribal segments that continued a nomadic existence and even toward Wahhabi townsmen. The first well-attested attempts to tame the Ikhwan's wild idealism took place in 1914, when Ibn Saud and Wahhabi ulama sent instructions to the hijras to refrain from attacking nomads.[59] In one letter, he warned against deviating from the shari'a and the guidance of the ulama. Another letter admonished the Ikhwan for regarding believing nomads as infidels; for attacking nomads and forcing them to settle down; for refusing to have dealings with nomads and townsmen on the pretext that they had committed an act of unbelief; for viewing the inhabitants of hijras as superior to villagers and townsmen; and for discriminating against Najdis who wore a black rope instead of a white turban over their headdress.[60] The ulama concluded by warning against further transgressions because the ruler, Ibn Saud, had the legitimate authority to punish them. It appears that these letters did not lower the temperature in some hijras, and two years later Ibn Saud dismissed a number of religious instructors for sowing extremist ideas.[61]

Then, in 1919, Ibn Saud held a meeting with leading ulama to discuss the continuation of Ikhwan attacks on tribes and oases they deemed fair game because of their religious laxity.[62] In the conventional fashion of scholastic discourse, the practical problem was given the form of questions about classes of people: emigrants and nomads, wearers of turbans and wearers of head ropes. On the question of the duty to emigrate, the Ikhwan had both Muhammad ibn Abd al-Wahhab and Ahmad ibn Hanbal on their side, but with respect to headdress, the religious texts did not support them.[63] The conclusion of the ulama marked the elevation of dynastic power over religious principle and is worth citing:

> He [the Muslim] should not be hostile or friendly except to those that the legal ruler orders. He who contravenes this goes against the way of the Muslims.[64]

Neither the Ikhwan nor even the Wahhabi ulama had the right to determine who is friend or foe, who is believer or infidel; that distinction was reserved to Ibn Saud. This assertion of dynastic prerogative did not sit well with the doctrinal legacy of nineteenth-century Wahhabism's sharp emphasis on enmity toward infidels. Moreover, Wahhabi authors had always defined infidelity on the basis of religious practice and belief, not according to the discretion of the ruler. The conclusion of the ulama in 1919, then, marked a new departure in Wahhabi thought. To clarify the difference between religious segregation from

Kuwaitis and Zubayris and regarding unsettled nomads as infidels, Ibn Saud paid for the publication of a prominent Wahhabi scholar's treatise. Ibn Sihman's essay examined errors in Ikhwan views, such as ostracizing people for minor slips and using physical coercion to enforce conformity.[65] The ruler also dispatched a prominent qadi, Abd Allah al-Anqari, to al-Artawiya in 1921 to dissuade its folk from fanaticism (ta'assub).[66] In 1926, Ibn Saud sent a young member of Al al-Sheikh, Muhammad ibn Ibrahim ibn Abd al-Latif, to the Ikhwan hijra at al-Ghatghat to tone down their zeal.[67]

In the second, violent phase of the Ikhwan's relations with Ibn Saud, a number of authors suggest that, in a sense, a clash became inevitable when Ibn Saud completed his Arabian conquests and recognized international borders. At that moment, the Najdi tribesmen's customary patterns of migrating to grazing areas in Iraq and raiding tribesmen there became violations of the international order. This left restless Ikhwan with no outlet for their martial impulses and no means for livelihood other than subsidies and the meagre gains of Najdi agriculture and petty trade.[68] The demobilized religious troops did not all rise as a body against the new order, just a handful of Ikhwan leaders, acting on either zeal or ambition. Perhaps the key element in the Ikhwan revolt was the unsatisfied ambition of the tribal leaders like Faysal al-Duwish and Sultan ibn Bijad, who resented Ibn Saud for using them to conquer his kingdom and then sending them back to their hijras. In this view, Duwish and Ibn Bijad expected to hold positions of authority in Hijaz. Another sore point for rank and file Ikhwan was Ibn Saud's barring them from seizing the booty they expected to gain by virtue of conquest.[69] In the case of the Ujman tribe that had dominated al-Hasa, Ikhwan restlessness may have stemmed from never adjusting to the loss of regional pre-eminence.[70] Finally, there is some evidence that Iraq's Hashemite ruler, Amir Faysal, conspired with Faysal al-Duwish to incite a rebellion to depose Ibn Saud, whereupon Duwish would rule Najd and the Hashemites would regain Hijaz.[71]

While mundane concerns permeate the reports of British observers, Saudi sources strike an official tone in their description of a series of conferences by restricting discussion to religious matters. In the first three years of mounting friction, both sides acted cautiously, attempting to resolve differences through two extraordinary summits convened in Riyadh to debate the religious legitimacy of their positions before a final violent climax. It is not clear if Ibn Saud consulted with

Wahhabi leaders ahead of the meetings, but they tilted in Ibn Saud's favour on issues underpinning his political authority while they sided with the Ikhwan on a number of important matters that required the ruler to tighten compliance with Wahhabi religious observance.

The trigger for the summits was a 1926 meeting of Ikhwan leaders at al-Artawiya, where they faulted Ibn Saud for not upholding the sharp separation of belief and infidelity. They noted that two of his sons travelled to idolatrous lands (Faysal to England, Saud to Egypt) and that idolatrous Iraqi and Transjordanian nomads were permitted to pasture their animals in the abode of Islam. They also blamed him for his lenience toward Shiites and the introduction of modern inventions (car, telephone and telegraph). Finally, they objected to what they considered illegal taxation of nomadic tribes.[72] To resolve the confrontation, Ibn Saud invited the Ikhwan leaders to Riyadh for a conference with Wahhabi ulama in January 1927, which ended with a religious decree confirming the validity of several Ikhwan grievances. The decree ordered the imposition of a much stricter regime on Shiites, banning Iraqi Shiites from entering Najd and instituting mandatory instruction in Wahhabi doctrine for al-Hasa's Shiites. Recently conquered lands in Hijaz were also to receive the blessings of Wahhabi education. Furthermore, the ulama agreed with the Ikhwan that Ibn Saud's taxes on the nomads were illegal. But on the central political issue, they upheld his right as the sovereign to collect these taxes and denied the Ikhwan any right to disobey. And crucially, the ulama affirmed that only the ruler could declare a jihad.[73] Even though the religious leaders did not rule on the new inventions, Ibn Saud banned the telegraph for the time being.

A number of tribes disobeyed the Wahhabi ulama's ruling on jihad and launched raids into Iraq under that banner. In October 1927, Faysal al-Duwish led a devastating attack on a police post at Busayya in Iraq. The British retaliated with bombings inside Najd and the Ikhwan pressured Ibn Saud to persuade the British to dismantle Busayya and other posts.[74] This exchange embodied the collision of new international realities with Wahhabi ideology and nomadic custom. With respect to the international situation, Britain had negotiated border agreements between Ibn Saud and the Hashemite rulers of Transjordan and Iraq and with the Al Sabah ruler of Kuwait. The boundary treaty with Iraq included a stipulation that neither side erect military posts in the vicinity of the border. In the wake of Ikhwan raids against tribes inside Iraq, the British set up a series of police posts 30 to 80 miles from the border on the assumption that such a distance complied with the treaty language. Ibn Saud protested the action, but the British insisted that Busayya's distance and character as a police post and not a military one meant that it conformed to the treaty.[75] The Ikhwan cared nothing for the niceties of the treaty or even the general principle of an international border. In their minds, they were pursuing jihad against infidels and the notion of a legal shield behind which infidels' lives and property were safe had no place in either the jihad tradition or the custom of tribal raiding.

If religious principles alone did not suffice to stir the Ikhwan to military activity, their economic situation was deteriorating as the internal pacification of Ibn Saud's realm left them without other sources of booty. That economic factors played an important role in Ikhwan restlessness is evident in a June 1929 letter to Ibn Saud from Faysal al-Duwish, who complained about the impoverishment of his folk since Ibn Saud prohibited raids on Bedouins and infidels (the betrayal of religious ideals also features in the letter). Again, the economic factor appears in a report on a meeting between an Ikhwan leader and the British agent in Kuwait, H.R.P. Dickson. The Ikhwan leader offered the following explanation for raids into Iraq, 'How could we help it when our grazing grounds and wells had been taken from us and seeing that we were persistently encouraged to do so [to raid]?' He also asserted that Ibn Saud had previously commanded raids against Iraq and Kuwait, so he was puzzled at the prohibition on such raids due to the treaties on boundaries.[76]

Ibn Saud and the British exchanged a series of diplomatic messages between April and November 1928. The British were unwilling to leave Iraq's tribes and towns exposed to Ikhwan raids. Having failed to move the British to solve his mounting domestic problems, Ibn Saud convened a second conference at Riyadh in November 1928, attended by thousands of tribesmen, Ikhwan, townsmen and ulama. An atmosphere of political crisis at the event foreshadowed the prospect of civil war, as Ibn Saud kept the tribesmen outside Riyadh's walls and reinforced its defences with men from other Najdi towns.[77] The situation revealed that, in one respect, the Ikhwan experiment had failed to convert all tribesmen into compliant political subjects, for a substantial body was ready to follow Ikhwan leaders in revolt against Ibn Saud. But in another respect, the experiment had succeeded because the explicit cause of revolt would be the imperative that the historically irreverent nomads remain true to religious principle.

The official Saudi newspaper reported that Ibn Saud opened the conference by offering to abdicate. The religious leaders expressed their satisfaction with his rule. Even if he had made certain mistakes, they were not so egregious as to warrant disobedience to him.[78] Ikhwan leaders also expressed their satisfaction with Ibn Saud's leadership up to that point in time, but they wanted to know if he would prohibit the telegraph, strictly enforce religious observance and morality, stand up to British pressure on the Iraqi frontier and wage jihad. The ulama declared that Islamic law did not expressly prohibit the telegraph and it was therefore not subject to prohibition. Ibn Saud declared that he was fulfilling his duty to send religious teachers to newly annexed regions. He also declared that the British had set up forts to guard Iraq because of wanton raids by a single Ikhwan leader, Faysal al-Duwish. The other Ikhwan agreed that he had transgressed but they also insisted that the forts come down because they posed a threat to their livelihood. On this point, the Wahhabi ulama took their side in stating that to fight for removing the forts constituted defending religion, not expansive jihad.[79] Most curiously, Ibn Saud declined to hold a public discussion of jihad but held a special private session, the substance of which was not announced.

The failure to completely mend the split between Ibn Saud and restless Ikhwan leaders paved the way for a showdown. What might have been the last straw for the ruler occurred in December 1928, when one of the rebellious chieftains led a ruthless Ikhwan attack on a caravan of merchants from al-Qasim, many of them from staunchly Wahhabi Burayda. To kill supposed infidels in Iraq complicated Ibn Saud's relations with the British; to massacre his subjects amounted to brazen defiance. He had to respond or admit that he was not the master of Najd.[80] He insisted that the aggressors restore the livestock stolen from the Buraydan traders and the Ikhwan responded with a call for the ulama to decide the issue. Efforts to mediate failed and the forces clashed at the Battle of Sibila on 30 March 1929. Ibn Saud mustered the sort of coalition of townsmen and allied tribesmen that his dynasty had relied upon ever since its first forays in the mid-eighteenth century. According to most accounts, the fighting was brief, almost anti-climactic, compressing into one hour a major defeat of the Ikhwan. Some of the rebel leaders got away, wounded but only slightly chastened.[81]

In al-Hasa, the embers of Ikhwan and tribal discontent burned among the Ujman tribe, who did not participate in the fighting at

Sibila and remained unbowed. A bout of rebellion flared as a result
of clumsy efforts by al-Hasa's governor to pre-empt such an event.
In the ensuing skirmish, the Saudi commander exacerbated matters
by executing the Ujman chief in captivity. When enraged Ujman
tribesmen launched a flurry of devastating raids on settlements in al-
Hasa, Ibn Saud turned to Britain, itself eager to pacify Saudi Arabia's
frontiers, for weapons to suppress yet another significant challenge
to his rule. By this time, rebellious Ikhwan were leaving their hijras
and returning to the desert and their old ways.

Before moving against the Ujman, Ibn Saud had to secure the tribal
area between Najd and Hijaz and that meant ensuring the loyalty of
the Utayba tribesmen, sections of which recognized Faysal al-Duwish
as their leader. Because not all sections of the tribe would declare
their loyalty, Ibn Saud tried to win them over through negotiation.
He gathered together the loyal Utayba tribesmen and announced that
any rebellious hijra would be evacuated and its inhabitants dispersed
to live with other tribes. To prevent further rebelliousness, he
announced that defeated rebels would have to surrender their arms
and their mounts. There remained the task of pursuing, cornering
and subduing unrepentant Ikhwan, whose desperation emerged in
a couple of opportunistic and futile efforts to win the backing of the
'infidels' of Kuwait and Britain. First, in June 1929, Duwish offered
his allegiance to Kuwait's Al Sabah ruler on condition that he accept
Islam and permit the Ikhwan into his country and protect them.
The next month, Ikhwan leaders even tried to strike a deal with
the British, offering a treaty and a pledge to refrain from attacking
tribes in Iraq and Kuwait.[82] There followed a handful of inconclusive
battles in fall 1929, but Ibn Saud's forces were gradually pressing the
Ikhwan to retreat toward Kuwait. In January 1930, the main body of
Ikhwan surrendered to British forces on the Saudi-Kuwaiti frontier.
The revolt of the tribal puritans was now a diplomatic problem –
repatriating the rebels on condition that their lives be spared – for
the British and Ibn Saud to resolve. The British returned the rebel
leaders to Najd and Ibn Saud honoured the stipulation to refrain
from executing them, satisfying himself with their incarceration as
exemplary punishment.[83]

Ibn Saud sealed the military defeat of the Ikhwan rebels with a
deft mix of punishment and rehabilitation to complete the job of
rendering the larger body of Ikhwan – who did not join the rebellion
but sullenly looked on – docile in the political field. Duwish and Ibn

Bijad died in captivity in Riyadh while their tribal followers suffered the confiscation of the lion's share of their camels and horses. The majority of Ikhwan reportedly sympathized with the rebels and resented Ibn Saud for his abandonment of their zealous religious spirit and his cooperation with the British, but he managed to placate them. One former associate of Duwish, Faysal al-Shiblan, joined the royal entourage. Another former rebel, Majid ibn Khathila, served a brief spell of internal exile and then helped reorganize the Ikhwan into the Saudi National Guard. He even accompanied Ibn Saud on his trip to 'idolatrous' Egypt in 1945 to meet the 'infidel' American president Franklin D. Roosevelt. Relatives of Faysal al-Duwish became governors of al-Artawiya. Rank and file Ikhwan fighters formed units in a new military institution, initially the White Army, eventually the National Guard and veterans of Ibn Saud's conquests received regular lifetime pensions.[84]

The denouement to the Ikhwan rebellion took nearly a full year to play out after the Battle of Sibila and, in the end, there was no doubt that its suppression spelled a new phase in Arabian state building. The official Saudi newspaper drove home the meaning of the episode when it reported Ibn Saud's speech before religious dignitaries and military leaders right after Sibila. He announced that they owed obedience to the ruler and stated that they may not 'hold meetings either to discuss religion or worldly questions without permission from the monarch'.[85] A clearer declaration of the ruler's supreme authority and the subject's duty to obey is difficult to imagine.

Ibn Saud's consolidation of dynastic rule depended on two factors. First, in the most immediate sense, he displayed superb political skills as a leader in his growing domain and as a foe to Arabia's other powers in Ha'il and Hijaz. Second, in the longer term, his relationship with the dominant regional power, Great Britain, made it possible to put his newly conquered domain on a durable footing. As we have seen, his perception that his political survival required a modus vivendi with the British precipitated the rebellion of the Ikhwan. This definitive and explicit shift to a realist foreign policy, inscribed in a series of treaties with the British, guaranteed Saudi Arabia's political independence during a period when most Arab lands bore the heavy burden of European colonialism: France ruled Morocco, Tunisia, Algeria, Syria and Lebanon; Great Britain controlled Sudan, Iraq and Palestine and still had a dominant role in Egypt. The kingdom's standing as one of the few independent

Arab countries (alongside Yemen) made Ibn Saud a more attractive figure to other Arabs than any previous Saudi ruler. Furthermore, he surrounded himself with advisers from Iraq, Palestine, Syria, Egypt and Lebanon. This made him far better equipped to understand and deal with other Arab countries than his predecessors. Thus, during the interwar period, Saudi Arabia eased into a slot as a regular player in Arab regional politics. To be sure, the prolonged and bitter struggle with Sharif Husayn over Hijaz poisoned relations with the Hashemite kingdoms of Iraq and Transjordan for many years, but the quelling of the Ikhwan at least pacified the international borders.

The Wahhabi Religious Establishment under Ibn Saud

Ibn Saud's re-establishment of dynastic power over most of Arabia was a blessing for the Wahhabi mission, even if it involved crushing the Ikhwan's zeal, because it offered the ulama a secure foundation for maintaining control over religious life. While the Rashidi years had brought occasional hardship to Wahhabi ulama in al-Qasim, the amirs of Ha'il did not bear the kind of intense animosity toward the mission that characterized the early nineteenth-century Ottoman-Egyptian conquerors and, in fact, a number of Rashidi amirs positively embraced it. Consequently, the Wahhabi ulama were well situated to restore hegemony over religious life.

The pre-eminent Wahhabi personality of the twentieth century's first two decades was Abd Allah ibn Abd al-Latif. He and Riyadh's other leading sheikhs designated loyalists to positions in areas that Ibn Saud conquered. After Abd Allah died in 1920, the next major figure in Al al-Sheikh to provide continuity between the era of Saudi decline and the third state was his distant cousin Abd Allah ibn Hasan ibn Husayn (1870–1958).[86] His teachers in Riyadh naturally included his own kinsmen, such as his own father and Abd Allah ibn Abd al-Latif. When Ibn Saud regained control of Riyadh, he appointed Abd Allah ibn Hasan to act as imam, teacher and preacher at the mosque of the ruler's father. In 1919, the rising ruler dispatched him to the Ikhwan at al-Artawiya, presumably to temper their zeal. Other political missions included his participation in an expedition to suppress a revolt in the Asir region along the frontier of Yemen. After the conquest of Hijaz, Ibn Saud made him the imam and preacher for the chief mosque in Mecca and then the qadi for the entire province two years later. Abd Allah ibn Hasan's other responsibilities included appointing mosque imams, administering all personnel at Mecca's

Grand Mosque, a censorship role over books and publications from abroad and enforcing the duty to command right and forbid wrong. This last function had an ancient lineage in Muslim societies and entailed the enforcement of shari'a rules of public morality and fair trade. In Saudi Arabia, it would take the form of Committees for Commanding Right and Forbidding Wrong, commonly referred to as the religious police.[87]

A second eminent member of Al al-Sheikh in Ibn Saud's reign was Umar ibn Hasan (1902–1975). His upbringing offers a portrait of conventional Wahhabi religious instruction. He studied with his father, kinsmen and other prominent ulama of the era. Apart from the usual Hanbali works on jurisprudence, Hadith and Qur'anic exegesis, Umar ibn Hasan's curriculum included memorizing basic works by Muhammad ibn Abd al-Wahhab and treatises by second amirate ulama like Abd al-Latif ibn Abd al-Rahman. Umar acquired a reputation for zeal that made him a natural candidate for the task of commanding right and forbidding wrong and for nearly fifty years he headed the official 'religious police' institution for Najd and al-Hasa.[88]

The religious police is a term for one of Saudi Arabia's distinctive institutions, the Committee for Commanding Right and Forbidding Wrong. Its purpose is to compel attendance at daily prayers and to police public moral behaviour. The exact origin of this institution is difficult to pin down, but its doctrinal foundation is well established in the Qur'an and the Sunna and it is the subject of an extensive literature in Muslim religious writings under the rubric of *hisba* and the duty to command right and forbid wrong. The central question in those writings is how and in what circumstances a believer should carry out the duty.[89] Should a believer resort to the sword to command or forbid? Or is it sufficient to verbally admonish a wrongdoer? At the very least, a believer should be mindful of the duty. Muslim scholars thus set forth three options for carrying out the duty: with the hand, with the tongue, or with the heart.

In the light of the conspicuous profile of Saudi Arabia's 'religious police', a historical question arises. Are they a contemporary manifestation of a doctrine and practice dating to Muhammad ibn Abd al-Wahhab and the first Saudi amirate? Michael Cook's meticulous study of the question concludes that the duty is mentioned a few times in Sheikh Muhammad's writings and those of his pupils, but not in a manner to suggest that it was a central concern. Moreover, Cook finds the historical record for the duty's enforcement in Najd to be quite meagre. Saudi actions in Mecca and Medina in the early 1800s constitute an exception. There, the Wahhabis banned smoking in public and enforced attendance at prayer.[90] By contrast, Cook finds abundant evidence attesting to the duty's prominent place in Wahhabi writings and rulers' decrees during the second amirate. Letters from Turki and Faysal indicate that the amirs of towns were obliged to support ulama in commanding right and forbidding wrong, including the taking of a roll call at prayer time. Cook suggests that the duty received such emphasis in the second amirate because jihad was not then an option.[91]

In the early years of Ibn Saud's polity, foreign observers reported roll-calls at mosques and punishments for habitual absentees, but the first documented instance of a formal committee to enforce the duty dates to 1926, when the official Saudi newspaper in Mecca published the news of its establishment.[92] The motives for creating the Committee are not well established. According to Ibn Saud's Egyptian adviser Hafiz Wahbah, the ruler wished to temper the aggressive conduct of zealous Ikhwan toward pilgrims and the recently subjugated Meccans.[93] Other accounts describe them as an outgrowth of informal performance of the duty by leading members of Al al-Sheikh even before the conquest of Hijaz.[94] In this version, the Committees spread first in Najd and al-Hasa. The precise jurisdiction and organization of the Committees are also not well documented, but the broad mandate to ensure compliance with daily prayers and public morality is evident. So the Committees' enforcers, known as mutawwi'a, kept an eye out for improper behaviour between men and women, music, smoking and alcohol.[95] Cook's careful study of the available Saudi and foreign diplomatic sources depicts some oscillation in the Committee's rigor during its early years and some uncertainty about when it formed local branches in different parts of Hijaz, Najd and the rest of the kingdom. Nevertheless, it appears that by the late 1930s, the Committee's branches were a ubiquitous feature. As for the religious leadership's role, we find major figures from Al al-Sheikh like Abd Allah ibn Hasan, Umar ibn Hasan and Muhammad ibn Ibrahim deeply involved as well as the head of Hijaz's judiciary, Abd Allah ibn Bulayhid.[96]

While Ibn Saud institutionalized Wahhabi authority, his relations with the ulama were complicated by his willingness to experiment with the trappings of modern nation-states and to adopt technical means that would buttress his power. The ulama asserted their views forthrightly and at times persuaded Ibn Saud to act on them. For example, in the late 1920s, there was a sort of national holiday to celebrate the establishment of the kingdom. In 1931, however, the Wahhabi sheikhs implored Ibn Saud to end the practice because Islam approves only two annual festivals, one to mark the end of Ramadan and another to close the pilgrimage. On this symbolic matter, he was willing to give way.[97] On the other hand, he often disregarded the ulama's strong reservations concerning modern technology, government institutions and reliance on foreign Arab advisers, whom the Wahhabis blamed for influencing Ibn Saud against their views.[98] One of these non-Saudi Arab confidants of the king was the Egyptian Hafiz Wahbah. As a westernized Arab, he viewed the Wahhabis with ambivalence. He found it difficult to fathom what he considered the backward mentality of sheikhs like Abd Allah ibn Bulayhid, a firm believer in the earth's flatness. Wahbah acknowledged the depth of Najdi ulama's learning in Islamic lore at the same time he faulted them for what he considered their pointless, interminable wrangling on abstract matters of doctrine and for lacking the capacity for original thought.[99]

Wahbah reported instances of friction between the ulama and their ruler over education. As director of the new Ministry of Education in 1930, Wahbah wished to introduce what appeared to be harmless topics to the curriculum but he encountered strenuous objections from the ulama. At Ibn Saud's urging, Wahbah met with them and listened to their concerns about offering instruction in drawing, foreign languages and geography. The sheikhs told him that they considered drawing a prohibited activity because of its similarity to painting. He assured them that instruction in drawing would be designed to teach children how to read and draw a map (presumably the ulama wished to prevent the depiction of living figures). As for learning foreign languages, the ulama maintained that this could introduce schoolchildren to infidels' ideas and corrupt their morals. Wahbah reminded them that some of the Prophet's Companions knew foreign languages and that present circumstances required dealings with foreigners, so it was better to have specialists in their languages instead of relying on foreign translators. One of the ulama's objections to teaching foreign languages was that it would allow familiarity with modern science, which they felt contradicted Islam. Wahbah observed that many scientific works were already available in Arabic translation. Furthermore, the ulama had no reason to fear that European scientific ideas would corrupt schoolchildren because

Islam's truth is strong enough to withstand an encounter with any false notions that might lie embedded in modern science. On the question of teaching geography, the ulama anticipated that it would lend support to ancient Greek philosophers' views, which earlier generations of Muslim scholars had combated and suppressed. The Egyptian responded that children would learn basic geographical information about countries, towns, economic production and trade, not concepts that would upset the ulama. Wahbah tackled the basis of the ulama's argument, namely the shari'a principle of blocking means to something forbidden. He remarked that they were showing excessive zeal and even capriciousness: Why did they not object to cultivating dates and grapes since their products might be used to make forbidden alcoholic beverages? The ulama did not pursue the argument; they just said that it was up to the Imam (Ibn Saud) to decide. Naturally, they wanted him to side with them, but if he did not, they noted, it would not be for the first time. Ibn Saud considered the ulama's objections to Wahbah's education plan unconvincing and he approved it.[100]

Wahhabi opposition to the introduction of new technology collided with the king's pragmatism. Wahbah offers an illustration of that contradiction in the case of ulama resistance to wireless telegraphy. The advantages of this invention for a ruler were obvious to Ibn Saud, but apprehension of violent reaction from the Ikhwan had induced him to postpone installing it until the late 1920s.[101] At that point, the Wahhabi leaders expressed their concerns. Abd Allah ibn Hasan told Wahbah that instant communication across long distances could only be the work of Satan-worship. The Egyptian accompanied him to a wireless station near Medina to let him examine the area and see for himself that there were no signs of 'sacrificial offerings – no bones, nor horns, nor wool' to be found. The operator of the wireless showed Abd Allah ibn Hasan how to use the machine. He exchanged messages with Ibn Saud, who was in Jeddah at the time. This experiment did not assuage the Wahhabi sheikh's suspicions, for he thought it possible that Wahbah and Ibn Saud had somehow staged a fake demonstration. Therefore, he performed unannounced inspections of the wireless station and queried the operators before he finally became convinced that it was a harmless invention. He even apologized to Wahbah for suspecting him of wrongdoing.[102] Nonetheless, when the wireless was introduced to Riyadh, the ulama sent religious students to wireless stations to look for signs of demons. When they openly expressed their objections to Ibn Saud, he told them that he would brook no dispute. He added that motor vehicles were also vital inventions for the kingdom and that as far as he could tell, they did not violate the shari'a. Conservative resistance finally evaporated when the wireless proved its value in helping the authorities respond to and quell revolts in northern Hijaz and Asir in 1932.[103]

Wahbah also attested to the Wahhabis' animosity toward foreigners. He related an incident from 1928, when Wahbah was travelling in Hijaz with Abd Allah ibn Hasan. They encountered Ibn Saud's British adviser, H. St. John Philby, who had not yet converted to Islam at the time. Sheikh Abd Allah expressed astonishment that Wahbah would greet a Christian with a handshake and invite him to share a meal. The Egyptian contended that adopting a rude and distant manner would make it nearly impossible to win converts to Islam and that Ibn Saud himself sometimes stood up to honour a Christian visitor. The Sheikh answered that while he found the point about making converts persuasive, he discounted the second point because Ibn Saud often did things that the ulama found objectionable.[104] Clearly, Hafiz Wahbah and Ibn Saud's non-Saudi Arab advisers held very different views of Islam's bearing on everyday life from those of the Wahhabi establishment.[105]

To put the Wahhabi ulama's resistance to modern ways into perspective, we need to keep in mind their doctrine on avoiding the company of idolaters. From its first formulation by Sulayman ibn Abd Allah during the Ottoman-Egyptian invasion to its early twentieth-century manifestation in the Ikhwan movement, this doctrine rested on a cluster of verses from the Qur'an and hadiths that portrayed the danger to belief that resulted from mixing with idolaters. If nineteenth-century ulama frowned on travel to the land of idolatry, who could expect their pupils to favour the borrowing of foreign inventions and customs, or even worse, mingling with idolaters? Ibn Saud's suppression of the Ikhwan in 1930 gave him room to manoeuvre vis-à-vis the ulama. They faced a determined, gifted ruler who had overwhelmed his rivals. Moreover, the ulama knew they owed what influence they enjoyed to Ibn Saud. He, in turn, was careful to consult with Wahhabi leaders in order to keep his finger on the pulse of religious sentiment. Consequently, they acquiesced to his innovations without explicitly adjusting doctrine. As timid as these may have appeared to outsiders, they were bold, even upsetting, when viewed from the perspective of Wahhabi ulama and their followers. In sum, Al Saud and the Wahhabis had arrived at a tacit bargain wherein the latter might raise objections to change but would generally not protest loudly when he overrode them. This arrangement worked as long as the scope of change was limited.

During Ibn Saud's lifetime, the opportunities to change much in his kingdom were constrained by a dearth of financial and human resources. Nonetheless, his steps to consolidate power pointed in the direction of building more effective state institutions, especially in the fiscal and military spheres. Ibn Saud continued his predecessors' practice of collecting the religious tithe (*zakat*) from townsmen, cultivators and tribesmen in addition to duties on trade through the Red Sea and Gulf ports. During the years of military expansion, he benefited from British subsidies, to a greater extent when Britain desired his support in the First World War and then less so after its end. Fortunately for Ibn Saud, the conquest of Hijaz brought not only the prestige of protecting the Holy Cities and supervising the pilgrimage, but in connection with the latter, revenue from taxes on pilgrims. Since his nascent administration did not produce a budget until 1934, there are no precise figures for the early years, but observers agree on the preponderant weight of pilgrim taxes in the treasury's revenues. That situation prevailed to the eve of the Second World War.[106] The paltry sums at Ibn Saud's disposal barely sufficed to preserve the kingdom's peace by providing gifts and subsidies to nomadic tribesmen, thereby ensuring their quiescence. With respect to military forces, Ibn Saud relied on a blend of levies of Najdi townsmen, tribal auxiliaries and, until the late 1920s, the Ikhwan. When he conquered Hijaz, he offered the defeated Iraqi and Syrian officers of the Hashemite army positions in permanent military units and when he formed a directorate of military affairs, many of these officers filled positions there.[107] By 1935, Saudi Arabia had the core of a ministry of defence, which took definitive form in 1946. These modest steps toward a modern army naturally generated second order initiatives in the fields of aviation and radio communications, both technologies offering the means to contain traces of unrest.

When it came to developing the kingdom's instruments of government, Ibn Saud moved in a purely ad hoc fashion, creating and dissolving administrative and consultative bodies to meet the needs of particular circumstances in one part of his realm or the other. The result was a patchwork of functionally distinct directorates and departments unevenly distributed over various regions. Hijaz possessed the most elaborate set of institutions. One description of the government at Riyadh around 1930 names seventeen departments under a royal council, but in fact the 'departments' were little more than compartments in the king's palace: horse-breeding, camels, motor vehicles, telegraph, radio, health (not public health but the palace household), hospitality and so forth. This arrangement made sense since Ibn Saud's 'government' consisted of his extended family, trusted advisers and retainers. He appointed relatives as governors of the most politically sensitive regions – Hijaz, al-Hasa, al-Qasim – so central authority flowed through members of the dynasty from Riyadh to the local districts. The rudimentary character of the early Saudi polity is evident from its treasury, managed for decades by a Qasimi trader, Abd Allah Sulayman, as a personal enterprise. To deal with foreign powers, Ibn Saud relied on expatriate Arabs from Egypt (Hafiz Wahbah), Iraq (Abd Allah al-Damluji), Syria (Yusuf Yasin) and Palestine (Fuad Hamza).

As long as Riyadh's treasury depended on pilgrims, zakat and foreign subsidies, Ibn Saud would lack the means for a more robust approach to state-building. The turning point in Saudi Arabia's development into a modern state was the discovery of petroleum. Much has been written on petroleum, the American oil companies that developed it and US-Saudi relations arising from the black fuel.[108] The modern kingdom's economic fortunes and place in international politics depend on petroleum wealth and American power. A few details about the famous 1933 concession to Standard Oil of California are worth noting here. First, the timing was fortunate as it came during the global depression, which had caused a drastic reduction in the number of pilgrims travelling to Mecca and a fall in treasury revenues. The opportunity for an injection of cash was propitious and an annual royalty payment would put Ibn Saud's fiscal affairs on firmer ground. Second, the initial contacts and talks between Ibn Saud's representatives and oil company officials occurred outside the kingdom's heartland, first in London, then in Jeddah. Third, the capital intensive character of petroleum extraction meant that American activities could be contained to the oil fields and ports.

There is an eerie silence in the many published accounts by American oil company writers and scholars about the attitudes of Wahhabi ulama toward the oil concession in the first place, and the trickle of American engineers and businessmen that followed.

The ulama cannot have been indifferent to Ibn Saud's decision to open the doors. Indeed, as the economic consequences triggered irresistible forces for social, cultural and moral shifts, Saudi ulama strained to judiciously assess these changes to discriminate between the acceptable and the unacceptable. Given the Wahhabi principle of enmity toward and avoidance of infidels, it was natural that contact between Americans and Saudis was minimal. Aramco, the consortium of American companies holding the concession, constructed enclaves for employees in the Eastern Province (al-Hasa), the centre of oil exploration and production and at pumping stations that dotted TAPLINE, the oil pipeline that traversed the kingdom and passed through Jordan and Syria before terminating at depots in Lebanon. In their colonies, Americans reconstructed the physical world of the mid-twentieth-century USA, complete with golf courses and swimming pools, not to mention American-style residential neighbourhoods.[109] The residential enclaves formed a sealed environment in which the foreigners worked and lived and from which they were forbidden to venture except on organized outings. Within the compound, Americans might show movies in open-air settings, but they had to be remote from any curious Saudis.[110] The expatriate population expanded in the early 1950s, as oil wealth bloated the allowances of Saudi princes. The first signs of royal conspicuous consumption appeared, as princes contracted with foreign firms to construct palaces with luxuries like swimming pools and amenities like air conditioning. As reports of such free spending ways spread, European, American and Arab businessmen flocked to the kingdom. While their numbers were small compared to the influx of expatriate workers that flooded Saudi Arabia in the 1970s, the growing presence of infidels in the Wahhabi heartland inevitably disturbed the ulama.

One incident illustrates the unease fostered by the presence of foreigners. In 1944, reports reached Ibn Saud's court of a Wahhabi sheikh in southern Najd criticizing him for 'selling land to foreigners'.[111] The American legation's account of this incident named the sheikh 'Abu Bahz'. He denounced an American project to increase agricultural production in the al-Kharj region by digging wells and irrigation canals. When Ibn Saud heard about Abu Bahz's protest, he had the sheikh brought to Riyadh. In an audience before the king's advisers and leading ulama, Abu Bahz told the king that he was 'selling the land and his people, into bondage of Unbelievers and that this course of action is contrary to his obligation as a Muslim ruler

and protector of the holy places and traditions'. Ibn Saud then asked
the ulama if the Prophet Muhammad had not himself hired non-
Muslims for certain tasks and they agreed that he had. Ibn Saud then
asked if it was therefore permissible to hire foreigners to work for him
at al-Kharj to benefit the kingdom and again, the ulama agreed with
their ruler. Abu Bahz, however, steadfastly (or stubbornly) rejected
the ulama's reasoning, so Ibn Saud hinted at a dire punishment for
rejecting the verdict of the religious authorities. Abu Bahz relented.

2. SAUDI AND AMERICAN OIL PIPELINE WELDERS, AL-KHOBAR, 1952.
O. OXLEY, *SAUDI ARAMCO WORLD*/PADIA.

King Abd al-Aziz ibn Saud died in November 1953, more than fifty
years after his raid on Riyadh. One of the interesting 'what might
have happened' questions to ask about Arabian history is how
Wahhabism might have fared in the absence of a Saudi restoration.
What we do know is that Ibn Saud hewed to the dynastic tradition
of supporting Wahhabi ulama and giving them control over religious
institutions. At the same time, he tempered Wahhabi zeal when he

felt that it clashed with the demands of consolidating power in Hijaz and al-Hasa or the constraints of firmer international boundaries maintained by the era's dominant power in the region, Great Britain. Simply put, political considerations trumped religious idealism. The same principle governed Ibn Saud's approach to adopting modern technology, building a rudimentary administrative framework and signing the oil concession with the Americans. By the early 1950s, Saudi Arabia was by no means a modern state. Ibn Saud lacked the resources to pay for its physical development and the expenses of staffing an extensive bureaucracy. Nevertheless, the twin pressures of controlling regions outside the Wahhabi heartland and navigating the currents of regional politics led him to take steps that punctured the seal between the internal land of belief and the outside land of idolatry. That Wahhabi ulama acquiesced indicates their recognition that, given the rocky history of Al Saud rule and the mission's dependence on dynastic power, half a loaf is better than none. Such recognition was not a new departure. We have no record of Wahhabi sheikhs raising an objection in the 1840s when Amir Faysal reached a tacit modus vivendi with Muhammad Ali and the Ottomans. The Ikhwan episode aside, the pre-eminent sheikhs had at least implicitly accepted the constraints on their mission imposed by political realities. In the mid twentieth century, as petroleum enriched Saudi Arabia, the Wahhabi mission would benefit from such realism through its incorporation into modern state institutions.

Chapter Four

Wahhabism in a Modern State

The historical Saudi amirates ruled their domains through a series of ad hoc arrangements with chiefly lineages and tribal leaders who affirmed political loyalty, provided military forces for expeditions, collected taxes for Riyadh's treasury and backed Wahhabi qadis and teachers. Such arrangements amounted to a set of bilateral relationships between Riyadh and local figures. Modern states, on the other hand, strive to wield authority through regular, uniform procedures and institutions. In the early twentieth century, Ibn Saud's achievement had been to re-conquer (in the Saudi narrative, to unify) much of Arabia and to hold his realm together with a blend of tactics: demonstrating royal largesse (subsidies to local leaders, hospitality and lavish banquets), forming political alliances through marriages with women from prominent tribes and supporting the Wahhabi mission.[1] After the suppression of the Ikhwan, he resorted to force on only a few occasions. In Hijaz, he preserved and modified a handful of administrative, educational and legal institutions dating from the late Ottoman period. Elsewhere, his manner of ruling followed the pattern of earlier Saudi amirates with one significant exception: rather than rely on local amirs to govern the provinces he appointed members of the royal family.

Ibn Saud's successors used the kingdom's growing petroleum revenues to create and staff national institutions, thereby initiating a transformation of the Saudi polity according to a pattern similar to that of Ottoman and Egyptian reorganization efforts during the nineteenth century. Those efforts modified and sometimes invented, administrative, educational and legal institutions in a bid to replicate the foundations of European power. One consequence of this trend was to open a rift between men with European-style education and men with traditional Islamic schooling. By the mid twentieth century, political elites, bureaucrats and professionals bore the stamp of the previous era's drive to westernize. Meanwhile, religious culture had also changed shape with the rise of modernist and revivalist currents and the decline of the ulama's traditional Islamic education.

When Saudi Arabia took the first steps to create the institutions of a modern state, much later than elsewhere, it too borrowed from western models and resorted to sending students abroad to acquire technical expertise, then importing western elements of statecraft. Whereas state reorganization in the Ottoman Empire and Egypt had resulted in the marginalization of the ulama, the deep historical connection between Al Saud and Wahhabism and perhaps Al Saud's own weak claim on the allegiance of their subjects, meant that the kingdom's religious component would not shift to the margins. Instead, the Wahhabi establishment would use its control over law, its influence on education and its moral legitimacy among a substantial portion of the population to hold fast against the tides of western-style modernity.[2] Nevertheless, the evolution of forms of governance from ad hoc to regular structures did affect the ways that Wahhabism operated in Saudi society. The process established Wahhabi civil servants in government agencies and while that might have placed them under official authority, it also supplied them with funds to hire staff and resources to amplify their message. Furthermore, the kingdom's unification through modern communications and transportation and the proliferation of national administrative bodies expanded Wahhabism's reach deeper into Saudi society.

Academic studies and journalistic writings on modern Saudi Arabia frequently draw on the modernization paradigm to frame the country's recent history. Part of the modernization paradigm's appeal as an explanatory framework arose from regional trends after the Second World War. During the years of decolonization, western political power receded, but western economic and cultural influences appeared as vigorous as ever. Thus, wherever one looked in the non-western world, secular tendencies were taken as evidence for the 'passing of traditional societies'.[3] Before the late 1970s, few western experts on the Middle East suspected that secularism would founder in the face of potent challenges from religious revivalists. We find a concise application of the modernization paradigm to Saudi Arabia in Ayman al-Yassini's monograph.[4] In his view, the kingdom followed the modernization path in the sense that the government centralized power, devised a national system of administration and promoted economic development. This endeavour naturally resulted in the emergence of a stratum with a secular, sometimes liberal, outlook. At the same time, Saudi rulers remained devoted (from conviction or political convenience) to sustaining the country's Wahhabi religious culture. Consequently, the country was plagued by endemic tension between proponents of steps to augment either a secular or a liberal religious vision of modernity on one hand and defenders of Wahhabism on the other.

This divide is reflected in parallel cultures of expertise that characterize the modern-educated, secular administration and the Wahhabi religious establishment. The political peril the former could pose to the monarchy rapidly emerged in the 1950s with the appearance of socialist and Arab nationalist tendencies. One of King Faysal's major accomplishments in his long career came when he was still the crown prince. He deflated calls for placing formal constraints on dynastic power with his Ten Point Programme of 1962. The document promised to introduce a constitution, a consultative council and local government along with guarantees to uphold religious institutions, invigorate economic development and abolish slavery.[5] While slavery was indeed banned, the measures that would have curbed royal power remained ink on paper. In the long view of Saudi history, however, the Ten Point Programme's promulgation underscored a substantial alteration in the political terrain compared to thirty years before when the dynasty confronted the Ikhwan.

Yassini presents a standard modernization argument when he observes that government organization, legal reform and modern education inevitably diminished the role of religion in Saudi public life. He traces the proliferation of ministries, bureaus and agencies with responsibility over matters such as petroleum, municipal affairs, public works and planning. None of these new bodies is grounded in Wahhabi norms. He also discusses the 'bureaucratization of the ulama' that took place through the establishment of government agencies for religious research, girls' education, mosques and religious foundations and so on.[6] In his reading, the incorporation of Wahhabi ulama into government institutions increased Al Saud's control over the religious estate. Likewise, shifts in the legal sphere such as regulations issued by decree and statutory courts to enforce those regulations signified a reduction in the ulama's influence, although we shall see that they have waged a protracted campaign to prevent statutory courts from encroaching on the domain of the shari'a. In the education field, Yassini describes the expansion of secular schooling according to quantitative measures like the number of schools and students and government expenditure. At the same time, he notes the integration of extensive religious instruction into the curriculum at the primary and secondary levels. The evidence for secular influence is stronger in the universities.[7] Yassini detects yet another gauge of religion's shrinking weight in the schooling and formative experiences of the royal family and the government's highest officials.[8] Throughout Ibn Saud's reign, members of the royal family and his personal confidants occupied the highest positions, but in the late 1950s and 1960s, King Saud and King Faysal appointed as ministers men educated at universities outside the kingdom. Moreover, Faysal represented a tendency in the royal family to send their children to Britain and the USA for secondary and higher education to prepare them for careers in government administration as ministers and provincial governors.

When Yassini wrote in the early 1980s, the modernization paradigm still dominated studies of Muslim societies and most observers considered religious revivalism to be an ephemeral reaction. Two decades later, the persistence of revivalism has jeopardized the paradigm. In Saudi Arabia, the Wahhabi mission certainly did not retreat before the tide of change but stood its ground and maintained a tenacious hold over essential, normative aspects of life in the kingdom.

Wahhabism in the Era of Government Expansion and Arab Nationalism

Modern state-building entails the creation of a uniform set of national institutions and administrative procedures that enable governments to exercise authority throughout the country. Before the 1950s, the Saudi polity consisted of the royal family, a handful of Arab advisers

from other countries, the heads of noble lineages, tribal leaders
and the Wahhabi establishment. The later 1950s witnessed the
proliferation of government ministries and agencies, some of them
quite ephemeral, designed to manage particular aspects of economic
development: communications, agriculture, education, petroleum
and finance. Naturally, it was revenue from oil royalties that made
such administrative expansion and differentiation both possible and
desirable. The same income funded the first educational overseas
missions in the mid 1950s. Saudis who acquired technical training
and expertise overseas and at Aramco schools in Dhahran formed a
new segment in society with a technocratic outlook. The ramification
of a technocratic sub-culture was embodied by the Institute of
Public Administration, created in 1961 on the recommendation of a
United Nations consultant on administration, to train a corps of civil
servants.[9] The crystallization of a technocratic segment coincided with
the growing influence of secular political trends in the Arab world
and their spread among that segment gave a political accent to the
cultural divergence between Wahhabi and technocrat. That cultural
divergence was epitomized by the pronouncement of a leading
Wahhabi sheikh, Abd al-Aziz ibn Baz. In 1966, when he was vice
president of Medina's Islamic University, he wrote an essay asserting
the geocentric view of the universe and condemning the secular
Riyadh University for teaching students the Copernican view.[10]

At the same time that Riyadh was experimenting with modern
administrative forms, the kingdom's domestic politics began to reflect
those of the wider Arab world, where secular nationalist forces
were ascendant. Ibn Saud's final pacification of the Ikhwan in 1930
heralded the end of tribal nomadic politics. Modern political dynamics
emerged in the 1940s in al-Hasa, where American oilmen created an
enclave economy and society marked by a strict ethnic, if not racial,
hierarchy. In Dhahran, American, Italian and Arab workers lived in
segregated residential compounds. This was not merely a measure to
shield Saudis from exposure to corrupt western ways, as the company
prohibited Saudis from entering American residential areas even if
they wished to. It took very little time for the stark contrast between
American and Arab conditions to spark a strike. In July 1945, a protest
snowballed from a hundred or so to over two thousand workers in
a few days.[11] There followed modest improvements in medical care
and housing conditions, but Saudi workers would not be permitted
to have family members live with them until well into the 1950s.[12]

In an effort to raise the skills and technical expertise of the Arab work force, Aramco sent some Arab employees to Egypt and Lebanon in the early 1950s.[13] When they returned, they occupied higher positions but continued to endure inferior living conditions. Therefore, in summer 1953, a number of these workers protested systematic discrimination by submitting a petition to King Abd al-Aziz, just months before his death in November, requesting better wages and housing. The outcome was a stormy meeting with Crown Prince Saud, and he had them thrown into prison. In response, a massive strike erupted in October involving some 13,000 Aramco employees. The strike collapsed after just two weeks and its leaders were fired. Nevertheless, soon after ascending the throne, Saud agreed to meet many of the strikers' original demands on wages, living conditions and schools for workers' children.[14]

The emergence of modern politics jolted the kingdom's rulers and they responded by clamping down on sources of dissent. For instance, they blamed the demonstrations of 1953 on foreign ideologies like communism and Arab nationalism, rather than objectively abhorrent conditions. Consequently, the government decided to limit the number of young Saudis permitted to study outside the country. It also expelled many Arab, especially Palestinian, workers from the Eastern Province on suspicion of subversive political activity. In addition to striving to harden boundaries between the kingdom and the outside world, now for political rather than religious reasons, the government reinvigorated the Committees for Commanding Right and Forbidding Wrong. In 1957, Riyadh pronounced a ban on women driving.[15]

The arrival of modern politics in the kingdom coincided with the appearance of another aspect of modernity: mass media. Arabian newspapers appeared in Hijaz in the late Ottoman period. In 1924, the Saudis published a quasi-official gazette, *Umm al-Qura*, in Mecca. The newspaper had the field to itself until some other periodicals devoted to religion and culture came out in the 1930s. Print media did not arrive in Najd until the early 1950s, when a monthly periodical made its debut in Riyadh. Demand for newspapers and periodicals remained weak well into the 1960s because of Saudi Arabia's low level of literacy. During King Faysal's reign, the number of daily newspapers rose from three to seven and quadrupled in circulation.[16] As in other modern sectors of Saudi society, foreign Arabs assumed a dominant role and in the case of newspapers, Egyptian journalists and print workers were ubiquitous. Consequently, when Egypt's Gamal Abdel Nasser rose to prominence in regional affairs, Saudi newspapers often expressed admiration for him and his policies. This situation became particularly sensitive when Egypt and Saudi Arabia clashed over the 1962 revolution in Yemen. That same year, the Saudi government created the Ministry of Information and then, in 1964, it issued a code to regulate the press by setting basic standards that newspapers had to meet.[17]

Radio and television broadcasting appeared later than print media and they proved much more controversial. The first radio station set up in Jeddah in 1948 reached only a handful of towns in Hijaz.[18] Whereas print media seem not to have stirred opposition from Wahhabi ulama, the radio broadcast of a woman's voice in 1963 prompted a delegation of ulama to declare their outrage to Crown Prince Faysal. He reportedly dismissed their objection, noting that the Prophet Muhammad had delighted in the voice of a woman poet.[19] Two years later, a more violent reaction greeted the first public television broadcast. Aramco employees and United States military personnel at Dhahran had had access to private programs since 1957.[20] A few years later King Faysal wished to bring the medium to his kingdom. In 1965, stations at Jeddah and Riyadh broadcast the first television programme, triggering a violent protest, even though programs were subject to strict censorship to prevent the airing of men and women in romantic situations. A group of zealots led by Prince Khalid ibn Musa'id, one of the late King Abd al-Aziz's grandsons, attacked the television station in Riyadh. In the melee, a policeman shot and killed the prince. While the incident passed without much notice outside the kingdom at the time, Khalid's brother would avenge his death ten years later by assassinating King Faysal. Despite the incident at the Riyadh television station, additional stations followed at Medina, Mecca, Ta'if, Burayda and Dammam.[21]

The expansion of modern media occurred, in part, to satisfy Saudis educated abroad who returned with a cosmopolitan outlook. In order to diminish antagonism from religious quarters, King Faysal (r. 1964–1975) devoted a large portion of broadcast time to religious programs and increased the ratio of secular ones only gradually, thereby preventing the new medium from turning into a contentious and divisive emblem of cultural polarization. In the early years, television aired just five hours daily, broadcasting mostly news, religious shows, music and series produced in Arab countries, the

USA and Britain.[22] A second purpose for introducing television was to counter Nasserist radio propaganda. With the Saudi government controlling all television news and information, King Faysal gained a medium to broadcast the government's positions on regional and local issues.[23] Programs largely focused on official duties of the king and princes, notably including international travels. A staple of television throughout the Arab world is the head of state greeting guests and departing and returning from diplomatic missions, as though government functions primarily occurred at airports. For all media, Wahhabi norms set limits. Photographs of women did not appear in newspapers, television did not show people drinking alcohol and discussion of religion outside the official framework did not occur.

The modernization paradigm applied to Saudi Arabia emphasizes the emergence of formal religious institutions and assumes that these institutions would curtail the Wahhabi ulama's authority in general and that of Al al-Sheikh in particular. For the 1950s and 1960s, such an assertion is premature because one member of Al al-Sheikh, Muhammad ibn Ibrahim ibn Abd al-Latif (1893–1969), dominated the Wahhabi religious estate and enjoyed unrivalled religious authority.[24] His life spanned decades of profound change. The Riyadh of his childhood differed little in size, population and material culture from the town of Amir Faysal's time. Indeed, the toll of dynastic strife in the 1870s and 1880s had reduced its population. By the time of Sheikh Muhammad's death in 1969, the Saudi political revival and the fortuitous discovery of the world's largest petroleum reserves transformed Riyadh and made Wahhabism's homeland the largest and wealthiest country in Arabia.

Muhammad ibn Ibrahim apparently did not view the creation of official religious institutions as portending a weakening of the kingdom's commitment to the Wahhabi mission. In fact, he participated in the development of these institutions. In the judicial realm, he supported the creation of a unified system in the 1950s that replicated the court structure and procedures established in Hijaz during the 1920s. Until this initiative, justice in Najd issued from qadis sitting in their homes or mosques and settling cases without recording them in writing. For three decades, the judiciaries in Najd and Hijaz operated separately, with the Hijaz courts under the authority of Abd Allah ibn Hasan until he died in 1957. The courts were then unified under a Higher Judicial Council to supervise procedures and judicial appointments. Muhammad ibn Ibrahim was head of the council. When the Saudis decided in 1963 to create a special office to issue fatwas (*Dar al-Ifta*), he presided over it in his capacity as grand mufti.[25] One of its primary functions was to examine unprecedented legal questions that came before the Saudi government. While the king appointed members of the Fatwa Directorate, the ulama performed their duties with greater regard for principles of Hanbali jurisprudence than royal preference.[26]

In addition to supporting initiatives to give religious bodies formal administrative shape, Sheikh Muhammad backed the government in its struggle against Arab nationalist regimes that threatened to undermine both the Saudis and Wahhabism. He represented the religious establishment's view that had long seen the destinies of Al Saud and Wahhabism as intertwined and he naturally supported initiatives designed to bolster both of them. During the 1950s, young Saudis were starting to view the older generation as reactionary and backward and were turning their backs on religious education, seeking instead to learn foreign languages and natural sciences. Sheikh Muhammad considered this trend a threat to Islam in its homeland and persuaded the government to create centres for teaching Islamic sciences and Arabic and to attract students with awards and other incentives. The graduates of these Islamic centres became instructors at a new Islamic Sciences college, religious court judges and teachers sent on missions abroad. Wahhabi outreach in the 1950s and 1960s went hand in glove with Saudi foreign policy initiatives to combat the wave of secular nationalism that swept the Arab world. A new Islamic university in Medina was created to train proselytizers and its regulations called for 75 per cent of its students to come from abroad. Sheikh Muhammad put his and the official Wahhabi leadership's imprimatur on the university and he entrusted its affairs to a rising star in the religious establishment, Sheikh Abd al-Aziz ibn Baz. He also backed the creation of the World Muslim League to set up cultural centres to revive Islam and to support beleaguered Muslim minorities. Sheikh Muhammad supplemented the League's efforts by supervising an office to dispatch Saudi-sponsored proselytizers to combat Sufism and religious innovations.

Even though Muhammad ibn Ibrahim favoured steps to give religious institutions a modern form, he was by no means a proponent of moderating Wahhabi positions. The conservative tenor of his outlook is evident in his fatwas on moral issues that came under the purview of the Committee for Commanding Right and Forbidding Wrong. He defended the Committees' work against assertions that they sometimes overstepped their bounds. For example, in one case where mutawwi'a levelled an adultery charge, they were technically guilty of slander. Muhammad ibn Ibrahim ruled that the broader purpose of upholding the duty of forbidding wrong would be diminished if committee members were punished.[27] On at least one occasion, however, he did part company with conservative ulama, when he approved the decision to open schools for girls.[28]

After Muhammad ibn Ibrahim's death in 1969, the government established a Ministry of Justice. This step and the creation of other new official religious bodies gave formal shape to a variety of functions that had customarily fallen under the authority of the Wahhabi leadership. The Ministry of Justice initially included within its domain the Presidency of the Judiciary, which held broad powers over religious life by issuing fatwas and appointing religious teachers, prayer leaders and mosque preachers. In the 1970s, these functions were divided and split from the Ministry of Justice. The Board of Senior Ulama and the Directorate of Religious Research, Fatwas, Propaganda and Guidance assumed the authority to issue fatwas. The Ministry of Pilgrimage and Religious Endowments took over supervision of mosque employees like preachers and prayer leaders. Education of girls was vested in yet another agency. The partition of functions reallocated but did not eliminate or even visibly diminish the influence of Wahhabism in Saudi public life.[29] Thus, the street enforcers of Wahhabi norms rose in standing in 1976, when the Al al-Sheikh director of the Committee for Commanding Right and Forbidding Wrong gained a seat on the cabinet.[30]

Religious Law in the Modern Kingdom

The modernization paradigm traces the creation of administrative and legal arrangements for Hijaz in the 1920s and their extension to the rest of the country from the 1950s onward, followed by the multiplication of non-religious government bodies managed and staffed by Saudis with modern education. This set of developments supposedly diluted Saudi Arabia's Wahhabi character. There is no question that modern processes of constructing bureaucracy and promulgating uniform regulations have affected the Wahhabi establishment, but it is not at all clear that they have undermined it. Rather, one could argue that the Saudi state has incorporated religious norms in ways that took advantage of their legitimacy without truly diminishing their authority in matters essential to Wahhabism. We find several episodes when the rulers indeed whittled down the ulama's power over one area or another, but the resilience of Wahhabi ulama and their tenacious grip on the loyalty of broad segments of society have enabled the ulama to recover from setbacks, reassert their authority and thwart the introduction of secular institutions. This is clearly the case in the legal sphere even though, as Frank Vogel notes, 'the biggest destabilizing factor in the modern Saudi legal system is a widely perceived need for drastic reforms... in spheres of law that have traditionally belonged to the ulama and the fiqh [Islamic jurisprudence].'[31]

One of the hallmarks of the modern nation-state is the development of a uniform legal system. In much of the Middle East, this occurred in two phases. First, during the nineteenth century, law codes and law courts in the Ottoman Empire and Egypt underwent a protracted process of change wherein sultans and their advisers created codes and courts as part of a broader reform movement called the *Tanzimat*, or reorganization. Second, in the Arab lands that came under British and French rule after the First World War, the Tanzimat framework stayed in place. It was only in the post-colonial period that independent governments began to modify it with new legislation and judicial structures. The more radical revisions of law and legal systems carried out in Turkey's Republic and Iran's Pahlavi monarchy beginning in the 1920s differed in substance from post-colonial Arab initiatives but they all followed comparable dynamics of centralizing and regularizing the authority to legislate and adjudicate.

Saudi Arabia presents a special case, not merely because of its Wahhabi character, but also because it did not evolve from an imperial tradition (the Ottoman and Iranian cases) and it never experienced direct European rule (the central Arab lands). Nevertheless, various forces have exerted pressure for the development of a modern legal system. First, Saudi Arabia's possession of the holy places compelled it to devise a regular administrative structure, including a judicial system, to reassure Muslim countries and colonial powers ruling Muslim lands that reasonable rules and procedures protected the rights of pilgrims and resident foreigners in Hijaz. Second, the kingdom's integration into the global economy created unprecedented legal, social and economic problems that demanded solutions. Third, in recent decades, urbanization, rural-urban migration, and the entry of an immense expatriate work force caused the crime rate to spike and overwhelm the capacity of religious courts or customary procedures of private mediation. In response to these pressures, Saudi Arabia did

not follow the path of other Middle Eastern countries in reforming its
legal institutions. Instead, it has allowed the religious law courts to
maintain their authority under Wahhabi qadis and it has improvised
a set of tribunals and statutory regulations to adjudicate matters
that fall outside the purview of the religious courts. The upshot is a
bifurcated legal landscape with poorly marked boundaries between
the religious and statutory courts.

Saudi Arabia lacks a constitution to define legislative authority and
processes. Wahhabi doctrine, however, possesses a political theory,
based on the views of Ibn Taymiyya, which requires Muslims to obey
the ruler, even if he is a sinner. Muhammad ibn Abd al-Wahhab
in *The Book of God's Unity* had declared that to obey the rulers in
permitting something forbidden by Islamic law is tantamount to
idolatry.[32] In Ibn Taymiyya's view, the only ground for disobedience
to a ruler is if he commands a believer to violate something prohibited
by the shari'a. Since believers owe the ruler obedience, he is free to
organize government as he sees fit as long as he does not cross that
line. While this appears to grant unlimited powers to the ruler, the
proviso for respecting shari'a limits is significant, since it includes, in
Wahhabi doctrine, respect for the independence of qadis in matters
within their jurisdiction. Hence, the ruler may not interfere in their
deliberations.[33] Building on this limitation on a ruler's power, the
ulama have preserved their autonomy in the legal sphere by refusing
to participate in the codification of law and the formation of a uniform
system of law courts.

Wahhabi qadis defend their autonomy on the basis of a principle
in Islamic legal theory, which Frank Vogel terms 'the rule against
ijtihad reversal'.[34] This principle establishes a presumption against
overturning a qadi's ruling when he bases it on ijtihad, or independent
legal reasoning, rather than an unambiguous text in the Qur'an or the
Sunna. The principle is crucial in two respects. First, it concentrates
the substance of the law in the hands of judges rather than legislators
because of the presumption that shari'a requires a judge to discover
God's will in the nexus of a specific case and relevant revealed texts.
For an individual (king) or collective body (parliament) to assume
the power to make law is to encroach on God's sovereignty. Second,
it severely limits the parameters of any appeals process, thereby
rendering the judge's determination practically immune to reversal.

In matters before religious courts, Vogel found a striking degree
of independence wielded by qadis because their mandate is not to

follow precedent or implement a uniform code but to discern the divine ruling in a particular incident. It is true that Wahhabi qadis generally follow Hanbali tradition, but they are not obliged to do so and there is no formal rule to ensure consistency in legal verdicts.[35] The persistence of qadi independence was evident when the Saudis unified the legal system in 1954. Since 1926, the Hijaz courts had complied with a regulation requiring them to adhere to rulings found in a handful of standard Hanbali legal texts. That regulation did not apply in Najd. Respect for qadi independence was maintained when the kingdom's courts were unified and that regulation lapsed.[36] Likewise, the presumption against reversing a qadi's verdict prevailed when Hijaz courts merged with courts in the rest of the country. Ibn Saud had experimented with appeals mechanisms in Hijaz, but these were suspended in 1954. Nevertheless, the head of the Wahhabi estate, Muhammad ibn Ibrahim, began to hear appeals from Najdi courts in that decade, perhaps indicating a slight weakening of the rule against ijtihad reversal. In 1962, a body called the Board of Review was created to hear appeals but it would not overturn a judge's verdict; at most, it would order a new hearing and only if it detected a violation of a clear text in the Qur'an, the Sunna, or consensus, thus preserving the rule against ijtihad reversal.[37] The persistence of this principle is evident in Vogel's survey of over 8,000 cases that went to review in 1979–1980: only one percent of cases were reversed.[38]

Foreigners frequently complain about the unpredictability of the Saudi legal system. Their grievance stems not only from its unfamiliar character but also from qadis' independence. The courts nevertheless achieve a de facto consensus that yields frequent but not consistent conformity to Hanbali law and to the fatwas of the most prestigious jurists. Vogel writes that this degree of uniformity 'seems to be achieved through education, group solidarity and through the mechanism of informal, non-binding leadership by powerful senior ulama, particularly those working at the upper levels of the hierarchy and close to the king and the legislative process'.[39] In the absence of a constitutionally binding source of legislation, consensus is built through the prestige and influence of individual senior religious scholars and the Board of Senior Ulama. In order to obtain something like a legal ruling that is binding on qadis, the government may request a fatwa from a single individual (like Abd al-Aziz ibn Baz in the 1980s and 1990s) or from the Board of Senior Ulama, as the government did when it wanted qadis to adopt a single line on the problem of construction contractors failing to complete work on schedule and figuring monetary penalties for such instances.[40]

The Wahhabi establishment's refusal to draft and enforce a uniform legal code is one cause of unpredictability in the Saudi legal system. A second cause lies in the reluctance of qadis to adjudicate issues that appear to fall outside the purview of the shari'a. In such matters, Islamic law recognizes the validity of dynastic law-making under the principle of *siyasa shar'iyya*, which permits a ruler to issue decrees as long as they do not contradict the shari'a.[41] This principle is the basis for thousands of statutory regulations issued by the government to cover matters that do not have any obvious bearing on Islamic law. Wahhabi ulama acknowledge that this principle gives a ruler the authority to craft regulations (called *nizam*s). In the 1930s, Ibn Saud began issuing regulations on matters like 'firearms, nationality, government collections and motor vehicles'.[42] It seems the ulama regarded such piecemeal bits of legislation as the ruler's prerogative according to the principle of siyasa shar'iyya, but they refused to adjudicate 'regulatory' matters in routine fashion, so Ibn Saud created special tribunals, or statutory courts, to enforce them, in effect dividing the kingdom's judicial system between religious and statutory courts.[43]

The ulama's reluctance to adjudicate statutory regulations contributed to the congealing of two distinct cultures of expertise, one based on statutory regulations and another based on Islamic law. Shortly before Ibn Saud died in 1953, he took a step that augured new efforts to unify and make consistent the kingdom's administrative and legal frameworks by establishing the Council of Ministers. In the 1950s, this body issued regulations for the petroleum sector; by 1970, it would author regulations on business enterprises, labour, traffic and customs duties. Because the ulama did not recognize such regulations as a legitimate basis for adjudication according to the shari'a, the Council created new statutory courts for each category of regulations. In doing so, the Council's initiatives expanded a distinctive legal culture based on expertise in regulations and possessing its own educational niche in the curricula of public administration faculties at Saudi universities.[44] Even with the expanding jurisdiction of statutory courts, religious law has remained the essential basis of legitimacy for Saudi rule. Therefore, if the ulama find that a regulation conflicts with a religious ruling, the latter prevails.[45] In the eyes of the ulama, regulations have a temporary air about them and it is merely a matter of time before they absorb into the domain of religious law the various aspects of life presently administered by the statutory courts.[46]

Since the 1960s, regulations have proliferated to keep pace with changes in Saudi society, economy and public administration. An illustrative list of areas covered by regulations might include 'defining unlawful narcotics, fixing rules for government procurement, setting up traffic laws and organizing government entities'.[47] The expansion of regulations naturally increased the authority of statutory courts. What had initially appeared to Wahhabi ulama in the 1930s as a negligible expression of dynastic authority mushroomed into a vast corpus of regulations governing huge swaths of daily life. Thus, even though the statutory courts conform to the principle of siyasa shar'iyya, they became a source of friction when the ulama grew alarmed at the expansion of those courts' jurisdiction. Some in the Wahhabi establishment questioned the rationale for a separate system of tribunals. In Vogel's concise statement of their reasoning, 'If these other tribunals do not apply shari'a, they should not exist; if they do apply shari'a, then why not abolish them and unify the courts of the country?'[48] But if the Saudi government were to permit religious courts to assume authority over regulations, its interest in predictable adjudication would be imperilled. One qadi might rule on a case according to his understanding of shari'a rather than the regulation at hand while another qadi considering the identical case might not discern a relevant religious law and refuse to hear it.

The creation of a body of regulations under the purview of statutory courts has plagued efforts to forge a unified system of law courts. Islamic law does not require such a system, but since it might benefit the public interest, the ruler may devise one as long as he does not violate shari'a.[49] Ibn Saud took the first step to regularize a system of courts in Hijaz. When the area was under Hashemite rule, the courts followed a pattern that was common in Arab lands under Ottoman rule. A chief judge from the Hanafi school presided, the bulk of local judges belonged to the Shafi'i school and the other two Sunni schools – Maliki and Hanbali – had representation as well. In the 1920s, Ibn Saud issued a quasi-constitutional basic law and formed a court system that preserved all four Sunni law schools, essentially keeping the late Ottoman judicial regime with only minor modifications.[50] The new Saudi system for Hijaz established two levels of courts. Ordinary criminal cases went before summary courts authorized to carry out lesser punishments while civil cases and serious criminal cases that could incur the most severe punishments of amputation or execution were heard by superior shari'a courts. Why Wahhabi ulama did not object to these measures is unclear. Vogel believes they accepted the quasi-constitutional Basic Law and a special system of courts for Hijaz as a temporary expedient.[51] It seems that Ibn Saud's pre-eminence and the sensitivity of Hijaz for international Muslim opinion gave him some leeway to uphold the validity of decrees issued by Ottoman sultans, but he annulled them in 1930, when he needed the ulama's backing for his final assault on the Ikhwan. Once that threat had receded, he took a bold step in 1931 with the establishment of the first tribunal, a commercial court resembling the Ottoman model, itself based on the French model. Wahhabi ulama did not regard the court or its regulations as binding, so it operated only in Hijaz.[52] An opportunity to place all law courts under a single authority came about in 1953, with the formation of the Council of Ministers, but Ibn Saud conspicuously omitted a Ministry of Justice, probably in deference to the prestige of Sheikh Muhammad ibn Ibrahim. Instead, when King Saud took steps to unify the legal system, he placed the religious courts under the Wahhabi leader's authority. It was only after Sheikh Muhammad's death in 1969 that the government created a Ministry of Justice and appointed a member of Al al-Sheikh to head it. As a result, the national administrative system has institutionalized parallel legal systems, one responsible for religious law and another for statutory regulations.

The existence of two distinct legal regimes complicates the task of fostering a regular, national system of law. To make matters even more perplexing, Saudi Arabia has seen a protracted tug of war between the growing demands of the national economy and the deeply entrenched authority of Wahhabi norms. The first factor pushes for the advance of regular legal procedures and secular principles. Religious forces assert themselves in the name of the second. Particularly with regard to commercial transactions, the application of Hanbali law has put religious judges at odds with Saudi business interests, the government and, most conspicuously, foreign trade.[53] Saudi commercial courts apply statutory regulations, but the ulama have succeeded at encroaching on that domain.

The first steps to create legal institutions outside the sole jurisdiction of ulama came in Hijaz with a commercial court in 1926; then a Commercial Court Regulation in 1931 instituted a new set of laws and courts with seven members, of whom only one was an expert in religious law while the other six were merchants. This system lasted until 1955, when the ulama reasserted their sole jurisdiction over commercial transactions. Then, in the mid 1960s, the government revived commercial courts under the secular Ministry of Commerce. By 1967, there were three such courts in Jeddah, Riyadh and Dammam. Initially, these courts were purely secular in that each one consisted of three members with training in the statutory regulations. The ulama won a concession in 1968 by gaining equal representation on the courts (they now had four members, two with religious training and two with public administration training). Finally, in 1969, membership of the courts was cut to just three, with two experts in religious law and one in regulations. As a result, the commercial commissions enforcing statutory regulations had a majority of religious experts. Vogel's review of cases from the courts in the late 1970s reveals notable contrasts between the courts in Jeddah and Riyadh. As one might expect, in Riyadh, the two ulama dominated and imposed shari'a norms and procedures so the rulings conformed to Hanbali fiqh and the process was very slow. In Jeddah the two ulama tended to yield to the legal expert on regulations, showed greater flexibility in searching for shari'a rules to conform to regulations and acted more swiftly. The Dammam court resembled Riyadh's.[54]

Experiments with various arrangements for commercial courts underscore the fluid character of authority and legitimacy in the kingdom, as the ulama and the dynasty negotiated, asserted and balanced contrary interests. In the 1980s, Wahhabi assertiveness in the legal sphere meshed with Al Saud's need for support from the religious establishment to cope with mounting social and political strains. Rather than concentrate power more decisively at the royal court, Saudi rulers shared it more conspicuously with the religious establishment. That tendency is evident in the way the government expanded the application of a category of capital punishment in traditional Islamic law called *siyasatan* punishment. The textual basis for this sort of punishment is the Qur'an, 5:33–4:

> Those who make war on God and His Apostle and spread corruption on earth shall be that they shall be slain, or crucified, or that their hands and feet be cut off on opposite sides, or that they shall be banished from the earth.[55]

Wahhabi ulama have interpreted the verse to permit the imposition of capital punishment for heinous crimes that are not covered by *hudud* and whose *ta'zir* penalty is deemed too light. For the most part, in order to broaden the scope of harsh punishments to combat new sorts of crime and political offences, the Saudis have relied on the religious leadership to issue fatwas.[56] Thus in 1981, King Khalid sought advice from the Board of Senior Ulama for a solution to the rising incidence of drug smuggling and abduction. In response, the Board issued a fatwa that extended the definition of 'brigandage' to bring abduction and assaults on sexual honour within the scope of hudud crimes warranting amputation or execution. Vogel notes that the fatwa maintained 'shari'a court jurisdiction over this broad range of new crimes'. The fatwa also 'seeks to shift to the courts jurisdiction over crimes that in the past led to decrees of execution by the ruler either *siyasatan* or as *ta'zir*'.[57] The Saudis thereby legitimized the escalation of harsh penalties by delegating their determination to religious courts.[58] The Board of Senior Ulama issued a fatwa in 1988 that placed terrorism and sabotage in the category of capital ta'zir crimes because they cause 'corruption in the earth', to use the Qur'anic phrasing. Under the rubric of sabotage, the Board's fatwa included 'blowing up houses, mosques, schools, hospitals, factories, bridges, storehouses of arms or water, sources of public revenue such as oil wells, or by blowing up or hijacking airplanes'.[59]

Vogel observes that the Board of Senior Ulama's fatwas, issued on its own as well as at the behest of the ruler, expand the scope of Islamic law's jurisdiction in a wholly 'unprecedented' fashion.[60] The definitions of sabotage, drug crimes and brigandage are much vaguer than traditional categories of Islamic law. The Saudi rulers essentially gave away their prerogative under siyasatan punishment. Perhaps they hoped that such an approach would legitimize a harsh crackdown on crime and political violence. It probably does. But at the same time it may have the paradoxical effect of weakening the legitimacy of official religious institutions by implicating them in measures that sustain the very political structure that has tenuous support from the population.

Vogel summarizes the problems stemming from the primacy of shari'a as:

> unpredictability of decisions; obscure if not occult doctrine;
> dissonance between many Saudi commercial norms and

those prevailing nearly everywhere else... huge costs on the Saudi economy. That the king and government have not been inclined, or able, to impose a solution to this widely known difficulty is an apt measure of the cultural and political influence of fiqh and ulama and of the centrality of the shari'a ideal for Saudi life public and private.[61]

This situation puts Saudi Arabia at odds with the rest of the Arab world, where modernizing governments have steadily hemmed in religious courts. It appears as though the Saudi rulers lack the confidence to challenge directly the Wahhabi ulama, perhaps from a sense that the dynasty's claim to legitimacy is questionable. Thus, contrary to the expectation of modernization theory, the state's expansion of administrative bodies and regular procedures has not marginalized religious law or reduced the moral authority of experts in such law. On the other hand, Wahhabi ulama have countenanced the evolution of statutory regulations and courts that cover broad areas of modern life. In the view of at least some ulama, this is just a temporary situation and in due time, religious courts will regain a monopoly over the entire legal field. Finally, it must be emphasized that the unusual aspect of Saudi Arabia's legal regime is not the Hanbali school's putative conservatism but qadis' retention of their independent authority over broad swaths of law that other Muslim countries have codified under secular courts.[62]

Wahhabism and Modern Education

Studies of education in Saudi Arabia tend to fall into two categories, before 11 September 2001 and after. The first category, governed by assumptions embedded in the modernization paradigm, concentrates on policy, expenditures, literacy rates and number of schools, teachers and pupils.[63] The second category, governed by the assumption that the 11 September hijackers represented the fruit of Saudi education, scrutinizes textbooks for messages of hatred toward non-Muslims and clues to the sources of al-Qaeda terrorism.[64] One element missing from both categories is a historical perspective that views modern education in the kingdom as a substantial departure from Wahhabi practice. The drive to achieve mass literacy, to create a uniform national system of schools, exams and textbooks and to incorporate science, foreign language and social studies into curriculum totally and rapidly transformed education.

What was traditional Wahhabi education? In most respects, it conformed to a model of learning that had evolved in Muslim societies in medieval times.[65] Education's purpose was to transmit eternal truths about God, His creation, man's place in creation and so forth. To achieve this purpose required deep familiarity with God's word (the Qur'an) and His messenger's example (the Sunna) as the authoritative sources for belief (theology) and conduct (jurisprudence). A rich array of language sciences devoted to untangling the complexities and subtleties of Arabic evolved to allow the pupil to attain correct understanding of the Qur'an and the Sunna. Arithmetic figured in education as well so that Muslims could accurately calculate inheritance shares and zakat payments according to shari'a rules.

In early Islamic centuries, learning usually took place at a mosque, a teacher's home, or even at a teacher's workshop. There was no such thing as a 'school' in the sense of a space dedicated to education until the twelfth century, when there appeared the *madrasa*, literally, a place to study. By the eighteenth century, one could find madrasas in much of the Muslim world, but a great deal of instruction continued to take place in mosques and homes. Whereas modern schools issue diplomas certifying that a pupil has completed a course of study, traditional Muslim education 'credentialed' the pupil with a certificate, or *ijaza*, literally, permission. In writing an ijaza, a teacher stated that a pupil had studied certain texts under him and he might add that the pupil's mastery of those texts qualified him to teach them to others. Thus, the student's credentials consisted of a collection of ijazas. In this fashion, a chain of authority was constructed that linked pupils to teachers and their teachers' teachers and so forth, stretching back to the Prophet Muhammad or one of his Companions.

Muhammad ibn Abd al-Wahhab was a product of this set of educational practices. The difference between the Wahhabi mission and other Muslims in this field initially lay in the former's adoption of Sheikh Muhammad's works as a canon on theology. He composed brief compendia on essential beliefs and Wahhabi sheikhs then taught those texts to pupils.[66] In al-Dir'iyya, the Saudis set up four madrasas where Sheikh Muhammad's four sons taught. The treasury paid salaries to teachers and stipends to needy pupils, not only in the capital but in other Najdi towns as well. Two of the early Saudi rulers instructed the governors of towns to select ten to fifteen youths to train at the treasury's expense.[67] When it came to Arabic language sciences, arithmetic and Hanbali law, the Wahhabis used the same standard texts found in other Muslim lands. As for theology, the ulama taught Sheikh Muhammad's *Book of God's Unity* and one of his treatises that refuted the views of his critics.[68] For Qur'anic exegesis, a topic of crucial importance for supporting Wahhabi views, the ulama taught the works of Ibn Kathir, al-Baghawi, al-Baydawi and al-Tabari.[69] In the field of jurisprudence, Wahhabis studied standard works by Hanbali authors like Ibn Qudama and al-Hujawi.[70]

During the second Saudi amirate, Wahhabi education preserved its original form and added a new element: polemical treatises by Abd al-Latif ibn Abd al-Rahman and Abd Allah ibn Aba Butayn entered the canon, apparently to equip pupils with arguments against Ottoman ulama.[71] Well into the twentieth century, Wahhabi ulama sustained the traditional forms and substance of education. The era's most influential sheikh, Muhammad ibn Ibrahim, gave lessons at a mosque near his home in Riyadh for nearly forty years, from 1921 to 1960. In the early morning after the dawn prayer, he taught grammar from classical texts, first to beginning students, then intermediate students and finally a more advanced group. At these lessons students recited texts from memory, a feat that he modelled for them. He explained obscure words and phrases. After the noon prayer, he taught more advanced texts on theology, including *The Book of God's Unity* and Hadith collections. He would go home before the afternoon prayer and then return to the mosque, where after prayer he gave lessons on technical matters in Hadith studies and theology. Again he would repair to his home and come back to the mosque for the sunset prayer, after which he taught inheritance law and Qur'anic exegesis until the evening prayer, after which he would go home for the night.[72]

Since the 1920s, Saudi education policy has reflected an amalgamation of values and interests. Ibn Saud agreed with his Arab advisers that the kingdom needed citizens familiar with the outside world and modern science, not just the subjects taught in traditional Wahhabi education. His backing enabled Hafiz Wahbah, head of the Directorate of Education, to overcome ulama opposition to the introduction of geography, foreign language and science to the curriculum.[73] Another Egyptian adviser, Muhammad Isa al-Nahhas, encountered similar resistance when he tried to open the first public school in the Eastern Province (al-Hasa) town of Hofuf in 1937.[74] The region had been under Ottoman rule for four decades, 1871–1913, during which Istanbul took large strides in opening state schools, but the wave of public education barely touched the Persian Gulf coast.

By one count, al-Hasa had just three state schools in 1900. Instead, education took place in mosques, Qur'anic schools and the Shiite *Husayniyyas*.[75] When Muhammad al-Nahhas declared the intention to establish a modern school, local ulama objected because their notion of such a school came from Bahrain, where a pronounced British missionary flavour prevailed. Not surprisingly, al-Hasa's religious teachers argued that the best way to safeguard Islam was to leave education under their complete control. In order to overcome these reservations, Nahhas met with the ulama and other townsmen at Hofuf's grand mosque after Friday prayer. He reminded them that Ibn Saud was committed to upholding salafi ways, so he would never permit Christian missionary influences into public education. He then reassured his audience by describing the curriculum: recitation and exegesis of the Qur'an, theology, Hanbali law, Arabic grammar and composition, the Prophet's life and the history of Islam. He also listed the texts that pupils would study: two works by Muhammad ibn Abd al-Wahhab and the conventional Wahhabi texts on exegesis and doctrine.[76]

Pressure for extending the Hijaz model of education came from two quarters. Aramco needed better-trained workers and was willing to send employees to the American University in Beirut and the USA. This affected a very small number of individuals in just one part of the country, the Eastern Province.[77] A more profound impulse for spreading modern education came from the dynasty's efforts to manage Saudi society via state institutions, and that required Saudis capable of working in them. Initial steps proceeded gradually and on a small scale. Thus, in 1948, education expenses consumed a mere three percent of spending.[78] In 1950, in the entire kingdom outside Hijaz, there were fewer than twenty elementary schools (six in Najd, six in al-Hasa, five in Asir). Hijaz had four secondary schools.[79] In order to justify these schools to the religious establishment, their curricula emphasized religion and Arabic, with as much as eighty percent of class hours on those subjects. Only in the fourth year of school did Qur'an instruction consist of fewer than ten hours per week.[80] Shortly after Saud ibn Abd al-Aziz succeeded to the throne in 1953, he folded the Hijaz-based Directorate of Education into a national Ministry of Education.[81] The kingdom devoted scant resources to the new ministry for a few years. Beginning in 1958, education received substantial allocations from the national budget and consequently the government made impressive gains in elementary education, in what might be termed a first phase of spreading schools to smaller provincial towns.[82] By the late 1960s, Saudis expected educational resources to continue expanding. Deep inroads into literacy rates had to wait for the sudden windfall of oil revenues in the 1970s that made it possible to pay for the construction of hundreds of schools and the hiring of thousands of teachers.

The Wahhabi leadership did not resist the quantitative expansion of schools, particularly since the curriculum incorporated the mission's doctrine and emphasized religious instruction. Creating schools for girls, however, aroused the ire of some ulama and the largely conservative population in general. Demand for girls' education had been building because educated Saudi men preferred to marry educated women and that usually meant non-Saudi Arabs. Within the royal family, Princess Iffat, the wife of the future King Faysal, advocated educating girls. She played a role in the opening of a school for orphan girls in Jeddah in 1956 and she later encouraged the expansion of opportunities at secondary and university levels.[83] A number of private schools for girls opened in the 1950s. When Faysal decided to create public schools for girls in 1960, he deflected criticism from conservative quarters by placing them under the supervision of Sheikh Muhammad ibn Ibrahim in an agency called the General Presidency of the Schools of Girls.[84]

Modern higher education came to Saudi Arabia in 1957 with the establishment of the kingdom's first university (originally named Riyadh University, renamed in 1982 King Saud University). The Wahhabi establishment pressed for the creation of a religious university to balance Riyadh University's anticipated secular character and, in 1961, the Islamic University was founded at Medina.[85] This institution also served a foreign policy purpose – offering a religious alternative to the Arab world's secular nationalist universities – by accepting and housing a large number of non-Saudi Arab students. A second religious university evolved in Riyadh from a cluster of colleges for theology and law first established in 1953. A special section to train shari'a court judges opened in 1965 and a special faculty for Arabic language studies followed in 1970. These various bodies were combined into a single entity called Imam Muhammad ibn Saud University in 1974.[86]

In the two decades after Ibn Saud, the kingdom made notable strides in the education field but it was only after the oil boom that more than half the population became literate. An astonishing sum of wealth suddenly became available. In 1970–1975, $2.5 billion was allocated to education. In 1976–1980, the figure was $28 billion.[87] In gauging the outcome of these expenditures, observers highlight the construction of more schools, the hiring of more teachers and the inclusion of more boys and girls in classrooms. Observers also note that in spite of generous budgets, Saudi education has been plagued

3. (LEFT) GIRLS' SCHOOL
CLASSROOM, UNDATED.
4. (BELOW) BOYS PLAY SCRABBLE
AT A JEDDAH BOYS' SCHOOL,
UNDATED.
KATRINA THOMAS, *SAUDI ARAMCO
WORLD*/PADIA.

by numerous problems: poorly trained teachers, low retention rates, lack of rigorous standards, weak scientific and technical instruction and excessive attention to religious subjects. Consequently, the kingdom has continued to depend on huge numbers of expatriate workers to fill technical and administrative positions.[88] It has been suggested that another effect of these problems is to amplify the influence of religious universities. Their less rigorous admissions criteria and the stipends they offer to needy students make them attractive to students from less prosperous, more conservative strata of society. Degrees in religious subjects leave graduates of Islamic universities less qualified for well-paying jobs in technical fields and the public sector than graduates of the secular universities. Thus, the cultural divide between secular and religious segments of Saudi society grows wider and disgruntled religious university graduates flock to dissident religious trends which harbour hostility toward the kingdom's secular segment.[89] In the 1970s and 1980s, as religious universities expanded so did the number of young Saudis with degrees in Islamic studies seeking employment. The modernizing economy, however, had little use for their expertise in the finer points of fiqh and Qur'anic exegesis. Because of the country's high birth rate, the kingdom needed school teachers and as long as religious subjects comprised roughly one-quarter to one-third of the curriculum, many shari'a-trained graduates could find jobs in education. Others staffed the expanding network of mosques and religious institutes, the patrols of Committees for Commanding Right and Forbidding Wrong, or the proselytizing offices of Saudi-funded organizations.[90] The economic woes of the 1980s and 1990s curtailed the government's ability to hire new graduates and they were poorly prepared for work in the private sector. In a sense, the Wahhabi mission's success in balancing secular higher education with an Islamic counterpart was to blame for the frustration of graduates ill-suited to employment in a business enterprise or in the petroleum sector. It was an instance where the political utility for Al Saud of placating their perennial Wahhabi backers created social and economic problems and in the long run, a political time bomb as disgruntled, young, unemployed men proved receptive to the agenda of modern Islamic revivalism, in both its non-violent and militant forms.

According to the modernization paradigm, the advance of modernity causes a redefinition of religion and its retreat to the private sphere.

Since the 1970s, however, both western and non-western societies have witnessed a wave of religious movements insisting on having a voice in the public arena. Apparently, the idea that secularism would inevitably advance in tandem with modernity expressed a western prejudice rather than an empirical finding. Nevertheless, modernity does affect religion inasmuch as believers interact with and respond to changing political, cultural and social conditions. In the particular case examined here, Wahhabism kept its doctrinal cohesion at the same time it adjusted to Al Saud's state-building measures. Contrary to the expectation that incorporating Wahhabi ulama into a network of government institutions would diminish their influence, the ulama turned institutions into vehicles to entrench and even expand their sway. They retained authority over those areas of the law they deemed relevant and left it up to Al Saud to devise mechanisms and rules for adjudicating areas the ulama chose not to touch. When it came to education, they ensured the incorporation of Wahhabi doctrine and a large element of religious instruction in the curriculum. They reacted to the creation of universities by developing a parallel set of religious schools of higher learning. The adoption by Saudis of western values and habits followed by the influx of expatriate workers triggered sporadic protests and endeavours to organize Committees for Commanding Right and Forbidding Wrong. What about the notion that modernity reshapes religion? Wahhabi ulama adapted to institutions, but they were yet to yield on essential doctrinal positions. To understand this dimension of religious change in Saudi Arabia, we must look to the ways that Muslim revivalist currents in the Arab East mixed with Wahhabism. Those currents, without question a product of the modern era, redefined Islam, not to admit the triumph of secularism but to assert the primacy of religion in the public sphere.

Chapter Five

The Wahhabi Mission and Islamic Revivalism

If you traced the long-term trend in relations between Wahhabism and the outside world from the mid eighteenth to the mid twentieth centuries, you would find a tendency toward accommodation.[1] The first Saudi amirate's own expansionist project meshed with the Wahhabi view of other Muslims as idolaters who must be conquered and converted. A more robust set of imperial neighbours in the nineteenth century compelled the second amirate to quell expansionist impulses and to settle for coexistence with 'idolatrous' neighbours. When it came to relations between Wahhabi and Ottoman ulama, however, no such corresponding modus vivendi evolved to mute doctrinal enmity until the 1880s and, as we have seen, throughout the nineteenth century, Wahhabi ulama wished to tightly control, if not prohibit altogether, travel to Ottoman lands. The only destination beyond the Pale of Najd that Wahhabi ulama considered legitimate was India, where a similar revivalist movement arose in the 1860s.

While the Wahhabis maintained their customary view of Ottoman Muslims as idolaters, there did emerge a tendency among a handful of religious scholars in the Arab East (Egypt and the Fertile Crescent) that initiated a reappraisal of the Najdi movement. This new religious tendency blended revivalism with an impulse to demonstrate Islam's compatibility with modern life. After the First World War, revivalists in the Arab East welcomed the Saudi rebirth, apparently dismissing the Ikhwan as ignorant Bedouins and as an aberration, not the essence of Wahhabism. These revivalists tried to rehabilitate the Wahhabis' reputation in the Muslim world. It appears, however, that the rapprochement was one-sided, with Wahhabi ulama confident that their conception of religious truth required no adjustment. Indeed, even in the decades after the Second World War, when Saudi Arabia became a refuge for Muslim activists facing persecution in Egypt and Syria, it is difficult to discern much flexibility in Wahhabi doctrine. Nevertheless, the infiltration of modern Islamic revivalism into the kingdom profoundly affected the country's religious culture and in fact, would shake Wahhabi hegemony in the later decades of the twentieth century.

Revivalist Trends in the Arab East

During the nineteenth century, Ottoman sultans and ministers undertook a reorganization of the empire's basic institutions of governance, defence, law and education. Known as the Tanzimat movement, this set of policies and initiatives borrowed extensively from European models, on the assumption that these constituted the foundations of superior European power and that for the Ottoman Empire to survive in a challenging international environment, it was necessary to strengthen itself by imitating the era's most powerful countries. The Tanzimat reduced religion's role in law and education. In the 1860s, there developed a reaction against the secularizing bent of the Tanzimat and an assertion that Islam was perfectly compatible with the necessities of the modern age. If Muslim societies had declined in relation to Europe and become backward, it was argued, the problem was not Islam but Muslims. They must have strayed from a correct understanding and practice of Islam. After all, the first generations of Muslims (the salaf), had enjoyed glorious worldly success. In Islam's first century, its faithful had created an empire that stretched from the Strait of Gibraltar to the Indus River. Muslim civilization had been a model of dazzling cultural achievement, scientific discovery and economic prosperity. But at some point, Muslims had taken a wrong turn along the path of history. It was therefore necessary to return to the ways of the Muslim ancestors, the salaf, in order to reproduce their worldly success. Late nineteenth-century Muslim reformers wished to re-examine the Qur'an and the Sunna to reinterpret law and doctrine in order to bring them into line with current notions about science, progress, governance and society. One dimension of Muslim reform in the Arab East, then, had largely pragmatic concerns when its proponents called for a revival of pure Islam. That would be the modernist thrust of the movement. At the same time, the idea that Muslims had strayed from true religion offered an opening for re-examining the sources and re-evaluating beliefs and practices. That second dimension meshed with an impulse to rid ritual behaviour of accretions and innovations, which dovetailed with the perennial Wahhabi thrust of eliminating forms of worship that violated monotheism.

The reform tendency in the Arab East began in the 1880s. Clusters of Sunni ulama in Egypt, Syria and Iraq gathered in mosques and madrasas to re-evaluate the historical legacy of religious scholarship in the light of Islam's textual foundation, the Qur'an and the Sunna. These men became fascinated with the works of Ibn Taymiyya, the medieval Hanbali scholar whose views informed Wahhabi doctrine. The Ottoman Arab reformers were attracted to his insistence on the right of qualified scholars to perform ijtihad on legal (shari'a) questions. They believed that if Muslims were to adjust to the demands of modern times, they needed the flexibility to revise Islamic law that ijtihad afforded. Interest in Ibn Taymiyya led to a search for rare manuscript copies of his writings. It was natural that the reformers would take an interest in the Wahhabis, who themselves were assiduous in seeking to justify their beliefs by citing Ibn Taymiyya.

Tracing the links among enthusiasts for Ibn Taymiyya reveals a network of ulama living in Baghdad, Damascus, Najd, Mecca and India.[2] In Baghdad, the recovery of Ibn Taymiyya's legacy was associated with a distinguished lineage of ulama, the Alusis. In 1880, Nu'man Khayr al-Din al-Alusi published a work that presented arguments to refute Ibn Taymiyya's medieval detractors, in particular for their rejection of his assertion that religious scholars could undertake ijtihad.[3] Alusi's interest in Ibn Taymiyya led to contacts with Wahhabi ulama, from whom he sought manuscripts missing from Baghdad's collections.[4] In Damascus, a religious scholar named Tahir al-Jaza'iri used his position as director of Syria's first public library to advance the revival of Ibn Taymiyya. In 1897, he compiled a list of twenty-two essays by the medieval scholar that he had uncovered. He noted that they had been copied in 1802 at the request of Muhammad ibn Abd al-Wahhab's son Ali.[5] Around the same time, a second Damascene sheikh, Jamal al-Din al-Qasimi, made a copy of a major work by Ibn Taymiyya.[6] Qasimi also initiated a correspondence with Khayr al-Din al-Alusi and his nephew, Mahmud Shukri al-Alusi.[7] Qasimi wrote to Mahmud al-Alusi in 1908, saying that he had heard of Alusi's desire to print and publish works by Ibn Taymiyya.[8] In reply, Alusi lamented the lack of financial resources to spread works by Ibn Taymiyya and his pupil Ibn al-Qayyim.[9] In another letter Alusi wrote that he was in touch with a member of Al al-Sheikh who had promised to send copies of Ibn Taymiyya's works.

The Ottoman Arab reformers' and the Wahhabis' common interest in Ibn Taymiyya does not mean that they concurred on doctrinal matters. Wahhabi positions on idolatry and viewing Muslims as infidels were at odds with the Ottoman Arab ulama's more inclusive outlook. But they did agree on the permissibility of ijtihad. That pitted them against the Ottoman religious law establishment that rejected ijtihad. They also agreed on the need to purify worship practices of innovation, which were particularly conspicuous in the ceremonies of Sufi orders. In the late nineteenth century, criticism of Sufi practices assumed a political aspect because Ottoman Sultan Abdulhamid II vigorously promoted Sufi orders to strengthen loyalty to Istanbul.[10] Arab religious reformers also fell foul of the sultan for supporting the constitutional movement to curtail the sultan's powers.[11] Defenders of customary religious practices and Sufi orders could attack the reformers on both doctrinal and political grounds.

When Ibn Saud launched his bid to regain Najd from the Rashidis, loyal vassals of the Ottomans, Istanbul became alarmed at the prospects of an alliance between the Saudi-Wahhabi cause and the religious reform camp. Conservative ulama opposed to that camp exploited this alarm to incite Ottoman authorities to persecute religious reformers on a number of occasions in Damascus and Baghdad on the ground that they were spreading Wahhabism, identified with the politically suspect Ibn Saud.[12] The Syrian reformers insisted that they were innocent of allegiance to Wahhabism, but they did have contacts with an emissary from Ibn Saud. Fawzan ibn Sabiq ibn Fawzan was not a religious scholar but a Buraydan trader who dabbled in religious studies. His commerce took him to Iraq, Syria and Egypt and it seems that his profile as a merchant-religious pupil offered good cover for political activity on behalf of Ibn Saud. In Damascus, he attended lessons with the teachers in the reform camp

(Jaza'iri, Qasimi and others) while at the same time he carried out secret political activities. During one of the episodes of Ottoman alarm over Wahhabi subversion, Fawzan fled to Egypt.[13]

While the political loyalties of Arab reformers were obscure, their religious views were clear and they marked a shift to a more sympathetic evaluation of Wahhabism. We find a sample of the revised attitude in a letter from Muhammad ibn Azzuz, a Tunisian sheikh residing in Istanbul, to Mahmud al-Alusi.[14] Ibn Azzuz wrote that he had heard that Wahhabis consider one who smokes tobacco to be an idolater and that they consider one who visits a grave and calls to God to be an infidel whose blood may be shed. But he had also heard that the Wahhabis were upholders of the Sunna, avoiders of innovations in worship, followers of the Hanbali school in law and adherents of salafi doctrine. To judge the issue fairly, Ibn Azzuz looked over some Wahhabi writings and concluded that their beliefs were sound. His letter gives a sense of how elastic the meaning of 'Wahhabi' had become. He noted that when he was in Mecca he asked an expert in Hanafi jurisprudence about another religious scholar. The Hanafi expert told him that the fellow was a Wahhabi. When Ibn Azzuz asked him what that meant exactly, the man said that he followed al-Bukhari (an authoritative ninth-century compiler of hadiths). Ibn Azzuz concluded that in Mecca, 'Wahhabi' was applied to anyone who followed hadiths or professed salafi doctrine.

The religious reform camp in Baghdad expressed the same view of Wahhabism. The leader of that camp around the turn of the twentieth century was Mahmud Shukri al-Alusi.[15] His affinity for the Wahhabi mission is obvious. In 1889, he completed an unfinished Wahhabi treatise by Abd al-Latif ibn Abd al-Rahman against the Baghdad Sufi Da'ud ibn Jirjis. The treatise's publication points to support for Wahhabism outside Najd: the amir of Qatar paid for the costs of its printing, which took place in India.[16] Around the same time, Alusi began a campaign against ritual innovations in Sufi orders like music, dance and veneration of saints' tombs.

Alusi's favourable view of the Wahhabis is most evident in *The History of Najd*, which was published posthumously in 1924.[17] The book is a compilation of scattered writings that Alusi's disciple Muhammad Bahjat al-Athari discovered after its author's death. We gather from Athari's preface that Alusi had written some of it before 1905. Athari noted that the work was believed to have been lost when Alusi was briefly expelled from Baghdad in that year. Athari later discovered sections on the tribes and rulers of Najd appended to a draft manuscript of Alusi's *History of Baghdad* and incorporated them into the work.[18] Internal evidence also confirms the early date of its composition. Alusi wrote that the current Rashidi ruler was Abd al-Aziz ibn Mit'ab, who reigned in Ha'il between 1897 and 1906. Alusi defended the Wahhabis against their Ottoman critics at the same time he mixed praise and censure for the Saudi rulers according to shifts in their relations with Istanbul.

The History of Najd begins with an overview of the region's topography, districts, towns and neighbouring lands.[19] In this section of the work, Alusi exhibited the attitude of a loyal Ottoman subject at the same time as he defended the Wahhabis. Thus, in his description of Jabal Shammar, the home region of the Rashidi amirs, he portrayed them as loyal subjects of the Ottoman Empire and devoted followers of the Hanbali legal school, as were all the folk of Najd (meaning the Wahhabis). The Rashidi amir referred legal issues to a Hanbali sheikh and implemented God's ruling as discerned by the sheikh, as was the case in all of Najd. Alusi observed that the Rashidi ruler, Abd al-Aziz ibn Mit'ab, was loyal to Istanbul and a just ruler familiar with matters of religion.[20]

When Alusi described al-Arid, the homeland of Al Saud, he explained the capital's shift from al-Dir'iyya to Riyadh as a result of the 'Egyptian' (he did not use the term 'Ottoman') invasion and Muhammad Ali's order to raze al-Dir'iyya to the ground, cut down its date palms and expel its inhabitants. The inclusion of exclamation points to punctuate the destruction of homes, the cutting of trees and the refusal to show mercy to children or the elderly indicates the author's sympathy for the vanquished party. Alusi described al-Dir'iyya in its heyday, when its markets bustled with traders from neighbouring lands. By contrast, Alusi had little to say about Riyadh, merely that it was a large town with wide streets, numerous homes, mosques, schools and ulama anchored in religion.[21] The descriptions of other regions of Najd – al-Qasim, Sudayr and Washm – name the amirs under Saudi rule. In the section on al-Arid, apart from the historical narrative about al-Dir'iyya, one would not know the region had been the cradle of Al Saud power. In enumerating the moral traits of Najdis, Alusi noted that they exhibited loyalty, zeal, honesty and valour. They protected strangers and they honoured the terms of contracts. Furthermore, they spoke the purest Arabic, so they excelled in poetry and eloquent speech.[22]

To describe the religion of the people of Najd (he did not use the term Wahhabi), Alusi relied on a treatise by Abd Allah ibn Muhammad ibn Abd al-Wahhab that set forth the main outlines of the mission's beliefs.[23] Alusi declared that his purpose was to point out misconceptions about Najd which arose from 'people of innovation and whim who take their religion as a plaything and who lie about religion'.[24] Distortions circulated by their adversaries included the following refrains, all familiar in anti-Wahhabi circles since the eighteenth century: they interpret the Qur'an according to personal opinion, they disrespect the Prophet, they do not respect the views of authoritative ulama, they consider everybody since the thirteenth century to be infidels except for those who agree with them, they prohibit lawful visits to graves and they do not accept the allegiance of anyone who does not affirm that they were formerly idolaters. Alusi asserted that whoever spent time with them saw that those charges were lies and slander spread by enemies of religion. Thus, he exonerated the Wahhabis from charges of extremism and called them *muwahhid* (monotheist) Muslims who followed the doctrines of the first Muslim generation (the salaf) on the essential matters of belief in God and the Prophet. As for Islamic law, they adhered to the Hanbali school and relied on well-established works of Qur'anic exegesis and Hadith. They did not blame others for adhering to any of the other three Sunni schools. If some Bedouins killed women and children in their raids, that was a result of their own ignorance and it was not condoned by the people of Najd in general.[25] To elaborate on the true nature of religion in Najd, Alusi reproduced excerpts from a nineteenth-century polemical work by 'the famous scholar' Abd al-Latif Al al-Sheikh[26] which refuted his Baghdadi nemesis Ibn Jirjis.

Besides attesting to the Wahhabis' religious rectitude, Alusi cast the history of Saudi rule in Najd in a mostly favourable light.[27] In the eighteenth century, Abd al-Aziz ibn Saud rescued the region from ceaseless tribal warfare and brought security to townsmen and nomads so that livestock could be tended safely by a single shepherd. When Saud ibn Abd al-Aziz conquered the Holy Cities, he erred in obstructing the pilgrimage, rebelling against the Ottoman sultan and excommunicating his opponents. His successor Abd Allah ibn Saud should have never attacked the sultan's domain or called their attacks on Muslims a jihad. Rather, they should have been content with a realm consisting of Najd, Bahrain and Oman, where they could teach the Bedouins to obey religion. In the second Saudi amirate, Turki

ibn Abd Allah succeeded in spreading proper religious observance
among the Bedouin tribes and Faysal ibn Turki was known for his
generosity to ulama, widows, orphans and the poor.[28] To substantiate
the case for the good rule of nineteenth-century Saudi amirs, Alusi
cited three epistles by Turki and Faysal exhorting their subjects to
perform prayer with a group, pay zakat and avoid sins like usury
and cheating with weights and measures, even in dealings with a
non-Muslim.[29]

In political terms, Alusi toed a fine line when we recall that he
wrote his work before the demise of the Ottoman Empire was on
the horizon. We find no such restraint to embrace Saudi Arabia as a
political cause in the post-Ottoman writings of his colleague in the
religious reform movement, Rashid Rida. This Syrian-born figure is
much better known than Alusi and had far-reaching influence on
the Muslim world through his monthly periodical, *al-Manar* ('The
Lighthouse'), which came out in 1898 and continued until Rida's
death in 1935. He had left his native Syria (in present-day Lebanon)
in 1897 and moved to Egypt in order to join the circle of the celebrated
Egyptian reformer-scholar Muhammad Abduh. They collaborated
on the first Muslim periodical to achieve a pan-Islamic reach, with
readers in Indonesia and the Muslim communities in the Americas.
Rida's political involvements in the Arab East are far too complex
for a thorough treatment here, but several incidents in his career
illustrate the tendency for Ottoman religious reformers to re-evaluate
Wahhabism. For one thing, conservative ulama put him in the same
category as others seeking to eliminate popular religious practices
and beliefs and tarred him with the Wahhabi label. These ulama
opposed the Ottoman constitutional movement and accused the
constitutionalists like Rida of being Wahhabis.[30] When Rida visited
Damascus a few months after the July 1908 constitutional restoration,
two conservative sheikhs interrupted his public lecture at the city's
ancient Umayyad mosque and 'Wahhabi-baited' him. The authorities
made matters worse by arresting one of the rabble-rousing sheikhs,
whose allies then drummed up protesting crowds at other mosques.
The rowdy mob frightened Rida into fleeing Damascus the next day
and with the Wahhabi tag attached to his local comrades in religious
reform, they retreated to their homes for several weeks before
venturing out.[31]

The Ottoman Empire's collapse at the end of the First World
War transformed the political status of the Arab East from Ottoman

provinces into European mandates with new boundaries and names: Iraq, Syria and Palestine. Among the major protagonists in post-war development were the sharif of Mecca, Husayn ibn Ali, and his sons. They aspired to project their dynastic authority over the Fertile Crescent and Arabia. At the conclusion of the war, Sharif Husayn ruled Hijaz and his son Faysal installed himself in Syria with the backing of Great Britain. Rashid Rida played a minor role in the brief life of Hashemite Syria, presiding over the Syrian National Congress, which affirmed Faysal's status as king of Syria. In July 1920, however, France invaded Syria and ousted Faysal, who then went to Baghdad to help Great Britain pacify Iraq. Meanwhile, the British allotted a portion of southern Syria, which they called Transjordan, to another of Sharif Husayn's sons, Abd Allah. In Arabia, the revived and expanding Saudi polity in Najd collided with Hashemite Hijaz and be-cause Hashemite clansmen ruled in Iraq and Transjordan as well, the struggle for Hijaz assumed a broader Arab dimension, not to mention the pan-Islamic significance of who would control the Holy Cities.

By the early 1920s, Rashid Rida had joined the ranks of Ibn Saud's boosters in the wider Arab world, if for no other reason than disenchantment with the outcome of Sharif Husayn's dynastic scheming for the Arab East: its partition into British and French spheres of influence. Hence, Rida's affiliation with the anti-Hashemite camp was born of frustration with the would-be dynasts' incompetence and perhaps a dose of opportunism. Ibn Saud must have realized the advantage of winning to his cause the publisher of *al-Manar*, with its pan-Islamic readership. By the time the new ruler of Hijaz convened a Muslim congress in Mecca in the summer of 1926, Rida was receiving funds from him.[32] Representatives of Muslim governments and popular religious associations attended the meeting, but no definitive resolutions passed and no subsequent congress in Mecca was ever held because of deep political and religious differences in the Muslim world. The congress represented Ibn Saud's bid to join the Muslim mainstream and to erase the reputation of extreme sectarianism associated with the Ikhwan. But the question of Wahhabi intolerance emerged as a problem when an Egyptian delegate reported harassment for uttering a phrase abhorrent to the mission's ulama.[33]

Rashid Rida's apologetic for Ibn Saud, *The Wahhabis and Hijaz*, set forth the case for the Saudi-Wahhabi side in the battle for Hijaz. It consists of a series of articles first published in *al-Manar* and Egyptian newspapers during the Hashemite-Saudi conflict. Whereas Alusi had written in an Ottoman context to vindicate Wahhabism's reputation, Rida addressed a controversial political struggle for control of Islam's holy places. Therefore, the bulk of his work focuses on political matters. Indeed, in the very first sentence, Rida acknowledged the significance of the political context for his pro-Saudi position when he wrote that if the Wahhabi incursion into Hijaz had taken place in the Ottoman era, the Islamic world would have been furious. Newspapers across the breadth of the Muslim world would have condemned the Wahhabis as infidels and financial contributions to fight them would have been gathered. After all, Muslims across the world had held a favourable view of the Ottomans and a dim view of the Wahhabis. But things were different now. The Wahhabis were known for pious adherence to religion and hostility to foreign influence. Their adversary Sharif Husayn was notorious for plotting with Islam's enemies for the sake of his ambition to gain the caliphate.[34] While Rida was overstating the case because of his personal antipathy toward the Hashemites, his portrayal of the impact of the post-Ottoman situation on Muslims' perceptions of the Wahhabis was accurate. The political-military contest between Sharif Husayn and Ibn Saud included mutual recriminations against one another's religious sincerity. The Hashemite ruler broadcast the litany of anti-Wahhabi accusations that dated to the eighteenth century whereas Ibn Saud played on the Meccan sharifs' reputation for corruption.[35] In order to set the record straight, Rida declared that he would rely on the writings of both sides and that he would only add comments buttressed by strong evidence.

To vindicate Wahhabism, Rida cited the same essay that Alusi had reproduced in *Tarikh Najd*, a treatise composed by Ibn Abd al-Wahhab's son Abd Allah. The noteworthy point in Rida's inclusion is that he informed readers that if they wished greater detail, they might consult Abd Allah's essay, which was available for free from al-Manar Press.[36] Rida boasted that he persuaded a number of anti-Wahhabi ulama at the Azhar to revise their views on the Wahhabis after he provided them copies of the essay. Except for this section, most of Rida's book has little to say about matters of religious belief or practice. Instead, it details how Sharif Husayn forfeited a rightful claim to rule Hijaz by betraying the Ottoman Empire during the First World War, delivering Arab Muslim lands to European rule in order to further his selfish ambitions, misgoverning the region and gouging pilgrims.

Rida's 'Wahhabiphile' treatise expresses deep anger toward Sharif Husayn and his family for selling the Arabs to western powers for the sake of dynastic ambition. Resentment toward Great Britain for betraying its World War I promises to the Arabs is also evident in the book. In fact, Rida discerned British manipulation as the cause of London's interwar dominance in the region. The purpose of Britain's intervention was to undermine Islam. The last thing London wanted, he asserted, was to see a faithful Muslim ruler, like Ibn Saud, who was not for sale, unlike the traitorous Husayn and his sons. A strong Muslim leader would prevent the realization of Britain's goal of erasing Islam from the earth, first as a religion of power and then as a religion of doctrine and belief.[37] The notion that ambitious western powers worked hand in hand with duplicitous Arab rulers to advance western interests and to crush Islam would become a pillar of Muslim revivalist and Arab nationalist discourses. Both searched for traitors to the community of believers and the nation, respectively, and they turned from one would-be hero to another to rescue the believers and the nation from betrayal.

The apprehension of a sinister alliance between voracious foreign powers and corrupt local rulers figures prominently in the outlook of the contemporary Muslim revivalist movements. The oldest and most influential such movement is the Muslim Brothers, founded in Egypt in 1928 by a twenty-two year old schoolteacher, Hasan al-Banna.[38] From modest origins as a small group of workers in the Suez Canal Zone, it mushroomed into a nationwide movement by the Second World War, calling for the revival of Islamic morality and resistance to western cultural inroads. In significant respects, Banna represented a new tendency in Islamic revivalism. First, his educational formation took place in state schools, not in the mosques or madrasas that had shaped the outlook of men like Rashid Rida and Mahmud al-Alusi. In the Sunni Arab realm, a lay education would become fairly typical for activists in the Muslim Brothers and related groups. Second, he created an organization to enact the revivalist agenda and he laid down rules for membership, leadership and specialized bureaus. During the twenty years that he led the Muslim Brothers, Hasan al-Banna made it a platform for advocating resistance to western cultural influences and summoning believers to recommit to Islam, which he defined as an all-encompassing way of life, not merely a set of rituals and rules for individual conduct. Islam had become an ideology.

Banna shared with the Wahhabis a strong revulsion against western influences and unwavering confidence that Islam is both the true religion and a sufficient foundation for conducting worldly affairs. Nevertheless, significant differences separate the Najdi movement from the modern revivalist agenda because the former stemmed from Muhammad ibn Abd al-Wahhab's distinctive views on doctrine whereas the Muslim Brothers were a reaction against European domination and cultural invasion. On the central Wahhabi doctrine of monotheism, Banna held that only the open proclamation of apostasy, denying well-known beliefs and religious obligations and deliberately twisting the meaning of the Qur'an rendered the believer an infidel. While he agreed with the Wahhabis on the need to purify religious practices of illegitimate innovations, he saw nothing wrong with visits to the tombs of holy men as long as one did not seek their intercession. Thus, unlike the blanket Wahhabi condemnation of Sufi practices, Banna only objected to those acts which deviated from the Qur'an and the Sunna. As a youth, he had been active in a Sufi order and although he would later criticize Sufism's 'corrupt' aspects, he maintained that its emphasis on asceticism and mindfulness of God made it an essential part of Islam. In fact, he exhorted Muslim Brothers to practise individual and group *dhikr*, a ritual 'mentioning' of God, to strengthen the believers' mindfulness of God and the Prophet's example. Dhikr is a hallmark of Sufi practice and considered by the Wahhabis an illegitimate innovation.[39] More generally, Banna's keen desire for Muslim unity to ward off western imperialism led him to espouse an inclusive definition of the community of believers. Thus, he would urge his followers, 'Let us cooperate in those things on which we can agree and be lenient in those on which we cannot.'[40] Banna did not share the Wahhabi view that most Muslims were idolaters.

Banna differed from the Wahhabis in his political ideas. He lived during Egypt's phase of constitutional parliamentary government and his writings reflect that context's influence. He believed that constitutional government was the best match with Islamic principles because it ensured a ruler's accountability to the people. He lamented the failure of the Egyptian constitution of his day to establish Islam as the fundamental basis for public life, but that did not invalidate constitutionalism in principle. It bothered Banna that Egyptian courts applied elements of both shari'a and western law. He regarded the latter as illegitimate and called on Muslim Brothers to boycott courts that enforced un-Islamic laws. The Wahhabis have never supported constitutional rule. Instead, they have always supported the Saudi monarchy, whereas Banna denied the legitimacy of hereditary monarchy in Islam, hardly a view that would be popular in Riyadh.[41]

A salient element in Banna's notion of Islam as a total way of life came from the idea that the Muslim world was backward and the corollary that the state is responsible for guaranteeing decent living conditions for its citizens. He argued that the government had the duty to minimize unemployment, guarantee a minimum wage and health care for workers and ensure the fair distribution of wealth.[42] Such notions are alien to Wahhabism. Other assumptions of the modern state permeated Banna's outlook. He considered public education a critical vehicle for bolstering Muslim society against western influences (which did not exist in eighteenth-century Najd). Muslim schools would teach pupils about Islam and encourage them to eschew foreign ways.[43]

The central area of accord between the Brothers and the Wahhabis is their moral zeal and rejection of western ways that threaten to erode piety and undermine Muslim custom. Western influences arrived in Saudi Arabia much later than Egypt, but when they did, the Wahhabis exhibited a similar revulsion toward them and agreed with the Muslim Brother view of European culture as one of godlessness, immorality and excessive individualism.[44] It is true that Muhammad ibn Abd al-Wahhab and Hasan al-Banna would have seen eye to eye on the ruler's responsibility to eliminate immoral habits. They would also concur on the duty of the ruler (or the state) to appoint (or employ) pious believers to responsible positions to ensure proper observance and enforcement of religious duties and principles.[45]

In the face of foreign forces that seemed to have the power to totally overwhelm every bastion of Muslims' lives – economic, political, cultural and moral – the revivalist assertion that Islam was not just a religion but an entire way of life represented a logical stance of resistance. The irony is that the position entailed reshaping Islam into religious nationalism and incorporating a notion of backwardness that made sense only in the context of the modern confrontation with the West. Briefly, to save Islam, Muslims had to change it. This reflects the different historical circumstances surrounding the appearance of the Muslim Brothers and Wahhabism. It is common for writers on Muhammad ibn Abd al-Wahhab to assert that he sought a social renewal of Arabia, but that characterization is never given specific substance, unless one considers ritual correctness and moral purity to constitute such renewal. The problem with such generalizations is they encourage facile comparisons with modern revivalist movements, when in fact Najd's eighteenth-century reformer would have found key elements in Hasan al-Banna's writings utterly alien.

Revivalist Trends in South Asia

British administrators and observers of Muslim revivalist trends in nineteenth-century India believed that they represented manifestations of Wahhabi influence. This perception resulted in an exaggerated impression of the Arabian mission's influence that has coloured writing on South Asian revivalism to the present day. Most historians trace its roots to the teachings of Shah Waliullah (1703–1762), a scholar at the Mughal Empire's capital of Delhi. His intellectual output would shape much of India's Islamic discourse for over a century.[46] A subtle and complex thinker, Shah Waliullah strove to lay the foundations for the unity of India's Muslims, who were divided between Sunni and Shiite, adherents of different Sunni legal schools and followers of various Sufi doctrines. His son Shah Abdulaziz perpetuated his legacy into the nineteenth century. In his lifetime (d. 1824), Britain's East India Company made huge strides in bringing large swaths of the subcontinent under its control.[47] He instructed his followers to cooperate with the British, but one of his pupils, Sayyid Ahmad Barelwi (1786–1831), took a militant turn and advocated jihad against the infidel British and Sikhs.[48] He also parted from Shah Waliullah's tradition in adopting a stricter, more exclusive view of monotheism that led British observers to posit a Wahhabi influence acquired on his 1821 pilgrimage to Mecca. Two details in Barelwi's life weaken the suggestion of Wahhabi influence. First, Sayyid Ahmad expressed his doctrinal views before his journey to Arabia. Second, while he agreed with the Wahhabis that Sufi ceremonies frequently consisted of illegitimate innovations, he did not condemn Sufism altogether. Nevertheless, the possibility of Wahhabi influence on him is still an open question.[49] At any rate, a definitely closer Indian analogue to Wahhabism appeared three decades after Sayyid Ahmad was killed in the course of his jihad against non-Muslim powers.

In the history of nineteenth-century India, the pivotal event was the 1857 Revolt, also called the Sepoy Mutiny, when Muslim princes, peasants and townsmen attempted to eliminate British power and influence throughout North India. The outcome was utter defeat for

Indian Muslims, the final destruction of the once mighty Mughal dynasty and the imposition of direct British imperial rule, known as the Raj. Muslims reacted to the loss of political power in several ways. Some attempted to accommodate British rule by espousing a modernist interpretation of Islam and establishing a college that would prepare Muslim youth for participation in the imperial system.[50] Others focused on reviving the community of believers through an educational campaign to purify religious practice. That tendency emerged in a town north of Delhi called Deoband and it is therefore known as the Deobandi movement. While they shared the Wahhabis' dedication to ritual correctness, their scrupulous adherence to the Hanafi legal school clearly set them apart from the Arabian Hanbalis.[51]

The first documented contact between the Wahhabi mission and an Indian revivalist movement relates to the *Ahl-i Hadith* (the 'Hadith Folk'), a name coined by its foremost religious teacher and a renowned scholar of Hadith, Nazir Husayn, in 1864.[52] He was famous for emphasizing the primacy of Prophetic traditions as the source for Islamic law. Like other purification movements, the Ahl-i Hadith strove to eliminate such religious practices as visits to Sufi shrines and intercessionary prayers, which it considered illegitimate innovations. Ahl-i Hadith scholars and Wahhabis agreed that Sufis and Shiites were not true believers. The movement also shared with the Wahhabis the desire to revive the teachings of Ibn Taymiyya and a tendency to express intolerance toward other Muslims (Ahl-i Hadith preachers compared Delhi's Muslims to idolaters).[53] On the other hand, its scholars insisted that to arrive at a correct understanding of Islamic law it was necessary to rely solely on the Qur'an and the Sunna, so they insisted on disregarding the four Sunni law schools.[54] The Wahhabis, of course, followed the Hanbali school and accepted the other Sunni schools as valid. This rejection of the legal schools did not interfere with the development of friendly ties with Wahhabi ulama but it did result in an intense controversy between the Ahl-i Hadith and the staunchly Hanafi Deobandis.[55]

In the independent Muslim principality of Bhopal, the Ahl-i Hadith enjoyed the patronage of Siddiq Hasan Khan (d. 1890). His ancestors belonged to the old Muslim elite surrounding Muslim princes and then fell on hard times with the imposition of direct British rule in 1857. Siddiq Hasan Khan frequented the lesson circle of a prominent Delhi sheikh before moving on to the court at Bhopal, where he

managed to marry his way into the ruling elite, first through a match
to the chief minister's daughter and then to the widowed princess
(known as the Begum) herself. With the resources of a principality at
his disposal, Siddiq Hasan Khan appointed Ahl-i Hadith scholars to
positions in religious institutions and subsidized the publication of
the group's favourite classical treatises.[56]

Around the same time that revivalists in the Arab East were
reappraising Wahhabism, a trickle of Najdi religious scholars were
making their way to India, fleeing the unsettled conditions of the late
second Saudi amirate to enjoy Siddiq Hasan Khan's hospitality at the
Bhopal court in Hyderabad. The compatibility of Ahl-i Hadith views
with Wahhabism became known through contacts between Indian
and Najdi Muslims in Mecca. The Wahhabi sheikh Hamad ibn Atiq
initiated a correspondence with Siddiq Hasan Khan. In one letter,
Ibn Atiq complimented him for his exegesis of the Qur'an, which
he reported receiving in 1880. The letter offers a glimpse into the
scarcity of classical religious works in the Wahhabi realm. Ibn Atiq
lamented that Najdis had very few books and requested that Hasan
Khan send copies of three classical works through a Najdi resident
of Mecca, Ahmad ibn Isa.[57] About a year after this correspondence,
Sheikh Hamad's eldest son, Sa'd, travelled to India and spent nearly
nine years there, mostly in Bhopal but also briefly with the Ahl-i
Hadith circle of Nazir Husayn in Delhi. Another son went to Bhopal
a few years later.[58] The Indian connection also attracted a member
of Al al-Sheikh, Ishaq ibn Abd al-Rahman.[59] When the Rashidis
conquered Riyadh in 1891, he travelled to India, where he attend
Nazir Husayn's lessons and then went to Bhopal to study with Ahl-i
Hadith scholars.[60] The Wahhabis were not the only Arab revivalists
interested in the Ahl-i Hadith movement. The Baghdad scholar Khayr
al-Din al-Alusi came across Hasan Khan's exegesis of the Qur'an
during a visit to Cairo in 1878. Their common interest Ibn Taymiyya
resulted in a correspondence and Hasan Khan's inclusion in Arab
revivalists' short list of important religious reformers.[61]

Wahhabism and the Revivalist Movements
in the Twentieth Century

The emergence of Islamic revivalism in the late nineteenth century
paved the way for cooperation among Wahhabis, Muslim Brothers and
South Asian movements in the mid twentieth century when the entire
Muslim world was swept by a wave of western cultural influence.

Alien norms, values and habits of consumption and leisure threatened to erase cherished customs. The Muslim Brothers reflected the mood of cultural defensiveness and developed the model of a grassroots movement to push back against the West. During the last years of British imperial rule in India, a similar programme for stemming Islam's retreat was formulated by Abu Ala Mawdudi. His writings found a sympathetic response among Egyptian Muslim Brothers, especially Sayyid Qutb, during a period of persecution at the hands of the Nasser regime. The ideas of Mawdudi and Qutb reshaped modern revivalist tendencies throughout the Muslim world, including Saudi Arabia, where they subtly challenged Wahhabism's hegemony.

Born in 1903, Mawdudi grew up in the shadow of British imperial power, as had Hasan al-Banna in Egypt. When Mawdudi scanned India's political landscape in the late 1930s, the two major forces were the Hindu-dominated Indian National Congress and the Muslim League. The former had the backing of Deobandi ulama, but Mawdudi viewed the Congress's platform of Indian nationalism for adherents of all religions as a phoney slogan to cover its Hindu essence. He held a dim view of the Muslim League as well, finding its secular leadership ill-suited to establish a homeland for Muslims. Consequently, Mawdudi created his own political party, the Jamaati Islami, in 1941.[62] The party's achievements in Pakistani elections have been modest compared to the impact of its creator's voluminous writings, which set forth a vision of a complete Islamic social, political, economic and cultural system.

Mawdudi held a standard Muslim view of history as a struggle between belief and unbelief. His assertion that traditional Islam fell into the category of unbelief marked a point of agreement with Wahhabism. But his writings bear little trace of concern for the finer points of theology and worship practices that preoccupied the Najdi movement. True, he wished to see the elimination of the usual assortment of illegitimate innovations in Sufi ceremonies, but he did not consider Sufism in itself such an innovation.[63] Mawdudi's primary objective was to demonstrate that Islam represented a distinctive set of principles rooted in eternal, divine truth as opposed to democracy, capitalism and socialism, which he deemed western ideologies and as such, modern manifestations of unbelief. His originality as a revivalist thinker lay in setting forth a detailed plan for the Islamic state in which God is sovereign. The essential purpose of such a state is to apply shari'a. Mawdudi's blueprint for the Islamic state

included a constitution and a government consisting of three branches
– legislative, executive and judicial – that would exert checks and
balances on each other. The novelty of such a plan in Islamic political
thought is obvious and it bears no relation to any notion ever espoused
by a Wahhabi sheikh. Establishing the Islamic state required a long
preliminary campaign to reconvert society to Islam. Otherwise, the
state would have to coerce citizens to comply with shari'a and that
would complicate the project. So instead of a sudden, violent seizure
of power, Mawdudi sought gradual conversion of citizens through
education and persuasion. Over time, true believers would infiltrate
and take over public institutions to put them at the service of the
task of Islamizing society (a key demand of Saudi Islamists in the
1990s). Once there was an Islamic state of true believers as citizens,
compliance with shari'a duties and values would come naturally to
all and there would be no need for harsh hudud punishments like
severing the hand of a thief. Again, this vision of a Muslim Utopia is
alien to Wahhabi doctrine.[64]

Notwithstanding differences between Mawdudi's thought and
Wahhabism, their common dedication to combating western influence
provided a foundation for friendly relations. In 1949, an Indian sheikh
named Mas'ud Alam Nadvi visited the Wahhabi leader Muhammad
ibn Ibrahim Al al-Sheikh in Riyadh. The host queried his guest about
the fortunes of the Ahl-i Hadith movement, perhaps because the
Wahhabi sheikh's teachers included men who had studied with the
Indian movement's scholars.[65] During Nadvi's stay, he met Sheikh
Abd al-Aziz ibn Baz, then a young qadi posted to a provincial town.
Ibn Baz praised Mawdudi's book on Islamic political systems. Nadvi
asked how Ibn Baz knew about Mawdudi. The Wahhabi sheikh told
him that when Nadvi had presented a copy of Mawdudi's book to
Crown Prince Saud (when that occurred is not mentioned in the
source), the latter had passed it along to Sheikh Umar ibn Hasan Al
al-Sheikh to make additional copies. Ibn Baz obtained his copy from
Umar ibn Hasan.[66]

Wahhabi ulama were not the only ones interested in Mawdudi's
writings. They circulated among Egyptian Muslim Brothers as well
and sparked a novel turn in the thinking of some members, who
confronted an entirely new political situation after a group of army
officers overthrew the monarchy in July 1952. Although members
of the 'Free Officers' had cordial contacts with the Muslim Brothers
before the *coup d'état*, the new regime's authoritarianism and lack

of interest in a religious agenda put it on a collision course with the Brothers. In 1954, a factional struggle among the Free Officers resulted in Gamal Abdel Nasser's consolidation of power. That same year, he cracked down on the Muslim Brothers for allegedly plotting against the government. In the cells of Egypt's prisons, a leading Muslim Brother writer, Sayyid Qutb, steered revivalist ideology down a more militant path by coming to view contemporary Muslim society as, in fact, not Muslim at all but a new form of religious barbarism, jahiliyya.[67] The idea that jahiliyya was not a bygone era but a current condition connects Qutb to both Wahhabism and Mawdudi. There is no question that Mawdudi influenced Qutb: He had shepherded the Pakistani author's works to publication in Arabic translation. Qutb agreed that twentieth-century Muslims were like the first generation of believers in the Prophet Muhammad's divine message, a vanguard waging jihad to establish a divinely ordained social order based on the shari'a.[68] While Qutb and Mawdudi agreed on the jahili condition of modern times and on the duty to replace jahili political systems with an Islamic one, they had different ideas of how to proceed. Mawdudi advocated a gradual approach through education. Qutb called for a revolution led by a vanguard Islamic party to overthrow jahili governments and to then remake society according to Islamic principles.[69]

The stark proclamation that Muslims are living in a jahili condition and hence are idolaters, makes it natural to see affinities between the outlook of Sayyid Qutb and Muhammad ibn Abd al-Wahhab. Both men realized how startling their views had to appear to their contemporaries. In words that would apply to the Najdi reformer, Charles Tripp wrote of Qutb, 'Precisely because he believed that he had come across a truth which had not only eluded others, but ignorance of which continued to delude many, he saw it as imperative that he should alert people to the fact that not everything was as it seemed.'[70] Similarities and affinities aside, Qutb and Muhammad ibn Abd al-Wahhab lived in different historical circumstances and had different concerns and intellectual methods.[71] Whereas Sheikh Muhammad never had an inkling of European intrusion into Najd, Qutb lived through the era of European colonialism and saw Arab countries gain political independence. In the post-colonial era, however, they retained western (jahili) legal, cultural, economic and political forms instead of restoring Islam. In Qutb's eyes, Saudi Arabia was included in the roster of jahili countries because of its close relations with the USA.[72] Thus, while Qutb and Ibn Abd al-Wahhab both viewed their respective contemporaries as defenders of jahiliyya who had to be converted to Islam, their reasons for holding that view were quite different. For the Wahhabis, the key issue was correct understanding of monotheism and conforming to the requirements of that understanding, that is, refraining from any action or saying that suggested the worship of a being other than God. Qutb's writings say nothing about these matters. For Qutb, acting on the monotheist imperative meant establishing a social and political order in conformity with God's will as expressed through the shari'a. His programmatic approach, in line with Mawdudi's presentation of Islam as a total ideological system, had the same objective as Wahhabism, to convert jahili society to Islam. But Qutb diverged from Wahhabism in defining what conversion exactly entailed.

Furthermore, Qutb's method for interpreting the Qur'an and the Sunna was utterly unacceptable to Wahhabi ulama. His rejection of traditional scholastic reasoning for a personal, subjective, even intuitive, approach made him an original thinker and probably accounts for the popularity of his works. But some of the lessons he drew from the Qur'an and his theological views appalled the Wahhabi ulama. Therefore, leading Wahhabi scholars displayed a cool attitude toward Qutb's writings because they contained what they considered grave errors in essential doctrine and offensive characterizations of Muhammad's Companions. Perhaps the most alarming facet of Qutb's popularity among religious educated youth in the 1980s and 1990s was the praise lavished on him by young preachers. The pre-eminent Wahhabi sheikh of the early 1990s, Abd al-Aziz ibn Baz, publicly faulted Qutb for errors in his widely read commentary on the Qur'an. For instance, on a doctrinal point pertaining to God's unity, Qutb interpreted the Qur'anic verse that describes God sitting on a throne as a metaphor for God's hegemony over creation. The Wahhabis insisted on a literal interpretation and rejected anything else as a distortion of God's word. Ibn Baz also objected to Qutb's discussion of the first Muslim civil war in which Muawiya defeated Ali. According to Qutb, Muawiya prevailed by resorting to deception and bribery whereas Ali refused to sink to that level. Ibn Baz called this a repulsive slander against Muawiya, one of the Prophet Muhammad's Companions. Another terrible mistake in Qutb's writing, according to Ibn Baz, occurred in his commentary on the Qur'an. The Egyptian writer interpreted a passage about

Moses to suggest it meant that he represented an impulsive, hot-tempered leader; Ibn Baz considered this an unforgivable slight of a prophet. The Wahhabi sheikh lamented Qutb's influence on young people enamoured with his books because of his smooth style and ability to stir emotions. Whereas other sheikhs saw some merit in Qutb's works, Ibn Baz argued that they contained so many gross errors that they could easily lead astray those lacking deep training in religious sciences. In fact, several prominent Wahhabi sheikhs considered Qutb's errors to stem from a lack of formal training in those sciences. They underscored that he was a literary critic well-versed in contemporary studies but certainly not a religious scholar.[73]

Such circumspection about Qutb's method may account for the very few Saudi editions of his works in spite of their popularity throughout the Arab world since the 1970s. A study of Saudi religious publications in the decade 1979–1989 reveals a tendency to reproduce classical texts in Islamic sciences. Publications must pass screening by the Ministry of Information, so the range of published topics and authors reflects Wahhabi censorship. Signs of contemporary revivalism in the form of books by Sayyid Qutb or Mawdudi are minuscule: three books by Mawdudi and one apiece by Qutb and Hasan al-Banna. The single volume by Qutb was a collection of essays recording his impressions from a visit to the USA, not one of his more influential and radical works like *Milestones* or *In the Shade of the Qur'an*. This does not mean that books by these and other writers were not to be found in Saudi Arabia. Rather it demonstrates that the official Wahhabi establishment ensconced in the Ministry of Information did not promote their views.[74]

In spite of differences among Mawdudi's Jamaati Islami, the Muslim Brothers and Wahhabism, they shared a common enemy – western cultural influence – and given the ascendance of western power and wealth over the globe in the twentieth century, Muslims eager to defend customary ways have proved willing to combine forces even if they do not have identical motivations, tactics, or objectives. Prior to the early 1960s, these doctrinal cousins interacted via networks of personal contacts resembling those of ulama in previous centuries. Teachers and pupils, authors of revivalist tracts and their audience exchanged ideas and information in an essentially closed circuit of religious enthusiasts. Profound changes in Saudi Arabia's foreign and domestic political contexts, however, would prompt Riyadh to appropriate Islam as an instrument of policy. This entailed funnelling considerable financial and human resources to new organizations that built on and expanded ties between the Wahhabi mission and revivalist movements in other Muslim lands.[75]

Ever since the eighteenth century, Wahhabism contributed to Al Saud power through religious, educational and legal institutions. The risk of giving Wahhabism a role in foreign relations stemmed from its doctrine toward others. Ibn Saud's clash with the Ikhwan largely centred on the question of who would decide matters of war and peace with neighbouring powers. He and his successors handled foreign relations with regard to *raison d'état* and took little note of Wahhabi qualms that policy reflected mundane considerations rather than religious principles. Then, in the 1950s and 1960s, two dramatic shifts in Arab regional and Saudi domestic politics brought Islam to the fore as an element in the kingdom's international relations. The two shifts were, in regional politics, the polarization of Arab politics between revolutionary (republican, nationalist) regimes and conservative monarchies and, in the domestic realm, the assimilation of political ideologies sweeping nearby Arab lands.

In the first decade after the Second World War, Saudi Arabia formed part of an alignment with Syria and Egypt against the Hashemite monarchies in Iraq and Jordan. A central issue in regional politics was the ambition held by each Hashemite kingdom to draw Syria into its orbit. To block the augmentation of Hashemite influence, Saudi Arabia and Egypt bolstered the position of Syrian politicians determined to steer a neutral course. This pattern continued for several years after Egypt's July 1952 Free Officers revolution brought Gamal Abdel Nasser to power. As Nasser's prestige grew and his message of nationalist revolution gained a pan-Arab following, he naturally incurred the resentment of less popular Arab leaders, including Al Saud. Riyadh's rulers disapproved of Nasser's steps toward closer relations with the Soviet Union, whose atheist communist ideology made it a natural object of Wahhabi enmity. At the same time, the Ba'ath Party in Syria was gaining popularity with its slogan of unity, freedom and socialism. Nasser's defiance of the western powers when he nationalized the Suez Canal in 1956 and his decision to forge a union with Syria in 1958 made him a heroic figure throughout the Arab world.

The problem that Nasser posed for King Saud and then King Faysal was compounded by the growing significance of Arab regional dynamics for the kingdom's domestic politics. Segments of Saudi

Arabian society became attuned to Arab political trends dominated by the ideas and voices of Nasser and the Ba'ath. It seemed natural for Al Saud to have responded with an Islamic voice and for Wahhabism to become an instrument in the dynasty's struggle against Nasser and the Ba'ath. It was also natural for Saudi Arabia to develop a symbiotic relationship with the Muslim Brothers wherein the Wahhabi kingdom offered asylum to Brothers fleeing repression in Egypt and Syria while the Brothers served Riyadh's interest in combating Arab nationalist and secular influences. When this relationship developed in the early 1960s, nobody could possibly have predicted that the mixture of Wahhabism and Muslim Brother revivalism would turn against the Saudi monarchy, both inside and outside the kingdom.

In the 1940s and 1950s, the Muslim Brothers had sent envoys to Mecca during the pilgrimage to spread their views, win recruits and establish branches in other Arab countries. Their revivalist message did not exactly mesh with Wahhabi ideas, but their opposition to secular, socialist and communist forces put them on the same side of the Arab world's political and cultural divide. Thus, in the very early years of Egypt's nationalist Free Officer regime, shortly before Nasser had emerged as its leading figure, King Saud intervened on behalf of the Brothers to secure their leader's release from prison.[76] When Arab nationalist regimes harshly suppressed the Brothers and criticized pro-western conservative monarchies, like the Saudi one, a political layer was added to the religious affinity between the Egyptian revivalists and the Wahhabis.

The author of Saudi Arabia's Islamic policy was King Faysal, the royal with the most experience in foreign affairs. Since the 1920s, he had represented Al Saud to diplomats stationed in Hijaz and visited Arab countries as the king's envoy. Faysal developed the Islamic policy in 1962 in response to Nasser's adoption of socialism and intervention in Yemen's civil war.[77] The policy's formal birth took place at a May 1962 conference that the Saudis organized at Mecca to discuss ways to combat secularism and socialism. The conference resulted in the establishment of the World Muslim League, a religious organization that would fund education, publications and Islamic cultural centres. The Wahhabi leadership of the World Muslim League made it an instrument for exporting the Najdi doctrine. In South Asia, the League supported such groups as the Deobandis, Ahl-i Hadith and Jamaati Islami to combat Sufism and eliminate popular religious practices. The League also sent missionaries to West Africa, where it funded schools, distributed religious literature and gave scholarships to attend Saudi religious universities. These efforts bore fruit in Nigeria's Muslim northern region with the creation of a movement (the Izala Society) dedicated to wiping out ritual innovations. Essential texts for members of the Izala Society are Muhammad ibn Abd al-Wahhab's treatise on God's unity and commentaries by his grandsons.[78] In Ghana, it recruited sympathizers to diminish the influence of the popular Tijani Sufi order. The Wahhabi organization made similar efforts in Ivory Coast, Guinea and Mali.[79] In 1972, the Saudis created the World Assembly of Muslim Youth to warn the new generation against 'false' ideologies.[80] Except for the focus on young Muslims, its function of propagating Wahhabi views overlaps with the World Muslim League's. A notable aspect of the World Assembly of Muslim Youth is its publication list, which features Muslim Brother rather than classic Wahhabi works. The World Assembly of Muslim Youth figures as an important institution for distributing the works of Sayyid Qutb and another influential Muslim Brother author-martyr, Abd al-Qadir Awda.[81]

By the time of King Faysal's assassination in March 1975, he had put Saudi Arabia at the centre of a robust set of pan-Islamic institutions, contributed to a new consciousness of international Muslim political issues, ranging from Jerusalem to Pakistan's troubles with India over Kashmir to the suffering of South Africa's Muslims under the apartheid regime. In the early 1970s, his pan-Islamic efforts dovetailed with a conservative mood in Arab politics, epitomized by the successions in Egypt and Syria of Anwar Sadat and Hafiz al-Asad, respectively. Faysal had not merely succeeded in fending off Arab nationalist intrusions into the kingdom and deflecting external pressures from Cairo, Damascus and Baghdad; he had made Saudi Arabia a significant player in regional and international affairs. And he had achieved this even before the enormous windfall of wealth generated by the 1973–1974 increase in petroleum prices, which in turn opened new opportunities for projecting Saudi and Wahhabi influence abroad.

On the surface, it is odd that the Wahhabi mission should have improved its standing in the Muslim world at the same time that modern forces reshaped Muslim societies. True, most Muslims still viewed Wahhabi doctrine on monotheism as excessively rigid. True, the Wahhabis and their revivalist cousins differed in substantial ways. Nevertheless, five basic changes in local, regional and global circumstances account for the augmentation of Wahhabism's influence outside Saudi Arabia. First, in the late nineteenth century, Ottoman religious culture changed as revivalists and modernists challenged ulama and Sufi loyalists, paving the way for a redefinition of religious culture in the post-war Arab East. Second, Wahhabism's earliest and most effective doctrinal resistance had emanated from Ottoman ulama loyal to Istanbul. The destruction of the Ottoman Empire at the end of the First World War eliminated that adversary. Third, during the interwar period, former ulama loyalists and some Sufis tended to ally with revivalists in the Arab East. Other Sufis would continue a hostile campaign against Wahhabism, but they had lost their political patronage with the demise of the Ottoman Empire. Fourth, western cultural pressure evoked a defensive reaction that disposed revivalists and Wahhabis to overlook disagreements that had previously obstructed cooperation in other circumstances. This defensiveness found expression in a streak of xenophobia common to Wahhabism and Islamic revivalism. In the nineteenth century, major figures in Al al-Sheikh had warned against contact with outsiders and stood alert to the dangers posed by infiltrators like the Baghdadi Sufi Da'ud ibn Jirjis. In the twentieth century, the xenophobic mood has focused on the West as the force posing the greatest danger to Islam. Fifth, Al Saud's vulnerability to Arab nationalist tendencies at home and abroad led to an alliance with the Muslim Brothers in an Islamic foreign policy campaign to fight secular ideologies and to propagate the mission in defence of the monarchy. That policy would return to haunt Al Saud, beginning in 1979. By opening the kingdom to Muslim Brother revivalism, the policy would also diminish the legitimacy and prestige of the Wahhabi establishment, compromised by its identification with the rulers of Riyadh.

Chapter Six

Challenges to
Wahhabi Hegemony

In the 1960s and 1970s, Wahhabism reached new heights of influence. As one observer has noted, Wahhabi ulama became less combative toward the rest of the Muslim world:

> Having given up violence against fellow Muslims early this century, Wahhabi views have become much more acceptable internationally, partly because the doctrine gained converts beyond the peninsula and partly because it has served well as a platform to confront the challenge of the West.[1]

More specifically, cooperation with Middle Eastern and South Asian revivalist movements punctured the historic barrier between Wahhabi Najd and the Muslim world while King Faysal's Islamic foreign policy breathed life into efforts to proselytize. The influx of oil wealth amplified those efforts, funding mosques, Islamic centres, publications and staff dedicated to spreading Wahhabi doctrine. Within Saudi Arabia, official religious institutions under Wahhabi control multiplied at the same time that ulama maintained their hold on religious law courts, presided over the creation of Islamic universities and ensured that children in public schools received a heavy dose of religious instruction. The underpinnings of Wahhabi influence, however, were shaky in two respects. First, its dependence on the Saudi government disposed leading Wahhabi clerics to support its policies. As political discontent in the kingdom intensified, the Wahhabi establishment found itself in the awkward position of defending an unpopular dynasty. Second, the relationship with Muslim revivalist movements was based on sharing a common adversary (western influence), not a common doctrine. As long as Riyadh's policies suited the revivalists, doctrinal differences could be glossed over. In the 1990s, however, the Saudi/Wahhabi-revivalist alliance unravelled because of Riyadh's decision to solicit United States military intervention against Iraq. The same issue divided the kingdom's religious camp between traditional Wahhabis loyal to the monarchy and recruits to the revivalist outlook. Both inside and outside of Wahhabism's homeland, its alliance with Al Saud, hitherto a source of power, diminished its credibility.

The gradual erosion of Wahhabi credibility has been punctuated by three major crises that struck Saudi Arabia between 1979 and 2001. First, in November 1979, millenarian zealots seized and briefly held Mecca's Grand Mosque in a bid to overthrow Al Saud. Second, in 1990–1991, the kingdom confronted its most serious external threat of the twentieth century when Iraq invaded Kuwait. The rulers' decision to invite United States military forces to defend the country triggered a period of political unrest that revealed the extent to which Islamic revivalist ideas had penetrated the country and gained popularity with young people. Third, al-Qaeda's 11 September 2001 attacks on the USA unleashed unprecedented strains in relations between Riyadh and Washington and nudged Al Saud to relax constraints on public discussion of the kingdom's affairs. Any delusions harboured by Saudis that al-Qaeda was Washington's problem and not theirs exploded in a wave of suicide bombings and attacks on foreigners in the kingdom in 2003 and 2004. The religious dimension of each crisis stemmed not so much from Wahhabism as it did from modern Islamic revivalism's advances in the kingdom. In each case, the Wahhabi establishment rallied to support the dynasty's efforts to suppress religious dissent.

Having opened the kingdom's doors to broader Islamic revivalist trends, Saudi Arabia was not immune to further developments in those trends, most notably the rise of a militant stream commonly referred to as 'jihadist', or 'jihadi salafi'.[2] The ideological inspiration for this offshoot of Islamic revivalism came from Egypt in the 1960s and 1970s in the writings Sayyid Qutb and Abd al-Salam al-Faraj. The jihadist stream gathered momentum in the Afghan war during the 1980s, when it found a new champion in Abd Allah Azzam, a Muslim Brother Palestinian propagandist for the Afghan cause. The jihadist movement assumed a transnational character after the Afghan war as veteran mujahidin returned to their home countries and dispersed to other sites of Muslim insurgency such as Algeria, Bosnia and Chechnya. It was from the transnational jihadist stream, not from the Wahhabi religious establishment, that Osama bin Laden and al-Qaeda emerged to confront the Saudi dynasty and its American allies.

Development Programmes and Dynastic Legitimacy

The rise of Islamic revivalism, with its emphatic positions on social justice and economic development, is related to Saudi Arabia's efforts to resolve an intractable knot of political, economic, social and cultural crises. In that respect, the kingdom is typical of trends in the Middle East during the 1970s and 1980s when governments reduced spending on health, education, employment and subsidies for food items. Those cuts signified a step away from an implicit social contract between governments and citizens that had evolved since the late nineteenth century.[3] In Saudi Arabia, beginning in the 1920s, King Abd al-Aziz ibn Saud distributed gifts and subsidies to tribesmen and Ikhwan. Petroleum royalties made it possible to turn selective patronage into a general programme of social welfare. The 1962 Ten Point Programme expressed an official commitment to economic development and to improving the standard of living. Point Seven declared:

> The government feels that one of its most important duties is to raise the nation's social level. The state has provided free medical and educational benefits. Recently the Social Security Regulations were promulgated for the aged, the disabled, orphans and women who have no means of support. The state will present to the working class a law protecting them from unemployment.

An ambitious vision for advancing the kingdom's infrastructure is contained in Point Nine:

> Measures for reform that will continuously spur economic activity will continue to be adopted. Among these are: an

extensive road program to link all parts and cities of the
Kingdom; the study of water resources for agricultural and
drinking purposes; the construction of dams for the preservation of rain waters and the creation of pasture lands; help
to heavy and light industries. Aside from State allocations for
these projects, all additional amounts the government will
receive from Aramco in satisfaction of the rights it claims
from that company for previous years will be put into a
special production budget for development. The creation of
an industrial bank and an agricultural bank is now in its final
stages and the General Petroleum and Mineral Agency will
soon come into being. These, together with other private
agencies, will take part in this development plan.[4]

In the 1960s, the resources for realizing the Programme's vision
were fairly modest. Naturally, the main source for government
budgets was income from petroleum sales. Between 1959 and 1970,
revenues grew from $655 million to $1.2 billion. Compared to the
financial austerity of the 1930s and 1940s, those were certainly robust
figures, but the dramatic rise in oil prices during the mid 1970s would
dwarf them. In 1973, revenues amounted to $4.34 billion. In just one
year, they quintupled to $22.5 billion; they peaked in 1981 at $108
billion.[5] With such vast sums pouring in, the government embarked
on a massive development programme to expand the communications
and transportation infrastructure, industry, education and health.
Social welfare spending ballooned as well. In the late 1970s, the
government began to pay housing allowances and subsidies to
businesses; university graduates were guaranteed positions in
government agencies.[6] By turning the state into the engine for
economic development, Saudi Arabia was part of the regional trend
that led citizens to expect the government to provide for their needs.
Then, in the 1980s, weak demand for oil and lower prices drove
down revenues and squeezed budgets. Revenues fell to $70 billion
in 1982, $37 billion in 1983 and hovered around $16 to $18 billion
in 1986–1988.[7] In the face of recession the government maintained
its commitment to social welfare policies for fear of stoking unrest.[8]
Nevertheless, government resources were unable to shield ordinary
Saudis from the recession's impact on the private sector. And if the
rulers took credit for the bounty of the 1970s, they were sure to get
the blame for the hard times that followed.

The influx of oil wealth transformed the social landscape, in part because the kingdom lacked the manpower to complete its ambitious projects. Unskilled Saudis refused jobs that paid low wages for exhausting work. Few Saudis possessed the technical expertise to supervise and manage construction projects. Consequently, foreigners flocked to the kingdom to build roads, expand ports, erect buildings and staff the growing network of schools, clinics and hospitals. In 1971, the kingdom's foreign labour force numbered around 300,000.[9] A few years later, the kingdom's resident population of nearly six million included 1.5 million foreign workers.[10] By 1979, the number of foreign workers had increased to around 2.5 million, as compared to a total Saudi population of 5.5 million.[11] It is difficult to fathom the cultural impact of this influx when we recall the powerful impulse in Wahhabi doctrine to shun infidels.

Aggravating the situation was the disorganized, indeed chaotic, atmosphere surrounding the development effort. A huge backlog of freight accumulated at Saudi ports. Airports became scenes of frequent quarrels as passengers scrambled for seats on flights. Traffic in cities became choked with vehicles as road building lagged behind the pace of automobile purchases. The arrival of expatriate workers drove up housing prices.[12] The pressure of so much petroleum revenue chasing the goals of a national development plan generated an inflationary spiral that cut into Saudis' purchasing power.[13] Contributing to the climate of disruption in the 1970s was the new face of expatriate labour. The kingdom had previously depended on Arab workers from Yemen for unskilled labour and from Egypt, Lebanon, Syria and Palestine for technical tasks. The 1970s, however, brought in thousands of workers from Pakistan, India, Turkey, the Philippines, Thailand and South Korea.[14] The proportion of Saudi nationals in cities dropped. From their perspective, the urban streetscape assumed an alien multinational aspect, transformed by the mushrooming of shopping malls, supermarkets, luxury hotels and restaurants.[15] As in other historical episodes of economic boom, the later 1970s witnessed a crime wave and rising incidences of divorce and alcohol and drug use along with corresponding growth in police force and prisons.[16]

Rising social tensions were aggravated by a culture conflict over the proper role of women. King Faysal had deftly handled the issue of girls' education in the 1960s by placing it under the authority of a special government body headed by a Wahhabi sheikh. By the 1980s, however, the graduates of those schools were pursuing careers in

5. (FACING PAGE, TOP) UNAYZA, 1935. J.W. "SOAK" HOOVER, *SAUDI ARAMCO WORLD*/PADIA.
6. (FACING PAGE, BOTTOM) UNAYZA, 1970S. TOR EIGELAND, *SAUDI ARAMCO WORLD*/PADIA.
7. (ABOVE) RIYADH MARKETPLACE, 1950. T.F. WALTERS, *SAUDI ARAMCO WORLD*/PADIA.
8. (LEFT) RIYADH, *C*.1980. S.M. AMIN, *SAUDI ARAMCO WORLD*/PADIA.

9. (TOP) TRADITIONAL PRODUCE STAND, AL-HASA, 1980. TOR EIGELAND, *SAUDI ARAMCO WORLD*/PADIA.

10. (ABOVE) SUPERMARKET PRODUCE SECTION, 1981. BURNETT H. MOODY, *SAUDI ARAMCO WORLD*/PADIA.

medicine, education, business and mass media. Liberals, men and women alike, began to broach sensitive topics in newspapers and magazines. For example, Islamic law permits a man to have up to four wives and in the event of divorce, a man has custodial rights over school-age children. Reformers wondered if those provisions should not be modified. Conservatives expressed outraged at any suggestion of altering divinely ordained rules and countered by formalizing custom as legislation through regulations forbidding a woman from spending a night in a hotel without a male guardian.[17]

In the 1980s, falling oil prices and high population growth rates cramped Riyadh's capacity to sustain welfare programmes. As in other Middle Eastern countries, the withdrawal of the government from its share of the social contract triggered a political reaction rooted in citizens' sense of moral grievance at betrayal by the rulers, who in the meantime apparently felt none of the pain. Princes continued to erect lavish palaces from absurdly excessive 'allowances'. Cultural tensions arising from the large expatriate presence, the rapid transformation of city spaces and women entering the modern workplace poured salt on economic and moral wounds. In Saudi Arabia and the rest of the region, popular political protest against this combination of tendencies took the form of Islamic dissent.[18]

The 1979 Crisis

Iran's pro-American monarchy fell to anti-western religious leaders in February 1979. Nine months later, on 4 November, Iranian revolutionary militants stormed the American embassy in Tehran and took diplomats hostage, fixing the world's attention on the ensuing international crisis. Then, at dawn on the first day of the fifteenth century in the Islamic calendar (20 November 1979), a band of millenarians seized control of Mecca's Grand Mosque, seeking to overthrow the Saudi dynasty. It appeared that the other pillar of western interests in the oil-rich Persian Gulf was in jeopardy. On 5 December, however, security forces regained control of the shrine and suppressed the uprising. A perceptive observer of the Saudi scene dubbed the incident 'the return of the Ikhwan', alluding to the movement whose abortive revolt occurred fifty years earlier.[19] It is important to emphasize, however, that the 1979 rebels were not literally a reincarnation of the Ikhwan and to underscore three distinctive features of the former: They were millenarians, they rejected the monarchy and they condemned the Wahhabi ulama.

The millenarian leader was Juhayman al-Utaybi, born around 1940 in an Ikhwan settlement in al-Qasim, not far from one of the old eminent hijras.[20] Like quite a few other young men of Ikhwan background, he served for a time in the National Guard. In the early 1970s, he attended religion courses at the Islamic University of Medina, a haven for Muslim Brother refugees from Egypt. Among his teachers at the university was Sheikh Abd al-Aziz ibn Baz.[21] Juhayman first attracted official suspicion in 1976 for issuing a pamphlet that condemned Al Saud. Since the 1950s, anti-monarchy groups had come and gone, so, in that respect, Juhayman fitted a familiar pattern. But he broke new ground when he blamed the Wahhabi religious establishment for twisting Islam to prop up an illegitimate regime. Two years later, security forces arrested him and about 100 others for interrogation. During their detention, Ibn Baz was summoned to meet with them. After ascertaining their views, he apparently recommended that they be released and the authorities set them free.[22] It is not clear if Ibn Baz misunderstood what sort of threat his former pupil posed to the government or if Juhayman's thinking evolved between his 1978 confinement and the 1979 uprising.

Exactly how or under whose influence Juhayman worked out his views is unclear. His writings blend nineteenth-century Wahhabism's deep revulsion at any contact with infidels, the Ikhwan's zeal for jihad and a strain of millenarianism altogether foreign to Wahhabism. There are also the traces of Muslim Brother ideas. In a statement broadcast at the Grand Mosque, the group called for eliminating western cultural influences and severing ties to western governments that exploit the country. It declared that Al Saud were not fit to rule because they countenanced foreign exploitation. The ulama were culpable for failing to protest policies that betrayed Islam. Therefore, it was necessary to overthrow the Saudi monarchy and replace it with a true Islamic regime that would hold the fallen dynasty accountable for the wealth it plundered. The country had to end oil exports to the USA until it reversed its hostility toward Islam. Finally, the statement called for the expulsion of foreign experts from the country.[23]

Wahhabism had always maintained that Muslims owe obedience to a ruler, no matter how that ruler might have gained power, as long as he did not command a subject to violate basic commands and prohibitions of Islamic law.[24] Juhayman rejected that line of thought. Instead, he maintained that rulers fall into two categories: those who follow the Qur'an and the Sunna and those who rule according to whim. Echoing Sayyid Qutb and Mawdudi, he asserted that in his time there were no true Islamic governments and that the Muslim world lived under regimes that used foreign systems, occasionally making a show of respect for Islam when it suited their purposes. In the specific case of Saudi Arabia, he argued that its illegitimate regime began when Abd al-Aziz ibn Saud refused to launch a jihad against the Ottomans and undermined the position of Sharif Husayn of Mecca.[25]

Wahhabi doctrine maintained that only the ruler may decree a jihad. As for why no Saudi ruler had declared a jihad in many years, recent Wahhabi leaders offered different reasons: Muslim countries needed time to coordinate their resources; Saudi Arabia alone lacked the means to carry it out.[26] Juhayman considered Al Saud's essential faults to be the suspension of jihad, 'the alliance with Christians and... the pursuit of worldly things'.[27] It is on these points that Ibn Saud's 'betrayal' of the Ikhwan resonates most clearly. According to Juhayman, Ibn Saud:

> called upon the Ikhwan, may God rest their souls, to support him on the basis of the Holy Qur'an and the tenets of the religion as the Imam of all Muslims. They fought for him, spread the faith and opened [conquered] the country for him. But as soon as his power was established and as soon as he secured what he wanted, he allied himself with the Christians and stopped the jihad outside the Peninsula.[28]

From the Saudi case, Juhayman drew a more general conclusion about monarchy as an illegitimate political regime:

> In a hereditary rulership, the Caliph is not chosen by the Muslims, but it is he who imposes himself on them. They are obliged to offer him their bay'a. If they are unhappy with him, he is not deposed. No! Because the whole thing is compulsory.[29]

The rejection of monarchy, characteristic of the Muslim Brothers' ideology,[30] was not the only radical facet in Juhayman's outlook, for he also blamed the Wahhabi ulama for lending support to the dynasty and concluded that they were opportunistic hypocrites. He used the term 'state Islam' for a situation where Muslims accept the rule of an infidel state and the ulama offer loyalty to corrupt rulers in exchange for honours and riches.[31] While they possess knowledge of the Qur'an and Sunna as well as advanced religious sciences, their knowledge was useless when they countenanced a government that routinely violated basic religious principles. Juhayman's attitude toward Abd al-Aziz ibn Baz was particularly telling in this regard. He apparently sent his first small treatise to Ibn Baz, who replied that while it had some merit, it was not proper to single out the Saudi regime for criticism. This led Juhayman to conclude that even though the senior cleric undoubtedly possessed profound learning, believers could not trust him because he made excuses for Al Saud's squandering the country's wealth on palaces rather than building mosques.[32]

As might be expected, a strict puritanical streak runs through Juhayman's writings on satanic innovations. Thus, he expressed outrage that an Islamic university would require a student to produce copies of his photograph in order to enrol even though, to his mind, Islam forbids reproducing the human image. Likewise, he objected to the appearance of the king's likeness on the country's currency.[33] As for the availability of alcohol, the broadcast of shameful images on television and the inclusion of women in the workplace, Juhayman considered them all instances of Al Saud's indifference to upholding Islamic principles.[34]

Much of Juhayman's thinking can be traced to nostalgia for the Ikhwan and sympathy for Muslim Brother positions. The unique aspect of his thought was its millenarianism. A doctrine of the Hidden Imam's return as the *mahdi* (the rightly guided one) is central to the denomination of Shiism prevalent in Iran and Iraq (and among Saudi Arabia's Shiites as well), but it has been rarer in Sunni history.[35] Nonetheless, mahdist movements did arise among Sunnis in the course of history. The millennial figure's advent would spell the end of tyrannical rule and inaugurate a chain of events leading to the reign of God on earth. Exactly how Juhayman became seized of the idea is unknown, but he evidently came to believe that one of his followers bearing the name of the expected mahdi, Muhammad ibn Abd Allah al-Qahtani, was indeed the millennial figure.[36] In a treatise entitled 'Call of the Ikhwan', Juhayman collected hadiths about the coming of the mahdi. The hadiths report various details about the mahdi's physical appearance, his name (the same as that of the Prophet, Muhammad ibn Abd Allah) and circumstances surrounding his coming:

The Mahdi will appear. His group will take refuge in the *Haram* [Mecca's Grand Mosque]. An army which is not Jewish, nor Christian, nor communist, but rather Muslim will attack them in the Haram. But Allah will order the earth to open and to engulf it, saving, by so doing, the Mahdi and his followers.[37]

While the insurrection came with such surprising suddenness that it jolted the Saudi rulers and shocked the broader Muslim public, its course did not follow the plot scripted by ancient traditions. In the days before the Muslim New Year, members of Juhayman's group trickled into Mecca and blended into the throngs as the annual pilgrimage wound down. After taking control of the mosque, Juhayman and his band hunkered down, taking advantage of the Haram's intricate network of subterranean passages and chambers as well as Al Saud's reluctance to order a full scale assault when hundreds of innocent Muslims were caught in the middle. Before resorting to violent measures against the rebels, King Khalid sought backing from the official religious establishment. It was practically a political necessity to obtain that backing and he requested a fatwa from the Board of Senior Ulama, headed by Abd al-Aziz ibn Baz, on the proper course of action.

The question before the ulama was formulated in terms favourable to the government.[38] How should the authorities respond to the violent takeover of the Haram and to Juhayman's call for a pledge of allegiance to the Mahdi? In the fatwa announced on 24 November, the ulama did not consider Juhayman's accusations against Al Saud and the official religious institution as justification for his actions; instead, they noted that Juhayman's group shot and killed government personnel outside the mosque. The fatwa declared that the militants should surrender and submit to the judgment of Islamic law. If they refused, then the authorities could use any means to overwhelm and kill them. The edict cited two proof-texts that would permit the government to resort to violence in suppressing the militants. First, the Qur'an 2:19:

And fight them not at the Holy Mosque unless they first fight you there, but if they fight you, slay them. Such is the reward of the disbelievers.

It seems that the verse applied to the present situation because Juhayman's group had initiated an attack and thereby fulfilled the condition for a counterattack. The final phrase specified the disbelievers as deserving such treatment and nowhere does the fatwa explicitly explain how Juhayman's group fell into that category. The commentary on it asserts that it applies to anybody who acts in a similar fashion. The second proof-text is a Hadith, 'He who comes to you while you are unanimous in your opinions and wants to divide you and disperse you, strike off his neck.'[39]

The senior ulama attached a declaration to the fatwa defining the incident as the work of an 'oppressive and aggressive clique which encroached on the sacredness of the Holy Place of God...shed prohibited blood in the prohibited month on the sacred land within the honoured Ka'ba'. They stated that to terrify Muslims in that place was a violation of the Qur'an and the Sunna. Because prayers at the Haram were suspended during the siege, the aggressors were as those described in the Qur'an, 'And who is more unjust than those who forbid that God's name be celebrated in places of worship, whose goal is in fact to ruin them?'[40]

With the Wahhabi religious leadership's approval, the government ordered security forces to retake the sacred shrine. In the tunnels and storerooms beneath the Haram, Juhayman and his followers held out for nearly a week until they finally surrendered in the early morning hours of 5 December.[41] Security forces captured 170 men, including Juhayman, but not the mahdi, who died in the fighting. Official Saudi figures put the casualty toll at 26 pilgrims, 127 government forces and 177 rebels. Juhayman and 62 others in his group were sentenced to execution; most of the condemned, 41, were Saudis; the next largest group consisted of ten Egyptians, followed by handfuls from Yemen, Kuwait, Sudan and Iraq.[42] To issue sentences for the rebels, the government obtained a decree from the Board of Senior Ulama. They found the defendants guilty of seven crimes: violating the Haram's sanctity; violating the sanctity of the month of Muharram; killing fellow Muslims; disobeying legitimate authorities; suspending prayer at Haram; erring in identifying the Mahdi; and exploiting the innocent for criminal acts.[43] In both this decree and the previous fatwa permitting the government to use armed force in the Haram, the Wahhabi establishment unwittingly and quite ironically vindicated Juhayman's accusation that it was a servant of dynastic power.

In the uprising's immediate aftermath, the government shuffled a number of senior officials, including the governor of Mecca, the director of public security and some high-ranking generals.[44] On the more essential matter of the country's drift in a secular direction, observers maintain that even before the Mecca incident, authorities had begun to institute stricter regulations on public morality like gender segregation and a ban on women studying outside the country.[45] That tendency deepened after Juhayman's revolt. Earlier, fairly timid steps to allow women to appear on television were reversed. Funding for religious universities increased to expand teaching staffs and student enrolments and that in turn fuelled demand for jobs for their graduates in religious institutions. The government also placated conservative religious forces by allowing the mutawwi'a to more rigorously enforce a strict regime of compliance with Wahhabi norms, enforcing the closure of offices, stores and restaurants during prayer time.[46] In 1981, Ibn Baz issued a decree forbidding women to drive with foreign chauffeurs.[47] But could such piecemeal measures quench the desire to enact the religious imperatives embedded in the Wahhabi reading of Islam's basic texts? Could the monarchy and the religious establishment control the pace and substance of change in habits of consumption and leisure when revenues from oil production unhinged the very real material restraints that had previously made austerity a destiny and not a choice? As long as the rulers tugged the country along an even path of incremental change, the contradiction between religious ideals and worldly interests could be managed. Once unimaginable wealth accelerated the pace of change, it was as though the entire country had, in an instant, turned down a steep, twisting road to an uncertain destination.

The situation in Mecca still hung in the balance when large demonstrations erupted among the kingdom's Shiite population in the oil-rich Eastern Province (al-Hasa). While the petroleum industry had opened new job opportunities for the region's Shiites, few rose to responsible positions in Aramco. Their exclusion was aggravated by anti-Shiite prejudice in hiring for government and civil service positions, even though these rapidly expanded in the 1960s and 1970s.[48] Of course, discrimination against Shiites reflected the Wahhabi view of them as idolaters who must convert to Islam.[49] Therefore, the public school system teaches Wahhabi doctrine and omits any reference to Shiite religious belief or events of importance to Shiism in early Islamic history. Traditional Shiite schools in al-Hasa closed in

11. Boys play guitars at a Jeddah boys' school, undated.
Katrina Thomas, *Saudi Aramco World*/PADIA.

the 1950s and, according to some reports, government schools barred Shiite teachers from leading classes on religion and history.[50]

In addition to measures to exclude Shiism from public education, Saudi authorities acted on Wahhabi decrees to dismantle vestiges of Shiite religiosity in and around Medina. For instance, in 1975, pressure from Wahhabi ulama led to the destruction of a Shiite imam's tomb.[51] About one year later, a high-ranking member of Al al-Sheikh, Abd al-Aziz ibn Abd Allah ibn Hasan, signed an order to cut down ancient palm trees that, according to local legend, the Companion Salman al-Farisi had planted under the direction of the Prophet Muhammad himself. Shiite pilgrims had visited the grove for generations because of its association with Salman and the Prophet.[52] In the 1990s, leading Wahhabi clerics like Ibn Baz and Abd Allah ibn Jibrin reiterated the customary view that Shiites were infidels.[53] Thus, Shiites could not publicly express their religious beliefs or practices; nor could they have their own mosques. They were permitted to gather in private assembly houses as long as their appearance did not indicate that they were designed for Shiite celebrations.[54]

Official discrimination essentially made Saudi Shiites second-class citizens. It was logical that Iran's Shiite revolution should inspire them to push for their rights. Ayatollah Khomeini and his circle championed the cause of their disenfranchised Shiite brothers ('the revolutionary masses, heroic people in Qatif') across the Gulf. Tehran's efforts to export the revolution through leaflets, radio broadcasts and tape cassettes castigating Al Saud for corruption and hypocrisy found a receptive audience in the Eastern Province.[55] On 28 November 1979, Saudi Shiites summoned the courage to break the taboo on public religious expression by holding processions to celebrate the Shiite holy day of Ashura (commemorating the martyrdom of the third imam, Husayn, at Kerbala, Iraq). Political protests against official religious and economic discrimination broke out in several towns and cities. The broad scale and intensity of the protests caught Saudi authorities off guard and they responded with a large show of force against protesters calling for solidarity with Iran. After a two-month lull, on 1 February, the one-year anniversary of Ayatollah Khomeini's return to Iran, violent demonstrations again erupted. Crowds attacked banks and vehicles and hoisted placards with Khomeini's picture.[56] The government responded to the February protests with a mix of coercion and cooptation. On one hand, leading Shiite activists were arrested. On the other, a high official from the Interior Ministry met with Shiite representatives and acknowledged that Riyadh had neglected the region's development needs. In a bid to stabilize the oil-rich province, the government implemented projects to extend the electricity network (note the irony of the world's major source of petroleum itself lacking adequate infrastructure to provide energy for its own population), build more schools and hospitals and improve sewage disposal. A year later, on the eve of Ashura, Saudi television broadcast a programme highlighting improvements in al-Qatif. At the same time, the government released many activists detained after the February demonstrations. Over the long term, the government's decision to co-opt Shiites with material benefits succeeded in preventing further outbreaks of popular protest.[57] Wahhabi preachers, however, criticized the lenient treatment of folk they consider idolaters.[58]

The Rise of the Jihadist Tendency in Islamic Revivalism

Saudi political and religious leaders may have heaved sighs of relief when they got past the twin crises in the kingdom's western and eastern provinces. Whether they believed that they had a handle on the sources of the militant mood that Juhayman tapped is hard to gauge. The 1979 seizure of the Haram, with its echoes of the Ikhwan, certainly had a 'made in Saudi Arabia' stamp on it. At the same time, his pronouncements and actions indicated that a combustible mix of Wahhabi and modern Islamic revivalism was brewing in the niches of Saudi mosques. Exactly how and when these elements combined has not yet been established beyond the common knowledge that Saudi Arabia opened its doors to members of the Muslim Brothers fleeing repression by secular regimes in Egypt and Syria in the late 1950s and 1960s. They spread their ideas by occupying influential positions in educational institutions and circulating their literature.[59]

Islamic revivalism did not remain static in the 1970s and 1980s. During those decades, a militant movement of jihadists arose in Egypt and spread to other Muslim countries. Tracing the origins and evolution of the jihadist stream in late twentieth-century Islamic revivalism is essential to comprehending the historical background to its most earth-shaking manifestation: al-Qaeda's 11 September 2001 attacks on the USA. Because Osama bin Laden and most of the hijackers are Saudi nationals, it was assumed that al-Qaeda is an expression of Wahhabism. That is not the case. Wahhabi ulama have maintained that it is the prerogative of the ruler to determine when conditions warrant jihad. Bin Laden and others in the jihadist tendency have unmoored the authority to declare jihad from the state and assumed that authority because they deem Al Saud and other Muslim rulers to be apostate. Hence, al-Qaeda is part of the jihadist tendency whose intellectual roots go back to the Sayyid Qutb.[60] He viewed regimes in Muslim lands as a modern form of jahiliyya (pre-Islamic barbarism) and he argued that Muslims must undertake jihad to overthrow them in order to restore Islam.[61] In the 1970s, militants inspired by Qutb elaborated the argument for waging jihad against 'apostate' regimes. In *The Neglected Duty*, Muhammad Abd al-Salam Faraj cited Ibn Taymiyya and Qutb to assert that jihad is an essential religious duty on par with the traditional five pillars of Islam.[62] Faraj met a similar fate to that of Qutb when the Egyptian government executed him in 1982 for his part in the conspiracy to assassinate President Anwar al-Sadat the previous autumn, but the jihadist stream survived in militant circles. Its advocates include Sheikh Umar Abd al-Rahman, best known for his role in plotting the 1993 World Trade Center bombing, and Ayman al-Zawahiri, the former Egyptian surgeon and deputy to Osama bin Laden in al-Qaeda.[63]

The precise trajectory of Islamic revivalism and its jihadist offshoot in Saudi Arabia is not fully clear, but glimpses come from an interview with the leader of a radical revivalist organization.[64] Omar Bakri Mohammed was born in Syria and became active in that country's branch of the Muslim Brothers as a high school student in the mid 1970s. At that time, Islamic militants were challenging the secular Ba'ath Party regime in Damascus. Pressed by the Ba'athist regime's harsh measures against the militants, Mohammed moved to Lebanon, where he joined a small, secretive organization called the Islamic Liberation Party (*Hizb al-Tahrir al-Islami*). This party first appeared in Jerusalem around 1952 and established branches in Syria and Lebanon. Its distinctive concept is the call for re-establishing the caliphate (abolished in Turkey in 1924) in order to revive Islam and Muslim political power on the world stage.[65] From this emphasis on the caliphate as the only true form of Islamic government, it follows that all existing political systems in the Muslim world are illegitimate, including the Saudi monarchy with its Wahhabi affiliation. In 1979, the young militant went to study at the Azhar in Cairo, but he clashed with his teachers and moved on to Saudi Arabia, arriving in Mecca in December 1979. Mohammed has stated that he was in Mecca during Juhayman's uprising and that he admired the millenarian rebel. The Syrian activist established cells of the Islamic Liberation Party, recruiting among followers of Juhayman and self-styled salafis who believed that Wahhabism was not sufficiently rigorous in adhering to the Prophet's example. After three years, Mohammed had managed to recruit only 38 new members. His efforts were hampered by having to operate clandestinely because of the Saudi ban on all political parties. In addition, the Islamic Liberation Party's branch in Kuwait discouraged his activities. When he persisted, the party suspended him. In 1983, on the anniversary of Turkey's abolition of the caliphate (3 March 1924), he and about thirty others created a new organization called Al-Muhajiroun, or 'The Emigrants', named after the believers who had joined the Prophet Muhammad on his emigration from Mecca's hostile infidel milieu to Medina. Omar Bakri Mohammed and his followers saw themselves as emigrants from infidel Arab nationalist lands to Islam's birthplace. They challenged the Saudi government with a propaganda campaign, posting leaflets critical of infidel governments, including the Wahhabi dynasty. The authorities detained him briefly in 1984 in Jeddah and a second time in December 1985 in Riyadh, where they found Islamic Liberation Party literature. After a week of interrogation, the Saudis ordered Mohammed to leave the country. He moved to Britain and mended ties with the Islamic Liberation Party's leadership in Europe (based in Germany).

Omar Bakri Mohammed's itinerary and doctrine fitted the profile of thousands of young men in the Muslim world's burgeoning revivalist trend that took off in the 1970s. The critical catalyst for that trend's 'jihadist' turn was the war in Afghanistan. In the eyes of western observers, the anti-Soviet jihad was significant primarily as part of the cold war contest between the USA and the Soviet Union. That the Afghan resistance drew on nationalist and religious inspiration was obvious as well. What observers of the war minimized, or missed completely, was its function as a crucible for the synthesis of disparate Islamic revivalist organizations into a loose coalition of like-minded jihadist groups that viewed the war as a struggle between Islam and unbelief. In brief, the war in Afghanistan amplified the jihadist tendency from a fringe phenomenon to a major force in the Muslim world.

The jihad's headquarters were in Peshawar, a Pakistani city near the Afghan border. Pakistan's Inter-Services Intelligence Agency and Saudi Arabia's Ministry of Intelligence coordinated efforts with revivalist organizations (the Muslim Brothers, Jamaati Islami) and Afghan mujahidin factions: altogether, these official bodies and revivalist groups became known as the Peshawar Alliance. Pakistani intelligence started recruiting fighters for the jihad in 1982. The American CIA contributed weapons and money. Saudi Arabia benefited from this alliance against communism because it would bolster relations with Washington and rid the kingdom of its own young militants.[66] The passage to Peshawar for thousands of young idealistic men was organized and funded by the World Muslim League and the Muslim Brothers. In all, perhaps 35,000 Muslim fighters went to Afghanistan between 1982 and 1992, while untold thousands more attended frontier schools teeming with former and future fighters.[67] Nobody knows exactly how many of those Muslim volunteers came from Saudi Arabia; estimates range between 12,000 and 25,000.[68]

The leading Muslim Brother in Peshawar (and an important influence on Osama bin Laden) was Abd Allah Azzam (1941–1989). He was born in the Palestinian West Bank and attended the theology faculty at Damascus University. At the Azhar in Cairo he became acquainted with relatives of Sayyid Qutb and met Sheikh Umar Abd al-Rahman, the militant preacher who was part of the conspiracy to bomb the World Trader Center in New York City in 1993. After completing his studies, Azzam went to Jordan for a brief spell as a university instructor before joining the faculty at King Abd al-Aziz University in Jeddah. After the Soviet invasion of Afghanistan, Azzam met with mujahidin organizers who came to Saudi Arabia seeking support. He moved yet again, this time to Pakistan, where he spent the 1980s coordinating an international Muslim campaign from his offices, known as the Services Centre, in Peshawar. He visited Afghanistan several times and mediated disputes between the fractious mujahidin groups.[69]

Azzam published the periodical *al-Jihad* to disseminate news about Afghanistan in the Arab world and to spread jihadist ideology. His location in Peshawar, the gathering place for mujahidin from many countries, meant that his views would spread to distant corners of the Muslim world and he consequently became the most influential voice in the 'transnational salafi jihadist movement'.[70] Azzam considered the Afghan jihad a religious duty binding on all Muslims, not just those of Afghanistan. In terms of Islamic law, he was making a radical argument, weaving together texts from the Qur'an, Ibn Taymiyya and Sayyid Qutb.[71] As a religious duty, jihad is normally a collective obligation that is fulfilled when sufficient numbers of people undertake it on behalf of the entire society. Azzam, however, asserted that when a Muslim land is under attack, jihad becomes the duty of each individual in that land and then in other lands if the Muslims enduring aggression prove unable to repel it alone.[72] He went further when he argued that the Afghan jihad was merely one phase in a much broader effort to restore Muslim sovereignty to 'Palestine, Bokhara, Lebanon, Chad, Eritrea, Somalia, the Philippines, Burma, Southern Yemen, Tashkent and Andalusia'.[73] In addition to espousing global jihad, Azzam travelled widely in the Gulf and the USA, where he mobilized youths to join the Afghan cause and exhorted the faithful to donate funds. Back in Peshawar, he funnelled donations from Muslim charities, Saudi intelligence and the World Muslim League to the mujahidin.[74]

For ten years the war in Afghanistan consumed the energies of young, idealistic Muslim men. With the withdrawal of Soviet forces 1989, the jihadist movement dispersed to other battlefields in the Balkans, Kashmir and the Caucasus to defend Muslim populations against Christian and Hindu foes. Thousands of veteran Arab mujahidin returned to their countries and filled the ranks of Islamist groups that regarded the governments as apostate, a view rooted in Sayyid Qutb's writings and one that gave impetus to jihadist rebellions striving to install what their partisans considered true Islamic regimes. At the time, it was not clear that one long-term effect of the Afghan war would be to provide a large pool of recruits for jihadist movements, like the one Osama bin Laden would launch in the mid 1990s against Saudi Arabia and the USA.[75]

The Wahhabi-Revivalist Schism

The Afghan jihad marked the apex of cooperation between Wahhabis and Muslim revivalist groups. When the Soviet Union agreed to withdraw in 1988, there was no reason to anticipate a deep schism between the doctrinal cousins. The occasion for that unexpected turn was Iraq's 2 August 1990 invasion of Kuwait. Saddam Hussein's annexation of the oil-rich amirate alarmed Riyadh and Washington, in large measure because his intentions were unclear: Did he intend to push south to seize the oil fields in Saudi Arabia's Eastern Province? Or did the annexation of Kuwait represent his maximum ambition? A delegation of political and military leaders from Washington persuaded the Saudi rulers that prudence required a massive American military build-up in the kingdom. In secular terms, Al Saud could explain requesting support from the USA as a necessary expedient to protect the country. But Wahhabi doctrine made it difficult to justify what in shari'a terms amounted to seeking infidels' assistance against a Muslim power. The identical doctrinal issue had sparked controversy in the 1870s when a member of Al Saud allied with the Ottoman Empire against another member of the ruling family. Furthermore, the USA's unpopular foreign policy in the Middle East, particularly support for Israel, ensured that broad sectors of the public would object on nationalist grounds to having American forces in the country. The Saudi rulers pressed the Wahhabi establishment to issue a fatwa to validate seeking help from the USA. The Board of Senior Ulama complied and published a suitable fatwa on 14 August.[76] The fatwa cited the 'heinous matters and serious crimes' suffered by Kuwait and stated that Saudi Arabia's leaders could 'request the assistance of Arab and non-Arab countries to repel the expected danger'. It does not mention the USA, nor does it say that non-Muslim, i.e. infidel, forces would provide assistance. Instead, there is a vague allusion to 'qualified forces with equipment that bring fear and terror to those who wish to commit aggression against this country'.[77]

The first clear sign of a schism between Islamic revivalists and the

Saudis surfaced outside the kingdom among Arab and South Asian organizations. Islamic parties initially condemned Iraq's invasion of Kuwait and some even offered volunteers to defend Saudi Arabia against a possible Iraqi attack. At the same time, they opposed western military intervention because they believed it would bolster western domination. When Riyadh invited thousands of non-Muslim (infidel) troops into the land of the holy places, the Muslim Brothers in Jordan and Egypt moved into the pro-Iraqi camp, thus putting the Islamic revivalist movement in the odd position of supporting a secular Ba'athist regime against the Wahhabi monarchy that had for decades provided a safe harbour and financial backing. A Jordanian Muslim Brother expressed the revivalists' perspective when he declared, 'This battle is not between Iraq and America but between Islam and the Crusades... It is not between Saddam and Bush but between the infidel leaders and the Prophet of Islam.'[78] He boldly went beyond this implicit criticism of the Saudis when he proclaimed that they had forfeited their credibility by inviting American troops, who were, he claimed, infecting the holy land with AIDS.[79] In February 1991, Jordanian Muslim Brothers published a statement vowing 'to purge the holy land of Palestine and Najd and Hijaz from the Zionists and imperialists'.[80] The notion of a clever American plot to manipulate the crisis over Kuwait in order to control Gulf oil supplies, promote Israel's interests and strengthen Washington's regional hegemony took hold throughout the Muslim world. Thus on 17 February 1991, the Muslim Brothers assembled with other Islamic groups in Pakistan to label the war on Iraq part of a campaign waged by infidels against Islamic causes in Palestine and Kashmir.[81]

Criticism from abroad annoyed the kingdom's rulers but did not pose a threat to the religious foundations of royal authority. The crisis over Kuwait did, however, set off an unprecedented, intense and public debate inside the kingdom that included challenges to senior Wahhabi ulama from radical clerics and liberal reformers. A number of influential popular preachers, known as the sheikhs of the awakening (sahwa, in Arabic), found the fatwa utterly unpersuasive. They denounced the decision to invite infidel soldiers into the kingdom, essentially rejecting the authority of the Wahhabi leadership.[82] The pronouncements and writings of Saudi Arabia's religious dissenters signified not merely a collision with the government on a matter of enormous political import. They also revealed the ideological gains achieved by Muslim revivalist movements and the doctrinal fault lines between them and Wahhabism. Radical clerics were not the only ones expressing dissatisfaction with the Saudi authorities. The crisis atmosphere also emboldened liberals to urge Al Saud to enact sweeping reforms that would create institutions to constrain royal power. Hence, Iraq's invasion of Kuwait revealed deep fissures between liberal and conservative forces that had been simmering throughout the 1980s. For example, a prominent liberal diplomat, Ghazi al-Qusaybi, published articles in 1987 that accused religious conservatives of undermining the government. From the conservative side, A'id al-Qarni and Said al-Ghamdi lambasted the diplomat as the archetype of such foreign trends as liberalism, secularism, feminism and communism that were infiltrating the kingdom and undermining Islam.[83] The feuding camps harboured starkly different visions of reform, but it seemed that everybody in the kingdom except Al Saud sensed a palpable need for substantial change in basic institutions. There seemed to be ubiquitous frustration at the government's inability to cope with systemic problems: worsening economic conditions, financial corruption and moral hypocrisy in the ruling family and strains between liberal (westernizing) and conservative (Wahhabi) tendencies.[84] The airing of contending visions and blueprints for reform marked a departure in Saudi politics and took a number of forms: petitions to the government, books and cassette recordings of sermons and speeches.

The first public initiative came from a group of former government officials, Aramco technocrats, university professors and businessmen who articulated the outlook of Saudi Arabia's liberal tendency.[85] In December 1990, they submitted a petition addressing four main issues to King Khalid.[86] First, they called for a clearly defined government framework, essentially a constitution or basic law. Second, the petition urged the government to create representative institutions at the national and local levels. Thus, the authorities should create a consultative council, with members from all regions, which would draft laws and oversee government bodies to ensure they were performing their functions properly. In addition, the petitioners wished to see the restoration of municipal councils, the implementation of lapsed regulations for provincial administration and permission for professions to create associations like the chambers of commerce. Third, the government should do more to ensure equality among citizens so there would be no discrimination based on tribe, sect, social class, or ethnicity. The call for non-discrimination against sects challenged established deeply rooted Wahhabi prejudice against Shiites. Related to the principle of equality, the petition called for opening select spheres of public life to women's participation. Finally, basic institutions of cultural life, the schools and the media in particular, were in need of comprehensive review and greater openness. The petition's secular thrust was significant. It called for clarifying and limiting the role of religion in public life by contending it was important to distinguish between religious rules based on unambiguous texts in the Qur'an and the Sunna from those based on fallible human interpretation of those texts. Laws that did not have a foundation in unambiguous religious texts were open to flexible interpretation according to temporal circumstances. Furthermore, the petition called for legislation to delineate the exact functions and conduct of the Committees for Commanding Right and Forbidding Wrong.

The liberal petition boldly challenged the religious camp, which responded in May 1991 with its own petition, 'The Letter of Demands', bearing over 400 signatures, including those of leading ulama like Abd al-Aziz ibn Baz. The document's twelve points drew attention to the need for repairing many of the same institutions as the secular petition, but with the difference that the essential principles for the clerics were conformity to the shari'a and ascertaining the morality of office-holders. Thus, the religious camp also wished to see a consultative council to tackle issues of domestic and foreign policy, but insisted that shari'a serve as the basis for decisions. Likewise, both petitions called for reforming judicial institutions, but the religious one called for repealing any law or regulation that did not conform to shari'a. Media and foreign policy should serve the cause of Islam and the government should allocate sufficient financial resources and personnel to operate religious institutions in the kingdom and proselytizing ones abroad. The religious establishment's petition called on the authorities to strengthen the armed forces and develop a national arms industry so that the country could defend itself and the holy places against external threat (and thus not feel forced to rely on the USA). A salient point that is absent from the liberal petition is a call for the fair distribution of public wealth, the elimination of taxes, the reduction of onerous fees and the prohibition of usury.[87]

When the religious camp's petition reached the palace, King Fahd responded angrily. He had security forces banish many signatories from preaching and teaching; others were sent to prison; petitions and cassette tapes criticizing the government were banned. A chastened

Ibn Baz submitted a memorandum to apologize for the Letter of Demands' tone and for publishing it at all rather than adhering to the customary Wahhabi principle that counsel to a ruler should be private.[88] Repressive measures caused the religious camp to split into dissident and establishment factions. Dissidents continued to circulate cassette tapes criticizing the kingdom's relations with the USA and other policies like girls' education. In December 1991, Ibn Baz publicly condemned the dissidents for spreading 'lies and conspiracies against Islam and Muslims'.[89] That declaration dramatically marked the rift that was opening in Saudi religious circles.

Despite steps to suppress criticism, a third document calling for reform was published in September 1992. The Memorandum of Advice, signed by more than 100 religious figures, challenged the rulers on a range of policies: reliance on foreigners to defend the kingdom; royal corruption; and a foreign policy that serves western rather than Saudi interests. The Memorandum called for strengthening the armed forces, establishing a consultative council to represent the views of the people to the rulers and creating a Supreme Religious Court to ensure that treaties and statutory regulations comply with shari'a.[90] The government persuaded Ibn Baz to condemn the document's signers for breeding disunity in the kingdom, violating the rule against public criticism and overlooking positive aspects in the country.[91] Seven of his colleagues on the Board of Senior Ulama, however, refused to condemn the petition, signalling a split within the Wahhabi establishment between idealists and pragmatists. King Fahd expelled those seven ulama from the Board.[92]

In 1992–1993, it appeared as though Al Saud might be tilting in favour of the kingdom's liberal camp. First, in March 1992, King Fahd issued a Basic Law of Governance; then in October 1993, he appointed members of the *Shura* (Consultative) Council. The Basic Law states that Saudi Arabia is a hereditary monarchy ruling in accord with the Qur'an and the Sunna. Citizens owe the king their obedience and in return the state is to ensure their welfare by providing employment, education and health care. The document assigns extensive powers to the king. As for the judiciary, it is responsible for adjudicating according to the shari'a. The document does not provide for a legislative body, but it does foresee the creation of a consultative council.[93] When the king selected 60 men for the Shura Council, he crafted a body that would reflect the views of merchants, government servants and religious leaders.[94] Neither the Basic Law nor the Shura

Council substantially touched on royal prerogatives in a manner that might satisfy proponents of reform, but they seem to have diminished pressure from the liberal camp in the short term.

Parallel to the collective endeavours embodied in the various petitions, individual dissidents campaigned for reform under the banner of returning to the ways of the salaf. The two most influential spokesmen for this tendency, Safar al-Hawali and Salman al-Awda, became known as the 'sheikhs of the awakening'.[95] The Arabic word for awakening is 'sahwa' and the term has become a standard label for the Islamic revivalist tendency in Saudi Arabia. Al-Hawali and Awda studied and taught at religious universities, strongholds of the Muslim Brothers and their sympathizers. Hence, they represented not traditional Wahhabism but the impact of Muslim Brother ideas on young Saudis.[96] Hawali attended the Islamic University in Medina and Umm al-Qura University in Mecca, where he obtained an appointment to teach theology.[97] Awda studied at Imam Muhammad ibn Saud University in Riyadh and taught shari'a at the branch campus in al-Qasim.[98]

In September 1990, as American troops were arriving by the thousands, Safar al-Hawali declared at a Riyadh mosque that the chief threat to Saudi Arabia came not from Iraq but from the USA, which was using the Kuwait crisis as a pretext to occupy the kingdom and set up military bases.[99] His argument, couched in the same terms as those of the Muslim Brothers and Jamaati Islami, reflected the penetration of modern revivalist views into Saudi Arabia, with their emphasis on religious nationalism instead of Wahhabism's focus on matters of ritual correctness and punctilious adherence to Islamic law.[100] The Gulf crisis was part of a broader western plot to dominate Muslims, a phase in a modern Crusade that is motivated by thirst for oil, evangelical Christian fervour and support for Israel.[101] The West no longer relies on military power. Echoing a well-established Muslim Brother critique of cultural imperialism, Hawali declared that the West now possesses subtler, insidious means such as the Internet and satellite television to infiltrate Muslim homes and spread western ideas and values. The most potent threat to Islam comes from cultural traitors on the inside: Muslim proponents of liberal and secular ideas. Believers must combat these agents of cultural imperialism.[102]

The other awakening sheikh, Salman al-Awda, agreed with Hawali that Saudi Arabia had to eliminate liberal, secular influences. Awda called for re-Islamizing society by purging liberals from government offices, schools (he believed that schools needed to increase time devoted to religious instruction) and positions in the media. It may be noted that the call for 'Islamizing' state institutions also amounts to a jobs programme for graduates of religious universities.[103] What makes Awda stand out from other dissidents is his proposition that Saudi Arabia has a divine mission as the cradle of Islam because its people possess an instinctive appreciation for religion. That quality made Arabians the perfect audience for the Prophet Muhammad's revelations, which erased religious ignorance (jahiliyya) from the land once and for all. In this respect, Awda contradicted the standard Wahhabi version of history, which holds that Arabia had lapsed into jahiliyya, thus necessitating Muhammad ibn Abd al-Wahhab's revivalist mission. On the other hand, Awda reproduced the Wahhabi view that the Saudi-Wahhabi alliance made Arabia a bulwark for Islam and that the kingdom's special character made it essential to block the infiltration of foreign cultures, to eliminate the non-Muslim presence (expel foreign workers and advisers) and to rid the country of Shiites. His Saudi nationalist narrative praised the Arabs' genius and their special physical powers engendered by surviving in a harsh environment.[104]

Hawali, Awda and other sahwa sheikhs articulated widespread dissatisfaction with the Wahhabi leadership's focus on ritual correctness at a time when Muslims suffered under foreign occupation and domination in Palestine, Iraq, Kashmir and Chechnya. That divergence typified the gap between Wahhabism and modern Islamic revivalism. A corresponding difference lay in the degree of expertise in religious sciences. None of the sahwa sheikhs could question the superior knowledge of ulama like Ibn Baz in that sphere, but they did consider him and his colleagues to be out of touch with more pressing realities affecting Muslims.[105] That Saudi youth were more attuned to the political commentary of Hawali than the senior clerics' defence of Al Saud indicates that social and political changes had altered the kingdom's discursive landscape in ways that undermined Wahhabism.

In 1994, the authorities decided to suppress the sahwa sheikhs. Al Saud convened the Board of Senior Ulama to examine their writings and taped sermons. The Wahhabi leaders determined that the sheikhs had expressed deviant views and ordered them to recant. When they refused, Abd al-Aziz ibn Baz banned them from speaking in public. Shortly thereafter, the government threw them into jail.[106] Consequently, voices of dissent relocated outside the kingdom in London. The Saudi exile who attracted the most attention was Muhammad al-Mas'ari, the spokesman for the Committee for the Defence of Legitimate Rights (CDLR). In the United Kingdom, he was free to broadcast his ideas and interact with like-minded Muslim dissidents. He used modern communications technologies – faxes, e-mails, an Internet web site – to disseminate his message back to Saudi Arabia. Mas'ari mingled with leaders of other Muslim revivalist movements in 'Londonistan' and drifted away from purely Saudi issues. This led to a rupture with Sa'd al-Faqih, the other major figure in the CDLR, in March 1996 and Faqih left to form his own organization, the Movement for Islamic Reform (MIRA). For his part, Faqih claimed that MIRA, not CDLR, now represented the movement that had begun with the Letter of Demands, the Memorandum of Advice and the speeches of Hawali and Awda.[107]

Sa'd al-Faqih grew up in the Iraqi town of Zubayr, which contains a substantial population of Najdi ancestry. At high school, he came into contact with teachers espousing the views of the Muslim Brothers and he became acquainted with the works of Sayyid Qutb. In 1974, his family moved to Saudi Arabia, where he studied medicine at King Saud University.[108] Faqih worked as a surgeon in Riyadh, where he participated in private discussions among Islamists about the need for reform in the wake of the Gulf crisis. This is clearly reflected in MIRA's May 1998 political programme, which parallels the 1992 Memorandum of Advice with calls for bringing the Saudi legal system into conformity with Islamic law (banning usury and making the judiciary independent of the government), reforming the political system (i.e., curbing the royal family's authority), economy (especially rampant corruption) and media, shifting foreign policy away from alliance with the USA, bolstering national defence and protecting individual rights.[109] Faqih was openly critical of senior ulama like Ibn Baz for siding with the government against Hawali and Awda and for opposing the Memorandum of Advice.[110]

The sahwa sheikhs bore the stamp not of Wahhabism but of Muslim Brother-style revivalism. It is true that their programme included traditional Wahhabi themes. They wished to see full implementation of shari'a. They rejected dependence on foreign powers (do not seek assistance from infidels). Nevertheless, Hawali, Awda, Mas'ari and Faqih had no use for Wahhabi political doctrine's quietism, which holds that if the ulama think that the ruler is sinning, they should advise him privately because a public reprimand is harmful to the public welfare.[111] By issuing memoranda, distributing copies of petitions to the royal family and publishing agendas for reform they broke the Wahhabi taboo. More importantly, the sahwa sheikhs enjoyed a large receptive audience thanks to the expansion of religious schools and universities in the 1980s. Many of their graduates had encountered and embraced Islamic revivalist ideas taught by Muslim Brother teachers and professors. Thus, by the 1990s, the marketplace of religious ideas offered more than a single product. The dissidents' complaints and aspirations emphasized efficiency, equity, calls for broader political participation and greater accountability of rulers to the people. These demands reflected the modern political concerns of Islamic revivalism.[112] Moreover, Islamic revivalism bears the imprint of nationalism's negative and positive impulses. Revivalists reject western influence and resent western domination because they threaten to erase Islam, which revivalists consider the essence of their culture. They condemn rulers for failing to safeguard Islam and selling it out for the sake of protecting selfish interests.[113] Saudi revivalists tap nationalist sentiments welling up against the shame of Riyadh's alliance with Washington. Nevertheless, their disenchantment with the kingdom's religious leadership is peculiar in one respect. After all, Wahhabism is a xenophobic doctrine and, as such, is in harmony with the revivalists' revolt against western influence. It seems, however, that the Wahhabi leadership had too much invested in the Saudi state to jeopardize by publicly denouncing the royal family for inviting American military forces.[114]

Osama bin Laden and al-Qaeda

As long as religious dissent consisted of sermons, tapes and publications, the outside world considered it a potential threat to Saudi Arabia's stability and hence an essentially domestic affair that drew the attention of foreign journalists, government officials and academic specialists. It certainly did not preoccupy ordinary people in the West. That changed in the mid 1990s, when jihadists struck in Saudi Arabia. On 13 November 1995, a truck bomb exploded in Riyadh outside the American training mission for the Saudi National Guard. Five Americans and two Indians were killed. Afterward, the government received fax messages demanding the withdrawal of all American forces. The Saudi government investigation resulted in the arrest and execution of four men, three of whom were reported to have been veterans of the Afghan jihad.[115] The transnational jihadist movement was gathering momentum in the mid 1990s as veterans of the Afghan jihad spearheaded Islamic causes from Algeria to Kashmir.[116] The emergence of Osama bin Laden and al-Qaeda is properly understood as part of that movement's aspiration to liberate Muslims from oppression under foreign or apostate regimes rather than as an expression of the Wahhabi mission's campaign to eradicate ritual innovations and inculcate its view of Islamic morality throughout the world.

The 11 September 2001 attacks on the USA were the culmination of a sequence of al-Qaeda terrorist actions that included the August 1998 bombings of United States embassies in Kenya and Tanzania and the October 2000 bombing of the USS Cole at Aden harbour. It soon emerged that 15 of the 19 hijackers on 11 September were Saudi nationals and that Osama bin Laden's organization was responsible for the attacks. This association with Saudi Arabia made it natural for many to see an intrinsic connection to the kingdom's affiliation with Wahhabism. But the ideology of Osama bin Laden and al-Qaeda is not Wahhabi. It is instead part of the contemporary jihadist tendency that evolved from the teachings of Sayyid Qutb and took shape in Egyptian militant groups that appeared in the 1970s and spread in the 1980s, thanks in large measure to the Afghan jihad. In other words, al-Qaeda belongs to an offshoot of twentieth-century Muslim revivalist ideology, not Wahhabism.[117] Al-Qaeda contradicts Wahhabi doctrine on two essential points. First, al-Qaeda's call for the overthrow of Al Saud contradicts Wahhabi doctrine and practice. Second, al-Qaeda's call for jihad against the West is illegitimate according to Wahhabi doctrine, which maintains that only a sovereign ruler may declare jihad. These may appear to be subtle distinctions, but in the forum of Muslim discourse, they are not. Nevertheless, Osama bin Laden's Saudi ties and support for al-Qaeda among religious circles in the kingdom created the impression that Wahhabism is a major factor in fomenting religious violence in many parts of the world.

A close examination of bin Laden's career reveals that his views have evolved. During the 1980s, he cooperated with Saudi Arabian intelligence to support the Afghan jihad, which of course had Washington's full support. When Iraq invaded Kuwait, he offered to defend the kingdom's borders, not a task he would undertake if he considered it an apostate regime at the time. But Riyadh turned to the USA instead to defend the kingdom and he followed the line of the sahwa sheikhs who blamed Al Saud for inviting infidel forces into the land of the two holy mosques. Bin Laden also adopted the sahwa sheikhs' view that Al Saud failed to rule according to Islamic law and managed the kingdom's oil reserves to suit America's needs. When the authorities cracked down on the dissidents, he condemned Al Saud for persecuting the ulama.[118] His affiliation with that tendency is evident in his choice of a MIRA periodical to publish his August 1996 declaration of jihad against the USA.[119] In concentrating on the imperative to wage jihad as a religious duty, bin Laden fitted the jihadist tendency that appeared in Egypt in the 1970s and spread more broadly as a consequence of the Afghan war in the 1980s.[120]

Bin Laden became familiar with Qutbist ideas while attending King Abd al-Aziz University in Jeddah, his home town, in the late 1970s. The university faculty included Sayyid Qutb's brother Muhammad and the Palestinian jihadist ideologue Abd Allah Azzam. Accounts of bin Laden's early years emphasize Azzam's influence on shaping his thinking more than Wahhabism.[121] It is also noteworthy that his encounter with militant revivalism at university coincided with the uprising of Juhayman and the Soviet invasion of Afghanistan. Not long after Red Army troops crossed into the Muslim nation, bin Laden travelled to Pakistan to meet with leaders of the resistance. For the next four years, he raised money in Saudi Arabia for the Afghan jihad and made periodic trips to Pakistan to handle the distribution of funds to mujahidin organizations. He also used his experiences and connections in the bin Laden family construction business to ship machinery, trucks and other equipment to the Afghan resistance. In 1984, bin Laden established a headquarters in Peshawar for volunteers and he assisted Azzam's Services Office with funds. He decided to resettle in Peshawar in 1986 and from there he directed the construction of a training camp inside Afghanistan. In 1987, he and his comrades withstood a Soviet attack for several days before retreating in the face of overwhelming firepower. The combat episode boosted bin Laden's reputation as a wealthy Saudi who risked his life for the sacred cause.[122]

It was not until after the Soviets left Afghanistan that bin Laden established al-Qaeda in order to gather information on the activities of Muslim volunteers for the jihad. At that point, the organization appeared to have a bland bureaucratic function. It would not evolve into a node for the transnational jihadist network for several years. There was no compelling reason for bin Laden to stay in Peshawar when Afghanistan was turning into the scene of a fractious civil war among mujahidin groups previously united by the common communist foe. Therefore, he returned to live in Saudi Arabia, where he gave public talks on the Afghan jihad and called on his countrymen to boycott American products. This was several years before he decided that economic measures were too mild for the infidel.[123] When Iraq invaded Kuwait in August 1990, he tried to persuade the Saudi government that he could recruit a force of 'Arab Afghan' veterans to defend the land of the holy places, but the rulers put little stock in the military capacity of such a force. After all, most analysts of the Afghan jihad had concluded that it was the Afghan mujahidin who, with arms and money from the USA, Saudi Arabia and Pakistan, had defeated the Soviets and that the Arab volunteers had played a marginal role. Bin Laden's offer nevertheless indicates that he did not yet consider the kingdom's rulers to be apostates.[124] When the royals spurned his offer, bin Laden joined the ranks of Saudi dissidents like Safar al-Hawali and Salman al-Awda, who condemned the rulers for opening the land of the holy places to American forces because Washington would use the kingdom as a base to dominate the entire Muslim world.[125]

Shortly after the Gulf War, bin Laden went to Pakistan for a few months before resettling in Sudan, where an Islamic regime had come to power in 1989. He contributed to the country's economic development with projects in construction, agriculture and food processing, transport and finance. Bin Laden's activities in Sudan and his network of trading contacts across Europe, Africa and Asia served as a cover for al-Qaeda's international financial transactions.[126] During his five years in Khartoum, he forged strong ties with jihadist groups in Chechnya, Tajikistan, the Philippines, Bosnia and several Arab countries.[127] He also established the Advice and Reform Committee as a platform to call for change in Saudi Arabia, adopting points set forth in the 1992 Memorandum of Advice issued by Saudi religious activists. For instance, a 1995 pronouncement by the Advice and Reform Committee called on the monarchy to revoke all man-made laws, to take steps to eliminate debt and unemployment and to stop wasting the country's wealth on lavish palaces for members of the royal family. The statement concluded by calling on King Fahd to abdicate.[128] Bin Laden also directly challenged the Wahhabi establishment. In a scathing letter to Abd al-Aziz ibn Baz, the Saudi renegade condemned the cleric for issuing a fatwa endorsing peace negotiations between Arab governments and Israel. He accused Ibn Baz of straying from Islam in order to please his masters, Al Saud.[129]

The USA and Saudi Arabia suspected bin Laden of using his base in Khartoum to direct terrorist operations like the November 1995 bombing of Riyadh's National Guard Building. So they pressured the Sudanese government to expel him from the country. In May 1996, these efforts resulted in his departure from Sudan and his return to Afghanistan, which was witnessing the rise of the Taliban, a new Islamic movement seeking to bring an end to the ceaseless fighting among former mujahidin factions.[130] A few months after arriving in Afghanistan, bin Laden announced a new phase in his mission when he issued his 'Declaration of War against the Americans Occupying the Land of the Two Holy Places' in August 1996.[131] This document blends verses from the Qur'an, hadiths and episodes from early Islamic history with indictments of sins committed by Al Saud and the USA. The basic thrust is straightforward. He called for rebellion against Al Saud and jihad against the USA. Bin Laden recited the same litany of grievances expressed in Saudi religious dissidents' letters and petitions of the early 1990s: mismanagement of the economy, resulting in inflation, unemployment and poverty; calibrating oil production and pricing to suit the interests of Washington rather than Muslims; and inept handling of national defence. The material 'policy' dimension of these issues hardly stems from a Wahhabi critique, but stands firmly in the Muslim Brother tradition. Likewise, the declaration echoes the Islamic revivalist depiction of traitorous, hypocritical Muslim rulers beholden to the West. Thus, bin Laden asserted that Al Saud had been betraying Muslim causes for sixty years. Abd al-Aziz ibn Saud allegedly helped the British quell the Arab Revolt in Palestine in 1936 by calming the mujahidin with false promises. Likewise, King Fahd lied when he declared in 1990 that American military forces would stay for a very brief time. The religious objections to Al Saud in the Declaration echo Sayyid Qutb's accusation that Muslim rulers governed through 'man-made' laws rather than the divine law of shari'a and that they allied with infidel powers against Muslims. Therefore, Al Saud had fallen into apostasy. To make matters worse, bin Laden noted that sincere Muslims had pointed out these errors to the rulers in a series of petitions and letters, but Al Saud rejected the advice and persecuted their authors. By refusing to treat sincere Muslims honourably, the ruling princes gave them no choice but to resort to force, thereby pushing the country to the brink of civil war.

When it came to the case against the USA, the leader of the Crusader-Zionist alliance, bin Laden recited a litany of crimes allegedly inspired by Washington and its underlings against Muslims in Bosnia, Chechnya, Palestine, Iraq, Tajikistan, the Philippines and elsewhere. The most recent aggression in this campaign was the American occupation of Saudi Arabia. On this point, he cited Safar al-Hawali's argument that Washington had planned this occupation for some time. In bin Laden's view, the US campaign against Islam included the trial and imprisonment of Umar Abd al-Rahman for the 1993 World Trader Center bombing, the assassination of Abd Allah Azzam and the decision of Saudi authorities to throw the sahwa sheikhs Safar al-Hawali and Salman al-Awda into jail. Bin Laden announced that the purpose of his movement was to rectify injustices inflicted on the Muslim world in general and the land of the two holy places (Saudi Arabia) in particular. He justified the 1995 and 1996 attacks in Riyadh and Khobar as defensive reactions to humiliation, oppression and poverty. In this condition, the foremost duty of Muslims is to liberate their lands from American occupation, which is intended to dominate, not protect.[132]

While the fatwa was a clear summons to jihad against the USA, it did not endorse violence against all Americans. In that respect, bin Laden was respecting the Muslim consensus on the rules for jihad that spare non-combatants from attack. In a 1997 interview, he stated that he wished Americans to leave Saudi Arabia, but he did not call for attacks on civilians.[133] He soon changed his mind on that point. In his February 1998 fatwa, he again depicted the USA as an aggressive power striving to destroy Islam. Its Crusader armies had invaded the Arabian peninsula to devour its wealth and use it as a base to launch further aggression against the Muslims of Iraq. Muslims therefore had to defend their religion by waging jihad, which was a religious duty in such circumstances. Bin Laden then dropped the exemption of civilians from attack, arguing that it was a duty for Muslims to kill civilian Americans as well as American military personnel because of the USA's own indiscriminate aggression against Muslims.[134] He later added in an interview that all Americans were complicit in their government's policies because they voted in elections and paid taxes to finance policies. If Americans wished to be safe from attack, they should elect a government that would end America's war against Muslims.[135]

The set of ideas and issues that matter most to Osama bin Laden are those of modern Islamic revivalism dating back to the early twentieth century: resisting western domination and combating regimes that fail to rule according to Islamic law. By contrast, the Wahhabi mission essentially aims to institute correct performance of worshipping God, to eliminate idolatry and to ensure compliance with Islamic law and morality. Muhammad ibn Abd al-Wahhab and his followers made correct understanding of tawhid the centre of their mission and their adversaries were other Muslims who rejected their views on tawhid. Bin Laden is preoccupied with defeating the USA and forcing it out of the Muslim world. The US and Muslim rulers allied to it are his adversaries. Bin Laden's point of reference is not a rigorous dogma of tawhid but the community of believers, the *umma*, whose rights and lives are trampled on by Washington and its servant regimes. Hence, bin Laden invokes injustices endured by Muslims in Lebanon, Palestine, Tajikistan, Kashmir and so forth, in order to summon believers for action. His language is that of an injured party retaliating against an aggressor, not a vigilant theologian eager to stamp out idolatry.[136] Bin Laden and Wahhabism do overlap on the question of ensuring the implementation of Islamic law, but when it comes to the criteria for evaluating a ruler's performance in that area, they diverge. Bin Laden follows the Qutbist line that a ruler who does not govern strictly according to Islamic law is an infidel who must be deposed. Wahhabi doctrine permits disobedience only if a ruler commands believers to violate a religious commandment. Thus, in the Qutbist view, a lax ruler is considered an infidel whereas in Wahhabi doctrine such a label applies only to a ruler who openly defies divine authority. By way of illustration, if the authorities tolerate video shops, Wahhabis find that objectionable but they do not view it as cause for deposing a ruler whereas the Qutbists do. The Wahhabis would only endorse disobedience if the authorities commanded a believer to consume alcohol or to steal.

The Wahhabi Mission Outside Saudi Arabia

Osama bin Laden's Saudi ties and support for al-Qaeda among religious circles in the kingdom created the impression that Wahhabism is a major factor in fomenting religious violence in many parts of the world. A closer look at regions where Wahhabi missionaries supposedly sow violence reveals this impression to be a distortion that replicates the tenor of earlier stereotypes of the mission. In this respect, we find a mixture of old Muslim animosity toward the mission's reformist agenda and more contemporary anxieties. For instance, when the Ikhwan first attracted the attention of British officials in 1918, they puzzled over their origin and objectives. Writing in the shadow of the Bolshevik Revolution in Russia, a British official in Baghdad compared the Ikhwan to socialists. The Hashemites did their utmost to stoke British fears by suggesting the Ikhwan threatened to destabilize Britain's position in Egypt, Afghanistan and India. Amir Faysal, who would clash with the Ikhwan after he became king of Iraq, likened Wahhabism to Bolshevism as a secretive, revolutionary movement.[137] More recently, Wahhabi influence in Afghanistan has been conflated with Saudi backing for the mujahidin. The Afghan jihad had plenty of fingerprints on it. The main Wahhabi contribution was to assist with fundraising in the kingdom; the military contribution of Wahhabi and jihadist volunteers was minimal; and only a handful of Afghan leaders held Wahhabi views.

When the Taliban rose to power and imposed a harsh regime of Islamic law and morality, it was common to view it as a manifestation of Wahhabism. While it is true that Saudi Arabia's government and Wahhabi establishment lent support to the Taliban, the Afghan puritans emerged not from Wahhabism but from the Indian Deobandi movement.[138] During the twentieth century, Deobandi schools spread from India to Pakistan and Afghanistan. A number of Deobandi ulama attended the coronation of Afghan king Zahir Shah in 1933 and shortly afterward they established several madrasas in the Afghan capital.[139] The movement picked up momentum after 1947, when the British partitioned South Asia into Hindu-majority India and Muslim-majority Pakistan, where Deobandis created an organization, the Jamaati Ulama Islam (JUI), to spread their views. They figured as a fairly minor part of Pakistan's religious scene until the regime of General Zia al-Haq (1977–1988), who used an Islamic policy to buttress his military dictatorship. Part of his policy to 'Islamize' Pakistan was a campaign to expand religious education with funds for thousands of new madrasas. Their numbers grew from around 900 in 1971 to over 8,000 official ones and another 25,000 unofficial ones in 1988. With financial support from Saudi Arabia, Deobandi madrasas were part of this vast proliferation in religious education, much of it located in Afghan refugee camps that sprang up in the 1980s. This rapid expansion came at the expense of the movement's doctrinal coherence as there were not enough qualified teachers to staff all the new schools. Quite a few teachers did not discern between tribal values of their ethnic group, the Pushtuns, and the religious ideals of Islam. The result was an interpretation of Islam that blended Pushtun ideals and Deobandi views, precisely the hallmark of the Taliban.[140]

In Russia and Central Asia, public figures and the media see Wahhabism as the inspiration for religious revival and Islamic political movements.[141] During the Soviet era, official apprehensions emerged about an 'Islamic threat' posed by Sufi orders as nests of secret conspiracies against the communist system. In the post-Soviet era, Sufism has assumed a positive connotation as a moderate form of Islam opposed to Wahhabism, which has become a sort of bogeyman in public discourse. Pejorative use of the term cropped up in the late Soviet era, when members of the official religious establishment castigated proponents of expunging ritual of non-scriptural elements for 'importing' Wahhabism, thus implying that it is alien to the region's heritage.[142] Many Russians believe that after the Afghan war, Wahhabis infiltrated Central Asia to spread their version of Islam. Thus, in 1998, political leaders of Russia, Uzbekistan and Tajikistan declared their readiness to confront 'a threat of aggressive fundamentalism, aggressive extremism and above all Wahhabism. This is what we have currently in Afghanistan and in troubled Tajikistan.'[143] The government of Uzbekistan tags unsanctioned religious activity with the Wahhabi label.[144] The problem with this outlook is that it conflates differences among a variety of Muslim religious movements, which include militant and reformist political tendencies alongside utterly apolitical ones. Thus, a leading Tajik modernist who favours a blend of democracy and Islam has been branded a Wahhabi even though he has ties to Sufi circles. An even more egregious instance of Wahhabi-phobia is the warning from a government minister in Kyrgyzstan about Wahhabi agitators from Shiite Iran.[145] The Russian media circulates stories about 'Wahhabi' villages in rebellious regions of Daghestan, where the inhabitants reportedly abide by a Taliban-style regime with a ban on television and compulsory veiling of women. When a journalist visited this village, he discovered religious pluralism: some women did veil while others did not; some men wore beards as a sign of piety while others were clean shaven; he even found some television viewers.[146]

Saudi-funded publications, schools and mosques on all continents have been blamed, with good reason, for spreading religious intolerance.[147] In the USA, the World Muslim League has bolstered conservative impulses in American Muslim communities. It recruits young men to Saudi religious universities for training as mosque imams and then sends them to the USA (and other countries). Moderate American Muslim opinion ardently opposes the rise of Wahhabi influence in American mosques. One critic of the Wahhabis has shown that what looks like an innocent charitable act, distributing free copies of English translations of the Qur'an, instead serves to spread Wahhabi views. The Saudi edition deletes passages in commentaries and exegeses on the Qur'an, such as a nineteenth-century scholar's reference to the Wahhabis as 'the agents of the devil'. Furthermore, the English translation substantially strays from the literal meaning of the Arabic text. Thus, in one instance, a literal translation of a verse would read:

> O Prophet, tell your wives, daughters and the women of the believers to lower (or possibly, draw upon themselves) their garments. This is better so that they will not be known and molested. And, God is forgiving and merciful.

The authorized Wahhabi version reads:

> O Prophet! Tell your wives and daughters and the women of the believers to draw their cloaks (veils) all over their bodies (i.e. screen themselves completely except the eyes or one eye to see the way). That will be better, that they should be known (as free respectable women) so as not to be annoyed. And Allah is Ever Oft-Forgiving, Most Merciful.

The Arabic term rendered 'cloak' or 'veil' in the Wahhabi translation actually means a dress or robe that one might use to cover one's legs or torso. Muslim commentators on the verse disagree on its exact implication. Some suggest that the verse orders women to cover everything but the 'face, hands and feet'. A less common position maintains that it means women must also conceal their faces.[148]

Pressures on Wahhabism inside Saudi Arabia

The 11 September attacks on the World Trade Center and the Pentagon and the crashed airliner in western Pennsylvania killed more than 3,000 people. In the mood of national shock and rage at the terrorists, the USA cared little for fine doctrinal distinctions between Deobandis,

Wahhabis and al-Qaeda. When the Taliban leadership rejected American demands to expel Osama bin Laden, it became the target of a United States invasion in the autumn of 2001. The American effort succeeded in deposing the Taliban but failed to capture bin Laden. Even though al-Qaeda lost its Afghan refuge, in the next three years it demonstrated the capacity to carry out terrorist attacks in Morocco, Spain, Turkey, Indonesia, Kenya and Egypt. For a year and a half after 11 September, most Saudis refused to believe that Osama bin Laden planned and that 15 Saudi nationals executed that day's attacks or that the country's official religious doctrine needed re-examination. Then al-Qaeda struck in the heart of Saudi Arabia in May 2003 with a series of suicide attacks on residential compounds. Even before then, liberal Saudi critics of the religious establishment had begun to press for curbs on its power. A tragic fire at a girls' school in Mecca in March 2002 provided an occasion for sweeping denunciation of the mutawwi'a. In that incident, 15 girls died when mutawwi'a prevented firemen and police from rescuing them: the girls were without their veils and the zealots refused to let them out or to admit emergency personnel to the school. Apparently, it was preferable to let the girls burn and suffocate to death rather than let them appear unveiled. Public outrage over the fire prompted the government to remove administration of girls' schools from the hands of the religious authorities and transfer it to the Ministry of Education.

In January 2003, a group of liberals pushed their agenda further by submitting a document to Crown Prince Abd Allah. The 'Strategic Vision for the Present and the Future' reformulated earlier proposals from 1990–1991 for reorganizing government.[149] Its authors couched their suggestions in religious terms by invoking a Hadith urging believers to advise rulers. They declared the purpose of devising a constitutional order as securing national unity, justice and equality. To reinforce the religious legitimacy of the Strategic Vision, the authors declared that shari'a is the basis of law for situations where the Qur'an or the Sunna contain a clear ruling. Furthermore, they reiterated the principle that the purpose of government is to ensure justice. They then contended that the surest way to do so is by amending the 1992 Basic Law of Governance by establishing separation of powers between executive, judicial and legislative branches. A specific recommendation in the Strategic Vision that marks a substantial change in the Basic Law is the creation of elected legislative bodies at the national and provincial levels. A second departure from the status quo is the need for a guarantee of freedoms of speech and assembly. The authors also repeated the call for reforms in the economy, the status of women and ending sectarian discrimination. While Al Saud did not embrace the Strategic Vision, it apparently inspired a group of Shiite reformers to issue their own petition in April 2003 at an audience with Crown Prince Abd Allah. The signatories included merchants, religious figures and university teachers seeking to end decades of discrimination against the kingdom's Shiite minority.[150]

The liberal and Shiite petitioners faced an uphill struggle because they lacked an institutional base of power vis-à-vis the royal family and the Wahhabi religious establishment.[151] As if to underscore the need for reform, just two weeks after the Shiite delegation presented its petition, al-Qaeda suicide bomb squads attacked three residential compounds for expatriates in Riyadh on 12 May 2003, killing 26 people, including nine Americans. Foreign Minister Prince Saud al-Faysal immediately acknowledged the Saudi nationality of the nine terrorists and pledged to crush their network. In the next few months, Saudi security forces conducted a massive manhunt that resulted in the arrests of militants and shootouts between fugitives and government forces. In the first week of November 2003, the holy city of Mecca was the scene of a fierce fire fight. Then, on 8 November 2003, a suicide car bomb attack on a Riyadh residential compound, this one housing mostly Muslim expatriates, killed 18 people. In spite of efforts to capture suspects and uncover caches of explosives and weapons, the militants continued their campaign in 2004 with a series of bombings, shootings and kidnappings in Riyadh, Yanbu on the Red Sea coast and Khobar in the Eastern Province.

The arrival of al-Qaeda's jihad on Saudi soil intensified a public debate that began in 1999, when the government decided to permit contending views in publications and on Internet websites.[152] The debate has revealed the contours of religious tendencies – Wahhabi, sahwa, jihadist and liberal Islamist – jockeying for influence. Of course, the Wahhabi establishment maintains a firm grip on the official religious institutions that emerged in the 1960s and 1970s, but in the forum of public opinion it has at least temporarily lost ground to the sahwa sheikhs' Islamic revivalist message. Abd al-Aziz ibn Baz and other senior figures had warned against the writings of Sayyid Qutb for some years (see Chapter Five). In the late 1990s, Sheikh Muhammad ibn Uthaymin attempted to dissuade young Saudis from listening to the recorded sermons of sahwa sheikhs because they expressed errant views.[153] As for al-Qaeda, Ibn Baz denounced its violent actions as transgressions of Islamic law.[154]

Whether and to what degree such pronouncements blunted the spread of revivalist or jihadist ideas is difficult to gauge, but the Wahhabi establishment's ability to combat them weakened when Ibn Baz and Ibn Uthaymin died, in May 1999 and January 2001 respectively. Since then, nobody of their stature has emerged to replace them as voices of the Wahhabi tradition.[155] To shore it up, the government appointed members of Al al-Sheikh to senior positions: Abd al-Aziz ibn Abd Allah Al al-Sheikh became the head of the Board of Senior Ulama and his kinsman Salih ibn Abd al-Aziz Al al-Sheikh became Minister of Islamic Endowments. While both men have publicly urged Saudis to eschew violence in the name of religion, they lack the authority of Ibn Baz or Ibn Uthaymin. After 11 September, Abd al-Aziz Al al-Sheikh denounced the hijackings and killing of thousands as crimes.[156] In retaliation Osama bin Laden condemned the Wahhabi sheikhs as corrupt puppets of an apostate government that refuses to acknowledge the duty to wage jihad against the USA.[157] Senior Wahhabi leaders have also faced sharp criticism from radical ulama inside the kingdom who proclaim that Al Saud are apostates for supporting the 2001 US invasion of Afghanistan and declare that Osama bin Laden is the true bearer of Muhammad ibn Abd al-Wahhab's legacy.[158] In the wake of al-Qaeda's May 2003 attacks in Riyadh, Abd al-Aziz Al al-Sheikh again urged believers to eschew violence and Salih Al al-Sheikh denounced any form of hatred.[159]

The most important factor eroding the standing of Wahhabi elders is the advance of Islamic revivalism, represented since the early 1990s by the sahwa sheikhs. The Saudi leadership appears to have recognized that Wahhabi elders were losing touch with a large section of public opinion more in tune with the sahwa sheikhs' politicized discourse. In 1999, the authorities released Safar al-Hawali and Salman al-Awda from prison in an effort to harness their popularity for dynastic ends. Precisely why the two men proved willing to cooperate is unclear. Perhaps they saw it as an opportunity to shut the door on any prospect for liberal reforms touching on education and women's status. Or perhaps they viewed the monarchy as a bulwark to reinforce religious institutions against liberal critics and considered minimal retreat in concert with Al Saud preferable to ceding ground to liberal reformers, whom they regarded as infidels.[160] At the very least, they gained a new opportunity to spread their views.

It is evident that they do not comprise a monolithic bloc. Awda, for instance, helped the regime by criticizing the 11 September attacks and composing a treatise calling for coexistence with the West. Hawali, however, has shown less willingness to support government positions.[161] Both men and about 50 other sahwa sheikhs publicly condemned al-Qaeda's May 2003 attacks in Riyadh; in June 2004, they joined six ulama to denounce al-Qaeda violence and efforts to overthrow Al Saud.[162] And in December 2004, they declared their opposition to anti-government demonstrations organized by MIRA's Sa'd al-Faqih in London. When al-Qaeda militants attacked the Ministry of Interior building in Riyadh that same month, Awda criticized them on an Internet website for threatening national stability and unity. At the same time, they oppose the Saudi government over relations with the USA even though Washington closed its military bases after the overthrow of Saddam Hussein in April 2003. The failure of the USA to stabilize Iraq and the eruption of a bloody insurgency provided a new point of contention between Islamic revivalists and Riyadh. The anti-American insurgency in Iraq is cast in terms of jihad against infidel occupation and, as might be expected, the sahwa sheikhs have declared their support for the jihad, but not against Iraqis cooperating with American efforts. At the same time, a handful of Saudi sheikhs have endorsed the jihadist agenda and brand as unbelievers anyone who does not support the global jihad.[163]

By rallying both Wahhabi and sahwa sheikhs to the Saudi banner, the government put al-Qaeda on the defensive in the arena of public opinion. Naturally, bin Laden's followers inside the kingdom, dubbed the al-Qaeda Organization in the Arabian Peninsula, had no access to the Saudi press or pulpits, so they broadcast their views on the Internet. The debate in cyberspace among Wahhabis, sahwa sheikhs and jihadists reiterated many of the arguments that contending religious circles set forth during the bloody Algerian civil war in the 1990s.[164] In April 2002, al-Qaeda issued a defence of the 11 September attacks in response to widespread condemnation by prominent Muslim spokesmen like the rector of Egypt's al-Azhar as well as by Islamic revivalist organizations like the Muslim Brothers and Hamas.[165] The declaration reiterated the familiar position that the USA was an aggressor against Muslims and that a defensive jihad was the proper response. The problem for al-Qaeda, then, was how to justify the killing of civilians, which is normally forbidden in the rules governing how Muslims are to wage jihad. Its statement asserted that the Qur'an permitted Muslims to use tactics normally forbidden if the enemy used such tactics. Since Israeli forces killed Palestinian civilians in its spring 2002 offensive to reoccupy West Bank towns, then it was permitted for mujahidin to target infidel civilians. Al-Qaeda also argued that the rules of jihad allow unintentional killing of civilians when they are mingled with the legitimate targets of attack. Furthermore, al-Qaeda contended that because Americans have an elected government to represent them, they are complicit in its actions and policies and thus participate in the US onslaught on the Muslim world.[166] The rhetoric justifying the 11 September attacks naturally permeates the Internet declarations of the al-Qaeda Organization in the Arabian Peninsula explaining its attacks on foreigners in the kingdom. Thus, its militants are mujahidin seeking to expel infidels, be they Christians (Crusaders), Jews (Zionists), or Hindus (cow worshippers who kill Kashmiri Muslims), from the land of the two holy mosques. Saudi security forces are idolatrous dogs serving an apostate regime. To place their actions in the context of a global jihad against the USA, they name their units after Jerusalem (al-Quds Brigade) and the centre of Iraqi anti-American resistance (Falluja Company). They regard their attacks on non-Muslim civilians in Saudi Arabia as part of a struggle to defend Muslims under siege in Palestine, Iraq and Afghanistan.[167]

Since 2001, a new wrinkle has appeared in Saudi religious discourse with the emergence of a liberal Islamist trend. Former jihadists, sahwa sheikhs and Wahhabis have come together to forge a religious argument for democratic reform to pave the way for national conciliation with Shiites and secular-minded reformers.[168] One member of this tendency, Mansur Nuqaydan, joined a commune of religious purists in Burayda that rejected modern technology. He moved out of his family's home in the late 1980s to live with 300 other families that had taken over a neighbourhood and set up their own school. He then refused to see family members because he deemed them insufficiently pious.[169] Nuqaydan began preaching at a mosque, urging families to boycott public schools for teaching things that God hates. It is a bit difficult to know what to make of that in the light of the criticism showered on Saudi schools for teaching hatred toward others. Perhaps it was their toleration of soccer, which he condemned in a fatwa. The doctrinal impulse behind this commune did not come from a return to the treatises of Muhammad ibn Abd al-Wahhab but from the works of Sayyid Qutb. The Egyptian thinker had urged true believers to 'separate themselves from the jahili society to escape its powerful hold over their minds'. He did not mean by this that believers must physically withdraw or emigrate but that they had to cultivate 'emotional separation'.[170] The Saudi purists, however, took the concept to the next step of creating their own living space purified of jahili influences. Moreover, Nuqaydan and his comrades considered the Wahhabi religious leaders a pack of hypocrites for forbidding attacks on purveyors of infidel influence like video stores. In 1992, he and some companions launched a minor jihadi blow against prohibited innovations by blowing up such a store in Riyadh. He was caught and sent to jail for a year and a half. After the November 1995 Riyadh bombing, Nuqaydan was apprehended in a dragnet of known militants. During his second stay in prison, he drifted away from jihadist doctrine and adopted a moderate view of Islam. After the 11 September attacks, he published articles in newspapers declaring that Wahhabism and Islamic revivalism were the sources of terrorism. He also stated that the Committees for Commanding Right and Forbidding Wrong are illegitimate innovations, or bid'a, using the very term that Wahhabis have used to ban ritual practices like supplication of holy men.[171] For his trouble, the government banned him from publishing.

12. TELEVISION AT HOME, 1999.
KRISTIE BURNS, *SAUDI ARAMCO WORLD*/PADIA.

A second figure in the liberal Islamist camp is a former qadi who once backed the sahwa sheikhs and al-Mas'ari's Committee for the Defence of Legitimate Rights. In the mid 1990s, Abd al-Aziz al-Qasim spent a few years in prison for his role in CDLR. Since his release, he has advocated democracy as the most effective means to ensure justice, which is the fundamental requirement of an Islamic political system. Whereas al-Qasim endorses liberalization in the political sphere, he adheres to conservative positions on such matters as gender segregation and women driving.[172] Yet another liberal Islamist, Hasan al-Malki, comes from the heart of the Wahhabi establishment, where he worked in the Ministry of Education. He came to the view that school curricula needed reform because schoolbooks inculcated hatred of Muslims outside the Wahhabi fold. Malki has even openly criticized one of Muhammad ibn Abd al-Wahhab's major treatises for espousing a rigid doctrine that recklessly denounces other Muslims as unbelievers.[173]

The liberal Islamists are few in number, but in one respect, they have staked out a sensible position in the Saudi context. They hold on to Islam as the guiding principle; they promote a doctrinally moderate interpretation of Islam; and they favour reform of basic institutions. Many ordinary Saudis were shocked by the wave of al-Qaeda violence in their midst and tried to comprehend how their society could breed extremism. A Saudi newspaper editorial written after the November 2003 bombing captured the main lines of thought:

> What has distorted the minds [of Saudi youth] to make it permissible for them to shed the blood of innocent women and children? We should probably start with the sources of ideas by placing responsibility on education, the media, mosques and the family. They should enlighten the young on the intellectual dangers of terrorism before the real dangers of terrorism, like murder and bombing, are manifested through their fanaticism, lack of comprehending the Other and recourse to violence as an alternative to dialogue.[174]

In the light of claims that Saudi classrooms instil hatred toward non-Muslims and therefore bear responsibility for the 11 September attacks, schoolbooks have been scrutinized for the seeds of terrorism. The alleged connection between al-Qaeda violence and lessons in Wahhabism begs the question of why the Najdi doctrine had not previously spawned a terrorist wave; it also misses completely the organic links between al-Qaeda and the transnational jihadist movement. Nevertheless, curriculum reform is on the agenda, if only to diminish the receptivity of Saudi youth to jihadist ideology. A study of high school texts (for ages 15 to 18) on religious subjects, namely Hadith (Prophet's traditions), fiqh (jurisprudence) and tawhid (monotheist doctrine), concluded that texts on the first two subjects contain very little material that exhibits hostility toward non-Muslims but that the doctrine books do.[175] The content analysis reveals both Wahhabi doctrine and Muslim Brother themes. In fact, the Muslim Brother imprint on this sample of Saudi schoolbooks is striking. Apparently, members of the organization secured positions in the Ministry of Education, which they used to propagate their ideas. Since the 1930s, the Brothers had emphasized the crucial role that education plays in shaping young minds and they made education policy a central focus in their lobbying to Egyptian governments as well as operating their own schools.[176] It was natural, then, that Muslim Brother refugees in the kingdom would seek to influence its schools. From the Najdi doctrine, the lessons enumerate idolatrous practices (seeking intercession, visiting shrines) and acts that make one an apostate (mocking religion, denying God's unity). Pupils learn the importance of avoiding the company of non-Muslims so that one does not become like them. One textbook exhorts the reader to never greet unbelievers on their holidays or offer them condolences on the death of a loved one. The Wahhabi discourse of separation had formerly been directed against Muslims of neighbouring lands, but modern Saudi textbooks define a new object of xenophobia, Christians and Jews, or in standard Muslim Brother terminology, Crusaders and Zionists. Pupils learn the Muslim Brother view of Islam's modern relations with the West. The foreign threat to Islam began with the Crusades and then resumed in the nineteenth century with missionary activity seeking to win converts to Christianity and undermine Islam. In recent times, foreign aggression has taken the forms of imported political ideologies (Arab nationalism, socialism, secularism), cultural imperialism (western forms of leisure and consumption) and Zionist expansionism. This Wahhabi/Muslim Brother hybrid exhibits a defensive mood, the sense that powerful alien forces threaten to totally uproot Islam.[177] Hence, the books teach that jihad is necessary to defend against an enemy seeking to corrupt morality (cultural imperialism) and expel Muslims from their homes (Zionism).[178] Of course, this aggressive defensiveness in turn evokes a sense of threat in foreign observers. The entire dynamic bears striking resemblance to historical enmity between Wahhabis and neighbouring Muslims: each felt the other was a threat and each adopted aggressive attitudes toward the other. In addition to the religious content of curriculum, a Saudi government study noted that conservative teachers frequently encouraged religious prejudice.[179]

The debate over religious intolerance in Saudi schools led to substantial changes in at least one text prepared for the 2003–2004 school year. The new edition of the text on doctrine for 15-year-old pupils removed entire sections that instructed pupils to bear enmity toward non-Muslims and Muslims who do not follow Wahhabi views. Instead, it emphasizes the common lineage that Islam shares with Christianity and Judaism, citing a Qur'anic verse that refers to the Torah, the Psalms and the Gospel as divine revelations.[180] Whether this sort of change will find its way into the entire religious curriculum is an open question, but it does indicate a willingness to inject a more tolerant spirit into the classroom and to challenge traditional Wahhabi positions. In fact, religious hardliners reacted with alacrity to the shift. In 2004, Safar al-Hawali supported a petition to protest education reform as surrender to demands from the USA, which desires to detach Saudi Arabia from its adherence to Islam and lure it into the infidel camp.[181] But the government was careful to secure the imprimatur of a senior Wahhabi cleric, Sheikh Salih ibn Fawzan, on the new version.[182]

Education reform is but one item in a larger agenda that emerged in the course of three National Dialogues convened by Al Saud in 2003–2004 in order to seek new ground for national unity. The agenda for these sessions included sensitive issues like terrorism, education and women's rights. More notable than the topics was the participation of Wahhabis, Shiites, Sufis, sahwa sheikhs and non-Wahhabi Sunni followers of Maliki and Shafi'i legal schools at the first session in Riyadh in June 2003. Hence, the dialogues recognized the country's religious pluralism.[183] Salman al-Awda attended a National Dialogue session in 2003 and met with Shiite religious leader Sheikh Hassan al-Saffar, but Safar al-Hawali refused to meet with Shiites, viewing them in traditional Wahhabi terms as infidels.[184] The second session took place in Mecca in December 2003. This forum convened religious figures from various groups as well as merchants and reformers. The discussion centred on the roots of religious violence and its relationship to endemic problems in the economy and the education system. In June 2004, a third National Dialogue was held in Medina to address women's issues, including employment, driving and their legal subordination to men (a woman may not go to school, get a job, or seek medical care without permission of a male guardian).[185] It seems doubtful that a set of sporadic dialogues could have much impact on deeply ingrained attitudes. Nevertheless, the official recognition of religious pluralism was a blow to the Wahhabi establishment, which could only view it as a compromise with idolatrous forces. On the other hand, the combined weight of Islamic revivalism and Wahhabi doctrine may curtail the pursuit of such inclusiveness.

Each crisis since 1979 has signalled a broadening of the field of religious discontent with dynastic rule and the Wahhabi establishment. Juhayman's revolt involved a few hundred men and was over in a matter of weeks. The ferment of 1990–1991, however, represented widespread dissatisfaction with Saudi policies and practices. More significantly, it demonstrated the inroads made by Islamic revivalism at the expense of Wahhabi ulama's legitimacy with pious Saudis. That the Najdi doctrine always felt oppressive to the kingdom's Shiites was natural. That a substantial segment of cosmopolitan Hijaz never embraced it was not surprising. But the novel aspect of the Gulf War controversies was the rise of a revivalist discourse that challenged the Wahhabi ulama. Developments since September 2001 have only confirmed the impression that Al Saud's historical alliance with the Wahhabi mission is paying diminishing returns. Al Saud has responded by opening the public sphere to a plurality of voices articulating a range of religious and liberal views. Behind this tactic lies an instrumental perspective of the Wahhabi mission. It is apparently showing itself to be unsuited to the shifting landscape and recent travails of Saudi society brought about by the inability of the government to manage the kingdom's resources to the benefit of many citizens. Wahhabism, with its focus on doctrinal and moral issues, does not have answers for rising levels of poverty, high unemployment and economic stagnation. Islamic revivalism has established firm roots among the graduates of religious universities that expanded in the 1980s, in large measure because of its explicit commitment to address modern political issues of development, government accountability, nationalism and anti-imperialism.[186]

The present debate signifies that the Najdi mission has become part of a globalized Muslim discourse. The Saudi government's deployment of Wahhabism as a foreign policy instrument amplified its influence. Conversely, Riyadh's decision to offer safe haven to Islamic revivalists unwittingly broadened the country's religious spectrum. These two developments combined with events in the Muslim world and the impact of such communications technologies as the satellite dish and the Internet that breach the walls of censorship to open Saudi Arabia to contemporary religious currents. How Wahhabism will fare in this particular marketplace of ideas remains to be seen. It still benefits from formidable institutional, material and political resources, but for a brief spell at least its hegemony is threatened by revivalist tendencies.

Conclusion

The Wahhabi mission's two-hundred-year reign as a hegemonic regional religious culture is in jeopardy. Behind a shield of Saudi authority, its doctrine, leadership, ulama and canon excluded rival Muslim perspectives well into the twentieth century. Wahhabi ulama discouraged travel to other Muslim lands to trade, let alone to pursue religious studies. Their doctrine of separation was rooted in the apprehension that idolatry spreads like a germ through contact with non-believers. The first line of communication with the Muslim world opened with the rise of sympathetic revivalist trends in Arab lands and India in the late 1800s. The wall between Wahhabis and other Muslims was lowered further as a result of Abd al-Aziz ibn Saud's pragmatic accommodation with the outside world. His desire for international legitimacy led him to suppress the Ikhwan and to adopt a flexible religious policy in Hijaz. His need for funds prompted him to invite American petroleum engineers into the kingdom. Meanwhile, Islamic revivalist trends like the Muslim Brothers afforded allies for combating western cultural advances. The decision to receive Muslim Brother refugees and then to use them as part of an Islamic foreign policy bolstered the Wahhabi mission outside its homeland, but it also undermined the Najdi doctrine's historical monopoly in Saudi

Arabia. The ostensible compatibility between the Muslim Brothers, Jamaati Islami and Wahhabism made them natural allies for many years, most of all in the triumphant Afghan jihad. But the Wahhabis' subordination of idealism to the interests of Al Saud, even to the point of endorsing the decision to request military assistance from the infidel USA, ruptured the alliance. By that time, Islamic revivalism had made inroads inside the kingdom. As Muslim Brothers obtained positions in schools and religious institutions (alternate cadres), and as young Saudis turned to books and cassettes by Islamic revivalists (an alternate doctrine and canon), Wahhabism lost its exclusive grip on public religious discourse. Revivalism's religious nationalist narrative of modern history and its critique of corrupt, inept rulers gained wide acceptance and steadily eroded Wahhabism's hegemony. That became evident in 1990–1991 when the dissident sahwa sheikhs deployed revivalism's vocabulary and schema of global events to express nationalist opposition to foreign domination in a religious idiom. When the Wahhabi leadership defended the dynasty, the Saudi revivalists denounced them both as corrupt. Nothing like a grassroots religious movement against the Wahhabi ulama had ever occurred before.

The internal challenge posed by the sahwa sheikhs was compounded by Osama bin Laden's denunciations of the Wahhabi ulama for endorsing an apostate regime. One might wonder if it makes sense to trace a militant thread from the early twentieth-century Ikhwan to Juhayman to bin Laden. There is a resemblance in that each one challenged the legitimacy of Al Saud on the grounds that they fell short in acting and ruling according to Islamic law. Furthermore, all three objected to Al Saud's accommodation to infidel foreign powers. The Ikhwan rebelled against the recognition of an international boundary when Abd al-Aziz ibn Saud deemed it necessary to coexist with the British in Iraq and Transjordan. Juhayman's band blamed Al Saud for permitting infidel cultural influences to spread in the kingdom. Osama bin Laden seeks to depose Al Saud for allowing infidel troops to occupy the kingdom and supporting United States foreign policy at the expense of Muslims' welfare. At the same time, we find significant differences between the three cases. The Ikhwan, for instance, came out of a cultural milieu of recently settled nomadic tribesmen and their revolt was, in part, an assertion by tribal nobility of their autonomy vis-à-vis Ibn Saud as well as refusal to abandon raiding as a means of livelihood. While Juhayman came from an old

Ikhwan settlement and lineage, he did not grow up in a nomadic milieu. Moreover, his movement did not challenge the international order, as the Ikhwan had done, but the morality of Saudi Arabia's internal order. In addition, the Ikhwan did not possess the millenarian streak that appeared in Juhayman's movement. Osama bin Laden presents yet another different set of concerns, not rejecting borders or asserting the arrival of the Mahdi. Instead, he belongs to the transnational jihadist movement that has spread across much of the Muslim world. The particular religious ideas that inspired the three militant episodes are not identical either. The Ikhwan were only recently absorbed into the Wahhabi discursive space before their revolt and the exact circumstances of their 'conversion' to Wahhabism remain frustratingly obscure. Juhayman's teachers certainly included Wahhabis, but his declarations bear the marks of modern revivalism. Bin Laden's ideas come from jihadist ideologues active in Egypt and the Afghan cause.

Since the 1970s, it has been commonplace to speculate about the legitimacy and longevity of Al Saud rule.[1] True, the kingdom has endured a prolonged stretch of unrest since 1990. And the arrival of al-Qaeda terrorism in May 2003 caught the authorities by surprise. Nevertheless, Al Saud have weathered many a crisis in their long history and they continue to skilfully wield a formidable array of resources. Petroleum income has proven to be a blessing and a curse. On one hand, it affords the government the revenue to employ a large, well-equipped internal security force to muzzle dissent and combat al-Qaeda. On the other hand, the spectre of princely extravagance at public expense has damaged the dynasty's legitimacy. Another asset for the Saudis is the splintered nature of the challenges to their regime. Liberal reformers lack an institutional base and a popular following. The criticisms of the sahwa sheikhs resonate with Saudis far more than the bloody campaign of al-Qaeda's jihadists. The Wahhabi establishment has thrown its full weight behind the dynasty's struggle against the jihadists and hopes it will keep liberal reformers in check. Except for the jihadists, none of these factions seeks to rid the country of dynastic rule. In sum, predictions of Al Saud's imminent demise miss the mark.[2]

Early in the twenty-first century, the truly novel element in the Arabian kingdom is not the dynasty's troubles but the debasement of Wahhabism's credibility. By recognizing religious pluralism in the 2003 National Dialogues, Al Saud demonstrated they possessed the power to subordinate the Wahhabi mission to dynastic interest. That step also implied a judgment that Wahhabism could no longer provide a sufficient foundation for the dynasty's legitimacy. Wahhabism lost that capacity because of the challenges from sahwa sheikhs and jihadists dissatisfied with senior clerics' unstinting loyalty to Al Saud. In that context, it made sense to expand the field of public religious expression to encompass Shiites, Sufis and non-Wahhabi Sunnis. These marginalized groups are eager to break down the walls of discrimination and persecution, so they participated in the National Dialogues. Whether this represents a strategic choice by Al Saud to develop a durable system of pluralism or a tactical manoeuvre in response to pressures of the moment remains to be seen. For as long as Wahhabi clerics dominate legal, educational and religious institutions, other Muslim groups will be on unsure footing. Were a period of political calm to set in, for instance, Al Saud might again close ranks with the Wahhabi establishment and force other Muslims behind closed doors.

But continued enforcement of public compliance with Wahhabi norms, even if the religious establishment were to negotiate the assimilation of the sahwa sheikhs, may prove to be untenable. This is not because the kingdom's Shiites, Sufis and non-Wahhabi Sunnis have marshalled the resources to assert themselves. On the contrary, they depend on the mood of Al Saud for the few bits of recognition they have obtained. In the long term, the fundamental problem for the Wahhabi mission's standing as the dominant religious culture of Saudi Arabia is more profound and may be resistant to resolution. That problem stems from the political bargain that made possible the mission's initial rise and consolidation in the eighteenth and nineteenth centuries. Muhammad ibn Abd al-Wahhab was able to propagate his call only after he was expelled from two Najdi settlements and he had the good fortune to find a patron at al-Dir'iyya. As Saudi power expanded in Najd, the Wahhabi doctrine not only accompanied it but also displaced the older religious tradition of the region. The Wahhabi mission was not about establishing itself as a legal school or Sufi order coexisting with other Muslims. Its exclusive claim to doctrinal truth endowed it with an impulse to exclude, or at least silence, other Muslim views where it had the political power to do so.

Much of Wahhabism's twentieth-century experience has been the story of trade-offs for the sake of consolidating the position of its political guardian. The ulama gained control over education, law, public morality and religious institutions. In return, they only mildly objected to the import of modern technology and communications and they did not hamper Abd al-Aziz ibn Saud's dealings with the British, non-Saudi Arabs and Americans. The long-term effect of their concession to the necessity of dealing with the outside world was Saudi Arabia's integration into the international political and economic system, but its isolation from modern norms, even those taking shape in other Muslim countries. That isolation did not persist, in part because of the political decision to receive Muslim Brother refugees and the ensuing infiltration of the transnational revivalist movement. Now there is no going back to the earlier historical phase of isolation because a generation of Saudi youth has assimilated the revivalist message alongside lessons in Wahhabi doctrine.

The introduction of the satellite dish and the Internet in the 1990s ensures a deepening of connections between Saudis and the outside world. Wahhabi ulama have used these and other communications technologies to proselytize. At the same time, they provide channels, into the kingdom, for ideas and images far more worrisome to Wahhabi ulama than anything contained in Ottoman polemical treatises. Unless Saudi Arabia were to electronically disconnect, the long term prospect for its citizens is increasing access to ideas about Islam and many other things, without travelling to study in infidel lands. The original condition of isolation and exclusion of other views has shattered. How the various factors of Saudi politics, economic distress, social tensions and cultural angst will play out is, of course, unforeseeable. Predicting the future is not part of the historian's job. The perils of 'present-minded' history are well known and, in this instance, unavoidable. The closer historians stand to events, the more obscure become the broad outlines that they seek to discern. From this vantage point, early in the twenty-first century, the religious field in Saudi Arabia appears to be in flux, its horizons hazy and the destiny of the eighteenth-century call from Najd uncertain.

Al al-Sheikh

The House of the Sheikh, the family of Muhammad ibn Abd al-Wahhab

Abd Allah ibn Abd al-Latif (1848–1921): Head of religious estate during period of Rashidi rule and the early years of King Abd al-Aziz ibn Saud

Abd Allah ibn Muhammad ibn Abd al-Wahhab (1752–1826): Head of religious estate after his father retired from public life in 1773; died in Cairo exile after the fall of the first Saudi amirate

Abd al-Latif ibn Abd al-Rahman (1810–1876): Head of religious estate in 1860s and early 1870s

Abd al-Rahman ibn Hasan (1780–1869): Head of religious estate in the second Saudi amirate

Muhammad ibn Abd al-Wahhab (1703–1792): Founder of the Wahhabi movement

Muhammad ibn Ibrahim (1893–1969): Head of religious estate in mid twentieth century

Sulayman ibn Abd Allah (1780–1818): Grandson of Muhammad ibn Abd al-Wahhab and author of influential treatises restricting travel to and residing in land of idolaters

Chronology

1744 Muhammad ibn Abd al-Wahhab and Muhammad ibn Saud make a pact to
support one another
1803 Saudi forces conquer Mecca
1804 Saudi forces conquer Medina
1811 Ottoman-Egyptian invasion of Arabia
1818 Ottoman-Egyptian conquest of first Saudi amirate
1824 Establishment of second Saudi amirate
1837 Second Egyptian invasion of Najd
1841 Egyptian withdrawal from Najd
1843 Amir Faysal comes to power
1865 Amir Faysal's death and Saudi succession struggle erupts
1871 Ottoman forces conquer al-Hasa
1891 Second Saudi amirate falls to Rashidis of Ha'il
1902 Abd al-Aziz ibn Saud seizes Riyadh
1913 Saudi forces conquer al-Hasa
1921 Saudi forces conquer Ha'il
1924 Saudi forces conquer Mecca
1925 Medina falls to Saudi forces
1929 Ibn Saud defeats the Ikhwan at Sibila
1932 Ibn Saud declares the kingdom of Saudi Arabia
1933 Oil concession to American consortium
1953 Ibn Saud dies; Saud ibn Abd al-Aziz becomes king
1962 Ten-Point Reform Programme promulgated; Muslim World League
founded
1964 King Saud deposed and Faysal ibn Abd al-Aziz becomes king
1979 Juhayman al-Utaybi's revolt in Mecca; Soviet Union invades Afghanistan
1988 Soviet Union withdraws from Afghanistan; fighting erupts among
mujahidin factions
1990 Iraq invades Kuwait; Saudi government requests United States military
assistance
1995 Saudi militants bomb National Guard building in Riyadh
1996 Saudi militants bomb Khobar towers; Osama bin Laden declares jihad
against the United States and the West; Taliban regime comes to power in
Afghanistan
1998 Al-Qaeda bombs American embassies in Kenya and Tanzania
2000 Al-Qaeda attacks USS Cole at Aden port

2001 Al-Qaeda carries out 11 September attacks against the USA; United States
       forces invade Afghanistan to overthrow the Taliban regime
2003 Saudi militants attack western residential compounds in Riyadh
2004 Saudi government holds National Dialogues recognizing religious
       pluralism

Glossary

Amirate	Principality
Bid'a	An illegitimate innovation in ritual
Fatwa	A jurist's legal opinion
Hadar	Settled folk of Arabia, in contrast to nomadic Bedouins
Hadith	A saying or action of the Prophet Muhammad
Hanbali	A school of law and theology named after a ninth century Baghdad scholar, Ahmad ibn Hanbal
Hijra	Emigration from a place of unbelief to a place of belief. The Prophet Muhammad and the first converts to Islam undertook a hijra from Mecca to Medina in 622. Hijra is also the term for an Ikhwan settlement in the early twentieth century
Hudud	Specific punishments prescribed in Islamic law for a finite set of crimes: adultery, theft, slander and so forth
Ifta'	The act of issuing a fatwa
Ijtihad	The exercise of personal judgment in arriving at a legal opinion or verdict on a case
Jahiliyya	Ignorance of God's unity, religious barbarism
Kafir	An unbeliever: idolater, apostate, Christian, or Jew
Kufr	Disbelief in God's unity and the obligation to worship Him alone
Madrasa	In modern Arabic usage, it is the general term for a school; it also has the connotation of a religious school
Mushrik	An idolater, one who associates creatures with God in worship, speech, or action
Mutawwi'a	Enforcers of Wahhabi norms in public; often called religious police
Muwahhid	A proclaimer of God's unity; a term Wahhabis have used to describe themselves
Qadi	In modern Arabic usage, it is the general term for a judge; it also has the connotation of a judge in matters of Islamic law
Salaf	The ancestors, the early, exemplary generations of Muslims
Salafi	One who claims to base his understanding and practice on the example of the early generations of Muslims and considers later Muslim tradition a departure from Islam; a term used by Wahhabis and by several other modern revivalist tendencies with varying agendas
Shari'a	Islamic law
Shirk	Idolatry, associating creatures with God; a form of unbelief

Sunna	The Prophetic Tradition; it is comprised of thousands of hadiths
Takfir	To consider somebody an infidel
Tawhid	The doctrine of God's unity
Ta'zir	Punishment for a crime at the discretion of a ruler or a judge
Ulama	Religious scholars

Notes

Preface

1. The term 'Wahhabi' is derived from the name of Muhammad ibn Abd al-Wahhab, the formulator of Wahhabi doctrine. He and his followers reject the term, coined by early Muslim opponents to disparage the reform movement. Their preference has been to call their movement either *salafi* or *muwahhid*. The first word refers to a Muslim who follows the ways of the first generations (*salaf*) of Muslims in the seventh century. This term has been appropriated by a number of modern revivalist movements with differing agendas. The second word means one who proclaims God's unity. Other Muslims see themselves as deserving that name as well. Some writers render it in English as 'Unitarian', but that term creates confusion with the modern western religious group of that name.

2. For an antidote to my western befuddlement, see the excellent discussion of Muhammad ibn Abd al-Wahhab's writings as a voice participating in an 'Islamic discursive tradition' spanning centuries. Haj, Samira, 'Reordering Islamic orthodoxy: Muhammad ibn 'Abdul Wahhab', *Muslim World* xcii (2002), pp. 333–336.

Introduction

1. Traboulsi, Samer, 'An early refutation of Muhammad ibn Abd al-Wahhab's reformist views', *Die Welt des Islams* xlii/3 (2002), pp. 373–396.

2. Al-Fahad, Abdulaziz H., 'The `imama vs. the `iqal: Hadari-Bedouin conflict in the formation of the Saudi state', in Madawi Al-Rasheed and Robert Vitalis (eds.), *Counter-Narratives: History, Contemporary Society, and Politics in Saudi Arabia and Yemen* (New York, 2004), pp. 42, 63 n. 44.

3. For a concise discussion of the jahiliyya concept, see Shepard, William E., 'Sayyid Qutb's doctrine of *jahiliyya*', *International Journal of Middle East Studies* xxxv/4 (2003), pp. 522–523.

4. Historians have proposed various explanations of Wahhabism's origins. Michael Cook suggests that the historical sources are too meager to venture a strong case for any particular causal argument. 'The expansion of the first Saudi state: The case of Washm', in C. E. Bosworth (ed.), *The Islamic World from Classical to Modern Times: Essays in Honor of Bernard Lewis* (Princeton, 1989); on the intellectual sources for Muhammad ibn Abd al-

Wahhab's doctrine, 'On the origins of Wahhabism', *Journal of the Royal Asiatic Society of Great Britain and Ireland* ii/2 (1992), pp. 91–202. On the other hand, Hala Fattah sees Wahhabism as the ideological justification for mercantilist policies pursued by Saudi rulers. *The Politics of Regional Trade in Iraq, Arabia, and the Gulf, 1745–1900* (Albany, 1997). Uwaidah M. Al Juhany situates the rise of Wahhabism more squarely in Najd's own long-term historical processes: the growth in the population and number of oasis settlements, incessant political strife and the increase in the number of religious specialists. In this scenario, Muhammad ibn Abd al-Wahhab had the solution to Najd's political instability with his call for a single, unitary political authority that would implement Islamic law. *Najd before the Salafi Reform Movement: Social, Religious, and Political Conditions during the Three Centuries Preceding the Rise of the Saudi State* (Reading, 2002). Khalid al-Dakhil cites the same historical processes as laying the foundation for state-formation. 'Social origins of the Wahhabi movement', paper presented at the Middle East Studies Association Annual Meeting, 2002. Abd al-Aziz al-Fahad emphasizes the detribalized character of oasis settlements and their vulnerability to nomads' frequent raids and extortion. In this view, Wahhabism and the unification of Najd's oasis settlements under Saudi rule provided the means for settled society to tame the region's nomadic tribes. 'The `imama vs. the `iqal'.

Chapter One

1. For an excellent portrait of pre-Wahhabi settled life, see Al Juhany, Uwaidah M., *Najd before the Salafi Reform Movement: Social, Religious, and Political Conditions during the Three Centuries Preceding the Rise of the Saudi State* (Reading, 2002), pp. 90–127.

2. For a useful overview of Najd ecology, climate and economy, see Steinberg, Guido, 'Ecology, knowledge and trade in Central Arabia (Najd) during the nineteenth and early twentieth centuries', in Madawi Al-Rasheed and Robert Vitalis (eds.), *Counter-Narratives: History, Contemporary Society, and Politics in Saudi Arabia and Yemen* (New York, 2004), pp. 78–85.

3. This point is emphasized in Al-Fahad, Abdulaziz H., 'The `imama vs. the `iqal: *Hadari*-Bedouin conflict in the formation of the Saudi state', in Al-Rasheed and Vitalis (eds.), *Counter-Narratives*, pp. 36–37, 39. The same argument is in Al-Dakhil, Khalid, 'Social origins of the Wahhabi movement', paper presented at the Middle East Studies Association Annual Meeting, 2002.

4. There are four legal schools in Sunni Islam. The Hanafi school was the official school of the Ottoman Empire. The Shafi'i school had a strong presence in Ottoman Arab lands and along the rim of the Indian Ocean. The Maliki school was dominant in North Africa. The Hanbali school, from which Wahhabism emerged, had ancient centres in Baghdad, Damascus and Palestine's Nablus region. The circumstances of the Hanbali school's establishment in Najd are unknown. Unlike the other three Sunni legal schools, the Hanbalis occupy a niche in the range of Islamic theological

groups and are known for espousing the most literal and least speculative positions. Each of the legal schools recognizes the legitimacy of the others. As we shall see, Wahhabism's peculiar character stems not from Hanbali law and legal theory but from Hanbali theology.

5. Sunnis are the largest Muslim sect, but Shiites comprise a majority in Iran, Iraq and Bahrain and substantial minorities in al-Hasa, Kuwait and Lebanon. Historical enmity between Sunnis and Shiites dates to the first generation of Muslims.

6. In Arabian nomenclature, 'Al Musharraf' means the folk of Musharraf. 'Al' means folk, family, or clan and is not to be confused with the Arabic definite article, transliterated with a hyphen, 'al-'.

7. Mutawa, Abdulla M., 'The Ulama of Najd from the Sixteenth Century to the Mid-Eighteenth Century', Doctoral dissertation, University of California, Los Angeles, 1989, pp. 153–158, 280–286.

8. For a summary of Muhammad ibn Abd al-Wahhab's life based on the two earliest Saudi chronicles, see DeLong-Bas, Natana J., *Wahhabi Islam: From Revival and Reform to Global Jihad* (New York, 2004), pp. 17–40.

9. For a meticulous discussion of the different versions of Muhammad ibn Abd al-Wahhab's travels, see Cook, Michael. 'On the origins of Wahhabism', *Journal of the Royal Asiatic Society of Great Britain and Ireland* ii/2 (1992), pp. 191–197.

10. Al Juhany, *Najd*, pp. 129–134.

11. A Hadith, or individual Prophetic tradition, has two parts. The first part is a list of men who heard and transmitted an action or saying of the Prophet. The second part consists of the reported words or acts of the Prophet. Muslim specialists in the study of hadiths rated their 'soundness', or reliability, according to the chain of transmission. Hadiths make up the Sunna, the concept of the Prophet's normative, authoritative practices that Muslims are supposed to follow. The Sunna is the second major source for Islamic belief and practice after the Qur'an, the word of God revealed to Muhammad. Sufi orders were widespread in the eighteenth-century Muslim world. They gave organized expression to Sufism, a diverse and complex dimension of Islam that may be characterized as the effort to purify one's moral character and attain a close relationship with God through religious ceremonies at which adepts 'mentioned' or 'remembered' God's name. The term *dhikr* applied to Sufi ceremonies means mention or remember in Arabic. Sufi orders had a hierarchy of spiritual leaders, assistants and lay members. The Wahhabis objected to the appearance of believers seeking to approach God through human intermediaries, either living Sufi leaders or dead saints believed to possess living grace at their tombs.

12. The possible influence of contact with Hadith scholars in Medina is explored in Voll, John, 'Muhammad Hayya al-Sindi and Muhammad b Abd al-Wahhab', *Bulletin of the School of Oriental and African Studies* xxxviii (1975), pp. 32–39. The Saudi chronicle by Uthman ibn Bishr relates an anecdote about a teacher in Medina who told Sheikh Muhammad that his 'sword' for

vanquishing heretical practices was his library of Hadith books. Cited by
DeLong-Bas, *Wahhabi Islam*, p. 21.

13. Ahmad Dallal offers a rigorous critique of the view that eighteenth century
     revivalists had common purposes or motives. He compares Ibn Abd al-
     Wahhab to India's Shah Wali Allah, Nigeria's Uthman dan Fodio and Libya's
     Muhammad al-Sanusi. Before my research on Wahhabism, I accepted the
     view that it was part of a broader revivalist trend, but I now consider that
     a hypothesis to be supported with more evidence. Dallal, Ahmad, 'The
     origins and objectives of Islamic revivalist thought, 1750–1850', *Journal of
     the American Oriental Society* cxiii/3 (1993), pp. 341–359. Bernard Haykel
     buttresses Dallal's scepticism of the hypothesis concerning a sweeping
     revivalism trend in his superb study of the Yemeni scholar Muhammad al-
     Shawkani (d. 1834). Haykel, Bernard, *Revival and Reform in Islam: The Legacy
     of Muhammad al-Shawkani* (Cambridge, 2003).

14. The imams are descendants of the Prophet Muhammad through his son-in-
     law Ali and daughter Fatima. Shiites believe that Ali and then his sons and
     their descendants were the rightful leaders of the early Muslim community
     but that corrupt Muslims had usurped power. Shiites honor Ali and his
     descendants with visits to shrines housing their tombs. Seeking the imams'
     intercession with God is legitimate in Shiite practice, but the Wahhabis
     consider it sheer polytheism.

15. Ibn Ghannam, Husayn, *Tarikh najd* (Cairo, 1961), p. 76.

16. Abd al-Rahman ibn Hasan Al al-Shaykh, *al-Maqamat* (Riyadh, n.d.), p. 6.
     Ibn Abd al-Wahhab, Muhammad, *Kitab al-tawhid: Essay on the Unicity of
     Allah, or What is Due to Allah from his Creatures*, translated by Ismail Raji
     al Faruqi (n.p., 1981); Arabic text, Ibn Abd al-Wahhab, Muhammad, *Kitab
     al-tawhid*, in Muhammad Rashid Rida (ed.), *Majmu`at al-tawhid al-najdiyya*,
     Reprint edition (Riyadh, 1999), pp. 19-95. Even if he did not compose the
     essay in Basra, it quickly became known to Basran religious scholars: one
     of the earliest attacks on Ibn Abd al-Wahhab's doctrine was written by a
     Basran sheikh. Traboulsi, Samer, 'An early refutation of Muhammad ibn
     Abd al-Wahhab's reformist views', *Die Welt des Islams* xlii/3 (2002), pp. 381–
     382. For another sample of eighteenth century anti-Wahhabi polemic in
     English translation, see Ebied, R.Y. and M.J.L. Young, 'An unpublished
     refutation of the doctrines of the Wahhabis', *Revista degli studi orientali* l
     (1976), pp. 377–397.

17. On the inspiration motif, see Cook, 'On the origins of Wahhabism', p. 202;
     on the view that he wrote the treatise in Huraymila after returning from
     Basra, see Ibn Ghannam, *Tarikh najd*, p. 77.

18. Vogel, Frank E., *Islamic Law and Legal Systems: Studies of Saudi Arabia* (Leiden,
     2000), p. 76. For a discussion of Ibn Abd al-Wahhab's legal method, see
     ibid., 72–76; DeLong-Bas, *Wahhabi Islam*, pp. 93–121.

19. For the proportion of verses from the Qur'an, hadiths and medieval
     authorities cited as proof-texts in *Kitab al-tawhid*, see DeLong-Bas, *Wahhabi
     Islam*, pp. 51–53.

20. I use idolatry for *shirk* throughout this study. On the concept of *shirk*, see Gimaret, D., 'Shirk', *Encyclopaedia of Islam*, CD-Rom Edition 1.0 (Brill, 1999) IX, 484b. Gimaret notes that the Qur'an does not refer to Christians and Jews as people who commit *shirk*, but that Muslim exegetes of the Qur'an blur the distinction. Christians and Jews are unbelievers, but the idolaters are the worst sort of disbeliever, or *kafir*. On the concept of *kafir*, see Bjorkman, W., 'Kafir', *Encyclopaedia of Islam*, CD-Rom Edition 1.0 (Brill, 1999), IV:407b.

21. The term 'companion' refers to believers who met the Prophet.

22. See *Kitab al-tawhid*, pp. 3–7. All references are to the English translation.

23. Ibid., pp. 22–24.

24. Ibid., p. 16. Chapter 34 relates a Hadith where the Prophet called shirk the gravest of all sins. Ibid., p. 101.

25. Ibid., p. 40.

26. Ibid., pp. 43–45.

27. Ibid., pp. 54–56.

28. Ibid., pp. 64–69.

29. Ibid., pp. 70–71.

30. Ibid., pp. 72–76. For an extensive, sympathetic examination of Muhammad ibn Abd al-Wahhab's writings on theology and law, see DeLong-Bas, *Wahhabi Islam*. For a concise analysis seeking to rescue his doctrine from misconceptions, see Haj, Samira, 'Reordering Islamic orthodoxy: Muhammad ibn `Abd al-Wahhab', *Muslim World* xcii (2002), pp. 333–368.

31. Ibn Ghannam, *Tarikh najd*.

32. For an analysis of how Ibn Ghannam implicitly compares Ibn Abd al-Wahhab's life to the Prophet Muhammad's, see Peskes, Esther, *Muhammad B. Abdalwahhab (1703–1792) im Widerstreit* (Stuttgart, 1993), pp. 375–377.

33. Ibn Ghannam, *Tarikh najd*, pp. 76–77; Rentz, George Snavely, 'Muhammad ibn Abd al-Wahhab (1703/4–1792) and the Beginnings of Unitarian Empire in Arabia', Doctoral dissertation, University of California, Berkeley, 1948, pp. 30–34. Rentz offers a close paraphrase of Ibn Ghannam and a later Saudi chronicler, Uthman ibn Bishr.

34. Al al-Sheikh, Abd al-Rahman ibn Abd al-Latif, *Mashahir `ulama najd wa ghayruhum* (n.p., 1974), p. 24.

35. Ibn Ghannam, *Tarikh najd*, p. 78; Rentz, 'Muhammad ibn Abd al-Wahhab', pp. 34–35, 39–43.

36. On Sheikh Muhammad in al-Uyayna, see Ibn Ghannam, *Tarikh najd*, pp. 78–79; Rentz, 'Muhammad ibn Abd al-Wahhab', pp. 42–46.

37. Ibn Ghannam, *Tarikh najd*, pp. 79–80.

38. Ibn Ghannam, *Tarikh najd*, p. 80; Rentz, 'Muhammad ibn Abd al-Wahhab', pp. 46–47.

39. Rentz, 'Muhammad ibn Abd al-Wahhab', pp. 48–52. In Rentz's translation of Ibn Bishr's account, 'Perhaps God has in store for you conquests and booty better than the share of the harvest'. A jihad would bring religiously sanctioned plunder and the power to levy taxes.

40.   A meticulous study of the gradual pace of Saudi expansion is in Cook, Michael, 'The expansion of the first Saudi state: The case of Washm', in C. E. Bosworth (ed.), *The Islamic World from Classical to Modern Times: Essays in Honor of Bernard Lewis* (Princeton, 1989).

41.   For Ibn Suhaym's life, see al-Bassam, Abd Allah ibn Abd al-Rahman, `Ulama' najd khilal thamaniyat qurun*, 6 vols. (Riyadh, 1997), 2:381–382. One source reports that Ibn Suhaym settled in Riyadh around 1737 and became the religious leader after 1745. Ibn Asakir, Rashid, *Tarikh al-masajid wa al-awqaf al-qadima fi balad al-riyadh ila `amm 1373* (Riyadh, 1999), p. 65.

42.   Rentz, 'Muhammad ibn Abd al-Wahhab', pp. 57–66, 68, 70–71, 78–79, 86–90, 98–99, 110–112, 116–118, 124–125, 136–138, 142–145, 149, 164–170.

43.   My discussion of Ibn Suhaym's criticisms of Ibn Abd al-Wahhab is based on Uthaymin, Abd Allah, 'Mawqif Sulayman ibn Suhaym', in Abd Allah Uthaymin (ed.), *Buhuth wa ta`liqat fi tarikh al-mamlaka al-`arabiyyah al-sa`udiyyah* (Riyadh, 1984), pp. 89–113. For more on Ibn Suhaym's efforts to mobilize ulama in Mecca and Basra to attack Ibn Abd al-Wahhab's doctrine, see Traboulsi, 'An early refutation'.

44.   Summarizing points set forth in Uthaymin, 'Mawqif Sulayman ibn Suhaym'.

45.   Ibn al-Qayyim is the medieval authority he cited.

46.   Bassam, `Ulama', 2:350–355.

47.   Saudis today interpret Sulayman's possessing his grandfather's name to suggest that he was older because it was customary to name the eldest son after one's father, or to argue that he was younger because it is not customary to name a child after his grandfather when he is still alive.

48.   Sulayman ibn Khuwayter was Sulayman ibn Abd al-Wahhab's ally in al-Uyayna who was killed at Muhammad ibn Abd al-Wahhab's order. Rentz, 'Muhammad ibn Abd al-Wahhab', p. 80.

49.   The treatise, found in Ibn Ghannam's chronicle, is *Mufid al-mustafid bi kufr tarik al-tawhid*, a title that may have been devised by later Wahhabi tradition.

50.   Ibn Abd al-Wahhab, Sulayman, *Al-sawa`iq al-ilahiyya fi al-radd `ala al-wahhabiyya*, Ibrahim Muhammad al-Bitawi (ed.), (Cairo, 1987). He sent the essay to a fellow sheikh, Hasan ibn Idan, who became the Wahhabi qadi at Huraymila.

51.   Ibid., pp. 22–26, 87–88.

52.   Ibid., pp. 28–30.

53.   Ibid., pp. 30–31, 33. On the concept of *takfir*, see Hunwick, J. O., 'Takfir', *Encyclopaedia of Islam*, CD-Rom Edition 1.0 (Brill, 1999), X:122a.

54.   On vows at tombs, Ibn Abd al-Wahhab, Sulayman, *Al-sawa`iq al-ilahiyya*, pp. 34–35; on slaughtering animals in the name of a creature other than God, p. 36; on the status of people who introduce innovations into worship, pp. 60–66; on the Kharijites, pp. 66–69; on takfir, pp. 70–76.

55.   Ibid., p. 96.

56.   Ibid., pp. 37, 40.

57. The Kharijites were a sect that fought both Sunnis and Shiites, so the comparison was designed to cast the Wahhabis as an extreme movement and it became a standard element in anti-Wahhabi polemics. For the explicit comparison to Kharijites in the treatise, see pp. 43–45.

58. The treatise is in Ibn Ghannam, *Tarikh najd*, pp. 429–464. Ibn Ghannam related that Sheikh Muhammad wrote it in 1167/1754 in order to counter his brother's epistle to al-Uyayna. Rentz, 'Muhammad ibn Abd al-Wahhab', pp. 80–81.

59. Ibn Ghannam, *Tarikh najd*, p. 438.

60. Ibid., pp. 453–461. For more on this theme, see Chapter Two.

61. Sheikh Muhammad had the satisfaction of seeing Sulayman's son Abd al-Aziz move to al-Dir'iyya, where he attended the reformer's lessons. Bassam, *`Ulama'*, 3:363–364.

62. For an extensive discussion of Ibn Abd al-Wahhab's writings on jihad, see DeLong-Bas, *Wahhabi Islam*, pp. 201–225.

63. Ibn Abd al-Wahhab, Muhammad, *Kitab al-tawhid*, pp. 18–24.

64. Ibn Ghannam, *Tarikh najd*, pp. 467–471.

65. Ibid., p. 477.

66. DeLong-Bas, *Wahhabi Islam*, p. 203.

67. Ibid., pp. 206–207.

68. Ibid., pp. 223–224.

69. Michael Cook remarks on the Saudi conquest's impact on religious life in one region of Najd, 'At a guess, the conversion of Washm may have been marked by something of the same lightness of touch as its conquest'. See 'The expansion of the first Saudi state', p. 675. The discussion below indicates that the Wahhabis resorted to more coercive measures to purge settlements of doctrinal opponents than suggested by Cook's phrase. Without Saudi conquest, it is difficult to imagine how Wahhabi doctrine might have triumphed.

70. Al-Isa, Mayy bint Abd al-Aziz, *al-Hayah al-`ilmiyya fi najd mundhu qiyam da`wat al-sheikh Muhammad ibn Abd al-Wahhab wa hatta nihayat al-dawla al-sa`udiyya al-ula* (Riyadh, 1997), p. 64.

71. The qadi in Huraymila and al-Hasa was Hasan ibn Idan, Bassam, *`Ulama'*, 2:51–52; the teacher who stayed in Ushayqir was Ahmad ibn Mani', Isa, *al-Hayah al-`ilmiyya*, p. 353; Ibrahim ibn Ahmad ibn Ibrahim ibn Yusuf died in Damascus, Bassam, *`Ulama'*, 1:264–267; Abd Allah ibn Ahmad ibn Ismail resettled in Unayza, ibid., 4:19–21. The sources disagree about the views of Uthman ibn Uqayl ibn Uthman al-Suhaymi, the qadi of Ushayqir before the Saudis conquered it. Bassam indicates he backed the Wahhabi mission, 5:139–140, but Isa suggests that he harboured doubts about it, *al-Hayah al-`ilmiyya*, p. 347 n. 31.

72. Michael Cook identifies the imam of Tharmada opposed to the Wahhabi mission as Muhammad ibn Id, 'The expansion of the first Saudi state', p. 696 n. 173; he also refers to this man as the qadi, p. 696 n. 170; Isa, *al-Hayah al-'ilmiyya*, pp. 349, 352 n. 29; perhaps referring to the same individual,

Bassam mentions Muhammad ibn Ubayd as a man who corresponded with Sheikh Muhammad and was killed fighting the Saudis, `Ulama', 6:274.

73. Abd al-Aziz ibn Abd al-Rahman ibn Ruzayn ibn `Adwan al-Ruzayni, Bassam, `Ulama', 3:406–409.

74. Abd al-Muhsin ibn Ali ibn Abd Allah al-Sharikhi, ibid., 5:28–29. One source gives the title of al-Sharikhi's rebuttal of Ibn Abd al-Wahhab as 'Radd ala taghiyat al-`Arid', or 'Refutation of al-`Arid's tyrant'. Ibn Humayd, Muhammad ibn Abd Allah, al-Suhub al-wabila ala dara'ih al-hanabila, Bakr Abd Allah Abu Zayd and Abd al-Rahman ibn Sulayman al-Uthaymin (eds.), 3 vols. (Beirut, 1996), 2:668.

75. Hamad ibn Ibrahim ibn Hamad Al Musharraf, from al-Marat, Bassam, `Ulama', 2:68–69.

76. Ibrahim ibn Hamad ibn Abd al-Wahhab ibn Musharraf would become qadi of al-Marat like his father and was killed in battle against the invading Ottoman-Egyptian forces in 1817, ibid., 1:294–295.

77. Ibrahim ibn Hasan ibn Idan (see note 71 on his father) was killed in an anti-Saudi revolt that erupted in al-Hasa in 1792, Isa, al-Hayah al-`ilmiyya, pp. 363, 364 n.1.

78. Representatives of the Aba Husayn lineage include Abd al-Rahman ibn Abd al-Muhsin ibn Uthman Aba Husayn. He was born in Ushayqir, studied there, then at al-Dir`iyya and became a qadi for the Saudis; Bassam, `Ulama', 3:121–122. His brother Uthman ibn Abd al-Muhsin ibn Uthman Aba Husayn also backed the Wahhabi mission, ibid., 5:128.

79. Hamad ibn Shabana, died around 1730s, ibid., 2:77–79; Uthman ibn Abd Allah ibn Shabana, probably a qadi before the first Saudi state, ibid., 5:113–114; Hamad ibn Abd al-Jabbar ibn Shabana, qadi for the first Saudi state, ibid., 2:80–81; Abd al-Jabbar ibn Hamad ibn Shabana, died around 1780s and was the father of two Wahhabi ulama, ibid., 3:7–8.

80. Muhammad ibn Suhaym and his son Sulayman ibn Suhaym (1718–1767), ibid., 2:381–382; Abd Allah ibn Ahmad ibn Suhaym (d. 1761) criticized the Wahhabis, ibid., 4:38–40.

81. Ibid., 4:364–369.

82. Ibrahim, Abd al-Aziz Abd al-Ghani, Najdiyyun wara' al-hudud: al-`Uqaylat, 1705–1950 (London, 1991), pp. 39–40; on the exile of the historian Ibn La`bun's lineage from the Sudayr region, see Bassam, `Ulama', 2:108–112.

83. On Sayf al-`Atiqi, Salih al-`Atiqi, Muhammad al-`Atiqi and Abd Allah ibn Da'ud, see the discussion of emigration from Najd to Zubayr in Chapter Two. A sixth individual may also have rejected the mission: Ahmad ibn Abd Allah ibn `Aqil (d. 1819) studied in Zubayr with anti-Wahhabi sheikhs Muhammad ibn Sullum and Uthman ibn Sanad and then settled in Medina; Bassam, `Ulama', 1:485–487.

84. Ibid., 4:26–27.

85. Ibid., 2:164–170.

86. On the expulsion of Al Rashid from Unayza in 1788, see Ibrahim, Najdiyyun, p. 44.

87. Ibn Humayd, *Suhub*, 1:380–384; Ibn Hamdan, Sulayman ibn Abd al-Rahman, *Tarajim muta'akhkhiri al-hanabila*, Bakr ibn Abd Allah Abu Zayd (ed.), (Al-Dammam, 2000), p. 54; Al-Qadi, Muhammad ibn Uthman ibn Salih, *Rawdat al-nazirin `an ma'athir `ulama' najd wa hawadith al-sinin*, 2 vols. 3rd ed. (Riyadh, 1989–90), 1:354.

88. Bassam, *`Ulama'*, 2:540–543.

89. Ibid., 6:443–445.

90. Sheikh Abd Allah witnessed al-Dir'iyya's destruction by an Ottoman-Egyptian army in 1818 and was transported to exile in Cairo, where he died. On his life and writings, see ibid., 1:169–179; Al al-Sheikh, *Mashahir*, pp. 48–71.

91. According to Wahhabi sources, Ali (d. 1829) refused to serve as qadi and was transported to Egypt. Bassam reports that he was the Sheikh's oldest son. According to a non-Wahhabi source, Husayn was the oldest son and followed as the chief of the religious estate. Anonymous, *Lam` al-shihab fi sirat Muhammad ibn Abd al-Wahhab* (Beirut, 1967), p. 173. Sources report that he was especially close to Amir Abd al-Aziz; Wahhabi sources merely report that he was a judge at al-Dir'iyya beginning in the time of Amir Abd al-Aziz. He died in al-Dir'iyya during the epidemic of 1809. The same source reports that on his death, Ali became head of the religious estate and that Amir Saud obeyed Sheikh Ali just as his father had obeyed Sheikh Muhammad even though this particular son was not so learned or scrupulous. He is supposed to have married and divorced frequently before he settled down with four more permanent wives; he also had a taste for fine clothes. Moreover, he had strong ties with the Qawasim of Ra's al-Khayma, for reasons left unexplained. Ibid., p. 177. Those ties would explain why his sons were able to find refuge there after al-Dir'iyya's destruction. Ibrahim was transported to Cairo.

92. Amir Saud ibn Abd al-Aziz called on Meccan townsmen to abandon idolatry, devote themselves to correct worship, command good and forbid evil. When they agreed, they swore an oath of allegiance to Saud on the Qur'an and the Sunna. The new Wahhabi rulers moved to ban intercessionary acts, to lift illegitimate taxes and to destroy hashish dens and break tobacco pipes. Sheikh Abd Allah instituted a new regime of religious education for Mecca: He distributed copies of his father's essays for the ulama to use for instruction to commoners. Al al-Sheikh, *Mashahir*, pp. 51–52.

93. For an English translation of his treatise, see O'Kinealy, J., 'Translation of an Arabic pamphlet on the history and doctrines of the Wahhabis, written by Abdullah, grandson [sic] of Abdul Wahhab, the founder of Wahhabism', *Journal of the Asiatic Society of Bengal*, xliii (1874), pp. 68–82. The treatise became an essential condensation of Wahhabi beliefs: in the early twentieth century, religious reformers in Egypt and Iraq would cite it as their source on the true nature of Wahhabism, as opposed to distortions circulated by its adversaries. See the discussion of Mahmud Shukri al-Alusi and Rashid Rida in Chapter Five.

94. For a detailed examination of these trends, see Isa, *al-Hayah al-`ilmiyya*, pp. 116, 124–128, 144, 150, 218–219.

95. According to Dina Rizk Khoury's research in Ottoman archives, the earliest mention of the Wahhabis is a March 1764 order from Istanbul to authorities in Baghdad and Basra. Khoury, Dina Rizk, 'Who is a true Muslim? Exclusion and inclusion among polemicists of reform in nineteenth century Baghdad', in Virginia Aksan and Daniel Goffman (eds.), *Early Modern Ottoman History: A Reinterpretation* (Cambridge, forthcoming).

96. Abun-Nasr, Jamil, 'The Salafiyya movement in Morocco: The religious bases of the Moroccan nationalist movement', *St. Antony's Papers*, 16 (1963), pp. 90–105.

97. For the response of an influential Sufi thinker to Wahhabi doctrine, see Radtke, Bernd, *The Exoteric Ahmad Ibn Idris: A Sufi's Critique of the Madhahib and the Wahhabis* (Leiden, 2000). On the arguments about visiting graves and venerating holy men, see the discussion of the Yemeni scholar Muhammad al-Shawkani's response to Wahhabi doctrine in Haykel, *Revival and Reform in Islam*, pp. 127–138. For the response from a Tunisian scholar, see Green, Arnold, 'A Tunisian reply to a Wahhabi declaration: Texts and contexts', in A.H. Green (ed.), *In Quest of an Islamic Humanism, Arabic and Islamic Studies in memory of Mohamed al-Nowaihi* (Cairo, 1984). For a response from a Syrian scholar in Damascus, see Commins, David, *Islamic Reform: Politics and Social Change in Late Ottoman Syria* (New York, 1990), pp. 22–23.

98. Al-Jabarti, Abd al-Rahman ibn Hasan, `Aja'ib al-athar fi al-tarajim wa al-akhbar*, 4 vols. (Cairo, 1999). Al-Jabarti's references to the Wahhabis are in Ghalib, Muhammad Adib, *Min akhbar al-hijaz wa najd fi tarikh al-Jabarti* (Riyadh, 1975), pp. 87–89, 94–98, 104–107, 111–118, 134, 145, 175–177.

99. Al-Jabarti, `Aja'ib*, 3:348.

100. Ibid., 3:373.

101. Ibid., 3:401–404.

102. Ibid., 3:549.

103. Ibid., 4:8–9. A European visitor to Jeddah in the 1850s heard reports that the Saudi conquest had been orderly: 'Their discipline within the Holy City was admirable and they did not commit the most minor excess'. Didier, Charles, *Sojourn with the Grand Sharif of Makkah*, translated by Richard Bouliad (New York, 1985), p. 99.

104. Al-Jabarti, 4:83.

105. Ibid., 4:84.

106. Ibid., 4:141–143.

107. Ibid., 4:219.

108. One of these men was a grandson of Muhammad ibn Abd al-Wahhab through his daughter. The grandson was Abd al-Aziz ibn Hamad. The other man was Abd Allah ibn Muhammad ibn Banyan. Ghalib, *Min akhbar*, p. 177.

109. Al-Jabarti, `Aja'ib*, 4:360–361.

110. Vassiliev, Alexei, *The History of Saudi Arabia* (New York, 2000), pp. 142–151.

111. Ibn Isa, Ibrahim ibn Salih, *Tarikh ba'd al-hawadith al-waqi'a fi najd* (Riyadh, 1999), p. 105.

112. Ibid., p. 106.

113. Sulayman ibn Abd Allah ibn Muhammad ibn Abd al-Wahhab, 'Fi hukm al-safar ila bilad al-shirk wa al-iqama fi-ha li al-tijara wa izhar `alamat al-nifaq wa muwalat al-kuffar', in Muhammad Rashid Rida (ed.), *Majmu`at al-tawhid al-najdiyya*, Reprint edition (Riyadh, 1999). Elizabeth Sirriyeh has translated this essay in her article, 'Wahhabis, unbelievers and the problems of exclusivism', *British Society for Middle Eastern Studies* xvi (1989), pp. 123–132. Sulayman ibn Abd Allah, 'Fi hukm muwalat ahl al-ishrak', in Muhammad Rashid Rida (ed.), *Majmu`at al-tawhid al-najdiyya*, Reprint edition (Riyadh, 1999).

114. Sheikh Sulayman and other Wahhabi writers seem to use idolater, *mushrik*, and infidel, *kafir*, interchangeably in many passages.

115. *al-rida bi al-kufr kufr.*

116. Sirriyeh translates the Hadith, 'He who consorts with the idolater and lives with him is like him'.

117. Sulayman ibn Abdallah, 'Fi hukm muwalat ahl al-ishrak', pp. 247–265.

118. Ibn Qasim, Abd al-Rahman ibn Muhammad (ed.), *Al-Durar al-saniya fi al-ajwiba al-najdiyya*, 12 vols. (Riyadh, 1995), 8:113.

119. Rida, Muhammad Rashid (ed.), *Majmu`at al-rasa'il wa al-masa'il al-najdiyya*, 4 vols. 3ʳᵈ ed. (Riyadh, 1996), 4:42–43.

120. Webster, Roger, '*Hijra* and the dissemination of Wahhabi doctrine in Saudi Arabia', in Ian Richard Netton (ed.), *Golden Roads: Migration, Pilgrimage, and Travel in Mediaeval and Modern Islam* (Richmond, 1993), p. 13.

121. Muhammad ibn Abd al-Wahhab cited the same Qur'anic verse, Ibn Qasim, *Durar*, 8:116.

122. Ibn Bishr, Uthman, `Unwan al-majd fi tarikh najd*, 2 vols. (Riyadh, 1999), 1:212.

123. Hatti Humayun 19698–A, Rajab 21, 1234 AH; Documents Section, King Fahd National Library, Riyadh; Arabic translation by Dr. Suheyl Sapan.

124. Ibn Bishr, `Unwan al-majd*, 1:341–342.

125. Sadleir, George Forster, *Diary of a Journey Across Arabia* (New York, 1977), pp. 79–82.

Chapter Two

1. Ra'uf, Imad Abd al-Salam, *al-Iraq fi watha'iq Muhammad Ali* (Baghdad, 1999), pp. 18–20.

2. Ali ibn Husayn Al al-Sheikh and Abd Allah ibn Ahmad al-Wuhaybi.

3. Ibrahim ibn Hamad ibn Abd al-Wahhab, Sheikh Muhammad's grandson through a daughter, had been a qadi for Amirs Saud and Abd Allah. He was killed in combat at the battle of al-Hinakiya in 1817; Al-Bassam, Abd Allah ibn Abd al-Rahman, `Ulama' najd khilal thamaniyat qurun*, 6 vols. (Riyadh, 1997), 1:295. Ali ibn Abd Allah Al al-Sheikh, a grandson of Sheikh Muhammad, died in combat at al-Dilam in 1819; Ibn Bishr, Uthman, `Unwan al-majd fi tarikh najd* (Riyadh, 1999), 1:344; al-Fakhiri, Muhammad ibn Umar, *al-Akhbar*

al-najdiyya, Abd Allah ibn Yusuf al-Shibl (ed.), (Riyadh, n.d.), p. 184. Ali ibn Hamad ibn Rashid al-`Urayni was the qadi at the southern Najdi town of al-Dilam. After the fall of al-Dir'iyya, he proclaimed his enmity toward the invaders, so Ibrahim Pasha had him put to death; Bassam, `Ulama', 5:179. Rashid al-Sardi was the qadi for the southern Najdi towns of al-Hawta and al-Hariq. He was executed at al-Dir'iyya; Ibn Bishr, `Unwan al-majd, 1:335; Bassam, `Ulama', 2:190–191. Abd al-Aziz ibn Rashid ibn Zamil was the qadi, imam and teacher at al-Rass in al-Qasim. He participated in the defense of his town against the Egyptian forces and is reported to have died from grief around October 1817 following Ibrahim Pasha's order to destroy his beloved garden outside of town; Bassam, `Ulama', 3:346–348. Abd al-Rahman ibn Nami was the qadi at al-Hasa. He was executed by the ruling Aray`ar clan when Ibrahim restored them to power in 1819; Ibn Bishr, `Unwan al-majd, 1:341; Bassam, `Ulama', 3:273. Ibrahim ibn Hamad ibn Musharraf was the qadi of al-Marat. He was killed at the battle of al-Mawiya, between Medina and al-Qasim, in 1817; Bassam, `Ulama', 1:501. In addition to these wartime casualties, another leading figure in al-Dir'iyya, Abd al-Aziz ibn Muhammad ibn Isa survived the invasion and its immediate aftermath only to be killed in an 1821 massacre perpetrated by a later Egyptian commander, Husayn Bey, at Tharmada; Ibn Bishr, `Unwan al-majd, 1:358.

4.   Ibrahim ibn Abd Allah ibn Ahmad al-Busaymi had been offered a post as qadi but he declined. Instead, he became amir in his ancestral town of Ushayqir at the time of the Egyptian invasion. He was killed in combat in 1818; Bassam, `Ulama', 1:375–376. Abd Allah ibn Hamad ibn Rashid al-`Urayni, a qadi's son, was killed at al-Dir'iyya; ibid., 2:73. Salih ibn Rashid al-Sardi, also a qadi's son, was tortured and executed at al-Dir'iyya; Al-Isa, Mayy bint Abd al-Aziz, *Al-Hayah al-`ilmiyya fi najd mundhu qiyam da`wat al-sheikh Muhammad ibn Abd al-Wahhab wa hatta nihayat al-dawla al-sa`udiyya al-ula* (Riyadh, 1997), p. 364 n. 8; al-Salman, Muhammad ibn Abd Allah, *al-Ahwal al-siyasiyya fi al-Qasim fi `ahd al-dawla al-sa`udiyya al-thaniya, 1238–1309/1823–1891* (Unayza, 1986–1988), p. 41, citing Ibn Bishr. Muhammad ibn Abd al-Rahman ibn Abd Allah Al al-Sheikh, a great-grandson of Sheikh Muhammad, was killed at al-Dir'iyya; Ibn Bishr, `Unwan al-majd, 1:335. Nasir ibn Husayn Al al-Sheikh, a grandson of Sheikh Muhammad, was killed after the fall of al-Dir'iyya; al-Fakhiri, *al-Akhbar al-najdiyya*, pp. 152, 184. Nasir ibn Hamad ibn Nasir ibn Uthman ibn Mu`ammar, the son of a leading sheikh, was killed in combat during the siege of al-Dir'iyya; Bassam, `Ulama', 2:127. Abd Allah ibn Muhammad ibn Suwaylim and Abd Allah ibn Ahmad ibn Kathir were also from ulama families and were killed in the war; Ibn Isa, Ibrahim ibn Salih, *Tarikh ba'd al-hawadith al-waqi'a fi najd* (Riyadh, 1999), p. 109; al-Fakhiri, *al-Akhbar al-najdiyya*, p. 151.

5.   In addition to Sheikh Abd Allah, his brothers Ibrahim and Ali: they all died in Cairo. The exiles included Sheikh Abd Allah's son Abd al-Rahman and his nephew Abd al-Rahman ibn Hasan. The latter's young son Abd al-Latif returned to Najd in 1848 and became the supreme Wahhabi sheikh.

According to a document from the Ottoman archives, the entire entourage of Al al-Sheikh numbered thirty-one, mostly servants (13) and children (9 sons, 3 daughters), just one wife, one daughter-in-law. Abd al-Rahman ibn Abd Allah and Abd al-Latif ibn Abd al-Rahman are not named in the document but are included in the list of sons. Hatti Humayun 19698–A, Rajab 21, 1234 AH; Documents Section, King Fahd National Library, Riyadh; Arabic translation by Dr. Suheyl Sapan.

6. Al al-Sheikh, *Mashahir `ulama' najd wa ghayruhum* (n.p., 1974), pp. 212–215; Bassam, `Ulama', 3:319–323; Salman, *al-Ahwal al-siyasiyya*, p. 48

7. This was the son of Sheikh Muhammad's adversarial brother Sulayman, Bassam, `Ulama', 3:363–365.

8. Ibid., 3:336–345. He remained in correspondence with members of Al al-Sheikh in Cairo, especially Abd al-Rahman ibn Hasan, who had been a close companion. The two sheikhs exchanged verse lamenting the woes of exile. Two more survivors died shortly after al-Dir'iyya's fall. Abd al-Aziz ibn Abd Allah al-Husayyin was one of the most important ulama, a qadi, the author of several works and teacher of large numbers of students. Ibrahim Pasha spared him on account of his advanced age (approaching 80 in 1818) and he died in Shaqra three years later; ibid., 3:454–464; Al al-Sheikh, *Mashahir*, pp. 206–210. The Egyptian military commander had the same reason for permitting Abd Allah ibn Hammad to leave al-Dir'iyya, but he died en route to Riyadh; Bassam, `Ulama', 4:322–323.

9. Sadleir, George Forster, *Diary of a Journey Across Arabia* (New York, 1977), p. 35.

10. The qadis were Ali ibn Husayn Al al-Sheikh and Abd Allah ibn Ahmad al-Wuhaybi. The other four ulama were Abd al-Rahman ibn Husayn Al al-Sheikh, Ahmad ibn Sirhan, Ahmad ibn Hudayb and Ibrahim ibn Sayf. Ibn Sayf had been posted to Ra's al-Khayma as qadi, so he was a familiar figure there. One of Sheikh Muhammad's daughters, Fatima, also fled with this group to Ra's al-Khayma. She is the only female member of Al al-Sheikh mentioned in the Saudi chronicles because of a story attesting to her religious steadfastness; Bassam, `Ulama', 5:364–366.

11. Ibid., 4:225–244; Al al-Sheikh, *Mashahir*, pp. 235–238; al-`Ajlan, Ali ibn Muhammad ibn Abd Allah, *al-Sheikh al-Allama Abd Allah ibn Abd al-Rahman Aba Butayn* (Riyadh, 2001), pp. 95–214.

12. Bassam, `Ulama', 4:166; Al al-Sheikh, *Mashahir*, p. 216.

13. Ibn Bishr, `Unwan al-majd, 2:22; Bassam, `Ulama', 5:79–82; Al al-Sheikh, *Mashahir*, p. 277.

14. Bassam, `Ulama', 1:501

15. Ibid., 5:415–422.

16. Ibid., 3:443–444.

17. Ibid., 6:393–399; Ibn Bishr, `Unwan al-majd, 2:21; Al al-Sheikh, *Mashahir*, p. 230. Several other men bridged the two Saudi amirates. Muhammad ibn Qirnas ibn Abd al-Rahman, son of the qadi of al-Rass, performed the pilgrimage to Mecca in 1819, but we do not know if he remained for long

in Hijaz. He later succeeded his father as qadi of al-Rass in 1846, serving until he died in 1858; Bassam, 'Ulama', 6:362–364. Muhammad ibn Abd al-Aziz al-'Awsaji came from al-Bir and studied at al-Dir'iyya. The sources do not mention his movements during the war, but he surfaced afterward as Turki's qadi in al-Mihmal, his home region; ibid., 6:94. Bassam has another entry on a man with a similar name as a qadi in the first state who died after 1830; ibid., 6:66. Another sheikh who returned to al-Bir was Muhammad ibn Abd al-Aziz ibn Sultan, a qadi in al-Dir'iyya for whom there is no further information after 1818; ibid., 6:71. The region of Washm had three transitional ulama. Muhammad ibn Abd Allah ibn Mani' seems to have remained in Shaqra; ibid., 6:212–217; Al al-Sheikh, Mashahir, p. 240. So too did Ibrahim ibn Hamad ibn Isa and he later became Faysal's qadi for al-Washm; Bassam, 'Ulama', 1:296–298. Muhammad ibn Abd Allah al-Husayyin, whose brother was a leading figure in the first amirate, had also been a qadi and he remained at al-Waqaf; ibid., 6:220–221. In the Sudayr region, Faris ibn Muhammad ibn Rumayh came from al-Attar, studied in al-Dir'iyya with the second generation of Al al-Sheikh and became an important teacher in the Saudi capital. After the city's destruction, he returned to al-Attar, then moved to Riyadh when Turki rose to power and spent the next four decades teaching religious students until he died in 1868; ibid., 5:358–359. Another figure to migrate from Sudayr to al-Dir'iyya and then return home is the historian Hamad ibn Muhammad ibn La'bun. He settled first in Hawtat al-Sudayr and five years later moved to al-Tuwaym, perhaps because of factional fighting in Hawta; ibid., 2:108–112. The qadi of Unayza, Abd Allah ibn Sayf, is reported to have left the town at the time of the invasion, but there is no report on him thereafter; ibid., 4:171. Abd Allah ibn Muhammad ibn Banyan was moved from al-Dir'iyya to Riyadh in 1818; ibid., 4:392–393.

18.   Ibn Bishr, 'Unwan al-majd, 1:357.

19.   Ibid., 1:358.

20.   Al-Ghunaym, Khalid Abd al-Aziz, al-Mujaddid al-thani: al-Sheikh Abd al-Rahman ibn Hasan Al al-Sheikh wa tariqatuhu fi taqrir al-'aqida (Riyadh, 1997); Bassam, 'Ulama', 1:180–201; Al al-Sheikh, Mashahir, pp. 78–86.

21.   Abd al-Rahman ibn Hasan Al al-Sheikh, Abd al-Rahman ibn Husayn Al al-Sheikh, Abd Allah ibn Abd al-Rahman Aba Butayn, Abd Allah ibn Ahmad al-Wuhaybi, Mahmud al-Farsi, Abd Allah ibn Sulayman ibn 'Ubayd, Uthman ibn Abd al-Jabbar ibn Shabana and Muhammad ibn Muqrin.

22.   Abd Allah, Ali and Husayn, sons of Sheikh Muhammad.

23.   Abd al-Rahman ibn Hasan ibn Muhammad ibn Abd al-Wahhab, Qurrat 'uyyun al-muwahhidin fi tahqiq da'wat al-anbiya' wa al-mursalin, in Muhammad Rashid Rida (ed.), Majmu'at al-tawhid al-najdiyya, Reprint edition (Riyadh, 1999), pp. 373–636.

24.   Ibn Bishr identifies members of Al al-Sheikh who emigrated to al-Hawta and al-Hariq: Abd al-Rahman ibn Hasan, Ali ibn Husayn (a former refugee to Ra's al-Khayma) and Abd al-Malik ibn Husayn. 'Unwan al-majd, 2:73.

25. On Hamad ibn Atiq, see Bassam, `Ulama`, 2:84–95; Al al-Sheikh, *Mashahir*, pp. 244–254; al-`Uqayli, Khalid ibn Zayd ibn Sa'ud al-Mani`, *al-Tahqiq fi ulama al-hilwa wa hawtat Bani Tamim wa na`am wa al-hariq: Ulama wa qudat al-hilwa* (Riyadh, 2000), pp. 11–19.

26. Ibn Atiq, Hamad, *Sabil al-najat wa al-fikak*, al-Walid ibn Abd al-Rahman al-Farayyan (ed.), (Riyadh, 1989), p. 9.

27. Abd al-Rahim, Abd al-Rahman Abd al-Rahim, *Muhammad Ali wa shibh al-jazira al-`arabiyya, 1234–1256/1819–1840*, 2 vols. (Cairo, 1986), 2:296.

28. Ibn Atiq, Hamad, 'Radd al-Sheikh Hamad ibn Atiq `ala Ibn Du`ayj', King Fahd National Library, Riyadh, Saudi Arabia, Manuscript section, 57/86. The date on the colophon is Rabi Awwal 1261/1845. The only Ibn Du`ayj I have come across in the biographical dictionaries is Ahmad ibn Ali ibn Du`ayj, 1776–1851/52, a Wahhabi qadi in Marat, Washm, from 1817 until his death. Both Imams Turki and Faysal retained him as qadi; Bassam, `Ulama`, 1:497–501. Salih ibn Muhammad al-Shithri's essay in the same manuscript suggests that Ibn Du`ayj studied in Iraq. For a discussion of Ibn Atiq's treatise as an expression of debate between moderate (like Ibn Du`ayj) and hardline Wahhabis, see al-Fahad, Abdulaziz H., 'Commentary: From exclusivism to accommodation: Doctrinal and legal evolution of Wahhabism', *New York University Law Review* lxxix/2 (2004), pp. 498–499.

29. Ibn Atiq, 'Radd', pp. 5–6.

30. Ibid., p. 11. Ibn Atiq's teacher, Abd al-Rahman ibn Hasan Al al-Sheikh, accused Hamad ibn Ali al-Mara'i (i.e., Ibn Du`ayj) of flattering and showing friendliness to 'lords of aggression and injustice against Muslims'. Ibn Qasim, Abd al-Rahman ibn Muhammad (ed.), *Al-Durar al-saniya fi al-ajwiba al-najdiyya*, 12 vols. (Riyadh, 1995), 8: 237.

31. Ibn Atiq, 'Radd', p. 19. It appears from this passage that some Najdis regarded Muhammad Ali (an ethnic Albanian) and the Ottomans as Turks, or at least used the ethnic label to denigrate them.

32. Ibid., pp. 6–10.

33. Ibid., pp. 9–10.

34. Ibn Bishr, `Unwan al-majd`, 2:93; Vassiliev, Alexei, *The History of Saudi Arabia* (New York, 2000), p. 175.

35. Ibn Bishr, `Unwan al-majd`, 2:95.

36. The Saudi historian Abd al-Fattah Hasan Abu Aliya uncovered a piece of correspondence in the Egyptian archives bearing on Faysal's escape. It is a letter dated 25 Muharram 1256 (30 March 1840) from Khurshid Pasha, the Egyptian viceroy for Arabia during the second occupation, to Muhammad Ali. The document indicates that Muhammad Ali ordered that Faysal be permitted to leave his confinement and return to Najd because he would establish and maintain friendly relations with the rulers of Egypt. Abu Aliya, Abd al-Fattah Hasan, *Dirasa fi masadir tarikh al-jazira al-arabiyya* (Riyadh, 1979), p. 78.

37. Bassam, `Ulama`, 2:373–380; al-Umari, Salim al-Sulayman, `Ulama' Al Salim wa talamidhatuhum wa `ulama' al-qasim*, 2 vols. (Riyadh, 1985), 1:196–199.

On Shatti's anti-Wahhabi views, see Weismann, Itzchak, *Taste of Modernity: Sufism, Salafiyya, and Arabism in Late Ottoman Damascus* (Leiden, 2001), pp. 65–67.

38. Salman, *al-Ahwal al-siyasiyya*, pp. 163–168.

39. Ibid., pp. 177–186.

40. Ibid., pp. 187–198.

41. Ibid., pp. 199–213.

42. Guarmani, Carlo, *Northern Najd: A Journey from Jerusalem to Anaiza in Qasim* (London, 1938), pp. 40–41.

43. The connection between Unayza's commercial character and the persistence of Najd's old scholastic tradition there is discussed in Steinberg, Guido, 'Ecology, knowledge and trade in Central Arabia (Najd) during the nineteenth and early twentieth centuries', in Madawi Al-Rasheed and Robert Vitalis (eds.), *Counter-Narratives: History, Contemporary Society, and Politics in Saudi Arabia and Yemen* (New York, 2004), pp. 83–85, 90–91, 94–98.

44. Al Juhany, Uwaidah M., *Najd before the Salafi Reform Movement: Social, Religious, and Political Conditions during the Three Centuries Preceding the Rise of the Saudi State* (Reading, 2002), pp. 125–126; Ibrahim, Abd al-Aziz Abd al-Ghani, *Najdiyyun wara' al-hudud: al-Uqaylat, 1705–1950* (London, 1991), p. 49.

45. Al Juhany, *Najd*, pp. 125–126; Ibrahim, *Najdiyyun*, pp. 8–9.

46. Ibrahim, *Najdiyyun*, pp. 40, 52.

47. Al-Bassam, Ahmad, 'Min asbab al-mu`arada al-mahalliyya li-da`wat al-sheikh Muhammad ibn Abd al-Wahhab fi `ahd al-dawla al-sa`udiyya al-ula', *al-Dir`iyya* iv/14 (2001), p. 32.

48. On immigration to Zubayr from Huraymila and Harma, see al-Nabhani, Muhammad ibn Khalifa, *al-Tuhfa al-nabhaniyya fi tarikh al-jazira al-`arabiyya* (Bahrain, 1986), p. 224; Ibrahim, *Najdiyyun*, p. 40; immigration from Rawdat Sudayr, ibid., 41; immigration from Unayza, ibid., 44; Steinberg, 'Ecology, knowledge and trade', p. 84. The Riyadh polemicist Sulayman ibn Suhaym wound up in Zubayr; Bassam, `Ulama', 2:381–382, 6:465. Ibn Suhaym's son Nasir was born in Zubayr in 1763 and travelled to al-Hasa to study under Ibn Fayruz before the latter's emigration. One source reports that when Riyadh's amir agreed to a truce in 1754, Ibn Saud demanded that Ibn Suhaym and some others come to al-Dir`iyya; Uthaymin, Abd Allah, 'Mawqif Sulayman ibn Suhaym', in Abd Allah Uthaymin (ed.), *Buhuth wa ta`liqat fi tarikh al-mamlaka al-`arabiyyah al-sa`udiyyah* (Riyadh, 1984), pp. 112–113. Another Najdi emigrant to Iraq, Abd Allah ibn Da'ud, moved from Sudayr to Basra, studied in Damascus and then returned to Basra, this time to study with Ibn Fayruz, before finally settling in Zubayr; Bassam, `Ulama', 4:114–115; Ibn Humayd, Muhammad ibn Abd Allah, *Al-Suhub al-wabila ala dara'ih al-hanabila*, 3 vols., Bakr Abdallah Abu Zayd and Abd al-Rahman ibn Sulayman al-`Uthaymin (eds.), (Beirut, 1996), 2:619–620. Abd Allah ibn Da'ud's harsh polemic against the Wahhabis won the praise of ulama in al-Hasa, Syria and Iraq; Abd Allah ibn Da'ud, 'al-Sawa`iq wa al-ru`ud fi al-radd `ala ibn Sa`ud', described in al-Abd al-Latif, Abd al-Aziz ibn

Muhammad ibn Ali, *Da`awa al-munawi'in li da`wat al-sheikh Muhammad ibn Abd al-Wahhab: `Ard wa naqd* (Riyadh, 1981), pp. 44–46.

49. Bassam, `*Ulama*', 6:236–245; Ibn Humayd, *Suhub*, 3:969–980. Ibn Fayruz and his students emigrated to Basra and Zubayr between 1785 and 1793, when the Saudis conquered al-Hasa.

50. Bassam, `*Ulama*', 6:292–302. He served as prayer leader at one of the town's two congregational mosques, 'al-Najada', a centre for the town's residents from Najd. Al-`Assafi, Muhammad ibn Hamad, *Masajid al-Zubayr*, Qasim al-Samarra'i (ed.), (Riyadh, 2001), pp. 56–57.

51. Bassam, `*Ulama*', 1:423–427. He was imam at Najada mosque from 1752 to 1772, before Ibn Sullum's arrival in Zubayr; 'Assafi, *Masajid al-Zubayr*, p. 57. Because of his anti-Wahhabi stance, he was the target of a Wahhabi sheikh's satirical verse; see Ibn Humayd, *Suhub*, 1:71–76. Writings by a member of Al al-Sheikh in the later nineteenth century identify him as an influential adversary; Abd al-Rahman ibn Hasan Al al-Sheikh, *al-Maqamat* (Riyadh, n.d.), p. 5. Ibn Jadid's anti-Wahhabi pupils included Muhammad al-Hudaybi (c.1766–1841) and Isa al-Zubayri (d. 1832). Both men taught dissident Unayzan religious pupils in Mecca. On Hudaybi, who studied with Ibn Fayruz in Basra, see Bassam, `*Ulama*', 5:508–511. On Zubayri, see ibid., 5:345–346. On Unayzan pupils who studied under them, see below on Abd Allah Aba al-Khayl and Muhammad ibn Humayd. Sayf ibn Ahmad al-`Atiqi (1694–1775) was an imam and jurist opposed to the Wahhabi mission in Sudayr who sent his son Salih (1750–1818) to al-Hasa to study under Ibn Fayruz; ibid., 2:415–416, 474–477; Ibn Humayd, *Suhub*, 2:417–418.

52. On Yahya ibn al-Zuhayr, see Nabhani, *al-Tuhfa al-nabhaniyya*, p. 225.

53. On the 1785 raid led by Muntafiq tribesmen, see ibid., p. 405; on the 1797 raid led by the governor of Baghdad into al-Hasa, see ibid., pp. 412–413.

54. Ibid., p. 225.

55. Bassam, `*Ulama*', 1: 423–427.

56. Ibid., 1:494–496. In the 1760s, Hamad ibn Ibrahim al-Bassam moved to Unayza, where the lineage became known for its prominent merchants; ibid., 1:528–532.

57. Ibid., 2:258 n. 1; Doughty, Charles, *Travels in Arabia Deserta*, 2 vols. (New York, 1979), 2:389.

58. Doughty, *Travels*, 2:367–368.

59. Ibid., 2:402, 404, 482. He also encountered a Wahhabi merchant named Rashayd with agencies at Basra, Zubayr, Kuwait, Aden; 2:449, 470.

60. Bassam, `*Ulama*', 2:528 n. 1.

61. Ibid., 4:426–430.

62. Salih ibn Hamad (1842–1919) is noted for his manuscript collection; ibid., 2:449–456; Salih ibn Abd Allah (1853–1890) gathered a huge private library; ibid., 2:495–497.

63. Eight members of Al Bassam studied under the clearly anti-Wahhabi Muhammad ibn Shibl at Unayza's al-Jawz mosque, apparently a centre for the old tradition; ibid., 6:129–130. Ibn Shibl's successor as imam, preacher

and teacher at al-Jawz mosque, Abd Allah ibn `A'id (1833–1904), depended on the patronage of Al Bassam; Doughty, *Travels*, 2:383, 385. Ibn `A'id studied in Unayza with Wahhabi sheikhs, then he went to Mecca, where he attended the anti-Wahhabi Ibn Humayd's lessons. Ibn `A'id's pupils included five members of Al Bassam, including three who also studied under Muhammad ibn Shibl; Bassam, `Ulama', 4:184–192.

64. Commins, David, 'Wahhabism as a Regional Religious Culture', Paper presented at the Middle East Studies Association annual conference, November 2004.

65. Bassam, `Ulama', 4:370–377; Ibn Humayd, *Suhub*, 2:641–644.

66. Muhammad al-Hudaybi and Isa al-Zubayri.

67. Ibn Hamdan, Sulayman ibn Abd al-Rahman, *Tarajim muta'akhkhiri al-hanabila*, Bakr ibn Abd Allah Abu Zayd (ed.), (Dammam, 1999), pp. 94–95.

68. Establishing firm dates on the movements of ulama depends on occasional discoveries of dated documents. In Aba al-Khayl's case, Ibn Humayd cites a document that locates him in Mecca in April 1832; *Suhub*, 2:641–644.

69. Bassam, `Ulama', 3:254.

70. Ibid., 5:484–486.

71. Ibid., 5:56–59. The ancestral opponent to Wahhabism was Humaydan.

72. The second member of Al Turki to study under Aba al-Khayl was his cousin Abd al-Aziz ibn Abd Allah ibn Turki (d. c.1844); ibid., 3:486–487. Another figure, Nasir ibn Muhammad ibn Turki, may have belonged to the same lineage. He supported the controversial Iraqi sheikh Da'ud ibn Jirjis discussed below; ibid., 6:481–482.

73. Ibid., 5:157–160.

74. Bassam, `Ulama', 6:477–478; al-Qadi, Muhammad ibn Uthman ibn Salih, *Rawdat al-nazirin an ma'athir ulama najd wa hawadith al-sinin*, 2 vols., 3rd ed. (Riyadh, 1989), 2:201–204.

75. Bassam, 'Min asbab al-mu`arada al-mahalliyya', p. 50.

76. Introduction by Abd al-Rahman al-Uthaymin, Ibn Humayd, *Suhub*, 1:11–70; Bassam, `Ulama', 6:189–204. His maternal uncle Abd al-Aziz ibn Turki belonged to the old scholastic tradition

77. Humaydan ibn Turki was a contemporary of Muhammad ibn Abd al-Wahhab; Ibn Humayd, *Suhub*, 1:380–383. The sources tell us nothing about Ibn Humayd's paternal lineage apart from an uncle, Uthman (d. 1835), who was a religious student; ibid., 2:642. Another member of Al Turki, Ibn Humayd's maternal uncle, Abd al-Aziz ibn Abd Allah ibn Turki, appears to have studied under ulama but himself fell short of attaining the standing of a scholar. Nonetheless, he had a hand in shaping his nephew's outlook; ibid., 1:20.

78. Ibid., 1:383–384. The chronicle is volume 4 in al-Bassam, Abd Allah ibn Abd al-Rahman ibn Salih, *Khizanat al-tawarikh al-najdiyya*, 10 vols. (n.p., 1999).

79. Bassam, *Khizanat*, 4:157–158.

80. Schacht, J., 'Dahlan, Ahmad B. Zayni', *The Encyclopaedia of Islam, New Edition*, B. Lewis et al (eds.), (Leiden, 1965–), 2:91.

81. He became the Hanbali imam in 1848 and the Hanbali mufti some time around 1866. Ibn Humayd, *Suhub*, 1:46, 48.

82. Hafsi, Ibrahim, 'Recherches sur le genre 'tabaqat' dans la litterature arabe', *Arabica* xxiv (1977), pp. 24–26; Makdisi, George, 'Tabaqat-Biography: Law and orthodoxy in classical Islam', *Islamic Studies* xxxii (1993), p. 388.

83. Preface to Ibn Humayd, *Suhub*, 1:78.

84. The editors list the main sources as Ibn Hajar's *al-Durar al-kamina*, al-Sakhawi's *al-Daw' al-lami` li ahl al-qarn al-tasi`*, al-`Ulaymi's *al-Durr al-munaddad*, Ibn al-`Imad's *Shadharat al-dhahab*, al-Muhibbi's *Khulasat al-athar fi a`yan al-qarn al-hadi `ashar* and al-Muradi's *Silk al-durar fi a`yan al-qarn al-thani `ashar*. Preface to Ibn Humayd, *Suhub*, 1:85–91.

85. In the eighteenth century, all the traffic was to Syria because the Hanbali school had just about vanished in Cairo by then. On the scarcity of Hanbali ulama in Cairo around 1740, see Perlmann, Moshe, 'Sheikh al-Damanhuri against the churches of Cairo (1739)', *Actas IV Congresso de Estudos Arabes e Islamicos* (Leiden, 1971), p. 29 n. 3.

86. Ibn Humayd has entries on just four Arabian ulama for the period before the Wahhabi mission. For a more detailed treatment of anti-Wahhabi aspects of Ibn Humayd's biographical dictionary, see Commins, David, 'Traditional anti-Wahhabi Hanbalism in nineteenth century Arabia', in Itzchak Weismann (ed.), *Ottoman Reform and Islamic Regeneration: Studies in Honor of Butrus Abu Manneh* (London, 2005). Ibn Humayd omitted Wahhabi ulama, honored men known for mystical attainments and praised the anti-Wahhabi ulama associated with Muhammad ibn Fayruz.

87. Ibn Humayd, *Suhub*, 2:686–687.

88. Ibid., 2:413–415. The other two early figures of Al Musharraf are Ibrahim ibn Sulayman ibn Ali (d. 1728/29), ibid., 1:31–33; and Abd al-Wahhab ibn Abd Allah ibn Abd al-Wahhab (d. 1712/13), ibid., 2:686–687.

89. Ibid, 2:675–681.

90. Ibid., 2:680.

91. Ibn Humayd became embroiled in a controversy with Wahhabi scholars over the religious legality of certain verses in *al-Burda*, a famous Sufi devotional poem to Muhammad. I have not found Ibn Humayd's treatise, but his views are cited in Wahhabi refutations. See Abd al-Rahman ibn Hasan Al al-Sheikh, 'Bayyan al-mahajja fi al-radd `ala al-lajja', in Muhammad Rashid Rida (ed.), *Majmu`at al-rasa'il wa al-masa'il al-najdiyya*, 4 vols. (Riyadh, 1996), 4:223–284. Ibn Humayd's former teacher Abd Allah ibn Abd al-Rahman ibn Aba Butayn also composed a refutation found in `Ajlan, *al-Sheikh al-`allama* (Riyadh, 2001), pp. 359–429.

92. Some sources refer to him as Da'ud ibn Sulayman al-Baghdadi. On Ibn Jirjis, see al-Alusi, Mahmud Shukri, *al-Misk al-adhfar fi nashr mazaya al-qarn al-thani `ashar wa al-thalith `ashar* (Riyadh, 1982), pp. 166, 459–462; al-Alusi, Ali Ala' al-Din, *al-Durr al-muntathar fi rijal al-qarn al-thani `ashar wa al-thalith `ashar* (Baghdad, 1967), p. 174 and 224 footnote; al-Haydari, Ibrahim Fasih ibn Sibghatallah, *Kitab `unwan al-majd fi bayan ahwal Baghdad wa al-Basra wa*

Najd (Basra, n.d.), pp. 90, 142; al-Bitar, Abd al-Razzaq, *Hilyat al-bashar fi tarikh al-qarn al-thalith `ashar*, 3 vols. (Damascus, 1961–1963), 1:610–611.

93. The episode is reported in Bassam, *`Ulama'*, 4:230–231.

94. Muhammad ibn Abd al-Wahhab, *Essay on the Unicity of Allah, or What is Due to Allah from his Creatures*, translated by Ismail Raji al Faruqi (n.p., 1981), pp. 122–123. On al-Busiri, the author of *al-Burda* and this devotional poem's significance in Muslim religious culture, see Danner, Victor, 'Al-Busiri: His times and his prophecies', in Robert Olson (ed.), *Islamic and Middle Eastern Societies: A Festschrift in Honor of Professor Wadie Jwaideh* (Brattleboro, Vt, 1987), pp. 41–61. An English translation of the poem is in Clouston, W. A. (ed.), *Arabian Poetry for English Readers* (London, 1986), pp. 320–341.

95. Ibn Jirjis, Da'ud ibn Sulayman, *Sulh al-ikhwan min ahl al-iman* (Bombay, 1888/89).

96. Abd Allah ibn Abd al-Rahman ibn Aba Butayn composed an epistle refuting Ibn Jirjis's claims about Ibn Taymiyya and Ibn al-Qayyim. Aba Butayn, Abd Allah, *al-Intisar li hizb allah al-muwahhidin al-radd `ala al-mujadil `an al-mushrikin* (Kuwait, 1989). For a description of the work and a list of printed editions, see `Ajlan, *al-Sheikh al-`allama*, pp. 163–169. Aba Butayn next composed an epistle disputing Ibn Jirjis's defense of *al-Burda* and his argument for considering it permissible to seek the intercession of dead saints. Published in ibid., as 'Radd `ala al-Burda', pp. 359–429. Aba Butayn composed yet another essay against Ibn Jirjis, *Ta'sis al-taqdis fi kashf talbis Da'ud ibn Jirjis* (Cairo, 1925/26). Then the anti-Wahhabi Hanbali mufti of Mecca and Unayzan native Muhammad ibn Humayd composed a refutation of Aba Butayn; Bassam, *`Ulama'*, 4:230–231, 6:482–483; Ibn Hamdan, *Tarajim*, 133. A second Unayzan, Nasir ibn Muhammad ibn Turki, also sided with Ibn Jirjis. The controversy continued with essays by Riyadh's top religious leader, Abd al-Rahman ibn Hasan and his son Abd al-Latif. Abd al-Rahman ibn Hasan's essay against Ibn Humayd is 'Bayan al-mahajja fi al-radd `ala al-lajja', in Rida, *Majmu`at al-rasa'il*, 4:223–284; a fuller response against Ibn Jirjis is *al-Qawl al-fasl al-nafis fi al-radd `ala al-maftari Da'ud ibn Jirjis* (Riyadh, 1985). The works by Abd al-Latif ibn Abd al-Rahman are *Tuhfat al-talib wa al-jalis fi kashf shubuh Da'ud ibn Jirjis* (Riyadh, 1990) and *Minhaj al-ta'sis wa al-taqdis fi kashf shubuhat Da'ud ibn Jirjis* (Bombay, 1891/2).

97. Ibn Qasim, Abd al-Rahman ibn Muhammad (ed.), *al-Durar al-saniya fi al-ajwiba al-najdiyya*, 12 vols. (Riyadh, 1995), 12:287–291.

98. Ibid., 12:292.

99. Ibid., 12:287.

100. Bassam, *`Ulama'*, 5:89–106; Qadi, *Rawdat al-nazirin*, 2:104–108. Qadi reports that Ibn Mansur attended the lessons of Muhammad ibn Sullum at Zubayr in 1826.

101. Both views are given in Bassam, *`Ulama'*, 5:92.

102. The only work by Uthman ibn Mansur that I could locate is 'Manhaj al-ma`arij fi akhbar al-khawarij', Dar al-Kutub, Cairo, Egypt, Manuscript number 28653. The colophon indicates that Ibn Mansur composed this work

in Basra in 1825 and revised it in 1839. Photocopy in author's possession. A second manuscript is attributed to him, 'Kashf al-ghumma fi al-radd `ala man kaffar al-umma'. It is this work that Abd al-Latif ibn Abd al-Rahman rebutted (see n. 103).

103. Abd al-Rahman ibn Hasan Al al-Sheikh, *al-Maqamat*; Abd al-Latif ibn Abd al-Rahman ibn Hasan Al al-Sheikh, *Misbah al-zalam fi al-radd `ala man kadhaba `ala al-sheikh al-imam* (Riyadh, n.d.). Qadi names the authors of additional rebuttals: Hamad ibn Atiq, Sulayman ibn Sihman, Abd al-Rahman ibn Muhammad ibn Mani', Ahmad ibn Isa, Abd al-Aziz ibn Hasan al-Milhami and Ahmad ibn Musharraf; Qadi, *Rawdat al-nazirin*, 2:108.

104. Ibn Mansur's papers also included a poem praising Ibn Jirjis; Bassam, `*Ulama*', 5:96–97.

105. Ibn Qasim, *Durar*, 4:425.

106. Until very recently, M. J. Crawford's superb study of the Wahhabi leadership's juridical writings on the Saudi succession struggle was a singular exception to scholarly neglect of the second amirate's religious tendencies. For a meticulous examination of the debate and its relationship to the writings of Ibn Taymiya, see Crawford, M. J., 'Civil war, foreign intervention and the question of political legitimacy: A nineteenth-century Sa'udi qadi's dilemma', *International Journal of Middle East Studies* xiv (1982), pp. 227–248. Al-Fahad also treats the debate among Wahhabi scholars in 'From exclusivism to accommodation', pp. 501–504.

107. Crawford, 'Civil war', p. 232.

108. Ibid., p. 233.

109. Ibn Qasim, *Durar*, 9:47–53.

110. Crawford, 'Civil war', p. 235; Ibn Qasim, *Durar*, 9:18.

111. Crawford, 'Civil war', p. 236.

112. Ibn Qasim, *Durar*, 8:319–327.

113. Ibid., 8:393.

114. Ibid., 8:385.

115. Ibid., 8:336–337, 343.

116. Ibid., 8:323.

117. Ibid., 8:325.

118. Ibid., 8:335, 354.

119. The sheikh was Abd al-Rahman al-Wuhaybi; ibid., 8:353–355.

120. Ibid., 8:383. Muslim theology maintains that God created the world in time and views the idea that the world is eternal as a denial of Qur'anic verses.

121. Bassam, `*Ulama*', 5:469–471; Al-Fahad, 'From exclusivism to accommodation', pp. 503–504.

122. Crawford, 'Civil war', p. 237.

123. Ibn Qasim, *Durar*, 8:364–368.

124. Ibid., 9:18–19.

125. Ibid., 9:29–30.

126. Ibn Hamdan, *Tarajim*, p. 16.

127. Bassam, `*Ulama*', 1:216–217.

128. King Faysal (r. 1964–1975) was the offspring of this match.

129. Vassiliev, History of Saudi Arabia, pp. 201–203; Salman, al-Ahwal al-siyasiyya, pp. 253–282.

130. Ibn Qasim, Durar, 9:83–84.

131. Wallin, Georg Augustus, Travels in Arabia (Cambridge, 1979), pp. 183–186.

132. Al-Rasheed, Madawi, Politics in an Arabian Oasis: The Rashidi Tribal Dynasty (London, 1991), pp. 91–94. This superb study is essential reading on late nineteenth and early twentieth century Najd.

133. Ibn Qasim, Durar, 8:385.

134. Umari, Ulama Al Salim, pp. 18–33; Bassam, `Ulama', 6:154–157.

135. Ibn`Ubayd, Ibrahim, Tadhkirat uli al-nuha wa al-`irfan bi ayyam al-wahid al-dayyan wa dhikr hawadith al-zaman, 5 vols. (Riyadh, n.d.), 2:279. For a documentary study of the controversy, see al-Zahiri, Abd al-Rahman ibn `Aqil, 'Dunya al-watha'iq', al-Dir'iyya i/2 (1998), pp. 264–326; for a concise summary, see al-Fahad, 'From exclusivism to accommodation', pp. 504–510.

136. Bassam, `Ulama', 1:277–293; Zahiri, 'Dunya al-watha'iq', pp. 303–316. Ibn Jasir served the Rashidi rulers as qadi for ten years: from 1898 to 1900 in Burayda, from 1900 to 1906 in Unayza, then from 1906 to 1908 in Burayda; ibid., pp. 310–311.

137. Zahiri lists religious pupils and scholars in Ibn Jasir's camp, four of them from Al Bassam; 'Dunya al-watha'iq', pp. 312–316.

138. Ibid., p. 302.

139. Ibid., pp. 273–275.

140. Bassam, `Ulama', 4:324–334; Zahiri, 'Dunya al-watha'iq', pp. 264–268.

141. Salman, al-Ahwal al-siyasiyya, pp. 275–276.

Chapter Three

1. Al-Bassam, Abd Allah ibn Abd al-Rahman, `Ulama' najd khilal thamaniyat qurun, 6 vols., (Riyadh, 1997), 5:384–386.

2. Al-Zahiri, Abu Abd al-Rahman ibn Aqil, 'Dunya al-Watha'iq', al-Dir'iyya i/2 (1998), p. 284, citing Al-Umari, Salim al-Sulayman, `Ulama' Al Salim wa talamidhatuhum wa `ulama' al-qasim, 2 vols. (Riyadh, 1985).

3. Bassam, `Ulama', 1:436–452; Abd al-Rahman ibn Abd al-Latif Al al-Sheikh, `Ulama' al-da'wa (n.p., 1966), pp. 84–87; Al al-Sheikh, Abd al-Rahman ibn Abd al-Latif, Mashahir `ulama' najd wa ghayruhum (n.p., 1974), pp. 260–264; on his father Ibrahim ibn Hamad ibn Isa, see Bassam, `Ulama', 1:296–298; Al al-Sheikh, Mashahir, p. 234.

4. Mahmud Shukri al-Alusi's Ghayat al-amani fi al-radd ala al-Nabhani. On his assistance to Nu'man Khayr al-Din al-Alusi to contact Siddiq Hasan Khan, see Commins, David, Islamic Reform (New York, 1990), pp. 24–25.

5. On Siddiq Hasan Khan, a leader of the Ahl-i Hadith movement in India, see Chapter Five. On Hamad ibn Atiq's correspondence in 1880 with Siddiq Hasan Khan requesting that he send a number of works via Ibn Isa, see Bassam, `Ulama', 2:89.

6. His pupils included Hamad ibn Atiq's son Sa'd; ibid., 2:220–222.

7.   Bassam gives the earlier date; Al al-Sheikh, *Mashahir*, gives the later date.

8.   Bassam, `*Ulama*', 5:223–224.

9.   Ibid., 4:503–508.

10. He studied with Khayr al-Din al-Alusi. On the Alusis and their connections to Wahhabism, see Chapter Five.

11. Bassam, `*Ulama*', 2:383–385; on his apology to Ibn Saud, see Al-Qadi, Muhammad ibn Uthman ibn Salih, *Rawdat al-nazirin `an ma'athir `ulama' najd wa hawadith al-sinin*, 2 vols., 3rd ed. (Riyadh, 1989–90), 1:142.

12. Steinberg, Guido, 'The Shiites in the Eastern Province of Saudi Arabia (Al-Ahsa'), 1913–1953', in Rainer Brunner and Werner Ende (eds.), *The Twelver Shia in Modern Times: Religious Culture and Political History* (Leiden, 2001), pp. 245–248.

13. Habib, John S., *Ibn Sa'ud's Warriors of Islam: The Ikhwan of Najd and their Role in the Creation of the Sa'udi Kingdom* (Leiden, 1978), p. 38.

14. Steinberg, 'The Shiites in the Eastern Province', pp. 248–254.

15. On the Holy Cities and Jeddah, see Kostiner, Joseph, *The Making of Saudi Arabia 1916–1936: From Chieftaincy to Monarchical State* (Oxford, 1993), pp. 66–70. On the Ta'if events, see Habib, *Ibn Sa'ud's Warriors*, pp. 113–114.

16. Kostiner, *The Making of Saudi Arabia*, pp. 101, 105.

17. Ibid., p. 118. For a study of Hijaz's institutions in the Hashemite Kingdom, see Teitelbaum, Joshua, *The Rise and Fall of the Hashemite Kingdom of Arabia* (New York, 2001), pp. 126–225.

18. Habib, *Ibn Sa'ud's Warriors*, p. 115.

19. Ibid., pp. 116–118.

20. Kostiner, *The Making of Saudi Arabia*, p. 110.

21. Ochsenwald, William, 'Islam and Saudi national identity in the Hijaz, 1926–1939', paper presented at the Middle East Studies Association Annual Meeting, 2004, pp. 13–15. For a novelist's treatment of daily life in one of Mecca's popular quarters during Ibn Saud's rule, see Bogary, Hamza, *The Sheltered Quarter: A Tale of a Boyhood in Mecca* (Austin, 1992).

22. Ochsenwald, 'Islam and Saudi national identity', pp. 4–7.

23. Sedgwick, Mark J. R., 'Saudi Sufis: Compromise in the Hijaz, 1925–1940', *Die Welt des Islams* xxxvii/3 (1997), pp. 349–368.

24. Ibid., pp. 363–364.

25. Ende, Werner, 'The *Nakhawila*, a Shiite community in Medina past and present', *Die Welt des Islams* xxxvii/3 (1997), pp. 263–348.

26. Ibid., pp. 277–278.

27. Ibid., pp. 293–298.

28. Ibid., p. 320.

29. Ibid., p. 294.

30. Ibid., p. 328.

31. Ibid., p. 287.

32. Ibid., p. 291.

33. This discussion of the Ikhwan relies on Habib, *Ibn Saud's Warriors*; Kostiner, *The Making of Saudi Arabia*; Helms, Christine Moss, *The Cohesion of Saudi*

Arabia: Evolution of Political Identity (Baltimore, 1981); and Al-Fahad, Abdulaziz H., 'The `imama vs. the `iqal: Hadari-Bedouin conflict in the formation of the Saudi state', in Madawi Al-Rasheed and Robert Vitalis (eds.), *Counter-Narratives: History, Contemporary Society, and Politics in Saudi Arabia and Yemen* (New York, 2004).

34. Al-Fahad, 'The `imama vs. the `iqal', pp. 42–43.

35. Al-Fahad discerns glimpses of religious shifts among some nomadic tribes as a result of Wahhabi efforts, ibid., pp. 50–51.

36. For one example of revisionist work, see Kostiner, Joseph, 'On instruments and their designers: The Ikhwan of Najd and the emergence of the Saudi state', *Middle Eastern Studies* xxi/3 (1985), pp. 298–323.

37. Al-Fahad considers the Ikhwan a secondary factor compared to the levies from Najdi towns and argues that Habib exaggerated their military significance, 'The `imama vs. the `iqal', p. 70 n. 88.

38. Habib, *Ibn Sa'ud's Warriors*, p. 6. For details on the Ikhwan as fighters and the significance of their contribution to Ibn Saud's conquests, see ibid., pp. 63–79, Helms, *Cohesion*, pp. 142–146 and Kostiner, 'On Instruments and their Designers'.

39. Webster, Roger, 'Hijra and the dissemination of Wahhabi doctrine in Saudi Arabia', in Ian Richard Netton (ed.), *Golden Roads: Migration, Pilgrimage, and Travel in Mediaeval and Modern Islam* (Richmond, 1993), p. 13.

40. Muhammad ibn Abd al-Wahhab, *al-Usul al-thalatha wa adillatuha*, cited in Habib, *Ibn Sa'ud's Warriors*, p. 17. This treatise went through two printings for distribution to the Ikhwan, first in 1918 and then in 1920; ibid., p. 81 n. 7. Sulayman ibn Sihman, *al-Hadiya al-Saniya*, cited in ibid., p. 32.

41. Umari, *`Ulama' Al Salim*, 1:101–102.

42. Ibid., 1:98–100.

43. Habib, *Warriors of Ibn Sa'ud*, p. 51.

44. Al al-Sheikh, *Mashahir*, pp. 142–143.

45. Photocopy in author's possession.

46. Habib, *Warriors of Ibn Sa'ud*, pp. 54, 107.

47. Abd Allah ibn Abd al-Aziz al-`Anqari went to the Ikhwan as Ibn Saud's emissary. `Anqari was descended from a line of amirs in the town of Tharmada; Al al-Sheikh, *Mashahir*, p. 382. On this important figure in the third state who studied with Al al-Sheikh at a time of Saudi eclipse (1893–1903), see Bassam `Ulama', 4:265–279. Also Abd Allah ibn Abd al-Wahhab ibn Zahim had a role in dealing with the Ikhwan. He was from al-Qasab in Washm and studied in Riyadh with Abd Allah ibn Abd al-Latif. See ibid., 4:298–303.

48. Bassam, *`Ulama'*, 4:490–496.

49. Ibid., 1:407.

50. Internal evidence in the account indicates the incident would have taken place in or before 1891. The account names the amir, Zamil Al Salim, who died in that year. See ibid., 6:173–174.

51. Helms, *Cohesion*, p. 135, citing Shamekh, Ahmed A., *Spatial Patterns of*

Bedouin Settlement in al-Qasim Region Saudi Arabia (Lexington, Ky, 1975).

52. Helms, *Cohesion*, p. 136.
53. Habib, *Ibn Sa'ud's Warriors*, pp. 42–43.
54. Ibid., pp. 80–81.
55. Ibid., p. 47.
56. Ibid., pp. 66–67.
57. Ibid., p. 79.
58. Ibid., pp. 40–41.
59. Helms, *Cohesion*, pp. 132–134.
60. On the question of headdress, see Al-Fahad, 'The `imama vs. the `iqal', pp. 35, 52–53.
61. Helms, *Cohesion*, p. 134.
62. Webster cites Hafiz Wahbah's observation in *Arabian Days*, p. 127, that Ibn Saud first tried to uproot extreme mutawwi'a in 1916.
63. Habib, *Ibn Sa'ud's Warriors*, p. 82.
64. Ibid., p. 83, citing Rihani, Amin, *Najd wa mulhaqatihu* (Beirut, 1964), p. 434.
65. Al-Fahad, 'The `imama vs. the `iqal', pp. 52–53.
66. Al al-Sheikh, *Mashahir*, p. 382. There is also a report that Ibn Saud dispatched Abd Allah ibn Hamad ibn Atiq to the hijra at al-Ghatghat to serve as guide, prayer leader and preacher in order to moderate their views, especially the idea that sinners were infidels. Qadi, *Rawdat al-nazirin*, 1:409.
67. Al al-Sheikh, *Mashahir*, p. 170.
68. Al-Fahad, 'The `imama vs. the `iqal', p. 54. It seems the first person to make this observation was the British resident at Kuwait, Dickson; Helms, *Cohesion*, pp. 211–212. Kostiner endorses this view as well, *The Making of Saudi Arabia*, p. 85.
69. Helms, *Cohesion*, p. 252.
70. Habib, *Ibn Sa'ud's Warriors*, p. 121.
71. Helms, *Cohesion*, pp. 238–242.
72. Helms, *Cohesion*, p. 253; Habib, *Ibn Sa'ud's Warriors*, p. 122.
73. Helms, *Cohesion*, p. 253, Habib, *Ibn Sa'ud's Warriors*, pp. 122–123.
74. Helms, *Cohesion*, p. 254.
75. Habib, *Ibn Sa'ud's Warriors*, pp. 124–125.
76. Helms, *Cohesion*, pp. 261–263.
77. Helms, *Cohesion*, p. 254, Habib, *Ibn Sa'ud's Warriors*, p. 130.
78. Habib, *Ibn Sa'ud's Warriors*, p. 132.
79. Ibid., p. 134.
80. Helms, *Cohesion*, p. 256; Habib, *Ibn Sa'ud's Warriors*, p. 137.
81. Helms, *Cohesion*, pp. 258–259; Habib, *Ibn Sa'ud's Warriors*, p. 140.
82. Helms, *Cohesion*, pp. 266–267.
83. Helms, *Cohesion*, pp. 259–260; Habib, *Ibn Sa'ud's Warriors*, pp. 144–155.
84. Habib, *Ibn Sa'ud's Warriors*, pp. 151–160.
85. Ibid., p. 141.
86. Bassam, `Ulama', 1:231–241, Al al-Sheikh, *Mashahir*, pp. 152–163. His sons

were Sheikh Muhammad, general director for Islamic education in the Ministry of Education; Sheikh Abd al-Aziz, a qadi, ministry of education; Sheikh Hasan, assistant to chief qadi in Hijaz and minister of education, author of religious works.

87. Sheikh Muhammad ibn Ibrahim emerged as the next dominant figure until his death in 1969; Bassam, `Ulama', 1:242–263. For details, see Chapter Four.

88. Ibid., 5:310–315; Al al-Sheikh, *Mashahir*, p. 144.

89. The definitive study on the subject is Cook, Michael, *Commanding Right and Forbidding Wrong in Islamic Thought* (Cambridge, 2001).

90. On the duty's minor place in Wahhabi writings, ibid., pp. 169–175. On its implementation in Mecca, ibid., p. 168, 168 n. 18.

91. Ibid., pp. 175–179.

92. Michael Cook identified the first specific information about such committees as a 1926 announcement in the official newspaper; ibid., pp. 183–184.

93. Ibid., pp. 181–184.

94. Al-Yassini, Ayman, *Religion and State in the Kingdom of Saudi Arabia* (Boulder, 1985), pp. 68–69.

95. Ibid., p. 69.

96. Cook, *Commanding Right*, pp. 186, 187 n. 135.

97. Wahbah, Hafiz, *Arabian Days* (London, 1964), p. 171.

98. Ibid., pp. 59–60.

99. Ibid., pp. 51–53.

100. Ibid., pp. 49–51.

101. Ibid., p. 132.

102. Ibid., pp. 57–59.

103. Ibid., pp. 59–60.

104. Ibid., pp. 54–55.

105. A more accommodating view toward innovations gradually took hold in ruling circles, if not among Wahhabi ulama. Holden, David and Richard Johns, *The House of Saud: The Rise and Rule of the Most Powerful Dynasty in the Arab World* (New York, 1981), pp. 169–170.

106. Vassiliev, Alexei, *The History of Saudi Arabia* (New York, 2000), p. 305.

107. Ibid., p. 308.

108. For a revisionist version of the early history of American petroleum enterprise in Saudi Arabia, see Vitalis, Robert, 'Black gold, white gold: An essay on American exceptionalism, hierarchy and hegemony in the Gulf', *Diplomatic History* xxvi/2 (2002), pp. 195–213.

109. Linabury, George, 'The creation of Saudi Arabia and the erosion of Wahhabi conservatism', in Michael Curtis (ed.), *Religion and Politics in the Middle East* (Boulder, 1981), p. 281.

110. Van Der Meulen, D., *The Wells of Ibn Saud* (London, 1957), pp. 147–148.

111. Al-Rashid, Ibrahim (ed.), *Saudi Arabia Enters the World, Secret U.S. Documents on the Emergence of the Kingdom of Saudi Arabia as a World Power, 1936–1949*, Part I (Salisbury, NC, 1980), pp. 201–203.

Chapter Four

1. On Ibn Saud's marriages as a political strategy, see Al-Rasheed, Madawi, *A History of Saudi Arabia* (Cambridge, 2002), pp. 75–80. On rituals of royal largesse, pp. 80–86.

2. In Chapters Five and Six, we will see that a modern revivalist current emerged in the kingdom.

3. The title of a highly influential work, Lerner, Daniel, *The Passing of Traditional Society: Modernizing the Middle East* (Glencoe, Ill, 1958).

4. Al-Yassini, Ayman, *Religion and State in the Kingdom of Saudi Arabia* (Boulder, 1985), pp. 107–110.

5. Ibid., p. 110. For an English translation of the programme, see 'Ministerial statement of 6 November 1962 by Prime Minister Amir Faysal of Saudi Arabia', *Middle East Journal* xvii/1 (1963), pp. 161–162.

6. Yassini, *Religion and State*, pp. 67–79.

7. Ibid., pp. 110–112.

8. Ibid., pp. 81–105.

9. Al-Sadhan, Abdulrahman M., 'The modernisation of the Saudi bureaucracy', in Willard A. Beling (ed.), *King Faisal and the Modernisation of Saudi Arabia* (London, 1980), p. 82.

10. Holden, David and Richard Johns, *The House of Saud: The Rise and Rule of the Most Powerful Dynasty in the Arab World* (New York, 1981), p. 262.

11. Vitalis, Robert, 'Black gold, white gold: An essay on American exceptionalism, hierarchy and hegemony in the Gulf', *Diplomatic History* xxvi/2 (2002), p. 201. Most accounts overlook this episode and trace labor unrest to 1953. The stark differences between Saudis' and Americans' living conditions are captured in Robert Vitalis's vivid description of 'reed huts in Saudi camps... California-style bungalows, school, pool, oleander hedges, dining halls, bowling alley, golf course, ball park, cinema... of Aramco's American Camp'. Ibid., p. 201.

12. Ibid., p. 202.

13. Ibid., p. 204.

14. Lackner, Helen, *A House Built on Sand: A Political Economy of Saudi Arabia* (London, 1978), pp. 96–97; Yassini, *Religion and State*, pp. 117–118.

15. Buchan, James, 'Secular and religious opposition in Saudi Arabia', in Tim Niblock (ed.), *State, Society, and Economy in Saudi Arabia* (New York, 1982), pp. 108, 111–112.

16. Rugh, William A., 'Saudi mass media and society in the Faisal era', in Willard A. Beling (ed.), *King Faisal and the Modernisation of Saudi Arabia* (London, 1980), pp. 125–127.

17. Ibid., pp. 133–134.

18. Ibid., p. 126.

19. Holden and Johns, *House of Saud*, p. 261.

20. Boyd, Douglas A., 'Saudi Arabian television', *Journal of Broadcasting* xv/1 (1970–71), p. 73; Rugh, 'Saudi mass media', p. 129.

21. Rugh, 'Saudi mass media', pp. 129–131; Holden and Johns, *House of Saud*,

pp. 261–262.

22. Boyd, 'Saudi Arabian television', pp. 73–78.

23. Rugh, 'Saudi mass media', pp. 132–133.

24. Al-Bassam, Abd Allah ibn Abd al-Rahman, `Ulama' najd khilal thamaniyat qurun, 6 vols. (Riyadh1997), 1:242–263; Al al-Sheikh, Abd al-Rahman ibn Abd al-Latif, Mashahir `ulama' najd wa ghayruhum (n.p., 1974), pp. 169–177.

25. The full name of the body is the Directorate of Religious Research, Ifta', Da`wa and Guidance. Abir suggests that the Directorate and a body called the Supreme Judicial Council were formed because the ulama refused to participate in a Ministry of Justice. Abir, Mordechai, Saudi Arabia: Government, Society, and the Gulf Crisis (London, 1993), pp. 46–47.

26. Yassini, Religion and State, p. 71; also see the discussion on law below.

27. Cook, Michael, Commanding Right and Forbidding Wrong in Islamic Thought (Cambridge, 2001), p. 190.

28. On the first girls' schools, see below.

29. Vogel, Frank E., Islamic Law and Legal Systems: Studies of Saudi Arabia (Leiden, 2000), p. 93. In spite of Islamic law's prominence in Saudi Arabia, we have few studies that explore the topic in any depth. Frank E. Vogel's monograph is the splendid exception and I have relied on his work for my discussion of law in the modern kingdom.

30. Yassini, Religion and State, p. 70.

31. Vogel, Islamic Law, pp. 279–280.

32. Muhammad ibn Abd al-Wahhab, Kitab al-tawhid: Essay on the Unicity of Allah, or What is Due to Allah from his Creatures, translated by Ismail Raji al Faruqi (n.p., 1981), pp. 109–110.

33. Vogel, Islamic Law, pp. 209–210.

34. Ibid., pp. 85–86.

35. Ibid., pp. 74–76, 84.

36. Ibid., p. 117.

37. Ibid., pp. 90–93, 95–96.

38. Ibid., p. 98.

39. Ibid., pp. 129–30.

40. Ibid., p. 124.

41. This section on siyasa shar'iyya, ibid., pp. 173–177, 205. Also see Layish, Aharon, 'Saudi Arabia legal reform as a mechanism to moderate Wahhabi doctrine', Journal of the American Oriental Society cvii/2 (1987), pp. 284–285.

42. Vogel, Islamic Law, pp. 285–286.

43. Ibid., pp. 175–176. The tribunals are also referred to as commissions. The first tribunal was the commercial court established in 1931.

44. Ibid., pp. 287–288, 290.

45. Ibid., p. 291

46. Ibid., p. 289.

47. Ibid., pp. 174–175.

48. Ibid., p. 176.

49. Discussion of the court system, ibid., pp. 88–98.

50. Layish, 'Saudi Arabia legal reform', p. 280.

51. Vogel, *Islamic Law*, pp. 282–283.

52. Ibid., pp. 284–285.

53. Ibid., p. 280.

54. Ibid., pp. 302–303.

55. Ibid., p. 251. The general discussion of this principle, pp. 250–253.

56. Ibid., pp. 252–255. Hudud crimes are 'adultery... theft, wine-drinking, slander involving imputation of adultery, brigandage, and apostasy.' The punishments are amputation for theft, flogging for adultery between people never before married, stoning to death for adultery between married or formerly married people, death for apostasy, death or exile for brigandage, and lashings for slander and alcohol. The punishments are mandatory and a ruler may not pardon someone convicted of a hudud crime, for to do so would overturn a divine decree. Ibid., p. 241. Ta'zir pertains to transgressions against shari'a prohibitions or against the ruler's decrees designed to protect society. Establishing the punishment for this kind of offence is up to the ruler but he may leave it to the qadi's discretion. Typically less severe than hudud measures, ta'zir punishments include fines, mild lashing, and imprisonment. Ibid., pp. 247–249.

57. Ibid., pp. 255, 257–258.

58. Ibid., pp. 271–275.

59. Ibid., p. 271.

60. Ibid., pp. 273–277.

61. Ibid., p. 306.

62. For the Hanbali school's essential similarity in legal method to other law schools, particularly on the use of analogy and syllogism to determining legal rulings, see Hallaq, Wael, *A History of Islamic Legal Theories: An Introduction to Sunni Usul Al-Fiqh* (Cambridge, 1997), pp. 33, 131, 140. On Hanbali divergence from other schools by continuing to practise ijtihad, pp. 143–144.

63. Abir, Mordechai, 'Modern education and the evolution of Saudi Arabia', in Edward Ingram (ed.), *National and International Politics in the Middle East: Essays in Honour of Elie Kedourie* (London, 1986), pp. 229–251. Roy, Delwin A., 'Saudi Arabian education: Development policy', *Middle Eastern Studies* xxviii/3 (1992), pp. 477–508.

64. Doumato, Eleanor, 'Manning the barricades: Islam according to Saudi Arabia's school texts', *Middle East Journal*, 57:2 (2003), pp. 230–247; Doumato, Eleanor Abdella, 'Are reformers challenging the legitimacy of the Saudi regime? A look at reforms in education', presented at the Centre for International Studies, MIT, 7 April 2005; Prokop, Michaela, 'Saudi Arabia: The politics of education', *International Affairs* lxxix/1 (2003), pp. 77–89; 'The West, Christians and Jews in Saudi Arabian schoolbooks', American Jewish Committee and the Centre for Monitoring the Impact of Peace (CMIP), 2002. www.edume.org/reports/10/toc.htm. For the controversy over Saudi education after 11 September, see Chapter Six.

65. For an extensive description of religious education in the early twentieth century, see al-Salman, Muhammad ibn Abd Allah, *al-Ta'lim fi `ahd al-malak Abd al-Aziz* (Riyadh, 1999).

66. Al-Isa, Mayy bint Abd al-Aziz, *Al-Hayah al-`ilmiyya fi najd mundhu qiyam da`wat al-sheikh Muhammad ibn Abd al-Wahhab wa hatta nihayat al-dawla al-sa`udiyya al-ula* (Riyadh, 1997), pp. 245, 300.

67. Ibid, pp. 250–252. The four sons were Ali, Abd Allah, Husayn and Ibrahim, p. 278.

68. The text is *Kitab kashf al-shubuhat*, ibid., p. 270.

69. Ibid., pp. 271, 301.

70. Ibid., pp. 296–298.

71. See the description of Umar ibn Hasan Al al-Sheikh's education.

72. Al al-Sheikh, *Mashahir*, pp. 170–172.

73. The debate is described in Chapter Three.

74. Abu Aliya, Abd al-Fatah Hasan, 'Nazara `ala ba`d watha'iq al-hayat al-fikriyya fi sanjak al-Hasa', *Revue d'Histoire Maghrebine* lvii-lviii (1990), pp. 65–67.

75. Ibid., pp. 58–60.

76. By Muhammad ibn Abd al-Wahhab, *al-Thalatha al-usul*, *Kashf al-shubuhat*; on theology, *Lam`at al-i`tiqad* and *al-Aqida al-wasitiyya*; on exegesis, the works of Ibn Kathir, al-Baydawi and *al-Jalalayn*.

77. Abir, 'Modern education', 230–231.

78. Trial, George T. and R. Bayly Winder, 'Modern education in Saudi Arabia', *History of Education Journal* i (1950), p. 125.

79. Ibid., Appendix B, p. 130.

80. Ibid., pp. 125–126.

81. Abir, 'Modern education', p. 231.

82. Holden and Johns, *The House of Saud*, p. 259.

83. Parssinen, Catherine, 'The changing role of women', in Willard A. Beling (ed.), *King Faisal and the Modernization of Saudi Arabia*, pp. 156–161.

84. Holden and Johns, *The House of Saud*, pp. 260–262.

85. Abir, 'Modern education', p. 237; al-Farsy, Fouad, *Modernity and Tradition: The Saudi Equation* (London, 1990), pp. 256–257.

86. Farsy, *Modernity and Tradition*, pp. 260–261; Layish, Aharon, '`Ulama' and politics in Saudi Arabia', in Metin Heper and Raphael Israeli (eds.), *Islam and Politics in the Modern Middle East* (London, 1984), p. 37.

87. Roy, 'Saudi Arabian education', p. 481.

88. Ibid., pp. 481, 485, 495; Abir, 'Modern education', p. 234.

89. Abir makes this argument, 'Modern education', p. 242. On religious dissent, see Chapter Six.

90. On Saudi-Wahhabi proselytizing through international Islamic organizations, see Chapter Five.

Chapter Five

1. For a meticulous study of Wahhabi doctrinal development in this area, see

Al-Fahad, Abdulaziz, 'Commentary: From Exclusivism to Accommodation: Doctrinal and Legal Evolution of Wahhabism', *New York University Law Review* lxxix/2 (2004), pp. 485–519.

2.   For the extent of this network, see al-`Ajmi, Muhammad ibn Nasir (ed.), *Al-Rasa'il al-mutabadala bayna Jamal al-Din al-Qasimi wa Mahmud Shukri al-Alusi* (Beirut, 2001), pp. 41–42, 61 (India), 68, 114 (India and Qatar), 170 (Basra), 182 (Najd), 183 (Egypt).

3.   Commins, David, *Islamic Reform* (New York, 1990), pp. 24–26. Itzchak Weismann has examined Alusi's treatise in the context of polemical exchange between Baghdad Sufis, including Da'ud ibn Jirjis, and members of the Alusi family since the 1840s. Weismann, Itzchak, 'The Naqshbandiyya-Khalidiyya and the Salafi Challenge in Iraq', *Journal of the History of Sufism* iv (2003–2004), pp. 229–240.

4.   In an 1893 letter from Khayr al-Din al-Alusi to Salih ibn al-Salim. Khayr al-Din al-Alusi also wished to obtain a copy of Sheikh Abd al-Latif ibn Abd al-Rahman's rebuttal to Uthman ibn Mansur. Al-`Anfan, Sa`d ibn Khalaf, *Al-Sheikh Salih ibn al-Salim (1275–1330)* (Riyadh, 1997), pp. 47–48

5.   Al-Jaza'iri, Tahir, 'Rasa'il Ibn Taymiyya wa al-kutub allati nuqila `anha fi badi` al-qur'an ghayr ma ishtahar', Manuscript no. 11726, Zahiriyya Library, Damascus, Syria.

6.   On Jamal al-Din al-Qasimi and Tahir al-Jaza'iri, see Commins, *Islamic Reform*. For the detail on Qasimi copying a work by Ibn Taymiyya, see ibid., p. 59. For the historical background to religious reform in Damascus, see Weismann, Itzchak, *Taste of Modernity: Sufism, Salafiyya, and Arabism in Late Ottoman Damascus* (Leiden, 2001).

7.   Al-`Ajmi, *al-Rasa'il al-mutabadala*, pp. 41–43; Commins, *Islamic Reform*, p. 60.

8.   Al-`Ajmi, *al-Rasa'il al-mutabadala*, p. 43.

9.   Ibid., p. 47.

10. Commins, *Islamic Reform*, p. 108.

11. Ibid., pp. 124–128.

12. Ibid., pp. 108–110.

13. Al-Bassam, Abd Allah ibn Abd al-Rahman, `Ulama' najd khilal thamaniyat qurun, 6 vols. (Riyadh1997), 5:379–382.

14. Al-`Ajmi, *al-Rasa'il al-mutabadala*, p. 104. The letter is on pp. 104–107.

15. Fattah, Hala, '"Wahhabi" influences, Salafi responses: Shaikh Mahmud Shukri and the Iraqi Salafi movement, 1745–1930', *Journal of Islamic Studies* xiv/2 (2003), pp. 127–148; on Alusi's career and some of his writings, ibid., pp. 138–146. For a translation of his writings on ijtihad, see Al-Alusi, Mahmud Shukri, '*Ijtihad* and the refutation of Nabhani', in Charles Kurzman (ed.), *Modernist Islam, 1840–1940: A Sourcebook* (New York, 2002), pp. 158–171.

16. *Fath al-manan tatimmat minhaj al-ta'sis radd sulh al-ikhwan*. Sheikh Abd al-Latif had not finished the treatise when he died. The treatise with Alusi's additions was published in 1309 (1891/92). Al-`Ajmi, *al-Rasa'il al-mutabadala*, p. 114 n. 2.

17.   Al-Alusi, Mahmud Shukri, *Tarikh najd* (Cairo, 1924). The publisher was
      Rashid Rida. Esther Peskes pointed out the significance of Alusi's book
      on Najd as a turning point in the appraisal of Wahhabism in the Arab
      East. Peskes, Esther, *Muhammad B. Abdalwahhab (1703–1792) im Widerstreit*
      (Stuttgart, 1993), p. 373.

18.   Alusi, *Tarikh najd*, p. 4.

19.   Ibid., pp. 19–36.

20.   Ibid., pp. 20–21.

21.   Ibid., pp. 24–26.

22.   Ibid. p. 39.

23.   Ibid., pp. 41–49; Alusi identifies Sheikh Abd Allah's treatise as his source
      on page 49 and indicates that it was recited upon the entry of Saudi forces
      into Mecca. For an English translation of the treatise, see O'Kinealy, J.,
      'Translation of an Arabic pamphlet on the history and doctrines of the
      Wahhabis', *Journal of the Asiatic Society of Bengal* xliii/1 (1874), pp. 68–82.

24.   Alusi, *Tarikh najd*, p. 49.

25.   Ibid., p. 46. Thus Alusi implies that even though Bedouins inhabit Najd,
      they do not represent it.

26.   '*Al-ʿalim al-shahir*', ibid., pp. 50–76. The work by Abd al-Latif ibn Abd
      al-Rahman is *Minhaj al-taʾsis wa al-taqdis fi kashf shubuhat Daʾud ibn Jirjis*
      (Bombay, 1891/92). This is the same treatise that Alusi had worked to
      complete in 1889.

27.   The section on Al Saud is in Alusi, *Tarikh najd*, pp. 90–96.

28.   Ibid., pp. 94–96.

29.   Ibid., pp. 97–105. Other points in the epistles include exhortation to
      command right and forbid wrong; to abstain from tobacco; to organize
      study sessions in mosques; to rebuild mosques in disrepair; to attain correct   –
      understanding of monotheism as explained by Muhammad ibn Abd al-
      Wahhab.

30.   Commins, *Islamic Reform*, p. 133.

31.   Ibid., pp. 129–132.

32.   Kramer, Martin, *Islam Assembled: The Advent of the Muslim Congresses* (New
      York, 1986), pp. 108–110. That Rida accepted money from Ibn Saud in 1926
      would have been ironic in the light of his assertion two years before that
      Sharif Husayn had to pay Egyptian journalists to spread his propaganda
      whereas Ibn Saud did not need to resort to that because his conduct spoke
      for itself; Rida, Muhammad Rashid, *al-Wahhabiyyun wa al-hijaz* (n.p., 2000),
      p. 94.

33.   Kramer, *Islam Assembled*, pp. 108–117.

34.   Rida, *al-Wahhabiyyun*, p. 11.

35.   Ibid., p. 12.

36.   He published it as *al-Hadiya al-saniya wa al-tuhfa al-wahhabiya al-najdiyya*,
      ibid., pp. 13–15; in a later chapter, he notes that many readers were seeking
      copies of this early Wahhabi treatise, p. 57.

37.   Rida, *al-Wahhabiyyun*, p. 53; the assertion that the British used Husayn in

order to seize Arabia appears at pp. 72 and 91 as well.

38. The essential work on Hasan al-Banna and the Muslim Brothers is Mitchell, Richard, *The Society of the Muslim Brothers* (New York, 1969). For a concise discussion of Banna's life and thought, see Commins, David, 'Hasan al-Banna', in Ali Rahnema (ed.), *Pioneers of Islamic Revival* (London, 1994).

39. Mitchell, *Muslim Brothers*, pp. 214–216.

40. Ibid., p. 217.

41. Ibid., p. 247.

42. Calls for such measures became central planks in the rhetoric of Saudi religious dissidents in the 1990s, indicating the influence of modern revivalism in Saudi Arabia. See Chapter Six.

43. Muslim Brother refugees from Egypt, Syria and Jordan would inject their ideology into Saudi schoolbooks. See Chapter Six.

44. Mitchell, *Muslim Brothers*, p. 223.

45. The call for Saudi rulers to purge the government of men with secular outlook and to replace them with pious men became common in the 1980s and 1990s. See Chapter Six.

46. Metcalf, Barbara Daly, *Islamic Revival in British India, 1860–1900* (Princeton, 1992), pp. 35–43.

47. Ibid., pp. 47–52.

48. On Sayyid Ahmad's ideas about jihad, see Metcalf, *Islamic Revival*, pp. 52–63; Noelle, Christine, 'The anti-Wahhabi reaction in Afghanistan', *Muslim World* lxxxv/1–2 (1995), pp. 24, 35–36, 42–43. Barelwi followed the Hanafi school in contrast to the Hanbali Wahhabis; Metcalf, *Islamic Revival*, p. 265.

49. Marc Gaborieau reopened the question with a close textual analysis of a treatise mistakenly ascribed to Shah Waliullah. Gaborieau concludes that multiple parallels to Wahhabi doctrine make it likely that the author had contact or familiarity with the Najdi movement. Gaborieau, Marc, 'A nineteenth-century Indian "Wahhabi" tract against the cult of Muslim saints: *Al-Balagh al-Mubin'*, in Christian W. Troll (ed.), *Muslim Shrines in India: Their Character, History and Significance* (Delhi, 1989), pp. 230–232. Against his generally compelling argument, the treatise cites the great Sufi saints. I have not seen Wahhabi authors resort to such texts, even as a rhetorical device. Ibid., pp. 209, 217.

50. Metcalf, *Islamic Revival*, pp. 317–335.

51. A thorough study of the Deobandi School is in ibid., pp. 87–263.

52. On Nazir Husayn, see ibid., pp. 268, 290–293; on his naming the movement, see ibid., p. 272 n. 11. For a full discussion of Ahl-i Hadith and late nineteenth century movements, see ibid., pp. 264–296; also see Noelle, 'Anti-Wahhabi', pp. 42–43 and 42 n. 91.

53. Metcalf, *Islamic Revival*, pp. 277–278, 283–284.

54. Ibid., pp. 270–272.

55. Ibid., pp. 271–272, 279. Given the animosity between the pro-Wahhabi Ahl-i Hadith and the Deobandists, it is ironic that an early twentieth century

treatise by an Indian Muslim attacking the Deobandists labelled them Wahhabis. Sanyal, Usha, 'Are Wahhabis kafirs? Ahmad Riza Khan Barelwis and his *Sword of the Haramayn*', in Muhammad Khalid Masud, Brinkley Messick and David S. Powers (eds.), *Islamic Legal Interpretation: Muftis and their Fatwas* (Cambridge, Mass, 1996), pp. 205–206.

56. Metcalf, *Islamic Revival*, pp. 268, 293.

57. See Chapter Three for details on Ahmad ibn Isa's role in connecting Wahhabis to sympathetic ulama in the Ottoman Empire as well.

58. On Sa`d ibn Atiq, see Bassam, `Ulama', 2:220–222; Al al-Sheikh, Abd al-Rahman ibn Abd al-Latif, *Mashahir `ulama' najd wa ghayruhum* (n.p., 1974), pp. 323–325; Al-Qadi, Muhammad ibn Uthman ibn Salih, *Rawdat al-nazirin `an ma'athir `ulama' najd wa hawadith al-sinin*, 2 vols., 3rd ed. (Riyadh, 1989–1990), 1:117. Qadi specifically states that Sa`d ibn Atiq left Najd because of the 'fitna' or civil war. On Abd al-Aziz ibn Atiq, see Bassam, `Ulama', 3:330–334.

59. Bassam, `Ulama', 1:557–563.

60. For other instances of Najdis who studied at Delhi and Bhopal, see ibid., 2:482–483; 5:305–308; 5:378–383; 6:407–408.

61. Commins, *Islamic Reform*, pp. 24–25, 40, 60.

62. Nasr, Sayyid Vali Reza, 'Mawdudi and the Jama`at-i Islami: The origins, theory and practice of Islamic revivalism', in Ali Rahnema (ed.), *Pioneers of Islamic Revival* (London, 1994), pp. 103–104.

63. Ibid., p. 105.

64. Ibid., pp. 106–108.

65. Wahhabi support for the Ahl-i Hadith continued in the 1990s, when the leading Wahhabi sheikh of the time, Sheikh Abd al-Aziz ibn Baz, had Saudi religious institutions fund their efforts in Pakistan. Roy, Olivier, *The Failure of Political Islam* (Cambridge, Mass, 1994), p. 118.

66. Barrak, Abd al-Aziz ibn Nasir ibn Rashid, *Ibn Baz fi al-Dilam* (Riyadh, 2000), pp. 79–81.

67. For an analysis of jahiliyya in Sayyid Qutb's thought, see Shepard, William E., 'Sayyid Qutb's doctrine of *jahiliyya*', *International Journal of Middle East Studies* xxxv/4 (2003), pp. 524–535.

68. Tripp, Charles, 'Sayyid Qutb', in Ali Rahnema (ed.), *Pioneers of Islamic Revival* (London, 1994), p. 164. Quintan Wiktorowicz notes that Qutb met one of Mawdudi's pupils in Egypt in 1951 and that he cited Mawdudi in his own exegesis of the Qur'an. Wiktorowicz, 'A genealogy of radical Islam', *Studies in Conflict and Terrorism* xxviii (2005), pp. 78–79.

69. Roy, Olivier, *Afghanistan: From Holy War to Civil War* (Princeton, 1995), pp. 34–36. Another key difference is that Mawdudi was far more explicit than Qutb about the shape an Islamic state would take. Sayyid Qutb never got to put his ideas into action. After eleven years in prison, the Egyptian government released him in 1964, apparently out of consideration for his failing health. Out of prison, Qutb returned to frequently meeting with Muslim Brothers. The regime suspected him of plotting to overthrow the

government and the authorities arrested him and several other Brothers, in August 1965, on sedition charges. One year later, he was sentenced to death and hanged. Tripp, 'Sayyid Qutb', pp. 164–165.

70. Tripp, 'Sayyid Qutb', p. 162.

71. For a comparison of Sayyid Qutb and Muhammad ibn Abd al-Wahhab on the concept of jihad, see DeLong-Bas, Natana J., *Wahhabi Islam: From Revival and Reform to Global Jihad* (New York, 2004), pp. 256–265.

72. Shepard, 'Sayyid Qutb's doctrine', p. 530.

73. Al-Sinani, Isam ibn Abd Allah (ed.), *Bara'at ulama al-umma min tazkiyat ahl al-bid`a wa al-madhamma* (Ajman, 2000); on Qutb's popularity in mosques, p. 7; on Ibn Baz's views about Qutb's writings, pp. 16, 20–21, 30–34; on other sheikhs' views, pp. 35–37, 49–51.

74. Ochsenwald, William, 'Religious publications in Saudi Arabia, 1979–1989', *Die Welt des Islams* xli/2 (2001), pp. 135–144; data on Qutb from p. 141.

75. Olivier Roy has noted the cooperation among Muslim Brothers, Jamaati Islami and the Saudi government to spread conservative religious views. Roy, *The Failure*, p. 110. Roy also observes that the Wahhabis and the Muslim Brothers cooperate on preserving morality and exhorting believers to correct religious practice. Ibid., p. 117.

76. The incident took place in March 1954. Mitchell, *Muslim Brothers*, pp. 130–131.

77. For a discussion of King Faysal's Islamic foreign policy, see Sindi, Abdullah M., 'King Faisal and Pan-Islamism', in Willard A. Beling (ed.), *King Faisal and the Modernisation of Saudi Arabia* (London, 1980).

78. Abd al-Rahman ibn Hasan and Sulayman ibn Abdallah are the authors of the commentaries. Kane, Ousmane, *Muslim Modernity in Postcolonial Nigeria: A Study of the Society for the Removal of Innovation and the Reinstatement of Tradition* (Leiden, 2003), p. 66, 123–125.

79. Sirriyeh, Elizabeth, *Sufis and Anti-Sufis: The Defence, Rethinking and Rejection of Sufism in the Modern World* (Richmond, 1999), pp. 158–160.

80. Yassini, Ayman, *Religion and State in the Kingdom of Saudi Arabia* (Boulder, 1985), pp. 72–73. The World Muslim League distributes free copies of the Qur'an and other religious texts. It also pays salaries for imams at mosques in Europe and North America. Roy, *The Failure*, p. 116.

81. Yassini, *Religion and State*, p. 73. Abd al-Qadir `Awda was an influential writer for the Muslim Brothers and rose to influence in their hierarchy during the early 1950s; Mitchell, *Muslim Brothers*, pp. 87, 117. `Awda was executed in December 1954 along with six other members on charges of plotting to assassinate Nasser. He is reported to have declared just before his hanging, 'Praise be to God that He has made me a martyr and may He make my blood a curse upon the men of the revolution'. Ibid., p. 161.

Chapter Six

1. Vogel, Frank E., *Islamic Law and Legal Systems: Studies of Saudi Arabia* (Leiden, 2000), p. 80.

2. In discussions of contemporary Islamic revivalist movements, the term 'salafi' refers to a different set of concerns than the late Ottoman 'salafi' trend. As seen in Chapter Five, the earlier salafis viewed a return to Islam's original sources as a way to combat ritual innovations and to justify an agenda for adapting institutions to modern conditions. Late twentieth century salafis share the aspiration to establish correct ritual practice but not the modernist dimension. Instead, they emphasize the imperative to overthrow secular regimes and replace them with an Islamic state based on shari'a. For a set of superb, meticulous studies on contemporary salafi trends, both non-violent and jihadist, see Wiktorowicz, Quintan, 'Anatomy of the salafi movement', *Studies in Conflict and Terrorism* xxix/2 (2006); page references in notes below are from the unpublished manuscript, December 2004; Wiktorowicz, 'A genealogy of radical Islam', *Studies in Conflict and Terrorism* xxviii (2005), pp. 75–97; Wiktorowicz, 'The new global threat: transnational salafis and jihad', *Middle East Policy* viii/4 (2001), pp. 18–38; Wiktorowicz and John Kaltner, 'Killing in the name of Islam: Al-Qaeda's justification for September 11', *Middle East Policy* x/2 (2003), pp. 76–92.

3. Gelvin, James L., *The Modern Middle East* (New York, 2005), p. 297.

4. 'Ministerial Statement of 6 November 1962 by Prime Minister Amir Faysal of Saudi Arabia', *Middle East Journal* xvii/1 (1963), p. 162.

5. Abir, Mordechai, *Saudi Arabia: Government, Society, and the Gulf Crisis* (London, 1993), pp. 66, 99.

6. Ibid., pp. 22, 73, 99.

7. Ibid., p. 99.

8. Ibid., p. 22, 100.

9. Linabury, George, 'The creation of Saudi Arabia and the erosion of Wahhabi conservatism', in Michael Curtis (ed.), *Religion and Politics in the Middle East* (Boulder, 1981), p. 282.

10. Holden, David and Richard Johns, *The House of Saud: The Rise and Rule of the Most Powerful Dynasty in the Arab World* (New York, 1981), p. 393.

11. Buchan, James, 'Secular and religious opposition in Saudi Arabia', in Tim Niblock (ed.), *State, Society, and Economy in Saudi Arabia* (New York, 1982), p. 148 n. 24.

12. Holden and Johns, *The House of Saud*, pp. 401–405.

13. Ibid., pp. 410–411.

14. Ibid., pp. 407–409.

15. Eleanor Doumato uses the term 'extraterritorialized space' to capture the sense that a foreign environment had suddenly sprouted up and erased familiar landscapes. Doumato, Eleanor, *Getting God's Ear: Women, Islam, and Healing in Saudi Arabia and the Gulf* (New York, 2000), pp. 10–11.

16. Yassini, Ayman, *Religion and State in the Kingdom of Saudi Arabia* (Boulder, 1985), p. 115.

17. Doumato, *Getting God's Ear*, pp. 2–7.

18. Gelvin, *The Modern Middle East*, p. 297.

19. Buchan, James, 'The Return of the Ikhwan', in Holden and Johns, *The House*

of Saud, pp. 511–526.

20. Holden and Johns, *The House of Saud*, p. 514. Al-Ghatghat was a centre for rebellious Ikhwan in the 1920s.

21. Ibid., p. 517.

22. Ibid., p. 518.

23. Kechichian, Joseph, 'Islamic revivalism and change in Saudi Arabia: Juhayman Al-Utaybi's 'Letters' to the Saudi people', *The Muslim World* lxx/1 (1990), p. 12.

24. Muhammad ibn Abd al-Wahhab, *Kitab al-tawhid: Essay on the Unicity of Allah, or What is Due to Allah from his Creatures*, translated by Ismail Raji al Faruqi (n.p., 1981), pp. 109–110.

25. Kechichian, 'Islamic revivalism', p. 13. The notion that Ibn Saud should have supported Sharif Husayn against the Ottomans is quite odd in the context of Wahhabi and Najdi religious thought and suggests that on this particular point Juhayman might have been influenced by non-Saudi Islamic trends.

26. Salame, Ghassan, 'Islam and politics in Saudi Arabia', *Arab Studies Quarterly* ix/3 (1987), pp. 317–318.

27. Kechichian, 'Islamic revivalism', p. 13.

28. Ibid., p. 13.

29. Salame, 'Islam and politics', p. 317.

30. Mitchell, Richard, *The Society of Muslim Brothers* (New York, 1969), p. 247.

31. Salame, 'Islam and politics', p. 315.

32. Ibid., p. 314; Kechichian, 'Islamic revivalism', p. 14.

33. Salame, 'Islam and politics', p. 316.

34. Ochsenwald, William, 'Saudi Arabia and the Islamic revival', *International Journal of Middle East Studies* xiii (1981), p. 276.

35. On the concept of the mahdi, see Madelung, W., 'al-Mahdi', *Encyclopaedia of Islam*, CD-Rom Edition 1.0 (Brill, 1999), V:1230b.

36. Holden and Johns, *The House of Saud*, pp. 519–520.

37. Salame, 'Islam and politics', p. 315.

38. The discussion of the ulama's handling of the crisis and their fatwa is based on Kechichian, Joseph, 'The role of the ulama in the politics of an Islamic state: The case of Saudi Arabia', *International Journal of Middle East Studies* xviii (1986), pp. 61–62, 66–68.

39. Ibid., pp. 66–68.

40. Ibid., p. 67.

41. Holden and Johns, *The House of Saud*, pp. 524–525.

42. Kechichian, 'The role of the ulama', p. 71 n. 21; Holden and Johns, *The House of Saud*, p. 527.

43. Salame, 'Islam and politics', p. 321.

44. Kechichian, 'The role of the ulama', p. 62.

45. Holden and Johns, *The House of Saud*, p. 530.

46. Abir, *Saudi Arabia*, p. 145; Okruhlik, Gwenn, 'Empowering civility through nationalism: Reformist Islam and belonging in Saudi Arabia', in Robert W.

Hefner (ed.), *Remaking Muslim Politics: Pluralism, Contestation, Democratization* (Princeton, 2005), pp. 194–195; Cordesman, Anthony, 'Saudi Arabia: Opposition, Islamic extremism and terrorism', in *Saudi Arabia Enters the 21st Century: Politics, Economics, and Energy* (Washington, 2002), p. 15; Jerichow, Anders. *The Saudi File: People, Power, Politics* (New York, 1998), pp. 71–72.

47. Salame, 'Islam and politics', p. 321.

48. Goldberg, Jacob, 'The Shii minority in Saudi Arabia', in Juan Cole and Nikki Keddie (eds.), *Shiism and Social Protest* (New Haven, 1986), p. 237. On Shiite demonstrations in 1979–80, see Abir, *Saudi Arabia*, pp. 82–88.

49. Ende, Werner, 'The *Nakhawila*, A Shiite community in Medina past and present', *Die Welt des Islams* xxxvii/3 (1997), p. 293.

50. Ibid., p. 326; Prokop, Michaela, 'Saudi Arabia: The politics of education', *International Affairs* lxxix/1 (2003), p. 81.

51. The imam was Ismail ibn Ja'far al-Sadiq. Ende, 'The *Nakhawila*', p. 294 n. 109.

52. Ibid., p. 297, 297 n. 128.

53. Ibid., p. 335.

54. Ibid., pp. 329–330.

55. Kechichian, 'Islamic revivalism', p. 5.

56. Goldberg, 'The Shii minority', pp. 239–240, 242–243.

57. Ibid., pp. 242–246.

58. Abir, *Saudi Arabia*, pp. 108–109.

59. Wiktorowicz, 'Anatomy', pp. 22–23; Kepel, *The War for Muslim Minds: Islam and the West* (Cambridge, Mass, 2004), pp. 174–177.

60. Wiktorowicz, 'Genealogy', pp. 78–79.

61. Ibid., p. 79.

62. Ibid., pp. 79–80. For a discussion and translation of Abd al-Salam al-Faraj's treatise, see Jansen, Johannes J.G., *The Neglected Duty: The Creed of Sadat's Assassins and Islamic Resurgence in the Middle East* (New York, 1986).

63. Wiktorowicz, 'Genealogy', pp. 80–81.

64. Abedin, Mahan, 'Al-Muhajiroun in the UK: An interview with Sheikh Omar Bakri Mohammed' (10 March 2004), www.al-muhaajiroun.com/articles/interview.htm, accessed on 10 June 2004.

65. Taji-Farouqi, Suha, *A Fundamental Quest: Hizb al-Tahrir and the Search for the Islamic Caliphate* (London, 1996); Commins, David, 'Taqi al-Din al-Nabhani and the Islamic Liberation Party', *Muslim World* lxxxi (1991), pp. 194–211.

66. Rashid, Ahmed, *Taliban: Militant Islam, Oil and Fundamentalism in Central Asia* (New Haven, 2000), p. 129.

67. Ibid., pp. 130.

68. Cordesman, 'Saudi Arabia', p. 14.

69. Bergen, Peter L., *Holy War, Inc. Inside the Secret World of Osama bin Laden* (New York, 2001), pp. 51–54; Roy, Olivier, *Afghanistan: From Holy War to Civil War* (Princeton, 1995), pp. 85–86.

70. Wiktorowicz, 'The new global threat', p. 23.

71. Wiktorowicz, 'Genealogy', pp. 84–85.

72. For an overview of the basic division between jihad as collective or individual duty, see Peters, Rudolph, *Jihad in Classical and Modern Islam: A Reader* (Princeton, 1996), pp. 29–30.

73. Wiktorowicz, 'The new global threat', p. 23; Bergen, *Holy War, Inc.*, p. 53.

74. Bergen, *Holy War, Inc.*, pp. 52–53; Roy, *Afghanistan*, pp. 85–86; Rashid, *Taliban*, p. 131.

75. Wiktorowicz, 'The new global threat', pp. 21–26

76. For a discussion and analysis of the fatwa and its significance in the development of Wahhabi doctrine, see al-Fahad, Abdulaziz H., 'Commentary: From exclusivism to accommodation: Doctrinal and legal evolution of Wahhabism', *New York University Law Review* lxxix/2 (2004), pp. 514–517. His analysis leads to him conclude that the ulama knew they stood on weak ground but bowed to the demands of *realpolitik*. An English translation is on pp. 518–519.

77. Ibid., p. 518.

78. Milton-Edwards, Beverly, 'A temporary alliance with the crown: The Islamic response in Jordan', in James Piscatori (ed.), *Islamic Fundamentalisms and the Gulf Crisis* (Chicago, 1991), p. 97.

79. Ibid., p. 98.

80. Ibid., p. 98.

81. Auda, Gehad, 'An uncertain response: The Islamic movement in Egypt', in James Piscatori (ed.), *Islamic Fundamentalisms and the Gulf Crisis* (Chicago, 1991), p. 119. For the similar reaction of South Asian revivalists, see Ahmad, Mumtaz, 'The politics of war: Islamic fundamentalisms in Pakistan', in James Piscatori (ed.), *Islamic Fundamentalisms and the Gulf Crisis* (Chicago, 1991), pp. 161–174, 179; the staunchly pro-Wahhabi Ahl-i Hadith movement blamed Saddam Hussein for the war and supported Riyadh; ibid., p. 184 n. 36.

82. On preachers criticizing the government for supporting western-led military action against Iraq, see Abir, *Saudi Arabia*, pp. 184–185.

83. Fandy, Mamoun, *Saudi Arabia and the Politics of Dissent* (New York, 1999), pp. 102–103. On the polemical exchange between al-Qusaybi and his religious critics during the crisis over Kuwait, see Dekmejian, Richard, 'The liberal impulse in Saudi Arabia', *Middle East Journal* lvii/3 (2003), p. 403.

84. Abir cites the economic hardship of the 1980s, royal corruption and the influence of non-Saudi revivalist tendencies, *Saudi Arabia*, pp. 181–182.

85. For the historical background of the liberal tendency, its social composition and programme, see Dekmejian, 'The liberal impulse', pp. 400–413.

86. For texts of the petitions, see Jerichow, *The Saudi File*, pp. 50–54.

87. The Letter of Demands is summarized in Champion, Daryl, *The Paradoxical Kingdom: Saudi Arabia and the Momentum of Reform* (New York, 2003), pp. 222–223. Dekmejian offers a useful discussion as well. Dekmejian, R. Hrair, 'The rise of political Islamism in Saudi Arabia', *Middle East Journal* xlviii/4 (1994), pp. 630–632.

88. Abir, *Saudi Arabia*, pp. 191–194.

89. Ibid., p. 198; Ibn Baz's rejection of these criticisms is also noted in Teitelbaum, Joshua, *Holier Than Thou: Saudi Arabia's Islamic Opposition* (Washington, 2000), p. 36.

90. Faksh, Mahmud A., *The Future of Islam in the Middle East: Fundamentalism in Egypt, Algeria, and Saudi Arabia* (Westport, Conn., 1997), p. 97; Dekmejian, 'The rise of political Islamism in Saudi Arabia', pp. 633–634. Dekmejian analyzes the social background of the signatories to the Letter of Demands and the Memorandum of Advice; ibid., pp. 635–637.

91. Teitelbaum, *Holier Than Thou*, pp. 38–39.

92. Faksh, *The Future of Islam*, p. 100; Cordesman, 'Saudi Arabia', p. 25.

93. The Saudi Constitution, www.the-saudi.net/saudi-arabia/saudi-constitution. htm

94. International Crisis Group, 'Can Saudi Arabia Reform Itself?', *International Crisis Group Middle East Report No. 28* (14 July 2004), p. 6.

95. Fandy, *Saudi Arabia and the Politics of Dissent*, pp. 48, 50, 102–103.

96. Kepel views the sahwa sheikhs' ideas as a 'hybrid of salafism and Qutbist thought'; *The War*, p. 178.

97. Hawali is also the author of two books; Fandy, *Saudi Arabia and the Politics of Dissent*, pp. 62, 67, 90.

98. Teitelbaum, *Holier Than Thou*, pp. 28–29.

99. Ibid., p. 30.

100. Kepel, *The War*, pp. 178–179.

101. Fandy, *Saudi Arabia and the Politics of Dissent*, pp. 67–73.

102. Ibid., pp. 63–65.

103. Ibid., pp. 98–99

104. Ibid., pp. 100–101.

105. Wiktorowicz, 'Anatomy', p. 26.

106. Ibid., p. 28; Cordesman, 'Saudi Arabia', p. 26.

107. Ibid., p. 151.

108. Ibid., pp. 151–154, 157.

109. Ibid., pp. 159, 167, 171.

110. Faqih included the prominent sheikh Muhammad Uthaymin in his criticism of apologists for the monarchy; ibid., p. 168.

111. Vogel, *Islamic Law*, p. 209.

112. Mahmud Faksh notes the modern features in the dissident camp's list of grievances. Faksh, *The Future of Islam*, pp. 94–95. On the foreign, especially Egyptian Muslim Brother influence, see Teitelbaum, *Holier Than Thou*, pp. 3–4.

113. For a discussion of the kinship between nationalism and modern Islamic political movements, see Gelvin, *The Modern Middle East*, pp. 291–299.

114. The exogenous origin of religious dissent was emphasized in 2002 by Saudi Interior Minister Prince Nayef. He criticized the Muslim Brothers for causing problems in Saudi Arabia and abusing its hospitality. One Saudi observer noted that the Muslim Brothers had never commented on corruption and abuse of power until the split over the Kuwait crisis. 'Is Saudi Arabia

divorcing political Islam?', *Arab Press Review*, 4 December 2002.

115. Cordesman, 'Saudi Arabia', pp. 33–35. Less than a year later, a more devastating blast in the Eastern Province town of Khobar killed 19 American military personnel and injured more than 300. In that instance, however, the truck bombing appears to have been the work of a Shiite group known as Saudi Hizballah, which had formed in the 1980s to protest discrimination against Shiites. Circumstantial evidence indicated that Iranian intelligence had a hand in the incident and that it was not part of a Sunni jihadist campaign. Ibid., pp. 36–43.

116. Wiktorowicz, 'The new global threat', pp. 24–26.

117. Ibid., p. 19. Anthony Cordesman concurs with this assessment, 'Saudi Arabia', p. 8. For a discussion that emphasizes Sayyid Qutb's imprint on Osama bin Laden, see DeLong-Bas, Natana J., *Wahhabi Islam: From Revival and Reform to Global Jihad* (New York, 2004), pp. 266–274. For analysis of Osama bin Laden's declarations, see Anonymous, *Through Our Enemies' Eyes* (Washington, D.C., 2002), pp. 45–88; Orbach, Benjamin, 'Osama bin Laden and al-Qa'ida: Origins and doctrines', *Middle East Revie of International Affairs (MERIA) Journal* v/4 (2001), pp. 54–68.

118. Anonymous, *Through our Enemies' Eyes*, pp. 46–71.

119. Ibid., p. 45.

120. Ibid., pp. 63–65; Wiktorowicz, 'The new global threat', pp. 19, 34.

121. Anonymous, *Through our Enemies' Eyes*, pp. 84–85; Wiktorowicz, 'Transnational', pp. 19, 26; Bergen, *Holy War, Inc.*, pp. 47–48.

122. Bergen, *Holy War, Inc.*, pp. 50–51, 56–57.

123. Ibid., p. 77.

124. Kepel, *The War*, pp. 181–182.

125. Bergen, *Holy War, Inc.*, p. 78.

126. Ibid., pp. 79–80.

127. Ibid., p. 86.

128. Ibid., pp. 88–89.

129. This incident took place in December 1994; Fandy, *Saudi Arabia and the Politics of Dissent*, pp. 187–188.

130. Bergen, *Holy War, Inc.*, p. 91.

131. 'Declaration of War against the Americans Occupying the Land of the Two Holy Places', www.pbs.org/newshour/terrorism/international/fatwa_1996.html

132. For the imperative to demonstrate the defensive posture of Muslims in order to justify jihad, see Wiktorowicz, 'The new global threat', pp. 34–35

133. Orbach, 'Osama bin Laden', pp. 59–60.

134. For the text of the 1998 fatwa, 'Jihad against Jews and Crusaders', see website of the Federation of American Scientists www.fas.org/irp/world/para/docs/980223-fatwa.htm

135. Orbach, 'Osama bin Laden', p. 60.

136. Anonymous, *Through Our Enemies' Eyes*, p. 28.

137. Habib, John S., *Ibn Sa'ud's Warriors of Islam: The Ikhwan of Najd and their Role*

in the Creation of the Sa'udi Kingdom (Leiden, 1978), p. 25–28.

138. Anthony Cordesman notes the misapplication of the Wahhabi label to the Deobandi and other revivalist currents; 'Saudi Arabia', pp. 8–9. On Deobandi influences in Nepal, see Gaborieau, Marc, 'A nineteenth-century Indian "Wahhabi" tract against the cult of Muslim saints: *Al-Balagh al-Mubin'*, in Christian W. Troll (ed.), *Muslim Shrines in India: Their Character, History and Significance* (Delhi, 1989), p. 201.

139. Rashid, *Taliban*, pp. 88–89.

140. Ibid., pp. 89–90.

141. Atkin, Muriel, 'The rhetoric of Islamophobia', *Central Asia and the Caucasus* i (2000), pp. 123–132; Knysh, Alexander, 'A clear and present danger: "Wahhabism" as a rhetorical foil', *Saudi-American Forum* xxiv (14 November 2003); Khalid, Adeeb, 'A secular Islam: Nation, state and religion in Uzbekistan', *International Journal of Middle East Studies* xxxv (2003), pp. 581, 587–591.

142. Khalid, 'A secular Islam', pp. 581, 590.

143. Atkin, 'The rhetoric of Islamophobia', p. 127.

144. Khalid, 'A secular Islam', p. 589.

145. Atkin, 'The rhetoric of Islamophobia', p. 129.

146. Ibid., p. 131.

147. Of course, the Saudis view their contributions to religious institutions as charitable deeds redounding to their credit. Thus, a quasi-official overview of King Fahd's achievements gives a long list of schools, academies, mosques, research institutes and Islamic centres to illustrate his bounty. The king has funded mosques and Islamic centres in North America, Africa, Europe and Asia. Al-Farsy, Fouad, *Modernity and Tradition: The Saudi Equation* (London, 1990), pp. 220–226.

148. Abou El Fadl, Khaled M., *Conference of the Books: The Search for Beauty in Islam* (Lanham, Md., 2001), pp. 290–293. Abou El Fadl notes that the verse had a specific purpose, namely that, by dressing a certain way, free women would distinguish themselves from slave women to spare them taunting by men at night. For two more examples of the slant in the Wahhabi translation, see pp. 294–301. The English translation carries Abd al-Aziz ibn Baz's seal of approval in his capacity as director of the Directory for Islamic Research, Ifta', Preaching and Guidance.

149. Dekmejian, 'The liberal impulse', pp. 404–407.

150. Ibid., pp. 411–412.

151. Ibid., pp. 408–410.

152. Lacroix, Stephane, 'Between Islamists and liberals: Saudi Arabia's new "Islamo-Liberal" reformers', *Middle East Journal* lviii/3 (2004), p. 358. On the relaxation of censorship in recent years, also see International Crisis Group, 'Can Saudi Arabia reform itself?' *International Crisis Group Middle East Report No. 28* (14 July 2004), pp. 21–22.

153. Wiktorowicz, 'Anatomy', pp. 20–21.

154. Ibid., pp. 37–38.

155. Kepel, *The War*, p. 186; Lacroix, 'Between Islamists and liberals', p. 345.

156. Wiktorowicz and Kaltner, 'Killing in the name of Islam', p. 76.

157. Wiktorowicz, 'Anatomy', pp. 29–30.

158. Kechichian, Joseph A., 'Testing the Saudi will to power: Challenges confronting Prince Abdallah', *Middle East Policy* x/4 (2003), p. 109.

159. Ibid., p. 104.

160. International Crisis Group, 'Can Saudi Arabia reform itself?', p. 25.

161. Kepel, *The War*, pp. 188–189.

162. International Crisis Group, 'Can Saudi Arabia reform itself?', p. 24; for a March 2003 declaration against strife inside the kingdom, see ibid., p. 24 n. 121.

163. Kechichian, 'Testing the Saudi will to power', p. 109; Jones, Toby, 'The clerics, the sahwa and the Saudi state', *Strategic Insights* iv/3 (2005).

164. Wiktorowicz, 'The new global threat', pp. 27–29; Wiktorowicz and Kaltner, 'Killing in the name of Islam', pp. 90–91.

165. Wiktorowicz and Kaltner, 'Killing in the name of Islam', pp. 76–77.

166. Ibid., pp. 84–91.

167. IntelCentre, 'Al-Qaeda in the Arabian Peninsula: Shooting, Hostage Taking, Kidnapping Wave', July 2004, www.intelcentre.com/reports-charts.html

168. Lacroix, 'Between Islamists and liberals', p. 346; International Crisis Group, 'Can Saudi Arabia reform itself?', pp. 13–15.

169. Rubin, Elizabeth, 'The jihadi who kept asking why', *New York Times Sunday Magazine* (7 March 2004).

170. Shepard, William E., 'Sayyid Qutb's doctrine of *jahiliyya*', *International Journal of Middle East Studies* xxxv/4 (2003), p. 530.

171. Lacroix, 'Between Islamists and liberals', pp. 352–354.

172. Ibid., pp. 347–348. Abd Allah al-Hamid is another former figure in the sahwa movement and the CDLR who prefers a vaguely defined form of consultation, or shura, to democracy. Ibid., pp. 348–350

173. Ibid., 350–352.

174. al-Madalij, Hafiz, *al-Riyadh* (15 November 2003).

175. Doumato, Eleanor, 'Manning the barricades: Islam according to Saudi Arabia's school texts', *Middle East Journal* lvii/2 (2003), pp. 230–247. For a study that focuses on religious xenophobia, see 'The West, Christians and Jews in Saudi Arabian Schoolbooks', American Jewish Committee and the Centre for Monitoring the Impact of Peace (CMIP), 2002. www.edume.org/reports/10/toc.htm

176. For Hasan al-Banna's views on education and on Muslim Brother efforts in that realm during the 1930s and 1940s, see Mitchell, *Muslim Brothers*, pp. 283–289.

177. Muslim Brother authors describe a 'Zionist-Crusading war against the Arab and Islamic peoples'. Sayyid Qutb wrote that 'the Crusader spirit runs in the blood of all westerners'. On the cultural imperialism motif, Banna called on Muslims to 'eject imperialism from your souls and it will leave your lands'. Banna opposed missionary activities while Qutb drew attention to

the ways that western academic experts (Orientalists) distorted Islam to mislead Muslims about its true nature. Ibid., pp. 227–231.

178. In the 1950s, Sayyid Qutb and other Muslim Brothers had written that United States foreign policy on Israel and Palestine was directed by 'Jewish gold and Zionist influence' and the 'Zionist-dominated' press. He claimed that Zionist fundraisers used the slogan, 'Pay a dollar and kill an Arab'. Mitchell, *Muslim Brothers*, p. 228.

179. Cordesman, 'Saudi Arabia', pp. 19–20.

180. Doumato, Eleanor Abdella, 'Are reformers challenging the legitimacy of the Saudi regime? A look at reforms in education', presented at the Centre for International Studies, MIT, 7 April 2005, pp. 5–7.

181. International Crisis Group, 'Can Saudi Arabia reform itself?', p. 25.

182. Doumato, 'Are reformers challenging', p. 10.

183. International Crisis Group, 'Can Saudi Arabia reform itself?' pp. 16–18.

184. Jones, 'The clerics'.

185. International Crisis Group, 'Can Saudi Arabia reform itself?', p. 17.

186. Wiktorowicz makes the same point in 'Anatomy', pp. 22–23.

Conclusion

1. Lackner, Helen, *A House Built on Sand: A Political Economy of Saudi Arabia* (London, 1978); Aburish, Said K., *The Rise, Corruption, and Coming Fall of the House of Saud* (New York, 1996).

2. Of course, it is not the historian's vocation to make predictions, so for this assessment I rely on political scientists and policy experts, among whom the consensus is that Al Saud will continue in power for quite some time. See Gause, F. Gregory, 'Be careful what you wish for: The future of U.S.-Saudi relations', *World Policy Journal* xix/1 (2002), pp. 37–50; International Crisis Group, 'Can Saudi Arabia Reform Itself?', *International Crisis Group Middle East Report No. 28* (14 July 2004).

Bibliography

Aba Butayn, Abd Allah, *Al-Intisar li hizb allah al-muwahhidin: al-radd `ala al-mujadil `an al-mushrikin* (Kuwait, 1989)

Aba Butayn, Abd Allah, *Ta'sis al-taqdis fi kashf talbis Da'ud ibn Jirjis* (Cairo, 1925/26)

Abd al-Latif ibn Abd al-Rahman Al al-Sheikh, *Minhaj al-ta'sis wa al-taqdis fi kashf shubuhat Da'ud ibn Jirjis* (Bombay, 1891/92)

Abd al-Latif ibn Abd al-Rahman ibn Hasan Al al-Sheikh, *Misbah al-zalam fi al-radd `ala man kadhaba `ala al-sheikh al-imam* (Riyadh, n.d)

Abd al-Latif ibn Abd al-Rahman Al al-Sheikh, *Tuhfat al-talib wa al-jalis fi kashf shubah Da'ud ibn Jirjis* (Riyadh, 1990)

Abd al-Rahim, Abd al-Rahman Abd al-Rahim, *Muhammad Ali wa shibh al-jazira al-`arabiyya, 1234–1256/1819–1840*, 2 vols. (Cairo, 1986)

Abd al-Rahman ibn Hasan Al al-Sheikh, *al-Maqamat* (Riyadh, n.d.)

Abd al-Rahman ibn Hasan ibn Muhammad ibn Abd al-Wahhab, 'Qurrat `uyyun al-muwahhidin fi tahqiq da`wat al-anbiya' wa al-mursalin', in Muhammad Rashid Rida (ed.), *Majmu`at al-tawhid al-najdiyya*, Reprint edition (Riyadh, 1999)

Abd al-Rahman ibn Hasan ibn Muhammad ibn Abd al-Wahhab, *Al-Qawl al-fasl al-nafis fi al-radd `ala al-muftari Da'ud ibn Jirjis* (Riyadh, 1985)

Abedin, Mahan, 'Al-Muhajiroun in the UK: An interview with Sheikh Omar Bakri Mohammed' (10 March 2004), www.al-muhaajiroun.com/articles/interview. htm, accessed on 10 June 2004

Abir, Mordechai, 'Modern education and the evolution of Saudi Arabia', in Edward Ingram (ed.), *National and International Politics in the Middle East: Essays in Honour of Elie Kedourie* (London, 1986)

Abir, Mordechai, *Saudi Arabia: Government, Society and the Gulf Crisis* (London, 1993)

Abou El Fadl, Khaled M., *Conference of the Books: The Search for Beauty in Islam* (Lanham, Md., 2001)

Abu Aliya, Abd al-Fattah Hasan, *Dirasa fi masadir tarikh al-jazira al-`arabiyya* (Riyadh, 1979)

Abu Aliya, Abd al-Fatah Hasan, 'Nazara `ala ba`d watha'iq al-hayat al-fikriyya fi sanjaq al-hasa', *Revue d'histoire maghrebine* lvii-lviii (1990) pp. 55–67

Abun-Nasr, Jamil, 'The Salafiyya movement in Morocco: The religious bases of the Moroccan nationalist movement', *St. Antony's Papers* 16 (1963), pp. 90–105

Aburish, Said K., *The Rise, Corruption and Coming Fall of the House of Saud* (New York, 1996)

Ahmad, Mumtaz, 'The politics of war: Islamic fundamentalisms in Pakistan', in James Piscatori (ed.), *Islamic Fundamentalisms and the Gulf Crisis* (Chicago, 1991)

Al-`Ajlan, Ali ibn Muhammad ibn Abd Allah, *al-Sheikh al-`Allama Abd Allah ibn Abd al-Rahman Aba Butayn* (Riyadh, 2001)

Al-`Ajmi, Muhammad ibn Nasir (ed.), *Al-Rasa'il al-mutabadala bayna Jamal al-Din al-Qasimi wa Mahmud Shukri al-Alusi* (Beirut, 2001)

Al al-Sheikh, Abd al-Rahman ibn Abd al-Latif, *Mashahir `ulama' najd wa ghayruhum* (n.p., 1974)

Al al-Sheikh, Abd al-Rahman ibn Abd al-Latif, *`Ulama' al-da`wa* (n.p., 1966)

Al-Alusi, Ali `Ala' al-Din, *al-Durr al-muntathar fi rijal al-qarn al-thani `ashar wa al-thalith `ashar* (Baghdad, 1967)

Al-Alusi, Mahmud Shukri, 'Ijtihad and the refutation of Nabhani', in Charles Kurzman (ed.), *Modernist Islam, 1840–1940: A Sourcebook* (New York, 2002)

Al-Alusi, Mahmud Shukri, *Al-Misk al-adhfar fi nashr mazaya al-qarn al-thani `ashar wa al-thalith `ashar* (Riyadh, 1982)

Al-Alusi, Mahmud Shukri, *Tarikh najd* (Cairo, 1924)

Al-`Anfan, Sa`d ibn Khalaf, *Al-Sheikh Salih ibn al-Salim (1275–1330)* (Riyadh, 1997)

Anonymous, *Lam` al-shihab fi sirat Muhammad ibn Abd al-Wahhab* (Beirut, 1967)

Anonymous, *Through our Enemies' Eyes* (Washington, D.C., 2002)

Al-`Assafi, Muhammad ibn Hamad, *Masajid al-Zubayr*, Qasim al-Samarra'i (ed.), (Riyadh, 2001)

Atkin, Muriel, 'The rhetoric of Islamophobia', *Central Asia and the Caucasus* i (2000), pp. 123–132

Auda, Gehad, 'An uncertain response: The Islamic movement in Egypt', in James Piscatori (ed.), *Islamic Fundamentalisms and the Gulf Crisis* (Chicago, 1991)

Barrak, Abd al-Aziz ibn Nasir ibn Rashid, *Ibn Baz fi al-Dilam* (Riyadh, 2000)

Al-Bassam, Abd Allah ibn Abd al-Rahman, *Khizanat al-tawarikh al-najdiyya*, 10 vols. (n.p., 1999)

Al-Bassam, Abd Allah ibn Abd al-Rahman, *`Ulama' najd khilal thamaniyat qurun*, 6 vols. (Riyadh, 1997)

Al-Bassam, Ahmad, 'Min asbab al-mu`arada al-mahalliyya li-da`wat al-sheikh Muhammad ibn Abd al-Wahhab fi `ahd al-dawla al-sa`udiyya al-ula', *al-Dir`iyya* iv/14 (2001), pp. 23–77

Bergen, Peter L., *Holy War, Inc. Inside the Secret World of Osama bin Laden* (New York, 2001)

Al-Bitar, Abd al-Razzaq, *Hilyat al-bashar fi tarikh al-qarn al-thalith `ashar*, 3 vols. (Damascus, 1961–63)

Bjorkman, W., 'Kafir', *Encyclopaedia of Islam*, CD-Rom Edition 1.0 (Brill, 1999), IV:407b

Bogary, Hamza, *The Sheltered Quarter: A Tale of a Boyhood in Mecca* (Austin, 1992)

Boyd, Douglas A., 'Saudi Arabian television', *Journal of Broadcasting*, xv/1 (1970–71), pp. 73–78

Buchan, James, 'The return of the Ikhwan', in David Holden and Richard Johns (eds.), *The House of Saud: The Rise and Rule of the Most Powerful Dynasty in the Arab World* (New York, 1981), pp. 511–526

Buchan, James, 'Secular and religious opposition in Saudi Arabia', in Tim Niblock (ed.), *State, Society and Economy in Saudi Arabia* (New York, 1982)

Champion, Daryl, *The Paradoxical Kingdom: Saudi Arabia and the Momentum of Reform* (New York, 2003)

Clouston, W. A. (ed.), *Arabian Poetry for English Readers* (London, 1986)

Commins, David, 'Hasan al-Banna', in Ali Rahnema (ed.), *Pioneers of Islamic Revival* (London, 1994)

Commins, David, *Islamic Reform: Politics and Social Change in Late Ottoman Syria* (New York, 1990)

Commins, David, 'Taqi al-Din al-Nabhani and the Islamic Liberation Party', *Muslim World* lxxxi (1991), pp. 194–211

Commins, David, 'Traditional anti-Wahhabi Hanbalism in nineteenth century Arabia', in Itzchak Weismann and Fruma Zachs (eds.), *Ottoman Reform and Islamic Regeneration: Studies in Honor of Butrus Abu Manneh* (London, 2005)

Commins, David, 'Wahhabism as a Regional Religious Culture', Paper presented at the Middle East Studies Association annual conference, November 2004

Cook, Michael, *Commanding Right and Forbidding Wrong in Islamic Thought* (Cambridge, 2001)

Cook, Michael, 'The expansion of the first Saudi state: The case of Washm', in C. E. Bosworth (ed.), *The Islamic World from Classical to Modern Times: Essays in Honor of Bernard Lewis* (Princeton, 1989)

Cook, Michael, 'On the origins of Wahhabism', *Journal of the Royal Asiatic Society of Great Britain and Ireland* ii/2 (1992), pp. 191–202

Cordesman, Anthony, 'Saudi Arabia: Opposition, Islamic extremism and terrorism', in *Saudi Arabia Enters the 21st Century: Politics, Economics and Energy* (Washington, 2002)

Crawford, Michael, 'Civil war, foreign intervention and the question of political legitimacy: A nineteenth century Saudi qadi's dilemma', *International Journal of Middle East Studies* xiv (1982), pp. 227–248

Dahlan, Ahmad ibn al-Sayyid Zayni, *al-Durar al-saniyya fi al-radd `ala al-wahhabiyya* (Cairo, n.d)

Al-Dakhil, Khalid, 'Social origins of the Wahhabi movement', paper presented at the Middle East Studies Association Annual Meeting, 2002

Dallal, Ahmad, 'The Origins and Objectives of Islamic Revivalist Thought, 1750–1850', *Journal of the American Oriental Society* cxiii/3 (1993), pp. 341–359

Danner, Victor, 'Al-Busiri: His times and his prophecies', in Robert Olson (ed.), *Islamic and Middle Eastern Societies: A Festschrift in Honor of Professor Wadie Jwaideh* (Brattleboro,Vt, 1987)

'Declaration of War against the Americans Occupying the Land of the Two Holy

Places', www.pbs.org/newshour/terrorism/international/fatwa_1996.html

Dekmejian, Richard, 'The liberal impulse in Saudi Arabia', *Middle East Journal* lvii/3 (2003), pp. 400–413

Dekmejian, R. Hrair, 'The rise of political Islamism in Saudi Arabia', *Middle East Journal* xlviii/4 (1994), pp. 627–643

DeLong-Bas, Natana J., *Wahhabi Islam: From Revival and Reform to Global Jihad* (New York, 2004)

Didier, Charles, *Sojourn with the Grand Sharif of Makkah*, translated by Richard Bouliad (New York, 1985)

Doughty, Charles, *Travels in Arabia Deserta*, 2 vols. Reprint edition (New York, 1979)

Doumato, Eleanor Abdella, 'Are reformers challenging the legitimacy of the Saudi regime? A look at reforms in education', presented at the Centre for International Studies, MIT, 7 April 2005

Doumato, Eleanor, *Getting God's Ear: Women, Islam and Healing in Saudi Arabia and the Gulf* (New York, 2000)

Doumato, Eleanor, 'Manning the barricades: Islam according to Saudi Arabia's school texts', *Middle East Journal* lvii/2 (2003), pp. 230–247

Ebied, R.Y. and M.U.L. Young, 'An unpublished refutation of the doctrines of the Wahhabis', *Revista degli studi orientali* l (1976), pp. 377–397

Ende, Werner, 'The *Nakhawila*, a Shiite community in Medina past and present', *Die Welt des Islams* xxxvii/3 (1997), pp. 263–348

Al-Fahad, Abdulaziz H., 'Commentary: From exclusivism to accommodation: Doctrinal and legal evolution of Wahhabism', *New York University Law Review*, lxxix/2 (2004), pp. 485–519

Al-Fahad, Abdulaziz H., 'The `imama vs. the `iqal: *Hadari*-Bedouin conflict in the formation of the Saudi state', in Madawi Al-Rasheed and Robert Vitalis (eds.), *Counter-Narratives: History, Contemporary Society and Politics in Saudi Arabia and Yemen* (New York, 2004)

Al-Fakhiri, Muhammad ibn Umar, *Al-Akhbar al-najdiyya*, Abd Allah ibn Yusuf al-Shibl (ed.), (Riyadh, n.d.)

Faksh, Mahmud A., *The Future of Islam in the Middle East: Fundamentalism in Egypt, Algeria and Saudi Arabia* (Westport, Conn., 1997)

Fandy, Mamoun, *Saudi Arabia and the Politics of Dissent* (New York, 1999)

Al-Farsy, Fouad, *Modernity and Tradition: The Saudi Equation* (London, 1990)

Fattah, Hala, *The Politics of Regional Trade in Iraq, Arabia and the Gulf, 1745–1900* (Albany, 1997)

Fattah, Hala, '"Wahhabi" influences, salafi responses: Shaikh Mahmud Shukri and the Iraqi salafi movement, 1745–1930', *Journal of Islamic Studies* xiv/2 (2003), pp. 127–148

Gaborieau, Marc, 'A nineteenth-century Indian "Wahhabi" tract against the cult of Muslim saints: *Al-Balagh al-Mubin*', in Christian W. Troll (ed.), *Muslim Shrines in India: Their Character, History and Significance* (Delhi, 1989)

Gause, F. Gregory, 'Be careful what you wish for: The future of U.S.-Saudi relations', *World Policy Journal* xix/1 (2002), pp. 37–50

Gelvin, James L., *The Modern Middle East: A History* (New York, 2005)

Ghalib, Muhammad Adib, *Min akhbar al-hijaz wa najd fi tarikh al-Jabarti* (Riyadh, 1975)

Al-Ghunaym, Khalid Abd al-Aziz, *Al-Mujaddid al-thani: al-Sheikh Abd al-Rahman ibn Hasan Al al-Sheikh wa tariqatuhu fi taqrir al-`aqida* (Riyadh, 1997)

Gimaret, D., 'Shirk', *Encyclopaedia of Islam*, CD-Rom Edition 1.0 (Brill, 1999) IX, 484b

Goldberg, Jacob, 'The Shii minority in Saudi Arabia', in Juan Cole and Nikki Keddie (eds.), *Shiism and Social Protest* (New Haven, 1986)

Green, Arnold, 'A Tunisian reply to a Wahhabi declaration: Texts and contexts', in A. H. Green (ed.), *In Quest of an Islamic Humanism, Arabic and Islamic Studies in memory of Mohamed al-Nowaihi* (Cairo, 1984)

Guarmani, Carlo, *Northern Najd: A Journey from Jerusalem to Anaiza in Qasim* (London, 1938)

Habib, John S., *Ibn Sa'ud's Warriors of Islam: The Ikhwan of Najd and Their Role in the Creation of the Sa'udi Kingdom, 1910–1930* (Leiden, 1978)

Hafsi, Ibrahim, 'Recherches sur le genre "tabaqat" dans la litterature Arabe', *Arabica* xxiv (1977), pp. 1–41

Haj, Samira, 'Reordering Islamic orthodoxy: Muhammad ibn `Abdul Wahhab', *Muslim World* xcii (2002), pp. 333–368

Hallaq, Wael, *A History of Islamic Legal Theories: An Introduction to Sunni Usul Al-Fiqh* (Cambridge, 1997)

Hatti Humayun 19698–A, Rajab 21, 1234 AH; Documents Section, King Fahd National Library, Riyadh, Saudi Arabia; Arabic translation by Dr. Suheyl Sapan

Al-Haydari, Ibrahim Fasih ibn Sibghatallah, *Kitab `unwan al-majd fi bayan ahwal baghdad wa al-basra wa najd* (Basra, n.d.)

Haykel, Bernard, *Revival and Reform in Islam: The Legacy of Muhammad al-Shawkani* (Cambridge, 2003)

Headley, R. L., 'Al-Djubayla', *The Encyclopaedia of Islam*, New Edition. Vol. 2, B. Lewis, Ch. Pellat and J. Schacht (eds.), (Leiden, 1965)

Helms, Christine Moss, *The Cohesion of Saudi Arabia: Evolution of Political Identity* (Baltimore, 1981)

Holden, David and Richard Johns, *The House of Saud: The Rise and Rule of the Most Powerful Dynasty in the Arab World* (New York, 1981)

Hunter, W. W., *The Indian Musalmans: Are They Bound in Conscience to Rebel against the Queen?* (London, 1871)

Hunwick, J. O., 'Takfir', *Encyclopaedia of Islam*, CD-Rom Edition 1.0 (Brill, 1999), X:122a

Ibn Asakir, Rashid, *Tarikh al-masajid wa al-awqaf al-qadima fi balad al-riyadh ila `amm 1373* (Riyadh, 1999)

Ibn Atiq, Hamad, 'Radd al-Sheikh Hamad ibn Atiq `ala Ibn Du`ayj', King Fahd National Library, Riyadh, Saudi Arabia, Manuscript section, 57/86

Ibn Atiq, Hamad, *Sabil al-najat wa al-fikak*, al-Walid ibn Abd al-Rahman al-Farayyan (ed.), (Riyadh, 1989)

Ibn Bishr, Uthman, `Unwan al-majd fi tarikh najd, 2 vols. (Riyadh, 1999)

Ibn Ghannam, Husayn, Tarikh najd (Cairo, 1961)

Ibn Hamdan, Sulayman ibn Abd al-Rahman, Tarajim muta'akhkhiri al-hanabila, Bakr ibn Abd Allah Abu Zayd (ed.), (Al-Dammam, 2000)

Ibn Humayd, Muhammad ibn Abd Allah, Al-Suhub al-wabila `ala dara'ih al-hanabila, 3 vols., Bakr Abd Allah Abu Zayd and Abd al-Rahman ibn Sulayman al-Uthaymin (eds.), (Beirut, 1996)

Ibn Isa, Ibrahim ibn Salih, Tarikh ba'd al-hawadith al-waqi'a fi najd (Riyadh, 1999)

Ibn Jirjis, Da'ud ibn Sulayman, Sulh al-ikhwan min ahl al-iman (Bombay, 1888/89)

Ibn Mansur, Uthman, 'Manhaj al-ma`arij fi akhbar al-khawarij', Manuscript no. 28653, Dar al-Kutub, Cairo, Egypt

Ibn Qasim, Abd al-Rahman ibn Muhammad (ed.), Al-Durar al-saniya fi al-ajwiba al-najdiyya 12 vols. (Riyadh, 1995)

Ibn `Ubayd, Ibrahim, Tadhkirat uli al-nuha wa al-`irfan bi ayyam al-wahid al-dayyan wa dhikr hawadith al-zaman, 5 vols. (Riyadh, n.d.)

Ibrahim, Abd al-Aziz Abd al-Ghani, Najdiyyun wara' al-hudud: al-`Uqaylat, 1705–1950 (London, 1991)

IntelCentre, 'Al-Qaeda in the Arabian Peninsula: Shooting, Hostage Taking, Kidnapping Wave', July 2004, www.intelcentre.com/reports-charts.html

International Crisis Group, 'Can Saudi Arabia Reform Itself?', International Crisis Group Middle East Report No. 28 (14 July 2004)

'Is Saudi Arabia divorcing political Islam?', Arab Press Review, 4 December 2002

Al-Isa, Mayy bint Abd al-Aziz, Al-Hayah al-`ilmiyya fi najd mundhu qiyam da`wat al-sheikh Muhammad ibn Abd al-Wahhab wa hatta nihayat al-dawla al-sa`udiyya al-ula (Riyadh, 1997)

Al-Jabarti, Abd al-Rahman ibn Hasan, `Aja'ib al-athar fi al-tarajim wa al-akhbar, 4 vols. (Cairo, 1998)

Jansen, Johannes J.G., The Neglected Duty: The Creed of Sadat's Assassins and Islamic Resurgence in the Middle East (New York, 1986)

Al-Jaza'iri, Tahir, 'Rasa'il Ibn Taymiyya wa al-kutub allati nuqila `anha fi badi` al-qur'an ghayr ma ishtahar', Manuscript no. 11726, Zahiriyya Library, Damascus, Syria

Jerichow, Anders, The Saudi File: People, Power, Politics (New York, 1998)

'Jihad against Jews and Crusaders', Federation of American Scientists Website, www.fas.org/irp/world/para/docs/980223-fatwa.htm

Jones, Toby, 'The clerics, the sahwa and the Saudi state', Strategic Insights iv/3 (2005)

Al Juhany, Uwaidah M., Najd before the Salafi Reform Movement: Social, Religious and Political Conditions during the Three Centuries Preceding the Rise of the Saudi State (Reading, 2002)

Kane, Ousmane, Muslim Modernity in Postcolonial Nigeria: A Study of the Society for the Removal of Innovation and the Reinstatement of Tradition (Leiden, 2003)

Kechichian, Joseph, 'Islamic revivalism and change in Saudi Arabia: Juhayman Al-Utaybi's "Letters" to the Saudi people', Muslim World lxx/1 (1990), pp. 1–16

Kechichian, Joseph, 'The role of the ulama in the politics of an Islamic state: The case of Saudi Arabia', *International Journal of Middle East Studies* 18 (1986), pp. 53–71

Kechichian, Joseph A., 'Testing the Saudi will to power: Challenges confronting Prince Abdallah', *Middle East Policy* x/4 (2003), pp. 100–115

Kepel, Gilles, *The War for Muslim Minds: Islam and the West* (Cambridge, Mass, 2004)

Khalid, Adeeb, 'A secular Islam: Nation, state and religion in Uzbekistan', *International Journal of Middle East Studies* xxxv (2003) pp. 573–598

Khoury, Dina Rizk, 'Who is a true Muslim? Exclusion and inclusion among polemicists of reform in nineteenth century Baghdad', in Virginia Aksan and Daniel Goffman (eds.), *Early Modern Ottoman History: A Reinterpretation* (Cambridge, forthcoming)

Knysh, Alexander, 'A clear and present danger: "Wahhabism" as a rhetorical foil', *Saudi-American Forum* xxiv (14 November 2003)

Kostiner, Joseph, *The Making of Saudi Arabia 1916–1936: From Chieftaincy to Monarchical State* (Oxford, 1993)

Kostiner, Joseph, 'On instruments and their designers: The Ikhwan of Najd and the emergence of the Saudi state', *Middle Eastern Studies* xxi/3 (1985), pp. 298–323

Kramer, Martin, *Islam Assembled: The Advent of the Muslim Congresses* (New York, 1986)

Lackner, Helen, *A House Built on Sand: A Political Economy of Saudi Arabia* (London, 1978)

Lacroix, Stephane, 'Between Islamists and liberals: Saudi Arabia's new "Islamo-Liberal" reformers', *Middle East Journal* lviii/3 (2004), pp. 345–365

Layish, Aharon, 'Saudi Arabia legal reform as a mechanism to moderate Wahhabi doctrine', *Journal of the American Oriental Society*, cvii/2 (1987), pp. 279–292

Layish, Aharon, '`Ulama' and politics in Saudi Arabia', in Metin Heper and Raphael Israeli (eds.), *Islam and Politics in the Modern Middle East* (London, 1984)

Lerner, Daniel, *The Passing of Traditional Society: Modernizing the Middle East* (Glencoe, Ill, 1958)

Linabury, George, 'The creation of Saudi Arabia and the erosion of Wahhabi conservatism', in Michael Curtis (ed.), *Religion and Politics in the Middle East* (Boulder, 1981)

al-Madalij, Hafiz, *al-Riyadh* (15 November 2003)

Madelung, W., 'al-Mahdi', *Encyclopaedia of Islam*, CD-Rom Edition 1.0 (Brill, 1999), V:1230b

Makdisi, George, 'Tabaqat-Biography: Law and orthodoxy in classical Islam', *Islamic Studies* xxxii (1993), pp. 371–396

Metcalf, Barbara Daly, *Islamic Revival in British India, 1860–1900* (Princeton, 1992)

Milton-Edwards, Beverly, 'A temporary alliance with the crown: The Islamic response in Jordan', in James Piscatori (ed.), *Islamic Fundamentalisms and the Gulf Crisis* (Chicago, 1991)

'Ministerial Statement of 6 November 1962 by Prime Minister Amir Faysal of Saudi Arabia', *Middle East Journal* xvii/1 (1963), pp. 161–162

Mitchell, Richard, *The Society of the Muslim Brothers* (New York, 1969)

Muhammad ibn Abd al-Wahhab, Kitab al-tawhid, in Muhammad Rashid Rida (ed.), *Majmu`at al-tawhid al-najdiyya*, Reprint edition (Riyadh, 1999)

Muhammad ibn Abd al-Wahhab, Kitab al-tawhid, *Essay on the Unicity of Allah, or What is Due to Allah from his Creatures*, translated by Ismail Raji al Faruqi (n.p., 1981)

Al-Munif, Abd Allah ibn Muhammad, 'Dawr a'immat Al Sa`ud fi waqf al-makhtutat fi mintaqat al-Riyad', *Nadwa al-Maktabat al-Waqfiyya fi al-Mamlaka al-`Arabiyya al-Sa`udiyya* (Medina, 2000)

Mutawa, Abdulla M., 'The Ulama of Najd from the Sixteenth Century to the Mid-Eighteenth Century', Doctoral dissertation, University of California, Los Angeles, 1989

Al-Nabhani, Muhammad ibn Khalifa, *Al-Tuhfa al-nabhaniyya fi tarikh al-jazira al-`arabiyya* (Bahrain, 1986)

Nasr, Sayyid Vali Reza, 'Mawdudi and the Jama`at-i Islami: The origins, theory and practice of Islamic revivalism', in Ali Rahnema (ed.), *Pioneers of Islamic Revival* (London, 1994)

Noelle, Christine, 'The anti-Wahhabi reaction in Afghanistan', *Muslim World* lxxxv/1–2 (1995), pp. 23–48

Ochsenwald, William, 'Islam and Saudi national identity in the Hijaz, 1926–1939', paper presented at the Middle East Studies Association Annual Meeting 2004

Ochsenwald, William, 'Religious publications in Saudi Arabia, 1979–1989', *Die Welt des Islams* xli/2 (2001), pp. 135–144

Ochsenwald, William, 'Saudi Arabia and the Islamic revival', *International Journal of Middle East Studies* xiii (1981), pp. 271–286

O'Kinealy, J., 'Translation of an Arabic pamphlet on the history and doctrines of the Wahhabis', *Journal of the Asiatic Society of Bengal* xliii/1 (1874), pp. 68–82

Okruhlik, Gwenn, 'Empowering civility through nationalism: Reformist Islam and belonging in Saudi Arabia', in Robert W. Hefner (ed.), *Remaking Muslim Politics: Pluralism, Contestation, Democratization* (Princeton, 2005)

Orbach, Benjamin, 'Osama bin Laden and al-Qa'ida: Origins and doctrines', *Middle East Review of International Affairs (MERIA) Journal* v/4 (2001), pp. 54–68

Parssinen, Catherine, 'The changing role of women', in Willard A. Beling (ed.), *King Faisal and the Modernization of Saudi Arabia* (London, 1980)

Perlmann, Moshe, 'Sheikh al-Damanhuri against the churches of Cairo (1739)', *Actas IV Congresso de Estudos Arabes e Islamicos* (Leiden, 1971)

Peskes, Esther, *Muhammad B. Abdalwahhab (1703–1792) im Widerstreit* (Stuttgart, 1993)

Peters, Rudolph, *Jihad in Classical and Modern Islam: A Reader* (Princeton, 1996)

Prokop, Michaela, 'Saudi Arabia: The politics of education', *International Affairs* lxxix/1 (2003), pp. 77–89

Al-Qadi, Muhammad ibn Uthman ibn Salih, *Rawdat al-nazirin `an ma'athir `ulama' najd wa hawadith al-sinin*, 2 vols., 3rd ed. (Riyadh, 1989–90)

Radtke, Bernd, *The Exoteric Ahmad Ibn Idris: A Sufi's Critique of the Madhahib and the Wahhabis* (Leiden, 2000)

Al-Rasheed, Madawi, *A History of Saudi Arabia* (Cambridge, 2002)

Al-Rasheed, Madawi, *Politics in an Arabian Oasis: The Rashidi Tribal Dynasty* (London, 1991)

Rashid, Ahmed, *Taliban: Militant Islam, Oil and Fundamentalism in Central Asia* (London, 2000)

Al-Rashid, Ibrahim (ed.), *Saudi Arabia Enters the World: Secret U.S. Documents on the Emergence of the Kingdom of Saudi Arabia as a World Power, 1936–1949*, Part I (Salisbury, NC, 1980)

Ra'uf, `Imad Abd al-Salam, *al-Iraq fi watha'iq Muhammad Ali* (Baghdad, 1999)

Rentz, George Snavely, 'Muhammad ibn Abd al-Wahhab (1703/4–1792) and the Beginnings of Unitarian Empire in Arabia', Doctoral dissertation, University of California, Berkeley, 1948

Rida, Muhammad Rashid (ed.), *Majmu`at al-rasa'il wa al-masa'il al-najdiyya*, 4 vols., 3rd ed. (Riyadh, 1996)

Rida, Muhammad Rashid (ed.), *Majmu`at al-tawhid al-najdiyya*, Reprint edition (Riyadh, 1999)

Rida, Muhammad Rashid, *al-Wahhabiyyun wa al-hijaz* (n.p., 2000)

Roy, Delwin A., 'Saudi Arabian education: Development policy', *Middle Eastern Studies* xxviii/3 (1992), pp. 477–508

Roy, Olivier, *Afghanistan: From Holy War to Civil War* (Princeton, 1995)

Roy, Olivier, *The Failure of Political Islam* (Cambridge, Mass, 1994)

Rubin, Elizabeth, 'The jihadi who kept asking why', *New York Times Sunday Magazine* (7 March 2004)

Rugh, William A., 'Saudi mass media and society in the Faisal era', in Willard A. Beling (ed.), *King Faisal and the Modernisation of Saudi Arabia* (London, 1980)

Al-Sadhan, Abdulrahman M., 'The modernisation of the Saudi bureaucracy', in Willard A. Beling (ed.), *King Faisal and the Modernisation of Saudi Arabia* (London, 1980)

Sadleir, George Forster, *Diary of a Journey Across Arabia* (New York, 1977)

Salame, Ghassan, 'Islam and politics in Saudi Arabia', *Arab Studies Quarterly* ix/3 (1987), pp. 306–326

Al-Salman, Muhammad ibn Abd Allah, *Al-Ahwal al-siyasiyya fi al-qasim fi `ahd al-dawla al-sa`udiyya al-thaniya, 1238–1309/1823–1891* (Unayza, 1986–88)

Al-Salman, Muhammad ibn Abd Allah, *al-Ta'lim fi ahd al-malak Abd al-Aziz* (Riyadh, 1999)

Sanyal, Usha, 'Are Wahhabis kafirs? Ahmad Riza Khan Barelwi and his *Sword of the Haramayn*', in Muhammad Khalid Masud, Brinkley Messick and David S. Powers (eds.), *Islamic Legal Interpretation: Muftis and their Fatwas* (Cambridge, Mass, 1996)

Saudi Constitution, www.the-saudi.net/saudi-arabia/saudi-constitution .htm

Schacht, J., 'Dahlan, Sayyid Ahmad B. Zayni', *The Encyclopaedia of Islam*, new edition, vol. 2., B. Lewis, Ch. Pellat and J. Schacht (eds.), (Leiden, 1965)

Sedgwick, Mark J. R., 'Saudi Sufis: Compromise in the Hijaz, 1925–1940', *Die Welt des Islams* xxxvii/3 (1997), pp. 349–368

Shepard, William E., 'Sayyid Qutb's doctrine of *jahiliyya*', *International Journal of Middle East Studies* xxxv/4 (2003), pp. 521–545

Al-Sinani, Isam ibn Abd Allah (ed.), *Bara'at `ulama' al-umma min tazkiyat ahl al-bid`a wa al-madhamma* (Ajman, 2000)

Sindi, Abdullah M., 'King Faisal and Pan-Islamism', in Willard A. Beling (ed.), *King Faisal and the Modernisation of Saudi Arabia* (London, 1980)

Sirriyeh, Elizabeth, *Sufis and Anti-Sufis: The Defence, Rethinking and Rejection of Sufism in the Modern World* (Richmond, 1999)

Sirriyeh, Elizabeth, 'Wahhabis, unbelievers and the problem of exclusivism', *British Society for Middle Eastern Studies* xvi (1989), pp. 123–132

Steinberg, Guido, 'Ecology, knowledge and trade in Central Arabia (Najd) during the nineteenth and early twentieth centuries', in Madawi Al-Rasheed and Robert Vitalis (eds.), *Counter-Narratives: History, Contemporary Society and Politics in Saudi Arabia and Yemen* (New York, 2004)

Steinberg, Guido, *Religion und Staat in Saudi-Arabien: Die wahhabitischen Gelehrten, 1902–1953* (n.p., 2002)

Steinberg, Guido, 'The Shiites in the Eastern Province of Saudi Arabia (Al-Ahsa'), 1913–1953', in Rainer Brunner and Werner Ende (eds.), *The Twelver Shia in Modern Times: Religious Culture and Political History* (Leiden, 2001)

Sulayman ibn Abd Allah ibn Muhammad ibn Abd al-Wahhab, 'Fi hukm muwalat ahl al-ishrak', in Muhammad Rashid Rida (ed.), *Majmu`at al-tawhid al-najdiyya*, Reprint edition (Riyadh, 1999)

Sulayman ibn Abd Allah ibn Muhammad ibn Abd al-Wahhab, 'Fi hukm al-safar ila bilad al-shirk wa al-iqama fi-ha li al-tijara wa izhar `alamat al-nifaq wa muwalat al-kuffar', in Muhammad Rashid Rida (ed.), *Majmu`at al-tawhid al-najdiyya*, Reprint edition (Riyadh, 1999)

Sulayman ibn Abd al-Wahhab, *Al-sawa`iq al-ilahiyya fi al-radd ala al-wahhabiyya*, Ibrahim Muhammad al-Bitawi (ed.) (Cairo, 1987)

Taji-Farouqi, Suha, *A Fundamental Quest: Hizb al-Tahrir and the Search for the Islamic Caliphate* (London, 1996)

Teitelbaum, Joshua, *Holier Than Thou: Saudi Arabia's Islamic Opposition* (Washington, 2000)

Teitelbaum, Joshua, *The Rise and Fall of the Hashemite Kingdom of Arabia* (New York, 2001)

Traboulsi, Samer, 'An early refutation of Muhammad ibn Abd al-Wahhab's reformist views', *Die Welt des Islams* xlii/3 (2002), pp. 373–396

Trial, George T. and R. Bayly Winder, 'Modern education in Saudi Arabia', *History of Education Journal* i (1950), pp. 121–133

Tripp, Charles, 'Sayyid Qutb', in Ali Rahnema (ed.), *Pioneers of Islamic Revival* (London, 1994)

Al-Umari, Salim al-Sulayman, '*Ulama' Al Salim wa talamidhatuhum wa `ulama' al-*

qasim, 2 vols. (Riyadh, 1985)

'Uqayli, Khalid ibn Zayd ibn Sa'ud al-Mani', *Al-Tahqiq fi 'ulama' al-hilwa wa hawtat Bani Tamim wa na`am wa al-hariq: `Ulama' wa qudat al-hilwa* (Riyadh, 2000)

Uthaymin, Abd Allah, 'Mawqif Sulayman ibn Suhaym', in Abd Allah Uthaymin (ed.), *Buhuth wa ta`liqat fi tarikh al-mamlaka al-`arabiyyah al-sa`udiyyah* (Riyadh, 1984)

Van der Meulen, D., *The Wells of Ibn Saud* (London, 1957)

Vassiliev, Alexei, *The History of Saudi Arabia* (New York, 2000)

Vitalis, Robert, 'Black gold, white gold: An essay on American exceptionalism, hierarchy and hegemony in the Gulf', *Diplomatic History* xxvi/2 (2002), pp. 195–213

Vogel, Frank E., *Islamic Law and Legal Systems: Studies of Saudi Arabia* (Leiden, 2000)

Voll, John, 'Muhammad Hayya al-Sindi and Muhammad b Abd al-Wahhab', *Bulletin of the School of Oriental and African Studies* xxxviii (1975), pp. 32–39

Wahbah, Hafiz, *Arabian Days* (London, 1964)

Wallin, Georg Augustus, *Travels in Arabia*, Reprint edition (Cambridge, 1979)

Webster, Roger, 'Hijra and the dissemination of Wahhabi doctrine in Saudi Arabia', in Ian Richard Netton (ed.), *Golden Roads: Migration, Pilgrimage and Travel in Mediaeval and Modern Islam* (Richmond, 1993)

Weismann, Itzchak, 'The Naqshbandiyya-Khalidiyya and the Salafi Challenge in Iraq,' *Journal of the History of Sufism* iv (2003–2004), pp. 229–240

Weismann, Itzchak, *Taste of Modernity: Sufism, Salafiyya and Arabism in Late Ottoman Damascus* (Leiden, 2001)

'The West, Christians and Jews in Saudi Arabian Schoolbooks', American Jewish Committee and the Centre for Monitoring the Impact of Peace (CMIP), 2002. www.edume.org/reports/10/toc.htm

Wiktorowicz, Quintan, 'Anatomy of the salafi movement', forthcoming in *Studies in Conflict and Terrorism* xxix/2 (2006)

Wiktorowicz, Quintan, 'A genealogy of radical Islam', *Studies in Conflict and Terrorism* xxviii (2005), pp. 75–97

Wiktorowicz, Quintan, 'The new global threat: transnational salafis and jihad', *Middle East Policy* viii/4 (2001), pp. 18–38

Wiktorowicz, Quintan and John Kaltner, 'Killing in the name of Islam: Al-Qaeda's justification for September 11', *Middle East Policy* x/2 (2003), pp. 76–92

Al-Yassini, Ayman, *Religion and State in the Kingdom of Saudi Arabia* (Boulder, 1985)

Al-Zahiri, Abd al-Rahman ibn `Aqil, 'Dunya al-Watha'iq', *al-Dir`iyya* i/2 (1998), pp. 264–326.

Index

Aba Butayn, Abd Allah ibn Abd al-Rahman ibn, 43, 58–9, 124

Aba al-Khayl, Abd Allah ibn Fa'iz ibn Mansur, 55–6

Abduh, Muhammad, 137

Abd Allah ibn Husayn (Hashemite), 138

Abd al-Rahman, Umar, 172, 174, 189

Abu Bahz, 101–2

al-Adwani, Sulayman ibn Muhammad, 75

Afghan war (jihad), 4, 157, 174–6, 185–7, 191–2, 206

al-Aflaj, 66, 83

Ahl-i Hadith, 144–5, 147, 152

Al Abu Ulayyan, Abd al-Aziz, 50

Al Bassam, 54–5, 68

Al Mu'ammar, Abd al-Aziz ibn Hamad, 42–3

Al Muqrin, 18

Al Musharraf, 10–11, 27, 57–8

Al Musharraf, Abd al-Wahhab ibn Sulayman, 11, 17, 58

Al Musharraf, Sulayman ibn Ali, 58

Al Sabiq, Fawzan ibn Abd al-Aziz, 73

Al Salim, 68, 73, 84

Al Saud, Abd Allah ibn Abd al-Aziz, 194–5

Al Saud, Abd Allah ibn Faysal, Amir, 61–6

Al Saud, Abd Allah ibn Saud, Amir, 33, 37, 40, 136

Al Saud, Abd al-Aziz ibn Muhammad, Amir, 136

Al Saud, Abd al-Aziz ibn Abd al-Rahman, King, 4, 66, 71–105, 107–10, 116–19, 124–6, 133, 138–40, 151, 157, 165, 188, 205–6, 209

Al Saud, Abd al-Rahman ibn Faysal, Amir, 65, 67

Al Saud, Fahd ibn Abd al-Aziz, King, 179–80, 187–8

Al Saud, Faysal ibn Abd al-Aziz, King, 77, 88, 106–7, 109–11, 126, 151–3, 155, 159

Al Saud, Faysal ibn Turki, Amir, 45–6, 49–51, 59–62, 64–7, 69, 71, 95, 103, 111, 137

Al Saud, Jiluwi ibn Turki, 51

Al Saud, Khalid ibn Abd al-Aziz, King, 121, 167, 178

Al Saud, Khalid ibn Musa'id, 110

Al Saud, Khalid ibn Saud, 46–7, 49, 51

Al Saud, Mishari ibn Abd al-Rahman, 45

Al Saud, Mishari ibn Saud, 41

Al Saud, Muhammad ibn Saud, Amir, 19, 22

Al Saud, Saud ibn Abd al-Aziz ibn Muhammad, Amir, 136

Al Saud, Saud ibn Abd al-Aziz, King, 88, 107, 109, 119, 125, 147, 151–2

Al Saud, Saud ibn Faysal ibn Abd al-Aziz, 195

Al Saud, Saud ibn Faysal ibn Turki, Amir, 61–6

Al Saud, Abd Allah ibn Thunayan, 49

Al Saud, Turki ibn Faysal, Amir, 43–5, 50, 55, 60, 95, 136–7
Al Shabana, 28
Al al-Sheikh, 29, 33, 37–9, 42–3, 45, 47, 49, 61–2, 65–6, 69, 71, 73, 83, 87, 93–5, 111, 113, 119, 133, 145, 154, 170, 196
Al al-Sheikh, Abd Allah ibn Abd al-Latif, 65–9, 75, 83, 93
Al al-Sheikh, Abd Allah ibn Hasan ibn Husayn, 93, 95, 97–8, 111
Al al-Sheikh, Abd Allah ibn Muhammad ibn Abd al-Wahhab, 29, 42, 136, 139
Al al-Sheikh, Abd al-Aziz ibn Abd Allah ibn Hasan, 170, 196
Al al-Sheikh, Abd al-Latif ibn Abd al-Rahman, 59–67, 74, 83, 94, 124, 134, 136
Al al-Sheikh, Abd al-Malik ibn Husayn ibn Muhammad ibn Abd al-Wahhab, 43
Al al-Sheikh, Abd al-Rahman ibn Hasan ibn Muhammad ibn Abd al-Wahhab, 42–3, 45–6, 49–50, 59–65
Al al-Sheikh, Hasan ibn Husayn, 69, 83
Al al-Sheikh, Ibrahim ibn Abd al-Latif, 68
Al al-Sheikh, Ishaq ibn Abd al-Rahman, 145
Al al-Sheikh, Muhammad ibn Ibrahim ibn Abd al-Latif, 87, 95, 111–13, 116, 119, 124, 126, 147
Al al-Sheikh, Salih ibn Abd al-Aziz, 196
Al al-Sheikh, Sulayman ibn Abd Allah ibn Muhammad ibn Abd al-Wahhab, 33–7, 42, 46–9, 81, 98
Al al-Sheikh, Umar ibn Hasan ibn Husayn, 94–5, 147
Al Suhaym, 28
Al Sulaym, 50–1
Al Turki, 55–6

al-Alusi, Mahmud Shukri, 133–40
al-Alusi, Nu'man Khayr al-Din, 132–3, 145
al-Anqari, Abd Allah, 87
Aramco, 101, 108–110, 125, 158, 169, 178
al-Arid, 17, 21, 26, 40, 46, 59, 135
al-Artawiya, 82–3, 87–8, 92–3
Asir, 46, 93, 98, 125
al-Awda, Abd al-Qadir, 153
Awda, Salman, 181–3, 187, 189, 196–7, 202
al-Azhar, 32, 45, 65, 139, 173–4, 197
Azzam, Abd Allah, 157, 174–5, 186, 189

Baghdad, 11, 52, 54–5, 58, 60, 63–4, 74–5, 132–5, 138, 153, 191
Bakri Mohammed, Omar, 173–4
al-Banna, Hasan, 140–3, 146, 150
Barelwi, Sayyid Ahmad, 143
Basic Law of 1992, 178, 180, 194
Basra, 11–12, 17–18, 20, 35, 52, 54, 60
al-Bassam, Abd Allah ibn Abd al-Rahman, 54
al-Bassam, Abd Allah ibn Muhammad, 54
Bin Laden, Osama, 6, 157, 172, 174, 176, 184–90, 194, 196–7, 206–7
Board of Senior Ulama, 113, 116, 121, 167–8, 176, 180, 182, 196
Book of God's Unity, The (Kitab al-tawhid), 12–16, 24, 45, 59–60, 115, 124
Burayda, 37, 44, 50–1, 61, 66–8, 73, 82, 84, 90, 110, 133, 198
al-Burda, 59
al-Busaymi, Abd Allah ibn Ahmad, 28

Cairo, 1, 7, 11, 27, 30–3, 37, 42–3, 45–6, 49, 65, 69, 145, 153, 173–4
Central Asia, Wahhabism in, 192
Committee for Commanding Good and Forbidding Wrong, 77, 94–5, 109, 112–13, 128–9, 179, 199

Committee for the Defense of Legitimate Rights (CDLR), 183, 200

Cook, Michael, 94–5

Dahlan, Ahmad ibn Zayni, 57, 74

Damascus, 1, 7, 11, 27–8, 30, 50, 132–3, 137, 153, 173

Dammam, 110, 120

Deobandi, 144, 146, 152, 191–3

Dhahran, 108, 110

al-Dir'iyya, 18–19, 22, 26–8, 30, 33, 36–40, 42–4, 53, 81, 123, 135, 208

Doughty, Charles, 54

al-Duwish, Faysal, 87–92

Education, 77, 94, 96–7, 105, 107–8, 112–13, 117, 122–9, 142, 144, 147–8, 159, 169–70, 172, 180, 194, 198, 200–2

al-Faqih, Sa'd, 183, 197

Far'a, 27

al-Faraj, Abd al-Salam, 157, 172

Faysal ibn Husayn (Hashemite), 87, 138, 191

al-Ghatghat, 87

Guarmani, Carlo, 51

Ha'il, 43, 60, 62, 65–70, 72, 74–5, 81, 84, 92–3, 135

Hajj (see Pilgrimage)

Hanbali, 10–12, 23, 28–9, 32, 50, 57, 94, 112, 116, 118–20, 122–5, 132, 134–6, 144

al-Hariq, 46

Harma, 28

al-Hasa (Eastern Province), 8–11, 18, 20, 27–8, 30, 35, 42, 46, 49, 53, 62–6, 72–3, 75–7, 80, 83, 87–8, 90–1, 94–5, 100–1, 103, 108, 124–5, 169, 176

al-Hawali, Safar, 181–3, 187, 189, 196–7, 202

Hawta, 43

Hijaz, 8–9, 30, 32–3, 37, 41–2, 46, 52, 54, 69–70, 72–4, 76–82, 87–8, 91–3, 95, 98–100, 103–4, 109–11, 113–14, 116, 118–19, 125, 138–9, 152, 177, 203, 205

Hijra (emigration as a religious duty), 34–6, 46–8, 69, 81–3, 86, 173, 199

Hijra (Ikhwan settlement), 81–7, 91, 164

Hilwa, 75

Hofuf, 66, 75, 124–5

Huraymila, 12, 17–18, 22, 27, 38, 42, 44, 53

Husayn ibn Ali (Sharif), 72, 93, 138–40, 165

Husayn, Nazir, 144–5

Ibn Abd al-Wahhab, Abd al-Aziz ibn Sulayman, 42

Ibn Abd al-Wahhab, Muhammad, 1–3, 10–29, 31, 35, 38, 40, 45, 48, 53, 56–60, 64, 80–2, 86, 94, 115, 123–5, 132–3, 141–2, 148–9, 153, 182, 190, 196, 198, 200, 208

Ibn Abd al-Wahhab, Sulayman, 11, 22–4, 56

Ibn A'id, Abd Allah, 69

Ibn Ajlan, Muhammad, 64

Ibn Akkas, Isa, 75

Ibn Amr, Abd Allah, 68–9, 73, 83

Ibn Atiq, Hamad, 46–9, 62–3, 66–7, 69, 145

Ibn Atiq, Sa'd ibn Hamad, 145

Ibn Azzuz, Muhammad, 134

Ibn Baz, Abd al-Aziz, 108, 112, 116, 147, 149–50, 164, 166–7, 169–70, 179–80, 182–3, 187–8, 195–6

Ibn Bijad, Sultan, 87, 92

Ibn Bulayhid, Abd Allah, 95–6

Ibn Dakhil, Abd Allah ibn Muhammad, 84

Ibn Dawwas, Dahham, 20

Ibn Du'ayj, Ahmad ibn Ali, 44, 47, 49

Ibn Duwiyan, Ibrahim, 84

Ibn Fawzan, Fawzan ibn Sabiq, 133–4

Ibn Fawzan, Salih, 202

Ibn Fayruz, Muhammad, 53
Ibn Ghannam, Husayn, 12, 16–17, 22
Ibn Humayd, Muhammad, 56–8
Ibn Isa, Ahmad, 73–4, 145
Ibn Isa, Ali ibn Abd Allah, 74
Ibn Isa, Muhammad ibn Abd Allah ibn
    Salih, 84
Ibn Jadid, Ibrahim, 53
Ibn Jasir, Ibrahim, 68
Ibn Jibrin, Abd Allah, 170
Ibn Jiluwi, Abd Allah, 75–6
Ibn Jirjis, Da'ud ibn Sulayman (al-
    Naqshbandi al-Baghdadi), 58–61,
    63, 74, 134, 136, 154
Ibn Kathir, Imad al-Din Ismail, 48–9,
    124
Ibn Mansur, Uthman, 60–1
Ibn Mazyad, Uthman, 56
Ibn Mu'ammar, Jawhara bint Abd
    Allah, 17
Ibn Mu'ammar, Uthman, 17–18
Ibn Mufadda, Abd Allah ibn
    Muhammad, 68
Ibn Muqbil, Sulayman, 50, 67
Ibn Muqrin, Muhammad, 44
Ibn Musharraf, Abd al-Aziz ibn Hamad
    ibn Ibrahim, 42
Ibn al-Qayyim al-Jawziyya, Shams al-
    Din Abu Bakr Muhammad, 23–4,
    59, 74, 133
Ibn Qirnas, Qirnas ibn Abd al-Rahman,
    44, 50
Ibn Qirnas, Salih, 69
Ibn Rashid, Abd al-Aziz ibn Mit'ab, 68,
    74, 84, 135
Ibn Rashid, Dukhayl, 28
Ibn Rashid, Muhammad, 66–9
Ibn Rashid, Talal, 60
Ibn Sa'igh, Salih, 28
Ibn Salim, Umar ibn Muhammad, 82–3
Ibn Sanad, Uthman, 56
Ibn Saud (see Al Saud, Abd al-Aziz ibn
    Abd al-Rahman)
Ibn Shabana, Uthman ibn Abd al-
    Jabbar, 43

Ibn Sihman, Sulayman, 68, 82, 87
Ibn Suhaym, Muhammad ibn Ahmad,
    28
Ibn Suhaym, Sulayman, 19–22, 28
Ibn Sullum, Muhammad ibn Ali, 53,
    55–6, 60
Ibn Suwaylim, Abd al-Aziz ibn Abd
    Allah, 44
Ibn Taymiyya, Taqi al-Din Ahmad, 23–
    4, 59, 64, 74, 115, 132–3, 144–5,
    172, 175
Ibn Turki, Abd al-Wahhab ibn Mu-
    hammad ibn Humaydan, 55–6
Ibn Turki, Humaydan, 28
Ibn Ubayd, Abd Allah ibn Sulayman,
    43
Ibn Uray'ar, Sulayman, 18
Ibn Uraykan, Muhammad ibn Ibrahim,
    55
Ibn Uthaymin, Muhammad, 195–6
Ibrahim Pasha, 37–8, 41–2, 44
Ijtihad, 22–3, 115–16, 132–3
Ikhwan, 75–7, 80–93, 95, 97–9, 103–4,
    106, 108, 119, 131, 138, 151, 157,
    163–6, 171, 191, 205–7
India, 4, 37, 74–5, 79, 130, 132, 134,
    143–6, 153, 159, 191, 205
Islamic foreign policy, 152–5, 204–5
Islamic Liberation Party (Hizb al-tahrir
    al-islami), 173–4

al-Jabarti, Abd al-Rahman, 31–2, 42
Jahiliyya, 3, 38, 63, 80, 148–9, 172, 182,
    199
Jamaati Islami, 146, 150, 152, 174, 181,
    206
Jamaati Ulama Islam, 191
al-Jaza'iri, Tahir, 132, 134
Jeddah, 54, 74, 77–8, 97, 100, 110, 120,
    126, 173, 175, 186
Jihad, 6, 24–6, 41, 63, 76, 88–90, 95,
    136, 148, 164–5, 172, 175, 185–6,
    188–9, 196–8, 201
Jihadist Movement, 156–7, 171–6, 184–
    7, 191, 195–7, 199, 201, 207–8

Juhayman al-Utaybi, 164–9, 171, 173, 186, 203, 206–7
Julajil, 43, 75

Kharijites, 23, 30, 41
Al-Kharj, 101–2
al-Khunayni, Abd Allah, 54
Kuwait, 5, 27, 48, 52, 71, 75, 83, 87–9, 91, 156, 168, 173, 176–8, 181, 185, 187

Labor Movement, 108–9
Law, 107, 111, 113–22
Letter of Demands, 179–80, 183
Liberal Islamists, 198–200
Liberal trend, 178–81, 194–6, 203, 207

Al-Majma'a, 19, 21, 28, 43, 74, 84
al-Malki, Hasan, 200
Marat, 44
al-Mas'ari, Muhammad, 183, 200
Mawdudi, Abu Ala, 146–50, 165
Mecca, 1–2, 7–8, 20, 28–35, 48, 53, 55–7, 59, 67–8, 72, 74, 77–8, 82, 84, 93, 95, 100, 109–10, 132, 134, 138, 143, 145, 152, 156, 163, 165, 167, 169, 173, 181, 194–5, 202
Mecca, November 1979 Incident, 163–9
Media, 109–11
Medina, 2, 7, 11, 16, 20, 30–4, 37, 42, 44, 48, 72, 77, 79, 82, 84, 95, 97, 108, 110, 112, 126, 164, 170, 173, 181, 203
Memorandum of Advice, 180, 183, 187
Al-Midhnib, 84
Movement for Islamic Reform in Arabia (MIRA), 183, 186, 197
Al-Muhajiroun, 173
Muhammad Ali, 32–3, 37, 39–41, 44, 46–7, 103, 135
Muhanna, Hasan, 66–8
Mulayda, Battle of, 67, 69
Muslim Brothers, 4–5, 140–2, 145–8, 150, 152–4, 157, 164–6, 172–4, 177, 181, 183–4, 188, 197, 201, 205–6

Mutawa, Abd Allah, 10
Mutawwi'a, 82, 95, 113, 169, 194
al-Muwaysi, Abd Allah ibn Isa, 28

Nadvi, Mas'ud Alam, 147
al-Nahhas, Muhammad Isa, 124–5
Nakhawila, 79
Nasser, Gamal Abdel, 110, 146, 148, 151–2
National Dialogues, 6, 202–3, 207–8
Nuqaydan, Mansur, 198–9

Pakistan, 4, 146, 148, 153, 159, 174–5, 177, 186–7, 191
Peshawar, 174–5, 186
Philby, H. St. John, 98
Pilgrimage, 7–10, 25, 31, 76–8, 95–6, 99–100, 113–14, 136, 139, 152, 167–8

al-Qaeda, 6, 122, 156–7, 172, 184–7, 190, 194–8, 200–1, 207
al-Qaeda Organization in the Arabian Peninsula, 197–8
al-Qahtani, Abd Allah, 166
Qarmatians, 30
al-Qasim, 28, 33, 37, 43–4, 46, 50–2, 54–5, 62, 65, 67–73, 75, 80, 83, 90, 93, 100, 135, 164, 181
al-Qasim, Abd al-Aziz, 200
al-Qasimi, Jamal al-Din, 133–4
al-Qatif, 75, 171
Qutb, Sayyid, 146, 148–50, 153, 157, 165, 172, 174–6, 183, 185–6, 188, 190, 195, 198

Ra's al-Khayma, 42–3
Rashidis, 60–2, 65–75, 81, 83–4, 93, 133, 135, 145
al-Rass, 37, 44
Rida, Rashid, 137–40
Riyadh, 5, 19, 28, 38, 43–7, 49–51, 54–5, 58, 61–8, 70–6, 81–4, 87–9, 92–3, 97, 100–2, 104, 108–11, 120, 124, 126, 135, 142, 145, 147, 150–2,

154, 156, 163, 171, 173, 176–7, 181, 183–5, 188–9, 195–7, 199, 202, 204
Russia, Wahhabism in, 192

Sadleir, G. Forster, 37
Sadus, 43
al-Saffar, Hasan, 202
Sahwa sheikhs, 177, 181–4, 186, 189, 195–8, 200, 202, 206–8
al-Salim, Muhammad ibn Abd Allah, 67–8
al-Salim, Muhammad ibn Umar, 67
al-Sanusi, Muhammad, 55
September 11 attacks, 5, 6, 122, 156, 172, 185, 193–4, 196–200
Shah Abdulaziz, 143
Shah Waliullah, 143
Shaqra, 27, 73, 84
Sharifs of Mecca, 8, 31, 51, 72, 74, 139
al-Shatti, Hasan, 50
Shiism, 2, 6, 10–11, 16, 26, 29–30, 64, 66, 73, 75–80, 88, 125, 143–4, 166, 169–71, 179, 182, 192, 195, 198, 202–3, 208
Sibila, Battle of, 90–2
Siddiq Hasan Khan, 144–5
al-Sinani, Muhammad ibn Ibrahim, 56
Sudayr, 27–8, 43, 52–3, 60, 66, 82, 135
al-Sulaym, Abd Allah, 51
Sulayman, Abd Allah, 100
Suq al-Shuyukh, 42
Sufism, 6, 11, 20, 55–6, 77–80, 112, 133–4, 141, 143–4, 146, 152–4, 192, 202, 208

Ta'if, 31, 76, 110
Taliban, 188, 191–2, 194

al-Tamimi, Abd Allah ibn Musallim, 74–5
Ten Point Programme, 106, 157–8
Tharmada, 27
Tripp, Charles, 148

Ujman tribe, 87, 90–1
Unayza, 27–9, 37, 42, 50–1, 54–6, 58–61, 67, 69, 73, 84
United States, 5, 107, 110, 149, 156, 164, 172, 174, 176, 179–81, 183–90, 193–4, 196–8, 202, 205–6
United States, Wahhabism in, 192–3
Ushayqir, 26–7, 54
Utayba tribe, 91
Uthayfiya, 27
al-Uyayna, 11, 17–18, 20, 22, 38, 56

Vogel, Frank, 114–16, 118–21

Wahbah, Hafiz, 95–8, 100, 124
Wahhabi political doctrine, 115, 141–2, 164–5, 180, 183–5
Washm, 26–7, 43–4, 47, 52, 60, 82, 135
World Assembly of Muslim Youth, 153
World Muslim League, 112, 152–3, 174–5, 192
al-Wuhaybi, Abd Allah ibn Ahmad, 66

al-Yassini, Ayman, 106–7

al-Zawahiri, Ayman, 172
Zayd ibn Khattab, 18, 20
Zia al-Haqq, 191
Zilfi, 22, 46
Zubayr, 17, 27–8, 48, 52–7, 75, 83, 183
al-Zubayri, Muhammad, 56